A Trumpet around the Corner

ALSO BY SAMUEL CHARTERS

MUSIC

Jazz: New Orleans 1885–1957
The Country Blues
Jazz: A History of the New York Scene
The Poetry of the Blues
The Bluesmen: The Story and the Music of the Men Who Made the Blues
Robert Johnson
The Legacy of the Blues: Art and Lives of Twelve Great Bluesmen
Sweet as the Showers of Rain
Spelmännen (The Swedish Fiddlers)
The Roots of the Blues: An African Search
The Blues Makers
The Day Is So Long and the Wages So Small: Music on a Summer Island
Blues Faces: A Portrait of the Blues
Walking a Blues Road: A Blues Reader, 1956–2004
New Orleans: Playing a Jazz Chorus

POETRY

The Children
The Landscape at Bolinas
Heroes of the Prize Ring
Days, or, Days as Thoughts in a Season's Uncertainties
To This Place
From a London Notebook
From a Swedish Notebook
Of Those Who Died: A Poem of the Spring of 1945

FICTION

Mr. Jabi and Mr. Smythe
Jelly Roll Morton's Last Night at the Jungle Inn
Louisiana Black
Elvis Presley Calls His Mother After The Ed Sullivan Show

CRITICISM

Some Poems/Poets: Studies in American Underground Poetry Since 1945

BIOGRAPHY

I Love: The Story of Vladimir Mayakovsky and Lili Brik (with Ann Charters)
Mambo Time: The Story of Bebo Valdés

MEMOIR

A Country Year: A Chronicle

TRANSLATIONS

Baltics (from the Swedish of Tomas Tranströmer)
We Women (from the Swedish of Edith Södergran)
The Courtyard (from the Swedish of Bo Carpelan)

ANTHOLOGY

Literature and Its Writers: An Introduction to Fiction, Poetry, and Drama (with Ann Charters)

A Trumpet

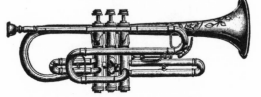

AROUND THE CORNER

THE STORY OF NEW ORLEANS

JAZZ

SAMUEL CHARTERS

UNIVERSITY PRESS OF MISSISSIPPI
JACKSON

Publication of this book is made possible in part by a gift from John N. Palmer.

AMERICAN MADE MUSIC SERIES

Advisory Board

www.upress.state.ms.us

The University Press of Mississippi is a member of the Association of American University Presses.

Unless credited otherwise, illustrations in this book are in the public domain, and they have been selected from materials in the collection of the Samuel and Ann Charters Archive of Vernacular African American Music and Culture in the Dodd Research Center, at the Storrs campus of the University of Connecticut. Their use in this book does not constitute any claim of ownership or reprint rights. The original examples of those illustrations identified as in the Samuel Charters Collection are owned by the author.

First printing 2008
∞
Library of Congress Cataloging-in-Publication Data

Charters, Samuel Barclay.
A trumpet around the corner : the story of New Orleans jazz / Samuel Charters.
p. cm. — (American made music series)
Includes bibliographical references (p.   ) and index.
ISBN 978-1-57806-898-2 (cloth : alk. paper) 1. Jazz—Louisiana—New Orleans—History and criticism. 2. Jazz musicians—Louisiana—New Orleans. I. Title.
ML3508.8.N48C44 2008
781.6509763'35—dc22   2007033564

British Library Cataloging-in-Publication Data available

In the 1950s, when New Orleans was quieter than it is today, if I found the place where the Eureka Brass Band was meeting for a parade, but I got there after they'd already started, if I just stood still and listened, I could hear a trumpet around the corner. . . .

For
Leonard Kunstadt
and Dave Van Ronk

who loved the music as I do—and would have argued with me about
something on every page.

Contents

Acknowledgments

David Evans, noted blues scholar and advisory editor to the University Press of Mississippi, approached me some time ago and asked if I would be interested in letting the Press reprint my first book on New Orleans music, *Jazz: New Orleans*, from 1958. I responded that although there was considerable biographical information in the original text that still was useful, there had been nearly as much music in New Orleans since the book was published as in the years that the book dealt with. I also explained that in the early book I hadn't included the city's white musicians, and they had certainly played as important a role in the development of New Orleans's music. In the 1950s many of us writing about jazz and blues reacted against the institutionalized racism we experienced in the South by placing special emphasis on the African American musical achievement.

David and Craig Gill at the press agreed to an extensive revision of the book, but after I began working on it I found there was so much new information that the original way of organizing the material into biographical segments didn't work. Without some context there was no way to follow the careers of the musicians through all their interactions with each other in the recording studios and on the bandstands. The obvious context would be a history of New Orleans jazz, incorporating the recent decades of research that have brought much more to our understanding of New Orleans music and its development. When I proposed this to David and Craig, they were both positive to the idea, and the result is this book. A great deal of the information in *Jazz: New Orleans* has made its way into this new text, but much detailed biographical information also had to be left out, and perhaps sometime in the future it would be useful for someone to reprint a small edition of the old book for specialist archives.

The greatest support for everything that I tried to do in New Orleans through the years came from the musicians themselves. They invited me into their homes and talked willingly about their careers; patiently enduring my interruptions when I asked for spellings of names or addresses of dance halls. In 1950 George Lewis was the first of many older musicians who opened the door for me to the

New Orleans story, and in 2005 it was drummer Johnny Vidacovich who gave me new perspectives on the enduring vitality of the New Orleans traditions. Frederic Ramsey Jr., one of the editors and writers of the seminal jazz history *Jazzmen*, was a close friend, and he was responsive and helpful as he showed me the first steps toward making use of my researches.

When I began the research for my first book there were only a handful of earlier sources to draw on. The amount of material available now is both exciting and daunting. This new book draws on the work that has appeared since the 1950s, and the materials that have been of particular help to me are listed in the bibliography. Individuals whose work has provided insights within certain areas have been cited in the text. All of them have my gratitude and admiration— particularly Lawrence Gushee, who explored many of the older New Orleans musical legends; Richard Sudhalter, who listened to many New Orleans recordings that other writers had ignored; and Lynn Abbott, whose scholarship in early New Orleans newspaper sources has been exemplary and invaluable.

Two individuals made significant contributions to the book's final text. Bruce Raeburn of the William Hogan Jazz Archive in New Orleans read the manuscript in its final stages, pointed out gaps in the story, and made helpful suggestions as to how to fill them—as well as correcting innumerable spelling errors.

Ann Charters read several drafts of the manuscript as it neared completion and acted as an attentive, sensitive, and patient editor for all textual matters.

My thanks.

A deep thanks also to my son Sam Charters, his wife Heidi, and their sons Andrew and Timothy, who for many years have continued to make New Orleans a home for me.

Samuel Charters

A Trumpet around the Corner

Counting Off the Beat

An Introduction

*This neighborhood when I was a kid was very mixed, you know, and it still is . . .
it was way more than fifty percent immigrants. I lived with my grandparents
and they were from Sicily. They were both from different cities in Sicily, and
the people next door to us were from Central America, the people next door to
them—the grandmother was from Ireland, the people next door to them Italy,
next door to them I don't know. The whole neighborhood was like that, and
there were no air conditioners so you'd hear music coming out of people's windows. We never got a TV 'til I was six, and I never was interested in it anyway.
I was out on the street, out on the porch. Go around the corner to the barroom
where I'd hear guys playing music. The windows were open and I could go sit
on the wood seat they had by the tree there, go up to the window and get a
bag of potato chips and a coke for ten cents. Nickel for the chips, nickel for the
coke. Sit there and have a drum lesson, and I'd be ten years old, sitting there.*

Drummer Johnny Vidacovich talking about
his childhood in New Orleans[1]

I f it seems difficult now in the flood of music that fills the air today to understand how someone like myself as a teenager could have become obsessively
drawn to traditional New Orleans jazz, it is important to remember that in
the late 1940s, if I looked for something beyond the expected assurances of the
popular music of those years, jazz was the only alternative I had to turn to. The
swing bands that had emerged from the first jazz era of the 1920s had already
become elaborate stage presentations, which featured more romantic vocals than

instrumental improvisation. The blues and its urban cousin, R&B, were completely inaccessible for someone living, as I was, in the California Central Valley: the music was without widespread radio play, and the recordings never appeared in any shop I knew about. Rock and roll had not appeared on the scene, and even the newer forms of jazz—Bop and Progressive jazz, the Cool Sound— still were only something happening in late night jam sessions in a handful of New York after-hours clubs. If I wanted something besides Vaughn Monroe singing "Racing With The Moon," then traditional jazz was what it would be.

When I turned to the Sacramento City Library for help, I found a handful of books that brought me back to the streets and neighborhoods, the dance halls and clubs in New Orleans, which for each of the books there on the shelves was the place where jazz had been born. What I found later, of course, is that nothing is beyond dispute, and that most opinions and attitudes, conclusions and surmises have the permanence of a message written in the sand. The usual cliches that the past is impervious to change and that the future is in our hands are actually the reverse of the reality, which is that we continually mold and remold the past like window putty, and the future is only an uncertain cloud. What we shape and reshape out of the past is our perception of it, and since perception is all that remains, why not remake it to suit whatever this moment seems to demand?

For many critics there is something close to contempt for the idea that jazz might have originated in New Orleans. The current perception is that jazz's origins were a common discovery that occurred simultaneously in many places. For some years I worked within this conceptual context; with all of the qualifications, however, I have found after years of vacillation that I have come back to about where I started so many years ago. My conclusion now is that, although many styles and variations of syncopated music emerged everywhere in the Americas in the late nineteenth century, the particular instrumental ensemble style nurtured in New Orleans was unique enough to be considered a distinct musical genre. In other words, I am comfortable with the conclusion that something with the distinct musical form of New Orleans jazz was created in New Orleans.

The New Orleans style has also been a long-lived form that has continued to define and sustain its identity, so that there is a direct lineage from those first New Orleans groups to the thousands of musicians everywhere in the world today who still play within its stylistic boundaries. It has also, over the years, absorbed many of the other syncopated idioms into its own stylistic definitions. In part, its uniqueness is reflected in its resilience and its ability to absorb and reshape so many of the elements that have marked the social changes reflected in the country's musical idioms.

I am aware that for many writers it has become virtually obligatory to emphasize the racial issue in any discussion of jazz, and I am conscious that anything I write will be considered first for its relevance to the present assumptions as to the nature and history of jazz as solely an expression of African American culture. I am also conscious, however, that in the particular racial and cultural environment in New Orleans at the moment in history when the city's jazz idiom emerges, the question of race becomes hopelessly blurred over the question of the Free Creoles of Color, a social group not present anywhere else in the United States. I have to agree with the introductory statement that Al Rose and Edmond Souchon M.D., the editors of the book *New Orleans Jazz: A Family Album*, wrote in their introduction in 1967:

> *We will not attempt to establish finally who was the inventor of jazz. (Some of our best friends have claimed this distinction.) Nor will we assert that we know who were the first to play it. We feel it was not invented at all, but that it came into being so gradually that any attempt to pin down a first time would be based on the most specious type of reasoning. Credit for the creation of jazz is due no individual man or race. If anything, it is a product, an inevitable product we think, of the avenues and alleys of a unique city, polyglot, multiracial, seething with love and conflict, a battleground of nations and cultures, a landscape of mire and magnolias.*[2]

I am also conscious that on the other side of this debate is the strongly voiced opinion of an African American musician, whom the writers don't identify, in the book *Bourbon Street Black*, by Jack V. Beurkle and Danny Barker: "A white guy doesn't play jazz; he imitates it. This is true for all whites. You can't name me a white musician who has contributed anything to jazz. He has copied—he has stolen from the black musician. And any white musician you name—any white cat who believes he plays jazz, I can tell you where he stole his music from!"[3]

Between these two considered opinions there is obviously no room for compromise or agreement.

Can we come to some common assumptions that would make a discussion of jazz in New Orleans possible? Is there any beat we can count off to get all of us tapping our feet at the same time? Probably that is assuming too much in the tide of emotions that we find ourselves in today, but it is useful to try.

In the many years that I've lived and worked and visited and enjoyed New Orleans I occasionally heard black musicians express some of the same feelings that were quoted in *Bourbon Street Black*, though almost always I found—as did the authors of that book—that among the majority of musicians it was generally a question of personal ability more than it was specifically a question of race when someone's talents were being considered. I spent much of the 1950s talking with black musicians as part of the research for my first book *Jazz: New Orleans*, and at the same time I often met and listened to the city's white musicians. The reality I found was that when anyone talked about the music they remembered and the dance halls and the bars where they'd played, I was continually faced with the unyielding reality that each of the city's social groups—white, Creole, and black—had spent most of their lives on different sides of an omnipresent racial barrier.

For an outsider it is difficult to comprehend how culturally segregated the city was, even though it was less rigorously segregated than most other cities in the

South. Until recent years, except for street encounters with marching bands or bands on advertising wagons, the different groups of musicians were expected to remain within the boundaries of their own society, and although they were conscious of each other and borrowed elements of their own styles from each other, they had almost no chance to sit on the same bandstands, or even share a night sitting and drinking in the same clubs and barrooms. I spent many hours in the kitchen of clarinetist George Lewis in 1950, listening breathlessly as he told me about his own music when he was a beginner, about the bands he'd played with, the dances and the parades—and in all the hours that he spoke, looking past me out of the window, quietly fingering his clarinet, he never mentioned the name of a single white musician.

What I feel now is that the development of jazz in New Orleans was a continual cultural interchange between societies linked in ways that were more complex than can be easily comprehended. Every musician in New Orleans in 1900, white, black, and Creole, was drawing from the same sources: the syncopated cakewalks and walk-around pieces of the minstrel show bands, the newly popular syncopated melodies of ragtime, the disciplined music of the ever-present marching bands, the popular songs that drifted into town like seeds in the wind with the traveling vaudeville shows, and the sheet music that was found in nearly every home in each of the city's social and ethnic groups. Although the blues is often included in the cataloging of the mix of early jazz, the blues as a song form emerges later, about ten years after what came to be called jazz appeared in New Orleans. The melodies of early New Orleans melodies that were commonly described as "blues" almost invariably, when someone sang them from memory, turned out to be a slow kind of ragtime song usually called "slow drag." What I found was that the term "blues" referred more generally to the use of a vernacular idiom in the song lyrics.

Gospel song is often also named as one of the sources of the New Orleans idiom, but as a Catholic city New Orleans had a much stronger tradition of Catholic ritual, with its chanted responses and sung liturgies. The Creole musicians, with their Catholic backgrounds, were separated from the emotionalism of the Baptist services, and the ragtime-inflected rhythms of the earliest New Orleans recordings maintain a considerable distance from the surging rhythms of the revival hymns. There were certainly influences from the Caribbean, and the syncopated rhythm of the Cuban habanera, but it was the European march and the banjo/piano rhythms of ragtime that had an even more decisive effect on the characteristic forms and the instrumental styles of the first jazz decades. What is just as relevant to the story of New Orleans jazz is the influence of the wave of Italian and Sicilian immigrants during this period. The popular Italian melodies and the lyric Italian trumpet sound left their mark on the playing of so many New Orleans jazz artists.

My own conclusion, after many years of turning over in my mind the questions of ownership and appropriation, is that each of the musical worlds in

New Orleans needed the others to create the city's distinctive musical style. What I have finally worked through for myself is what a black older musician quoted in *Bourbon Street Black*, and again not identified, described in *his* interpretation of the complicated relationship between the two groups. Since he knew the names of four of the five members of the Original Dixieland Jazz Band—cornetist Nick La Rocca, trombonist Eddie Edwards, clarinetist Larry Shields, and pianist Henry Ragas—he was probably familiar with some of the jazz writing that has carried on the perpetual discussion.

> . . . *some of the bands—they call 'em Dixieland. They play little pieces, and some of 'em have been listenin' to the Negro musicians playin' around—and they put it together. And, it was just a little bit more organized. LaRocca. He went up there (to the North). He wasn't no great musician. He just played a little straight horn, and I don't think he could read much. But some of the guys like Edwards, I think he was a fair musician. Larry Shields, he couldn't read much, but he had a nice tone. Ragas was one of them. They were a little bit organized. They got their harmonizin' voice—they got together. And they're the ones who put this stuff together, but it's not the way we play it.*[4]

He then went on to point out the differences between the way black musicians from different parts of the country also played differently from each other. For me, his consciousness of the "harmonizin' voice," which is the shaping of the harmonic and ensemble forms of the early music, is a major defining factor that describes the white contribution to the new style. He had his own comfortable explanation for the way music was played in New Orleans. "I think the climate may have somethin' to do with that," and his conclusion was an easy New Orleans compromise. "I think a lot of white musicians take pattern after Negro musicians, and a whole lotta Negro musicians take pattern after white musicians."[5]

Anyone familiar with my first book, *Jazz: New Orleans*,[6] is aware that its subject is the city's African American musical traditions. It is, in essence, a biographical dictionary of as many of the city's black musicians as I was able to trace between 1885 and 1957, and despite its limitations and errors it was helpful to a number of other writers. For much of the research I spent time with the veteran musicians themselves, and the book was the result of hours of interviews in front rooms, on verandahs, over kitchen tables, or sitting on the steps in the breaks during a long brass band funeral. It was centered on black musicians because I had been stunned by my first experience of institutionalized racism when I first came to New Orleans in 1950, and as I began doing research in newspaper files and in official records, I found that for these sources, the black world of the city did not really exist except as a kind of vague background sketched in the shadows behind the city's white world. Since this seemed to be a story that was fading from people's memories, I felt it was necessary to begin at that moment to do what I could to preserve something that lay outside of the ordinary social memory, and to write about the black musicians was a way for me to make some kind of statement about the racial situation that had forced its way into my consciousness.

At the same time, I felt that what I was doing was only a beginning, and that eventually the whole story should be told in much greater depth than I could achieve by myself. The Ford Foundation Grant in the late 1950s, designed to support this research that led to the creation of the oral history recordings at the William Hogan Jazz Archive at Tulane University, and the invaluable work of interviewing and collecting headed by Richard B. Allen and William Russell, fortunately came in time to preserve much more of the story.

When I was gathering material for that first book, I had so few sources to draw on—only the first slim discographies, a handful of books on jazz, and some musical journals that specialized in jazz but were largely devoted to chronicling and reviewing the current jazz scene. Now there is a flood of material, some careful and comprehensive, some considerably less so, but all of it with something that relates directly to the story of New Orleans jazz. So with all of these qualifications, can I still insist that there is a distinct New Orleans jazz style? Even after so many years have passed, is it still possible to tell its story? Obviously I think so. My hope with this introduction is at least to begin the story with all of us stepping off on the same beat.

JOE FRISCO "COUNTING OFF THE BEAT" FOR TOM BROWN'S JASS BAND ON THE STREETS OF CHICAGO, PROBABLY LATE AUGUST, 1915. THE FACE OF THE DRUMMER, BILLY LAMBERT, IS HIDDEN BEHIND FRISCO'S RIGHT HAND; BROWN, RAY LOPEZ, AND LARRY SHIELDS ARE VISIBLE OVER HIS LEFT ARM AND SHOULDER. AT THE EDGE OF THE CROWD TO THE RIGHT IS BASSIST DEACON LOYOCANO. THE FIGURE AT FAR LEFT, WITH HIS HAND ON THE TROMBONE CASE, IS AL CAPONE.

1

A City like No Other

What would you have me describe? the ancient part of the city, its narrow streets, French and Spanish-built houses, with their showy colored stuccoes, and iron balconies,—or the numerous Fauborgs, with their spacious pavements and tall ranges of handsome buildings? Would you look upon the square of the Cathedral, whitewashed and weather-stained without, and dusty within; the public edifices; the immense buildings erected by private companies for the pressing and warehousing of the produce of the cotton plantations? Or would you peep in upon the varieties of human race that crowd every avenue, and swarm along the levees? Were I to make choice of a spot, from which the scene passing upon or within sight of which you would glean the most vivid idea of the characteristic features of this strange city, I should lead you to the levee in front of the square of the Cathedral, and bid you post yourself for an hour in the vicinity of the markets.

CHARLES JOSEPH LATROBE, WRITING AS "THE RAMBLER,"
DESCRIBING HIS VISIT TO NEW ORLEANS IN DECEMBER, 1833[1]

It was a Frenchman who led the first European journey down the river, and who was the first to drift in an unsteady bark canoe past the bend in its current that became New Orleans. The leader of the small party, Rene-Robert Cavelier, sieur de la Salle, was a French entrepreneur—a fur merchant—who had floated the thousands of miles down the river in an effort to find a more economical way to ship his furs from the forests of the northern river valley to Europe. On March 31, 1682, they stopped at a village of the Tangipahoa tribe, the natives who lived along the river. The village was close to the site of what was to become known as the Bayou St. John portage, and the portage was to become New Orleans. La Salle continued down the river, and reached its mouth

9

on April 9, and before he made his way back to the native village he claimed all of the river valley of the Mississippi for Louis XIV, the king of France, naming it Louisiana. The land he proclaimed as French was occupied by the millions of native peoples who had lived on it for millennia, but in their rush to seize the continent, the only land claims the Europeans recognized were each other's.

What LaSalle found at the mouth of the river was that in reality there was no single mouth. As the current pushed out into the Gulf of Mexico the alluvial deposits the water had been carrying from the interior of the vast continent were dropped in uneven tongues of shifting mud and sand. As one channel became clogged the water shifted to another, and it continued reaching out into the gulf like outstretched fingers. The shallows were also thick with alligators, sliding through the mud, roaring at each other, eager to attack anyone who was forced to leave their boat. La Salle returned to the portage, and the natives led him away from the river bank, following the path they had worn as they walked north four or five miles to a small river which emptied into the large lake, later to be named Lake Ponchartrain, at the river's mouth. With their canoes the natives traveled down the river to Ponchartrain, less than three miles away, then east along its south shore to the opening of a second large lake to the east, which was later named Lake Bourne. Paddling east, the natives followed Bourne's northern shore, ending at the shores of the gulf, bypassing the morass at the mouth of the Mississippi.

The Bayou St. John portage finally became the site of the planned city. Physically, it was one of the least promising sites for a city that any of the first groups of colonists had chosen anywhere in North America. To the group of financiers thousands of miles away in Paris who were supporting the colony, however, the location might have seemed ideal. The new city was to be situated on the banks of the majestic Mississippi River, the opening to the still mostly unexplored continent. It was almost ninety miles from the river's mouth, and in the best years the land was only two or three feet above the river's seasonal floods, but despite the problems, which were never made clear to the potential investors, a decision was made in 1717 to begin work on a settlement, which was tactfully named for the royal regent, the Duc d'Orleans. Its role was to be a trans-shipping point for trade goods coming down the Mississippi River. The small craft bringing the trade goods would unload their cargoes at the new settlement at the portage, the goods would be carried to the small river, loaded again onto small craft that would bring the merchandise through the lakes to the gulf, and finally transferred to the oceangoing vessels that would carry the merchandise to France or the French colonies in the Caribbean.

The actual site for the city was selected by Jean Baptiste le Moyne, sieur de Bienville, whose titled name was to live on as one of the city's streets. Although the mouth of the river was already an obstacle to ships trying to overcome the current and sail upstream, the crescent of the river was also considered more easily defensible, since the settlement could be built on the level ground

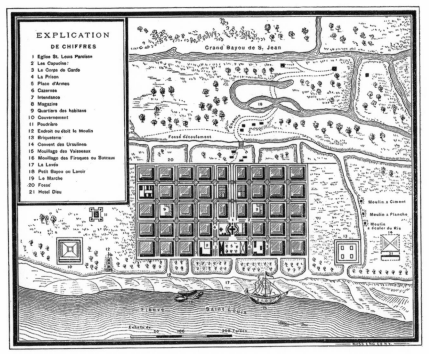

New Orleans, the newly planned city, 1728. Courtesy of the University of Texas Libraries, The University of Texas at Austin.

close to the river, and attacks would have to come overland through the swamps. Little was known about the river and its vagaries, but it was easily observable that at high water—in the spring months when the river was swollen with the runoff from the snows in its northern tributaries—some areas close to the river's crescent were less heavily flooded. The French noted where the native tribes living in the bayous had placed their scattered villages, and they realized that in the almost yearly flooding, these areas of the swamps suffered the least and drained quickly. Nearly three hundred years later, when the flooding of 2005 devastated the city after the winds of Hurricane Katrina, comparisons with old city maps showed that the parts of the city that had survived with the least damage were the sites where the natives had placed their villages.

The insoluble problem for the city—which the sketchy geological knowledge of the period could not have told the planners when the first proposals were drawn up—was that there is no solid ground beneath it. The whole of the delta at the lower stretches of the Mississippi is made up of loose deposits of mud, sand, and stones carried by the river's current, then dropped to the bed of the channel when the river's strength ebbs as it flows into the Gulf of Mexico. As one riverbed filled with silt the river changed course, first gouging out a new bed, then as inevitably filling it with the deposits of the yearly flooding. Over the tens of thousands of years that it had emptied into the sea, the Mississippi had changed its mouth many times, and the mushy layers of debris were spread over hundreds of miles.

The flow of the current was slower when the French made their first plans. Upriver, there were none of the levees or barrier walls that hem in the river today, that deepen it, and speed up its flow as the mass of water is continually squeezed into a narrower current. There was nothing upstream to impede its flow, so the spring flooding simply spread over the low banks into Arkansas and Mississippi. The twists and bends of the river changed each season, and the layers of soil that the river picked up in its first flush of the floods in the north were spread over a wide flood plain, creating what, a century later, would become one of the richest agricultural areas of the United States. The continuing flow of sediment into the narrow neck of debris below the crescent of the river where the settlement was to be placed simply added more miles to the narrowing fingers of earth at the river's mouth.

What the natives living along the river had learned was that close to the curve of the crescent the river had stayed within its banks for a relatively long period, and the flooding had brought new earth that was heaped on top of the first deposits. The sediment, year by year, became heavier and slowly rose into broad ridges that lifted a little above the other earth further from the river's banks. Although the ridgelines could not be traced through the mass of vegetation, the natives had slowly discovered their general shape. The areas in today's New Orleans that line this inside curve of the crescent—extending from the Carrollton district to the west, through the Garden District, the French Quarter, and through the Bywater to the East, known locally as "the sliver by the river"— escaped the prolonged flooding that drowned much of the rest of the city on August 29, 2005. Another low mound of relatively solid earth extended from the area that became the French Quarter toward Lake Ponchartrain. At the height of the city's prosperity, now named Esplanade Avenue, it was lined with elaborate mansions, which except for the damage from the winds also escaped most of the catastrophe of Hurricane Katrina.

The first clearing for the new settlement began in March 1718, but the work went slowly. The French were using convict labor, there were continual shortages of supplies, and they had to deal with two severe hurricanes in 1721 and 1722. They also were struggling with clouds of mosquitoes, deadly snakes, and land that was covered with a dense tangle of low brush, coarse-leaved vines, and saplings. Perhaps the only thing that finally helped keep some order in the clearing and the slow building was that, instead of permitting the settlement to sprawl in the usual muddle of shacks and meandering dirt paths, a French engineer, Adrien de Pauger, had prepared precise plans for what would become today's French Quarter. The fitful stages of the settlement's construction followed his drawings. The plan created, at least on paper, the center of the new city at a square named the Place d'Armes, now known as Jackson Square. By November of 1721, however, the settlement had been so lamed by the heat and diseases and desertions that it had only 470 people; 277 whites, 172 blacks, and 22 African slaves. The bayous around them still were inhabited by native villagers who traded food for European goods, and without whom it is difficult to know if the colony could have survived. The Europeans had learned from their other contacts with the natives that they made poor slaves, so the natives would ultimately have to be driven from their lands, but in these early exchanges the foreign diseases, against which the natives had no defenses, did much of the work of displacement.

The basic economic plan that lay behind the initial decision to construct a point where goods could be transferred from the river vessels to ocean vessels was sound, but, like so many of the French attempts at building a new France in North America, it foundered on the lack of people to fill the new settlements and the lack of realism in the planning. At this point, when their idea was that New Orleans was to fill with cargoes brought down the Mississippi, there was almost nothing to bring down. The fur trade of Canada was small and there were closer outlets through the rivers of French Canada. The other trade goods that were to have been part of the scheme, agricultural products and raw materials, arrived so desultorily that French ships finally began avoiding the long, difficult trip upstream from the gulf or the interminable delays at the ports close to the entrance to Lake Bourne. Although their arrival did not signal an economic upturn, there was an infusion of older French culture when the refugees from "Acadia," the island renamed Nova Scotia ("New Scotland") began to make their way to Louisiana after the invasion of the island and the destruction of their homes and crops by the British in 1755. Few of the "Acadians," however—the ancestors of today's Cajuns—stayed in New Orleans. The colonial government offered them grants of land along the Mississippi to the north of New Orleans and along the shores of Bayou Forche, one of the many streams that flowed through the bayous to the west. The distribution of their land to the new arrivals forced the natives further from their homes and pushed them west into an uneasy confrontation with tribes they had quarreled with centuries before.

In 1791 there was a new infusion of French blood in New Orleans, following the defeat of the French colonial militias in Haiti by the revolutionary black army led by the charismatic slave leader Toussaint l'Ouverture. More than six thousand French citizens and their French-speaking servants fled to New Orleans, one of several American cities where they were welcomed. The melodies that the brilliant nineteenth-century New Orleans composer Louis Moreau Gottschalk adapted for his early compositions were based on the Haitian songs he learned from his mother, who had been born into the Haitian white aristocracy, and from her servant, an African slave who had followed her from Haiti. The continuing wars in Europe, however, cast long shadows in the European colonies, including the one the French had built along the Mississippi. In 1763 the French government—entangled in the unsuccessful war that lost Canada to the English armies—in a secret treaty ceded the entire Louisiana territory, including what was still its unprofitable port in New Orleans, to Spain.

The Spanish administrators who took over the city—and rebuilt the French Quarter in the Spanish colonial style after a disastrous fire in 1788 that destroyed 850 homes—were much more efficient than the French, and the end of the American Revolutionary War made investment in the colony seem a little more promising. The look of the city changed with the fire and the rebuilding that followed. The original blocks that were laid out by de Pauger had been subdivided into twelve house sites, and in each the original settlers built heavy log houses surrounded by gardens and smaller structures. Thick hedges of orange trees divided the sites from each other. The houses, with their entrances open to the street, were built up to the edge of narrow wooden sidewalks that were constructed around each of the large blocks. The narrow streets were unpaved, and beside the wooden sidewalks there were deep ditches to provide drainage. The fire swept away the wooden houses, and in their place the Spanish built a new city of stucco and wood, with the severe Spanish lines that were typical of the style of construction in the Spanish colonies to the south. The new, substantial structures were built close enough to touch each other, and they crowded against the sidewalks that were now laid out with stone and gravel. It is this Spanish town that has survived into the modern era and is known today as the French Quarter, or by the French term "Vieux Carré," which means the old section. The ornamental ironwork that is one of the glories of the old section was added to the buildings in the 1840s and 1850s.

Even more important than the changes to the buildings, however, was the change occurring hundreds of miles up the river. The rush of settlers into the western territories of the newly created states of the rapidly expanding American republic brought them to the Ohio River and to the Mississippi. They succeeded in decimating the native tribes and, as quickly as they were able to clear the forests, utilized the land they had seized for European-style farming. The trade that the French had anticipated finally began in earnest, and frontier adventurers were soon bringing cargoes to land in New Orleans. The perception of the city as an exotic world, as a place of romantic adventure, took root in these years; and the perception of New Orleans as a place to leave the inhibitions of the communities to the north on the emptied boats also emerged at the same time.

The frontiersmen, some of them floating down the river on rafts of logs that they sold as timber, were usually Protestant, and often with a stiffly moralistic church background. When they stepped off the wharves into New Orleans, they were in a Catholic city with a less restrictive Caribbean attitude toward what to them was "sin." They had also finally been paid after their long, arduous, and risky trip, and they faced a more difficult trip back up the river, since there were no railroads, and hardly roads of any kind. New Orleans offered a moment's respite, and soon, like every other port in the Caribbean, it had become loose, seductive, raw, and irrepressible. To land their cargoes, the riverboat men had to have a "Right of Deposit" from the Spanish authorities, and several times in the three decades that the Spanish controlled New Orleans the right was denied to the boatmen in an effort to curb their drunken excesses when they were on shore.

Under pressure from the French government, Spain returned the territory in 1803, then a few months later the French sold it to the United States. The formal transfer took place in a ceremony at the Place d'Armes the same year. The Spanish years had been beneficial to the colony in every way. The population was now 8,000 people, divided between 4,000 whites, 2,700 slaves, and 1,300 free persons of color. The free persons of color generally spoke French, and they were later to be known as Creoles of Color, to distinguish them from the French settlers who also referred to themselves as Creoles. The language and musical culture of the two French societies were to have a decisive role in the development of the city's unique musical traditions. The new streets and the spread of buildings now began to resemble the dream of the conscientious French officer who had drawn the plans for the streets of the first city. In 1805, the city's government was separated from the administration of the Louisiana territories, and New Orleans became the self-governing entity that it is today. There was the first expansion into what the French settlers called the Fauborg St. Marie, using the French term "fauborg" for districts. This was the land across the broad commons that is now known as Canal Street. The new buildings and houses were the center of the rapidly growing American business community that was exploiting the new economic possibilities.

Two technical developments, however, also had to be in place before the city could realize its potential as the shipping center for the Mississippi Valley.

First, there had to be some important commodity that was being produced in the new areas upriver for the merchants in New Orleans to have something to sell. The new commodity turned out to be cotton. The invention of the cotton gin, which ended the ancient, exhausting problem of separating cotton fiber from the cottonseeds by hand, suddenly made the rich farmlands, dark in soil deposits from the annual Mississippi floods, the potential cotton kingdom of the future.

The second needed development was some improved way to ship the bulky cotton down the river, since the small boats relying on river currents, oars, and sails could not handle the large amounts of cotton that the land could produce. In 1812, as the second war with Britain was slowly being waged in the north, the first steamboat, named the *Orleans*, sailed down the river, starting its journey at Pittsburgh on the Ohio River, a tributary of the Mississippi that joins it south of St. Louis. The steamboat was to be the final piece in the economic construct that would lead to the city's growth. With the Battle of New Orleans in January 1815, when Andrew Jackson and a disorderly army of Cajuns, local militia, and a sprinkling of pirates defeated a major British force attempting to march through the swampy underbrush from the east in an effort to seize the city, there was a new self-confidence among the people who now began to think of themselves as Americans. The reality that the battle had taken place after the peace treaty ending the war had already been signed did nothing to stem the surge of bustling self-confidence.

With all of its new swagger, however, the city was still a servant to its situation along the river. The first small settlement had been protected by a crude dirt levee two feet high, but within a year it was raised another foot when spring floods swept away many of the rough houses. In 1853 a large *Gazetteer* of the United States discussed the city's situation in some detail, and described the precautions that had been taken in the intervening years: "The site of New Orleans, in conformity to other parts of the banks of the Mississippi in the same vicinity, is on an inclined plane; the declivity falling very gently from the margin of the river towards the swamp in the rear. When the river is full, the surface of the water is from 2 to 4 feet above the streets of the city; and at any stage it is above the swamps in the rear of the back streets. To prevent inundation, an artificial embankment, called the *Levee*, has been built upon the river, at a great expense, extending from Fort Plaquemine, 43 miles below the city, to 120 miles above it, which is 4 feet high and 15 feet wide."[2]

The "swamps in the rear of the back streets," despite the omnipresent danger of flooding, were to become the center of New Orleans, which was steadily expanding as the city continued to build on the unstable soil toward Lake Ponchartrain.

Despite these efforts to hem it in with levees, however, the river continued to dominate the life of the city. When Charles Latrobe, a popular London writer who used the pen name "The Rambler," visited the city in December 1833, he found that the water continued to be one of the hazards.

In this remarkable city we were detained a month; I say detained, because our curiosity was soon sated with its motley scenes, and we were anxious once more to reach a piece of dry solid ground. Well may New Orleans be called the 'Wet Grave.' With a thermometer between 70 and 80 degrees, and a constant drizzle, the surrounding country was a sheet of water; the streets were full of mud oozing up from the pavement, and it was a penance to be within its thick and unwholesome atmosphere. The last hours of December, an impenetrable mist rested on the city, through which frequent flashes of lightning glimmered portentously;—then came a terrific storm ushering in the New Year, but with no abatement in the heat till the following night, when the temperature fell below the freezing point.

Three days after the country was covered with snow, and many miserable wretches were found dead in the streets and under the porticoes. It continued freezing for four days, when the atmosphere again regained the former degree of heat. Such a chaos of mud can hardly be conceived.[3]

Despite its problems—or perhaps as a way to ignore them—the people of this continually threatened city gave themselves to the pleasure of dance, theater, and music with a fervor that startled its visitors. In his book *Music in New Orleans*, historian Henry A. Kmen recorded some of the wondering responses of the newcomers to the city's gaiety.

To a French refugee from Saint-Dominique who fled to New Orleans in 1803, it seemed that "they dance in the city, they dance in the country, they dance everywhere." The women especially would, he thought, "pass all their days and nights" at dancing if they could. An American Protestant thought that this ardor for dancing was carried to "an incredible excess. Neither the severity of the cold, nor the oppression of the heat, ever restrains them from this amusement, which usually commences early in the evening, and is seldom suspended until late the next morning." . . . Another observer who called himself "a Yankee" dourly remarked that New Orleanians managed during a single winter "to execute about as much dancing, music, laughing and dissipation, as would serve any reasonably disposed, staid and sober citizens, for three or four years," even if the latter were given all year to do it in. With less disapproval a French visitor noticed young mothers at a dance nursing their babies between waltzes—a feat made easy by the cut of their gowns and understandable by the assertion that they had dreamt of nothing but the balls since the age of seven. He could only characterize such fervor for dancing as "an inconceivable rage." Perhaps the best description though was provided by Louis Tasistro, an actor who played in New Orleans in the late 1830's. He simply called the city "one vast waltzing and gallopading Hall."[4]

Kmen's book documents balls of all kinds on all occasions. There were children's balls, colored balls, balls for slaves that insisted that the slaves have permissions from the owners to attend. There were also the widely famed "quadroon balls." Entrance to these balls was restricted to white men and free women of color, though often slave women also managed to be included in the excitement. In romantic accounts of these mixed balls, there was an emphasis on the decorum of the women present, many of them chaperoned by their mothers, as they sought a protector, since marriage was not to be considered. The reality was less orderly.

It wasn't however, solely the lure of flirtation, the heightened gaiety, and the easy informality that drew men to the quadroon balls. Judging from the descriptions of the wantonness and disorder that attended them, there were enough white balls replete with these qualities. It was quite simply that the quadroon affairs outdid the white ones when it came to lewdness and excitement. Alexis de Toqueville found the laxity of morals at these balls incredible. One of New Orleans's own newspapers honestly acknowledged them to be "inter-racial orgies." A man might even find himself dancing with a girl wearing only her nightgown it he didn't watch out.

In short, most of the quadroon balls, like the lower-class white balls, were fields of operation for prostitutes. Acting mayor John Culbertson denounced them in 1835 as "sinks of the most dissolute class of women." The Globe Ballroom was variously labeled "that most villainous of all establishments"; "the saturnalia of the depraved portion of our population," and a "moral fester on the community." The Louisiana Ballroom was called a "den of iniquity."[5]

The newspapers generally tried to present themselves as bastions of morality, and their accounts of anything relating to pleasure and excitement tended to take on an ominous tone; however, even allowing for a level of exaggeration it was clear that the quadroon balls were particularly problematic. Kmen notes that although all the balls were subject to fights and violent altercations of every kind—even with all weapons checked at the door—the quadroon balls were even more dangerous. Duels were occasionally fought over some of the most tantalizing women, adding to the heady flavor of the balls for many of the patrons, and despite the notoriety, the balls continued to be popular. In some of the white ballrooms the women found that so many men had deserted them that there weren't enough to make up the dance sets, and they began to join the ranks of free women of color, at first taking advantage of the widely practiced habit of masking at certain balls to protect their identity, then openly joining the crowds.

In 1840 there were more than eighty ballrooms offering dancing, at least on an occasional basis, and on Carnival night there were eleven balls competing for dancers. In all of the descriptions of the balls, however, there is little mention of the music. Kmen's suggestion is that the music was simply taken for granted, though early travelers' accounts that did notice the orchestras were less than impressed. A description of the orchestra from 1802 noted that the music for the ball the writer attended was played by

> *five or six fiddlers whom he called 'gypsies or persons of color.' He conceded their enthusiasm saying that they scraped away 'with all their might,' but he characterized the sound thus produced as 'squeaky.' . . . Often the advertise-ments of a ball promised that the orchestra would be a better one than last time; or boasted that 'no pains or expense' had been spared in hiring the musi-cians. . . . In spite of such pains, one of the lesser nobility of Europe, the Baron de Montlezun, who went to the Conde Street Ballroom in 1816 when that room was still the best in New Orleans, had this to say: 'The music was paltry and of a pitiable effect. Six crude fiddlers were all the orchestra, ruining some melo-dies, cold and slow and pitiful in contrast with the fire of the dancers.'*[6]

Occasionally the ballroom resorted to inviting the local military bands to per-form the waltzes for the dancers, but as musicians moved in greater numbers to the city, a ballroom that wanted to present itself as among the city's better establishments would have an orchestra of at least fifteen members, performing standard orchestrations.

Even more important to the city's musical life, however, was the widely famed opera. As Kmen noted,

> *Opera was New Orleans's cultural glory throughout the nineteenth century. This city had its own self-supporting, resident company which, for much of the century, offered the best opera to be found in America. Its superiority was especially marked before the Civil War when the presentation of opera in other American cities was sporadic and transient. At its prewar height, opera in New Orleans represented a cultural flowering in the old South that differed only in kind, not in degree, from the vaunted flowering in New England. Its presence in New Orleans was decisive in encouraging and setting the tone of numerous other music activities. Without it the city would not have been able to boast as it did in 1837 that "the little musical enthusiasm prevailing in the United States is nearly entirely encountered in New Orleans."*[7]

For nearly a century one of the proudest institutions of the Creole society was the French Opera House on Bourbon Street. The Swedish social reformer Fredrika Bremer, who traveled through much of the United States, visited the opera in 1850.

> *I was taken by some of my acquaintances to the French Opera, where I saw "Jerusalem," which was very well given. The prima donna, Mademoiselle D. is a great favorite with the public, and deserves to be so, from her lovely figure, the nobility of her demeanor, and her exquisite and melodious singing, though*

her voice in itself is not remarkable. Her hands and arms are of rare beauty, and their movement was in exquisite harmony with her singing.

The most interesting scene to me, however, was not on the stage, but in the theatre itself, where the ladies of New Orleans, seated in their boxes, presented the appearance of a parterre of white roses. They were all dressed in white, gauze-like dresses, with bare necks and arms, some of them very bare indeed, and some of them with flowers in their hair. All were very pale, but not unhealthy looking; many of the young were quite pretty, with delicate features, and round, child-like countenances. Beauty is scarce here, as it is all over the world. The white pearl-powder, which the ladies commonly use, gives to the complexion a great softness, in which, however, the art is too frequently apparent . . .[8]

The opera was much more central to the world of the "Free Persons of Color"—the group that came to be called Creoles—than simply as a social occasion. The orchestra members were largely drawn from the Creole community, and it was this group of well-trained, experienced musicians who were to give the emerging music of New Orleans a distinctive character that was not present in any other American city. When the opera house burned in 1919 one of the popular local writers lamented in his newspaper column, "The heart of the old French Quarter has stopped beating."

As trade on the Mississippi grew, the decades between 1840 and 1860 were to be New Orleans's golden age. In the Caribbean only Havana equaled its economic growth, and in the United States its only rival was the equally tumultuous New York City. New arrivals continued to remark on the city's musical life and on its mania for dances. The wondering accounts they sent home or in excited letters to their small town newspapers claimed emphatically that they had come to a city where there were balls and dancing every night. The advertising columns of the city's newspaper, the *Daily Picayune*, in January and February 1842 confirm that this was no exaggeration: there were public balls every night of the week. At the Chartres Street Ball Room, in the Orleans Hotel between St. Louis and Toulouse Streets, there were "Grand Dress and Masquerade" balls held on Tuesdays, Thursday, and Saturdays, with a special dance "for white ladies" on Sundays. At the Washington and American Ball Room, on St. Philip Street between Royal and Bourbon, there were dress and masquerade balls every Monday, Wednesday, Friday, and Saturday. The admittance charge for gentlemen was $1.50, and for ladies the admittance was "Gratis." At the Orleans Ball Room on Orleans Street there were balls on Monday, Wednesday, Friday and Saturday evenings. Ladies were again admitted gratis, but for gentlemen the admittance was "$2.00 the ticket." An energetic and indefatigable dancer who didn't tire of the excitement could attend thirteen dress balls every week, and the masquerade balls—which meant masks were permitted—opened the dances to almost anyone with the money for an admittance ticket.

There were also continual concerts and musical evenings, often employing a noted "French Orchestra." An enthusiastic review of a concert that appeared in the newspaper on February 16 singled out two orchestras for praise.

It was a matter to be fully anticipated that this concert would turn out brilliantly successful. The orchestra of the Orleans Theatre, the German Glee Club, Madame Fabj, and such a concentration of high musical talent as was combined to form the entertainment, could by no means fail to produce in New Orleans the exciting effect which accordingly took place. The overture to Otello, by the French orchestra, led by Prevost, was executed in a style of perfection, reflecting high honor upon the artistes engaged in the performance, and, indeed, the delighted silence of the thronged audience, while the composition was starting into ravishing sound from the instruments, together with the spontaneous applause that burst forth at its termination, attested unequivocally the lively appreciation which was present on the occasion.[9]

The newspaper columns also noted the din of music in the streets, sometimes by street peddlers, but also by itinerant groups of German musicians. This was a period of steadily increasing immigration from the duchies that constituted the still disunited Germany, and the musicians brought their instruments and the melodies with them. Many local merchants also used drummers or bands of instruments posted in front of their shops to advertise their wares, and generally the pounding of the drums was enough to drive the competing German troubadours on to the next block.

In his descriptions of New Orleans at this moment in its history, Latrobe's writing caught the raw excitement and the stubborn beauty, the din of voices and the mingling of peoples, that made New Orleans a city that was like no other. The immediacy of his response is still so fresh, and his impression of what he experienced so vivid, that the scenes he describes come to life on his pages, anticipating the excitements of the next decades of the city's story.

The lower end of the [Cathedral] square is open to the levee and the river whose margin appears lined for upwards of two miles with ships and boats of every size as close as they can float. Highest up the stream lie the flats, arks, and barges, and below them the tier of steam-boats, fifty of which may be seen lying here at one time. Then come the brigs ranged in rows, with their bows against the breast of the levee; these are succeeded by the three-masters, lying in tiers of two or three deep, with their broadside to the shore, and the scene presented by the whole margin of the river as you look down upon it from the levee or from the roof of Bishop's Hotel in a sunny morning after a night of storm, when the sails of the whole are exposed to the air, and their signals or national flags abroad, is one of the most singularly beautiful you can conceive. . . .

Here, amidst a melee of all classes and costumes—French, Spaniards, Americans, Creoles, Quadroons, Mulattoes, Mexicans, Negroes—you may note a double row of petty merchants disposed along the more open part of the Levee, while paving stones, masses of marble and granite coping stones, piles of lumber and bricks, log-wood, coffee, sugar, corn, and wheat, beef and pork, and mountains of cotton fill up the intervals. Here you see fruit stalls loaded with the produce of the tropics,—bananas, plantains, cocoa and pecan nuts, oranges and pines; there piles of butcher's meat and venison,—fish laid out upon clean fresh palmetto leaves,—eggs wrapped up in Spanish moss,—or lines of seed-sellers with their neat little packets arranged before them on a yellow mat. The Babel of languages is highly diverting, as well as the odd mixture of names appended over the neighboring shops. At every step you meet with something to catch the attention of a curious or idle man.

Here you note a cluster of mulatto women, sitting with kerchief heads and comfortable rabbit skin shawls folded around their persons before the mats which display their various articles of traffic to the passenger—there a group of insurgent market-women tossing their empty baskets at one another, or pale faced quadroon girls half veiled, followed by their duennas. On one side advances a negro, feathered from head to foot by the live turkeys hung upon his person; on the other, a string or mules, or a mulatto driving his dray in the primeval position of a Greek charioteer. Then comes a party of half-a-dozen coloured people, clothed in the brightest hues imaginable, seated with knees and chins in contact, in a car drawn by a single old horse boring its way through the press, or a gray-haired negro going home with his Christmas [sic] dinner, consisting of a fat hen and a string of onions, and grinning with delight from ear to ear. Nor will you fail to mark with astonishment the hubbub of voices and tongues broken in upon by that most indescribable of all joyous sounds, the negro's laugh.[10]

2

People, Faces

It may be a mere fancy, but it has always struck me as a fact, that in Louisiana nature itself is, in many elements, less steady and uniform than in the higher latitudes of our country. Not infrequently the alternations of health and sickness, joy and sorrow, commercial prosperity and misfortune, sweep over the Crescent City with the suddenness and fury of those autumnal hurricanes which occasionally visit it, by which in a few moments of time the strongest edifices are leveled with the dust, the majestic live-oaks and cypresses prostrated, and the vessels along the levee overwhelmed in the flood.

REVEREND THEODORE CLAPP, FROM HIS *AUTOBIOGRAPHICAL SKETCHES*, PUBLISHED IN 1857[1]

New Orleans was an exotic destination for most of the United States in these antebellum decades, but with the vagaries of transportation it also spent most of the nineteenth century, as far as much of the United States was concerned, as the destination at the end of a tedious journey. It was at the end of the Mississippi River, or at the end of the railroads that snaked over the southern fields of the Black Belt southwest from Atlanta, or at the end of the new railroad lines that straddled earth levees through the Mississippi delta south from Chicago. For someone journeying to the city by sea, New Orleans was at the end of dozens of ferry lines and shipping services that crossed the Gulf of Mexico from the south, and made New Orleans as much a part of that foreign world as it was the world of the states to the north.

As this kind of exotic destination, New Orleans had a compelling effect on the occasional young Americans who considered it the ending of something like a railroad line, but at the same time a beginning for what might be their own careers. At different periods, two of nineteenth-century America's most conspicuous literary artists, Walt Whitman and Mark Twain, visited the city. Whitman experienced New Orleans as a neophyte newspaper reporter in the 1840s, while Twain, as a young riverboat pilot and hopeful writer, contributed pieces to the same newspaper where Whitman had been employed, *The Crescent*, a decade later. A third talented young journalist, Lafcadio Hearn, arrived after the war, when so much had already changed. The sojourns of Whitman and Twain were only a pause in a longer journey, but Hearn found the city more to his liking. His descriptions of his dozen years there, both in his lengthy published articles and his letters, helped give many people outside of the city the sense of what it was like to walk the New Orleans streets, to feel its soft night air and to smell the layering of odors that hung in the streets.

Whitman was approached in 1887 by the New Orleans newspaper the *Picayune* and asked if he had any memories of the city that he could contribute to their fiftieth anniversary celebration. Whitman answered with pleasure.

. . . I went down to New Orleans early in 1848 to work on a daily newspaper, but it was not the Picayune, *though I saw a good deal of the editors of that paper and knew its personnel and ways. But let me indulge my pen in some gossipy recollections of that time and place . . .*

One of my choice amusements during my stay in New Orleans was going down to the old French Market, especially of a Sunday morning. The show was a varied and a curious one; among the rest the Indian and negro hucksters with their wares. For there were always fine specimens of Indians, both men and women, both young and old. I remember I nearly always on these occasions got a large cup of delicious coffee with a biscuit, for my breakfast, from the immense shining copper kettle of a great Creole mulatto woman (I believe she weighted 230 pounds). I have never had such coffee since. About nice drinks, anyhow, my recollection of the "cobblers" (with strawberries and snow on top of the large tumblers), and also the exquisite wines, and the perfect and mild French brandy, help the regretful reminiscence of my New Orleans experiences of those days. And what splendid and roomy and leisurely bar-rooms! particularly the grand ones of the St. Charles and the St. Louis. Bargains, auctions, appointments, business conferences, &c., were generally held in the spaces or recesses of these bar-rooms.

I used to wander a mid-day hour or so now and then for amusement on the crowded and bustling levees, on the banks of the river. The diagonally wedg'd in boats, the stevedores, the piles of cotton and other merchandise, the carts, mules, negroes, etc., afforded never-ending studies and sights to me. . . . Sundays I sometimes went forenoons to the old Catholic Cathedral in the French Quarter. I used to walk a good deal in this arrondissement; and I have deeply regretted since that I did not cultivate, while I had such a good opportunity, the chance of better knowledge of French and Spanish Creole New Orleans people . . .

THE NEW ORLEANS LEVEE, 1880S. MUGNIER PHOTO, COURTESY MAUDE FERRIER. SAMUEL CHARTERS COLLECTION.

Let me say, for better detail, that through several months (1848) I work'd on a new daily paper, The Crescent; *my situation rather a pleasant one. My young brother, Jeff, was with me; and he not only grew homesick, but the climate of the place, and especially the water, seriously disagreed with him. For this and other reasons (although I was quite happily fix'd) I made no very long stay in the South. In due time we took passage northward for St. Louis in the "Pride of the West" steamer, which left her berth at dusk. My brother was unwell, and lay in his berth from the moment we left till the next morning; he seem'd to me to be in fever, and I felt rather alarm'd. However, the next morning he was alright again, much to my relief.[2]*

Whitman's concern for his brother's health was well founded. Generally the descriptive writing by travelers like Whitman who visited the city during the antebellum years emphasized the pleasures of walks in the French Quarter or the colorful life along the river, but it was at the same time a period of continual struggle against the endemic flooding and the epidemic diseases that swept the city. In typical years like 1831 and 1832 there were outbreaks of cholera and yellow fever, and tens of thousands of people died. In his classic book *Fabulous New Orleans*, published in 1928, writer Lyle Saxon gave considerable space to a little known memoir about New Orleans life by a Presbyterian minister, Reverend Theodore Clapp, who wrote his reminiscences in 1857, after living through the series of contagions that threatened to destroy the city. He described the scene on October 25, 1832, shortly after he had discovered two men dying from what he recognized as "Asiatic cholera" when he was walking on the levee in the predawn light. They had been taken ill when they were on a river steamer, and they had been dragged onto the levee and abandoned by the ship's crew.

The weather, this morning, was very peculiar. The heavens were covered with thick, heavy, damp, lowering clouds, that seemed like one black ceiling spread over the whole horizon. To the eye, it almost touched the tops of the houses. Every one felt a strange difficulty of respiration. I never looked upon such a gloomy, appalling sky before or since. Not a breath of wind stirred. It was so dark, that in some of the banks, offices, and private houses, candles or lamps were lighted that day.

Immediately after breakfast I walked down to the post office. At every corner, and around the principal hotels, were groups of anxious faces. As soon as they saw me, the question was put by several persons at a time, "Is it a fact that the cholera is in the city?" I replied by describing what I had seen but two hours before. . . . That day as many persons left the city as could find the means of transmigration. On my way home from the post office, I walked along the levee where the two cholera patients had disembarked but two or three hours before. Several families in the neighborhood were making preparations to move, but in vain. They could not obtain the requisite vehicles. The same afternoon the pestilence entered their houses, and before dark spread through several squares opposite to the point where the steamer landed the first cases.[3]

Between October 27 and November 6, 1832, there were at least 5,000 deaths. Many more died without being included in the official count of bodies. Reverend Clapp noted that many victims simply were thrown into the river, with weights of some kind tied to their feet. One ingredient in the terror that greeted the outbreak of any of the feared killers was the reality that their cause was unknown. The city's appalling drinking water was certainly part of the problem, but there were long periods when people drank the water without falling sick. When the disease struck, its progress seemed relentless.

Persons were found dead all along the streets, particularly in the mornings. For myself, I expected that the city would be depopulated. I have no doubt, that if the truth could be ascertained, it would appear that those persons who died so suddenly were affected with what were called then premonitory symptoms hours, perhaps a day, or a night, before they considered themselves unwell. In this early stage, the disease is easily arrested; but when the cramps and collapse set it, death is, in most cases, inevitable. Indeed, that is death. Then, nothing was known of the cholera, and its antecedent stages were unnoticed and uncared for . . .

Nature seemed to sympathize in the dreadful spectacle of human woe. A thick, black atmosphere, as I said before, hung over us like a mighty funeral shroud. All was still. Neither sun, nor moon, nor stars shed their blessed light.

Not a breath of air moved, A hunter, who lived on the Bayou St. John, assured me that during the cholera he killed no game. Not a bird was seen winging the sky. Artificial causes of terror were superadded to the gloom which covered the heavens. The burning of tar and pitch at every corner; the firing of cannon, by order of the city authorities, along all the streets; and the frequent conflagrations which actually occurred at that dreadful period—all these conspired to add a sublimity and horror to the tremendous scene. Our wise men hoped, by the combustion of tar and gunpowder, to purify the atmosphere. We have no doubt that hundreds perished from mere fright produced by artificial noise, the constant sight of funerals, darkness, and various other causes.

It was an awful spectacle to see night ushered in by the firing of artillery in different parts of the city, making as much noise as arises from the engagement of two powerful armies. The sight was one of the most tremendous which was ever presented to the eye, or even exhibited to the imagination, in description. Often, walking my nightly rounds, the flames from the burning tar so illuminated the city streets and river, that I could see everything almost as distinctly as in the daytime. And through many a window into which was flung the sickly flickering of those conflagrations, could be seen persons struggling in death, and rigid, blackened corpses, awaiting the arrival of some cart or hearse, as soon as dawn appeared, to transport them to their final resting place.[4]

Earlier in that same year the city had already suffered a yellow fever epidemic that killed almost 8,000 people. New Orleans was the continual victim of storms and floods, and there were almost yearly outbreaks of cholera and yellow fever. A cholera epidemic of 1842 again claimed thousands of lives, but it was to be fifty years, 1892, before New Orleans belatedly began to install a sewage system. In 1853 New Orleans was ravaged by the worst siege of yellow fever in the history of the United States. More than 11,000 people died before the pestilence had spent itself. Throughout these years malaria was so common that it went almost unnoticed. The summers were generally the most deadly season, the stifling months when the "vapors" of the surrounding swamps hung over the city. Families with the means to escape sought some relief in the towns along the Gulf Coast to the east, where the ocean breezes kept the air clearer. It wasn't until medical research finally identified the causes of the diseases—the clouds of mosquitoes breeding in the standing water in the ditches along the streets and in the city's cisterns, the practice of relying on the river water for drinking after a crude purification process, the millions of rats that infested the old buildings—that there was a serious effort to deal with the problems. With the discovery in 1905 that the mosquito was the cause of yellow fever there was a determined effort to eliminate the insect's breeding grounds, and the fever became a thing of the past.

In the early period of his life when he was piloting on the river, Mark Twain couldn't have missed seeing New Orleans, since it was the destination of many of the steamboats he guided down the river's twisting shoals and bars. It was also the period of the city's greatest prosperity. Despite the continual epidemics, the hurricanes, and the nearly yearly flooding, the river brought the produce of the Mississippi River's banks to the city. Along the jammed levees, gangs of stevedores unloaded the steamboats and barges, and the flood of goods was inventoried and sold, or shipped onward by sea to the ports of the eastern United States or further on to Europe. These were the years when cotton became the staple of the English weaving mills, and the newly opened lands of the Mississippi delta, inland from Natchez, grew cotton in such abundance that it supplied the world. In the 1830s New Orleans was probably the wealthiest city in the country, and its population was the third largest. There was continual contention as to whether New Orleans or New York was the largest port city in the nation, but New Orleanians were satisfied that they were the leaders. The population by 1840 had grown to over 102,193, despite the omnipresent dangers of flooding and disease.

Although the rise of the railroads already presaged New Orleans's decline as a major shipping destination, it was the Civil War, erupting in 1861, and the early capture of the city by the Union forces in 1862 that put an end to the city's greatest period of prosperity. The war had also put an end to Mark Twain's piloting. In 1875, however, almost fifteen years later, he contributed several sketches titled "Old Times on the Mississippi" to a New York magazine, and there was considerable interest from his growing audience in a full-length book of his early experiences. He had been away from the river for so long he didn't think he had enough to write about, so after many delays he returned to the river in 1882, traveling as a passenger and already well-known writer. *Life on the Mississippi* appeared the next year. He was now doing some of the most concentrated and effective writing of his long and productive career. His classic *The Adventures of Tom Sawyer* had been published six years earlier and *Adventures of Huckleberry Finn* would appear a year later, in 1884.

Twain's own view of the city, in these years when the first outlines of what was to become its distinctive musical language were taking form, was a jambalaya of feelings. What he didn't like he told his readers without hesitation, but what he did find to enjoy he praised with the same fulsomeness. The business part of the city, close to the river, looked about the same to him. "The city itself had not changed—to the eye. It had greatly increased in spread and population, but the look of the town was not altered. The dust, waste-paper littered, was still deep in the streets; the deep, trough-like gutters alongside the curb-stones were still half full of reposeful water with a dusty surface; the sidewalks were still—in the sugar and bacon region—encumbered by casks and barrels and hogsheads; the great blocks of austerely plain commercial houses were as dusty looking as ever."[5]

When his eye turned to the New Orleans homes, he was as effusive about the shaded streets of the Garden District as he'd been skeptical of the commercial blocks. The cisterns he describes were a necessary way to store rainwater, since the city was still without a water system.

The domestic architecture in New Orleans is reproachless, notwithstanding it remains as it always was. All the dwellings are of wood—in the American part of town, I mean—and all have a comfortable look. Those in the wealthy quarter are spacious; painted snow-white usually, and generally have wide verandas, supported by ornamental columns. These mansions stand in the centre of large grounds and rise, garlanded with roses, out of the midst of swelling masses of shining green foliage and many-colored blossoms. No houses could well be in better harmony with their surroundings, or more pleasing to the eye, or more home-like and comfortable-looking.

One even becomes reconciled to the cistern presently; this is a mighty cask, painted green, and sometimes a couple of stories high, which is propped against the house corner on stilts. There is a mansion-and-brewery suggestion about the combination which seems very incongruous at first. But the people cannot have wells, and so they take rain-water. Neither can they conveniently have cellars, or graves; the town being built upon "made" ground; so they do without both, and few of the living complain, and none of the others.[6]

Although Twain spent several weeks in New Orleans he doesn't seem to have heard any music, except at the Ponchartrain resorts, West End and Spanish Fort, and he limits himself to a casual mention that thousands of New Orleanians took the train out to the lake every night to listen to the music of the brass bands, have something to eat, and "take strolls in the open air under the electric lights." The city might not have a water or a sewage system, but he found that in 1882 it already had more miles of electric lights than any city he'd visited in the United States.

It is also ominous to note that in his writings he was aware of the danger that New Orleans faced if the levees were to give way, a danger that became a bitter reality when the levees were breached in Hurricane Katrina.

The approaches to New Orleans were familiar; general aspects were unchanged. When one goes flying through London along a railway propped in the air on tall arches, he may inspect miles of upper bedrooms through the open windows, but the lower half of the houses is under his level and out of sight. Similarly, in high-river stage, in the New Orleans region, the water is up to the top of the enclosing levee-rim, the flat country behind it lies low—representing the bottom of a dish—and as the boat swims along, high on the flood, one looks down upon the houses and into the upper windows. There is nothing but that frail breastwork of earth between the people and destruction.[7]

For other people who came to New Orleans, the feeling of languor and pleasurable romance generally outweighed the filth of the streets and the smells of the open sewers. Lafcadio Hearn came to the city from Cincinnati, where he had been one of the city's best known newspaper journalists and where, in secret, he had married an African American woman. He somehow managed to live a clandestine life with her for some time before the relationship was discovered and he was forced to leave his job and Cincinnati itself. He picked up his career again in New Orleans, and was drawn to the social life he found in the French Quarter, where he lived during his early years. He first contribution to his new employer, the *Daily City Item*, in November 1878 was a tender sketch portraying "The Glamour of New Orleans."

The season has come at last when strangers may visit us without fear, and experience with unalloyed pleasure the first delicious impression of the most beautiful and picturesque old city in North America. For in this season is the glamour of New Orleans strongest upon those whom she attracts to her from less hospitable climates, and fascinates by her nights of magical moonlight, and her days of dreamy languors and perfumes. There are few who can visit her for the first time without delight; and few who can ever leave her without regret; and none who can forget her strange charm when they have once felt its influence.[8]

A year later he wrote an impressionistic piece that gave a glimpse of the life of the Creole families behind the building façades of the French Quarter.

Like many of the Creole houses, the façade presented a commonplace and unattractive aspect. The great green doors of the arched entrance were closed; and the green shutters of the balconied windows were half shut, like sleepy eyes lazily gazing upon the busy street below or the cottony patches of light clouds which floated slowly, slowly across the deep blue of the sky above. But beyond the gates lay a little Paradise. The great court, deep and broad, was framed in tropical green; vines embraced the white pillars of the piazza, and creeping plants climbed up the tinted walls to peer into the upper windows with their flower-eyes of flaming scarlet. Banana-trees nodded sleepily their plumes of emerald green at the farther end of the garden, vines smothered the windows of the dining-room, and formed a bower of cool green about the hospitable door . . . Without, cotton floats might rumble, and street cars vulgarly jingle their bells, but these were mere echoes of the harsh outer world which disturbed not the delicious quiet within . . . Without, roared the Iron Age, the angry waves of American traffic; within, one heard only the murmur of the languid fountain, the sound of deeply musical voices conversing in the languages of Paris and Madrid, the playful chatter of dark-haired children lisping in sweet and many-voweled Creole, and through it all, the soft, caressing coo of doves. Without, it was the year 1879; within it was the epoch of the Spanish Domination.[9]

The term "Creole" was used casually in New Orleans, but the diffuse interpretations of the word's meaning were also a reflection of the racial ambiguities that were part of the city's social fabric. Originally the Portuguese word *crioulo* was used to describe an African slave born in the Western Hemisphere. For some time it was also used to characterize anyone with a European background who had also been born in one of the new colonies. In Louisiana, the old French families became upset at the vagueness of the racial implications of the term and insisted it applied only to whites. They adopted the term *le gens libre de couleur* as the designation for the mulatto families of the French Quarter, and the phrase was commonly anglicized to Creoles of Color. Almost without exception, all of the early musicians referred to as Creoles would be more properly classed as Creoles of Color, although as the flamboyant political figure of the 1930s Huey Long once claimed, all of the "pure" white people in New Orleans could be fed on a half a cup of beans and a half cup of rice, and there'd be some left over.

Many visitors to the city described the music that they heard everywhere around them on the streets. It was the custom in New Orleans, as it was everywhere in the Caribbean, for street vendors to call out their wares with songs. In the 1950s there were still men and women calling out their offerings on the streets of the French Quarter. Hearn quoted some of the songs he heard in his newspaper columns. Most, of course, were in French, but he encountered a man selling coal and charcoal by the sack out of his horse-drawn wagon, and Hearn was struck that the man called out to the houses he passed in both French and English. Hearn's transcription of his song appeared in the *Item* in August 1880.

CHAR-COAL

Black—coalee -coalee!
  Coaly-coaly; coaly-coaly; coal-coal-coal
  Coaly-coaly!
  Coalee! Nice!
  Cha'coal!
  Twenty-five! Whew! . . .
  Cha-ah-ah-ahr-coal!
  Coaly-Coaly!
  Charbon! Du charbon, Madame! Bon
  charbon? Point! Ai-ai! Tonnerre de Dieu!
  Char-r-r-r-r-r-bon!
  A-a-a-a-a-w! High-ya-a-ah! High-yah!
  Vingt-cing! Nice coalee! Coalee!
  Coaly-coal-coal!
  Pretty coaly!
  Charbon de Parius!
  De Paris, Madame; de Paris![10]

CANAL STREET IN THE 1850S. (NOTE THE STORE ADVERTISING "PIANO FORTES.")

For many years the broad neutral ground on Canal Street continued to separate the two distinct cultures of New Orleans, and the term "neutral ground" itself was used to delineate the boundary. As the century passed, however, the old animosities that divided the city into French and American societies, each keeping to their side of Canal Street, were blurred in the flood of new immigrants and the increasing numbers of Americans leaving the eastern states to begin new lives on the Mississippi. In the 1840s and 1850s there was a flood of new immigrants from Germany and Ireland, the Germans fleeing the failed revolutions of the 1840s, the Irish fleeing a desperate famine. They quickly took over many of the waterfront jobs and the work for skilled laborers that had traditionally been the domain of black workers. In the late 1880s came a wave of Italian immigrants whose musical traditions and instrumental abilities were to leave a distinctive trace on the new music that was developing in New Orleans during this period. Their first years were marked by open hostility and discrimination, culminating in a recurrence of the mob violence that was a continual threat to the city's African Americans.

For others moving into New Orleans, however, it still had a charm and a feeling of romance they had experienced nowhere else. In 1892 a young bride, a woman named Maude K. Ferrier, moved with her husband into the Pontalba Apartments, which line Jackson Square on either side of the Cathedral in the French Quarter, and she never forgot the music that she and her husband heard every evening. "Every night I would see the Negroes going through the streets with their guitars, and they would stand under the galleries serenading. They sang sweet love songs, and I could hear their voices in the quiet. The first night I was in New Orleans my husband and I walked through the Vieux Carré together in the moonlight. It was a beautiful spring night. When we turned the corner in front of the Cabildo, right across the street from our flat, there was a man under the arches with a hurdy gurdy playing very softly, 'After the ball is over, after the dance is through . . .'" [11]

In this murmur of reminiscences and anecdotes of an older white New Orleans, however, there are a myriad of voices and faces that can be only dimly intuited as part of the background of every scene: the city's African Americans, who did so much of the city's work, crowded with their families into the wooden frame houses of many of its neighborhoods, and sang many of its songs and played as much of its music. On the other side of Canal Street, virtually all of the manual labor was done by African Americans. Many of them were of the caste of "free persons of color" that had been established by the French, but slaves were everywhere. The French Quarter streets were crowded with slaves out on errands, or with black street criers selling anything—like sacks of charcoal—that could be loaded onto a wagon. In the courtyards of nearly every French Quarter building there are still narrow wooden balconies leading to small, bare, shabby rooms. Even in the 1950s they were referred to as "slave quarters," where the house servants were given beds and space for their few possessions. Many of the slaves were owned by the better-established Free Persons of Color, to whom slavery was a fact of everyday life.

Two accounts have come down to us of the music and dancing that was part of the lives of the city's slaves early in the century in a cleared area across Rampart Street later known as "Congo Fields" or "Congo Square." One of the descriptions, George W. Cable's extravagantly detailed and romantic "The Dance in Place Congo," published in *Century Magazine* in 1886 with fervent illustrations by Edward Windsor Kemble, has been often cited but unfortunately is material borrowed from another source. Cable did state with some equivocation at the beginning of the piece that the practice had died out before he'd had the opportunity to witness the dancing himself, but he failed to make it clear that he had "borrowed" his descriptions of the dancing, the costumes, the music, and the tribal origins of the dancers from an account of African retentions in the French West Indies written by a traveler named Moreau de Saint-Mery.

The other account, by architect Benjamin Latrobe, is less often quoted, probably because even though Latrobe actually witnessed the slave dances in the summer of 1819, he didn't find what he saw very exciting. His description, with its extraordinarily detailed notes on the African instruments still in use, followed a lengthy digression in his journal on the habits of spending Sunday in New Orleans and his impassioned criticism of the practice of the owners to force their slaves to labor without an opportunity to help themselves in any way.

This long dissertation has been suggested by my accidentally stumbling upon an assembly of negroes, which, I am told, every Sunday afternoon meets on the Common in the rear of the city. My object was to take a walk on the bank of the Canal Carondelet as far as Bayou St. John. In going up St. Peter's Street and approaching the Common, I heard a most extraordinary noise, which I supposed to proceed from some horse-mill—the horses tramping on a wooden floor. I found, however, on emerging from the house to the common that it proceeded from a crowd of five or six hundred persons, assembled in an open space or public square. I went to the spot and crowded near enough to see the performance. All those who were engaged in the business seemed to be blacks. I did not observe a dozen yellow faces. They were formed into circular groups, in the midst of the four of which that I examined (but there were more of them) was a ring, the largest not ten feet in diameter. In the first were two women dancing. They each held a coarse handkerchief, extended by the corners, in their hands, and set to each other in a miserably dull and slow figure, hardly moving their feet or bodies. The music consisted of two drums and a stringed instrument. An old man sat astride of a cylindrical drum, about a foot in diameter, and beat it with incredible quickness with the edge of his hand and fingers. The other drum was an open-staved thing held between the knees and beaten in the same manner. They made an incredible noise. The most curious instrument, however, was a stringed instrument, which no doubt was imported from Africa. On the top of the finger board was the rude figure of a man in a sitting posture, and two pegs behind him to which the strings were fastened. The body was a calabash. It was played upon by a very little old man, apparently eighty or ninety years old. The women squalled out a burden to the playing, at intervals, consisting of two notes, as the negroes working in our cities respond to the song of their leader. Most of the circles contained the same sort of dances. One was larger, in which a ring of a dozen women walked, by way of dancing, round the music in the center. But the instruments were of different construction. One which from the color of the wood seemed new, consisted of a block cut into something of the form of a cricket bat, with a long and deep mortise down the center. This thing made a considerable noise, being beaten lustily on the side by a short stick. In the same orchestra was a square drum, looking like a stool, which made an abominable, loud noise, also a calabash with a round hole in it, the hole studded with brass nails, which was beaten by a woman with two short sticks.[12]

These kinds of slave celebrations, obvious survivals of African music and culture in the new hemisphere, were widespread, and the celebrations in the New England states, known as the "Pinkster" dances drew crowds that numbered in the thousands as they reenacted African tribal ceremonies. As the years passed, and in areas where there was no further importation of slaves, the African past became a dim memory, and the practices were gradually abandoned. Although dancing by groups of slaves in the square was occasionally reported on Sundays in later years, by the 1880s the dancing had often taken on a more social character.

THE CORNER OF DAUPHINE
AND ST. PHILLIP'S STREETS
IN THE FRENCH QUARTER,
1880S. SAMUEL CHARTERS
COLLECTION.

With the end of the Civil War in 1865 the slaves who had spent their lives on the plantations north of New Orleans were now legally free to make their own choices as to where they now would live, though in reality most still found themselves bound to the land where they had been indentured. In 1877, following the withdrawal of Federal troops who had attempted to enforce the new legal freedoms accorded to the ex-slaves in the Constitution, organized vigilante groups of white southerners under various names roamed the countryside, terrorizing the African Americans who hadn't managed to flee. The South soon became a violent, socially separate nation within the American political structure.

Even with the difficulties and the dangers, however, thousands of the new freedmen and their families found their way into New Orleans, where there was work, and some protection from the vigilante bands. Many of the newcomers found jobs on the levees, since the immigrants from Germany and Ireland who had reached the city a generation before had begun to move on to other occupations that were generally restricted to African Americans. To accommodate the influx from the countryside, new city districts were created to the north and the west of Canal Street, in what was generally known as Uptown, since it was upstream from the center of the median ground on Canal Street, just as Downtown was downstream.

The houses that were hastily built to meet the needs of the new arrivals were the inexpensive, simple one-story frame houses known as "shotgun" houses, since it was said that someone could fire a shotgun in the front door, and the pellets would fly harmlessly out the back door without touching anyone. The reason was that to save space—the houses were very narrow—there were no hallways, and all of the three or four rooms opened onto each other. If the doors were open at the same time the air could circulate through the house, giving it some ventilation in the summers. The houses were built directly on the street, and since the area where they were spreading was on low ground they were raised two or three feet on cement block pilings. The "shotguns"—often built in tandem, with two together sharing a roof, known as "double shotguns"—are still one of the characteristic sights of New Orleans's back streets, particularly in the Uptown neighborhoods where they seem to be the only style of house that was built. Since they were raised off the ground they proved to be remarkably resilient. If the doors were left open when the water from the occasional floods subsided, the house soon dried, since the air could circulate under the thin floorboards. The flooding of Katrina rose only to just below floor level in most of the Uptown areas.

The immigrant groups that were filling the city were becoming well enough established for their own music to become part of the city's sounds, and each group made their own distinctive contribution. As the German families became more integrated, they turned again to their familiar social customs, which included fraternal lodges with their busy musical activities. The complicated music funerals that are so central to the New Orleans image seem to have been introduced by the Germans, who brought with them the custom of using village brass bands to accompany the funeral cortege. The first bands that older musicians remembered playing the funerals were the German brass bands. The white bandleader Jack Laine, who was born in 1873, remembered hearing the bands when he was a boy. In answer to a question by William Russell, Laine answered,

> *Oh yes, there was brass bands.*
> *There were brass bands?*
> *Yes, white brass bands. I remember one, one colored band, I remember that, but the all-white bands, they had Professor Braun, and Brookhaven, people like that, white bands. They used to play funeral marches and stuff like that too, and I got so I got in that line too, playin' funerals . . .*[13]

Both Professor Braun and Professor Brookhaven were German musicians. The pattern of the funeral music was familiar. Dirges were played on the march to the cemetery with the body, then after the burial the bands performed standard marches on the return to the lodge hall. It was this tradition that was quickly adapted by the African American brass bands and became an indispensable part of the city's life.

Another band, one made up of visiting musicians, was also to play a role in the unique styles developing in New Orleans. On December 16, 1884, the "World's Industrial and Cotton Centennial Exposition" opened at Audubon Park, and until its closing on June 1, 1885, it filled the city with visitors. One of the popular attractions was a "Mexican Band," and it brought the syncopated rhythms of the other Caribbean societies to New Orleans, as well as offering the sight of a band with musicians of diverse skin color. Although slavery was abolished in Mexico decades before it was brought to an end in the United States, and it had never played as dominant a role in the Mexican social hierarchy, the city of Vera Cruz, on the Gulf of Mexico on the east coast, had a large Afro-Mexican population, and many of the rhythmic innovations of the Cuban orchestras were also popular in Mexico.

The Mexican Band was the concert band of the 8th Mexican Cavalry. The Mexican exhibition was one of the largest at the Exposition, in celebration of the inauguration of a new president, Porfirio Diaz, and the presence of the musicians was intended to emphasize Mexican achievements in the arts. The band was already in New Orleans at the beginning of December for a formal celebration of Diaz's presidency and played a concert before a large audience, even though the Exhibition had not officially opened. The *Picayune* reviewed their concert with breathless awe on December 4, 1884.

This band of eighty pieces is so admirably composed that it can render all classes and schools of music intelligently and with full effect. No band in the country has a more perfect capability for expressing the true language of music, its feeling, its sympathies, its soul. It is neither loudness or lowness of tone, nor is it the shrillness of the trebles nor the growling gruffness of the bass that make up expression, but the quality or timbre of each instrument's voice that must be taken into consideration. . . . Such a band can bray and bellow, and it can also sing of love, sorrow, hate and despair. It can lift up its voices in prayer, sing paens [sic] of praise, shout aloud its triumphs and swell with the rage of battle. To do all this and more is demanded of a great band of music, and the instruments as well as the musicians are necessary. Such a band is that presided over by the accomplished Prof. Encarnacion Payen, and in which every member is an artist and a dozen are eminent solo performers.

The band's program included opera selections, the overture to Rossini's opera *William Tell*, waltzes, polkas, mazurkas, and concluded with a dansa, the Mexican version of the syncopated Cuban *habanera*. Members of the band also quickly became part of New Orleans's musical life. On January 21, 1885, the *Picayune* noted that a concert "for the benefit of Miss Kate E. Bridewell, of this city, to aid her in completing her musical studies at the Cincinnati College" would be held at Odd Fellows Hall, and continued "Miss Bridewell will have the assistance, this evening, of two soloists from the Mexican Band."

In his book *The Latin Tinge*, John Storm Roberts emphasized the importance of the appearance of the Mexican musicians in the city. "That the 'Mexican band,' as it came to be called, was highly important to New Orleans music is beyond doubt. Within a year of its stay, local publishing houses had issued sheet music of many of its popular numbers, many of them arranged for piano by New Orleans composer W. T. Francis. The most prolific of these publishers, Junius Hart, also continued to issue other Mexican-inspired numbers, many of them strongly influenced by the Cuban Habanera." [14]

At the close of the Exposition the next summer, several of the members of the band decided to stay behind. One of them was a saxophonist named Joe Viscara or Joe Vascaro, and Roberts quotes Jack Laine as saying, "He hardly could speak American, but that son of a bitch could handle a horn." [15]

Although the differences in their language may have presented a problem, there was no difficulty for the Mexicans to find a place in the musical life of the city's Creole community.

For much of the nineteenth century the Creoles of Color were exempt from many of the laws enacted to control the lives, work, and social behaviors of the African Americans who had ostensibly been freed from slavery. The first attempt by the Creoles to play a role in the reconstruction government as elected representatives in 1866, a year after the end of the Civil War, ended when a peaceful gathering of lawmakers was attacked by the New Orleans police, which now included many Confederate war veterans, and nearly two hundred of the elected representatives were shot and killed. By the 1890s their freedoms had been severely restricted, and in 1894 they were reclassified as "Negro" by a change in the legislative code. With a legislative edict, their two hundred years of society and culture were thrust aside, and they were forced to accept the same discrimination in housing, jobs, and political rights that faced the rest of African American society.

The Creoles made a determined effort to seek recourse through the legal system, but the result, which they couldn't have foreseen, was the legalization of the principle of segregation everywhere in the United States. Among the onerous statutes that were enacted in 1890, was the "separate car law," which stated that African Americans, now including Creoles, could not ride in the same railway cars as whites in the state of Louisiana, though for the time New Orleans was still exempt from the prohibition. Leading the opposition to the new restrictions was a group of Creole business and professional men led by Louis A. Martinet, editor of a small newspaper, the *Crusader*. The group called itself the "Citizen's Committee to Test the Constitutionality of the Separate Car Law." Their decision was to challenge the law by disobeying it and forcing the courts to rule on its legality.

On June 7, 1892, a friend of one of the members of the committee, a Creole shoemaker named Homer Adolph Plessy, who lived on North Claiborne Avenue in the Treme district, boarded a first-class carriage on the East Louisiana Railway with a ticket to Covington, twenty miles away on the other side of Lake Ponchartrain. Plessy was immediately arrested, as the group had planned, and the strategy they had settled on was to force the courts to consider the law itself, by insisting that it violated the Thirteenth and Fourteenth Amendments to the Constitution. Their lawyer, Albion W. Tourgee, was a northern white veteran of the Civil War who had been wounded three times in combat, and ironically he was facing a judge, John H. Ferguson, who was from the state of Massachusetts. By choosing Plessy the committee had also complicated the issue, since he was seven-eighths white and nothing about his demeanor could be described as "Negro."

By insisting that it was the law itself that constituted the offense, Plessy's defense intended to force the issue to be decided by a higher court by making it virtually impossible for Judge Ferguson to dismiss the case with a fine or a light sentence. They claimed that the state didn't have the right to discriminate against its citizens, and the new law placed a stigma of inferiority on African Americans. The assistant prosecutor who presented the state's case insisted that the provision was only intended for the comfort of the passengers, and the law was intended to avoid friction between the races. His statement included the term "separate but equal." When Judge Ferguson pronounced Plessy guilty, his lawyers immediately appealed the case, confident that their arguments would prevail. In 1896, however, the Supreme Court, in a decisive and crushing decision, *Plessy v. Ferguson*, determined that segregation did not in itself place blacks in an inferior position. The court's decision, shared with an 8–1 majority, declared that it might be the opinion of African Americans that this left them with a badge of inferiority, but "if this be so, it is not by reason of anything found in the act, but solely because the colored race chooses to put that construction on it."

With its support for the concept of "separate but equal," *Plessy v. Ferguson* turned the United States overnight in an apartheid nation, and it became the basis for the maze of restrictive legislation that extended to housing, employment, education, and public services. Its terms were used to support restrictions against other groups as well, and many immigrant groups, Jews among them, were denied access to many schools and public organizations. For the committee, the legal battle to take the issue to the Supreme Court had been emotionally draining as well as financially disastrous. Within a few months of the decision the group disbanded. Following the conviction of Plessy in the initial trial in 1892 the *Picayune* had editorialized, "The sooner they (Negroes) drop their so-called 'crusade' against the 'Jim Crow Car,' and stop wasting their money in combating so well-established a principle—the right to separate the races in cars and elsewhere—the better for them."

In his presentation, the New Orleans prosecutor had pointed out that the law worked both ways—no whites would be permitted to sit in the cars designated for blacks, and the endorsement of this concept in *Plessy v. Ferguson* also lay behind the difficulties that white jazz enthusiasts sometimes encountered decades later when they met black musicians in New Orleans bars or at social gatherings in the black community. The way to handle the situation, which clarinetist Albert Burbank explained carefully to me in 1950, was that if a policemen found us talking in a bar in his neighborhood, I was to say that I was a full-blooded American Indian.

Plessy v. Ferguson cast a pall over American society for nearly sixty years. It was finally overturned in the historic Supreme Court decision of 1954, *Brown v. Board of Education*, which ruled that segregation in itself created the inferiority that was evident everywhere in the situation of African Americans. Even with its mantle of legality stripped away, however, the South continued its long-established practices. In the early spring of 1961 I was asked by Kenneth Goldstein of Prestige

Records to travel to Memphis to record blues artist Furry Lewis, and I decided to go by train from New York. Late that night, an hour south of Washington, D.C., in the state of Virginia, the train stopped in the middle of a field, and with a feeling of disbelief, I looked out of the window and saw the African American passengers walking back along the tracks to a Jim Crow car that had been coupled to the end of the train.

As the 1800s wound down, New Orleans was the same hazy web of contradictions it had been for generations—moving by fits and starts into the modern era, but tightly bound to its unique and complex past. By 1900 the population had grown to 287,000, the steady expansion of the sewage system had largely ended the threat of cholera, and the clearing of the channel at the mouth of the Mississippi by the Army Engineers had brought large ocean vessels to the levees for the first time. There were busy picnic grounds and resorts at Spanish Fort along Lake Ponchartrain, with their concert bands and their dance orchestras. Brass bands still assembled to lead processions through the streets for any conceivable occasion. Sundays still were a day for family visits among the Creole families of the Vieux Carre and the Treme, and there were almost nightly balls in the dozens of roomy, modestly decorated wood frame buildings meant for meetings or dances that were part of every neighborhood. The establishment of the Restricted District, generally known as Storyville, in 1898 had at least localized some of the endemic prostitution and gambling, and the cabarets and dance halls within its boundaries gave work to many New Orleans musicians. If the city still was poor and its future uncertain, and if the tensions that had risen after the disenfranchisement of the Creoles still hung in the muggy air, these darker aspects pushed into the background were accepted as part of the New Orleans life style—just as many of the city's continuing problems still are accepted with a sense of fatality today.

It was perhaps to be expected that the nineteenth century closed with an outburst of violence. The discomfort among New Orleanians at the increasing level of immigration was fanned by accounts of the secret criminal societies that the arrival of numbers of Sicilians, beginning in the 1870s, were said to have brought with them. By the early 1890s the number of Italians and Sicilians had grown to more than twenty thousand, including many families whose sons would become one of the largest and most ambitious groups of early jazz musicians. Two Sicilian groups fought among themselves in May 1890, and the newspapers reports of the violence increased the tension in the city. There were arrests and trials, and five months later the chief of police was shot on the street near his home. In a police sweep nineteen Sicilians were taken into custody, and nine of them were tried for the crime. The city watched their trial with growing tension, and in a surge of anger at the jury's verdict, which acquitted six of those accused, and declared a failure to reach a verdict on the other three, a mob of white New Orleanians, estimated at more than five thousand, broke into the Parish prison and killed eleven of the men who had been arrested, clubbing and shooting them to death.

THE RESORT AT WEST END, 1890S.

The continuing pressures on the African American community also aggravated the mood of distrust between white and black in the city, culminating in the Robert Charles riots that erupted in the summer of 1900. The beginning of the trouble was an encounter between a night police patrol and two African American men they found sitting in front of a house, waiting for the sister of one of the men to finish work. After an argument, a constable struck one of the men, a large, burly man named Robert Charles, who fought back. In his anger the constable drew his pistol and shot Charles in the leg. Charles also was carrying a pistol in his pocket and he shot the constable and stumbled off into the darkness, trailing blood. Charles understood that he wouldn't live long after shooting a police officer, and when he was traced to the house where he rented a room, he shot and killed the first two police officers who burst in on him, a police captain and a patrolman. In the confusion—it was 3 a.m.—Charles slipped away, and for the next two days the city was in turmoil as the frenzied search went on and mobs of white attacked the few black persons they could find on the streets.

Beside a drawing of Charles that was printed in the *Picayune* in July 25, 1900, to aid in the search for him, the large headlines read,

NEGRO KILLS
BLUECOATS
AND ESCAPES

Shoots Down Captain John T. Day and
Patrolman Peter J. Lamb

MURDERER, CURSING HIS VICTIMS, FIRES
INTO THEIR LIFELESS FORMS

Populace Inflamed and Armed Mobs Throng the
Streets . . .

The mayor offered a reward of $250 for the capture of Charles "dead or alive," and the governor of the state offered an additional $250. When the mobs swept into the District the women in the houses clustered on the balconies in their dressing gowns, pointing out any places where they felt some African Americans might have hidden. The only group known to be playing in the District that night, a dance orchestra led by a musician named Henry Peyton, escaped just in time, losing coats and instruments. Charles's room had been searched, and along with the offers of the rewards, a column describing him noted that he was "Fond of talking about race wrongs and Liberia emigration project." Pamphlets encouraging Liberian emigration as an escape from the South's institutionalized racism had been found among his papers, which meant that he was a racial agitator as well as a murderer of police officers.

Charles was finally tracked down to a house in the African American neighborhood, where he had retreated to an upper story He had taken with him a Winchester rifle and a quantity of ammunition. The rifle meant that the mob surrounding the house were within range, and Charles shot anyone who came out in the open. Before officers finally broke into the room where he was hidden he had shot more than twenty of the men who were returning his fire. In the three days of violence Charles killed nine men and wounded seventeen others. He was severely wounded when the officers found him, and he was killed in the final exchange of shots. His body was dragged into the street and mutilated. The Robert Charles riot became part of the city's lore of song and story, and for many days wreaths hung on houses in both the new black neighborhoods on the American side of Canal Street, and on houses on the Creole streets of the Vieux Carre.

New Orleans, in its headlong rise from a backward river town to a major American city, had experienced a hundred years of turbulence and prosperity, unchecked growth and as sudden decline, violence and disappointed hopes, all of it bound into New Orleanians' unique pleasure in a way of life that was like no other. Perhaps some of the confusion was reflected in one of the earliest accounts of what could be a beginning of the new musical style that would finally emerge from the New Orleans chrysalis as jazz. During the Carnival in 1898, the *Picayune* described the scene in one of the Uptown districts: "The air was freighted with a pandemonium of sounds, in which the ceaseless clang of the tramcars gong and the shrill music of a horrible cacophonous orchestra domiciled on one of the wagons played no inconsiderable part." [16]

3

A Society to Itself

. . . So I was invited to the rehearsal that night and I went to the place and I said to him, "What do you want me to do?" I said, "Do you want me to play my instrument? Is there any music?" He said, "Music? You don't need none." I said, "How am I going to play?"

ALPHONSE PICOU, DESCRIBING HIS FIRST BAND
REHEARSAL AT THE AGE OF SIXTEEN IN 1894[1]

In the Sunday morning edition of the *Daily Picayune* on May 15, 1910, there was an advertisement for "An Unusually Important MUSIC SALE" by D. H. Holmes Co., one of New Orleans's biggest music retailers. On Monday they were offering all of their best selling sheet music at ten cents a copy, with an additional five hundred titles of "Odds and Ends" at five cents a copy. To emphasize that this was their best-selling merchandise, they assured readers—in large letters—that the sale would include "the Big Song Hit 'MOTHER' The song adopted by the National Congress of Mothers." Sheet music sales were then the most important outlet for the music industry, and the list of titles included in the advertisement was the equivalent of a best-selling record chart a half century later. They were a glimpse into New Orleans's musical tastes in these years before the turmoil of the first World War. A few of the titles still have some luster, though most have been forgotten.

That Mesmerizing Mendelssohn Tune, MOTHER, I've Got Something in My Eye and It's You, Put On Your Old Gray Bonnet, Go On Good-a-Bye, I've Got Rings on My Fingers, Dandelions (Intermezzo), Garden of the Roses, My Alabama Rose, By the Light of the Silvery Moon, Same Old Way (new), Dear Old County Mayo (Irish ballad), Roses Bring Dreams of You, Chocolate

Creams Rag, When You Dream of the Girl You Love, Cherry Leaf Rag, The Songs My Mother Sang, etc., etc.

Although New Orleans, during these years, was beginning to hear a new kind of dance music in some of the cabarets, for most New Orleanians the city's musical culture seemed no different from the rest of the country. Although these years are often described as the "ragtime era," only three of the popular favorites were ragtime: Irving Berlin's raggy reworking of Mendelssohn's classic "Spring Song" as "That Mesmerizing Mendelssohn Tune," and two instrumental rags, "Chocolate Creams Rag" and "Cherry Leaf Rag." A handful of musicians might be picking up the popular tunes, turning them upside down and shaking them to see what different rhythms they could get out of them, but for anyone who didn't venture into the Restricted District or never passed the corner honkytonks on Gravier Street, the only time they heard any of the new musical sounds was when a "ballyhoo" wagon stopped at a street corner and the band tried out their different style of ragtime as part of the day's advertising.

Ragtime was to be the vernacular musical form that opened the way to jazz, but like jazz, its beginnings were obscure, and there was a gulf between improvised ragtime melodies and the later classic ragtime compositions by composers like Scott Joplin, James Scott, and Joseph Lamb. The beginnings of ragtime lay in the syncopated banjo melodies that emerged in the rural areas before the Civil War and were popularized by the first minstrel shows. The rhythms were based on African-influenced adaptations of Irish and English dance melodies, which probably were first performed by slave musicians who provided entertainment for their masters. The first ragtime pieces were generally short, songlike strains, but when the dance rhythms were wedded to popular instrumental forms like the march, with multiple strains and changes of key, ragtime became an international craze. Also like the beginnings of jazz, which are often difficult to distinguish from ragtime's infectious rhythms, ragtime had an immediate predecessor, the cakewalk of the minstrel show. One of the most enduring of the cakewalk melodies, Kerry Mills' "At a Georgia Camp Meeting," was published as a cakewalk in 1895, was then played for many years as a ragtime dance, and is still a staple of bands playing in the traditional style.

Ragtime was published as orchestrations and band arrangements, and the "Red-Backed Book," as the collection of orchestrations of classic rags published by John Stark in St. Louis was known, was a New Orleans standby. The published instrumental parts were difficult to play, and usually a noisy approximation of the notes was the best most bands could do. As Greenwich Village singer and ragtime guitarist Dave Van Ronk often blustered—half seriously—about early New Orleans jazz, "They were trying to play ragtime, and they couldn't!"

Like every other city in the country, New Orleans musicians worked in restaurants, theaters, dance halls, played for railroad excursions, in serious orchestras and concert brass bands. Many of the jobs in New Orleans were open to African

American musicians, though in the places that offered music in Storyville they usually alternated with white bands.

For the "legitimate" musicians who studied with the popular teachers, there was a wide choice of jobs. The pay, however, was very poor, the work was irregular, and musicians were regarded simply as a different kind of servant. The response to the music in the city clearly reflected the contrasting attitudes of each social group toward it. In the white community it was considered a near catastrophe if a son decided to seek a career as a dance hall musician, since it closed off any opportunity for economic security and a position of respect in society. For the Creoles, it was an acceptable profession, but only if meant performing "good" music. In the Uptown neighborhoods, strict Baptist and Methodist families had serious objections to music as a profession, but for most of the black families, deprived of schools and opportunities for anything beyond menial laboring jobs, a son who became a musician was the family's pride. For nearly all of them, however, music provided only a sporadic income, and they worked days at something that was steadier.

For the city's white musicians there were opportunities to work at several large theaters, among them the Dauphine, Tulane, Crescent, Orpheum, Colonial, Lyric, and the Lafayette, which changed to a policy of exclusively black audiences in 1919, as well as the French Opera House. In 1912 the pianists and violinists could also expect to find work at five new motion picture houses: the Trianon, Bijou Dream, Grand Theatre, Electric Theatre, and Dreamland. One of the early neighborhood moving picture emporiums, the Triangle, was immortalized by its house pianist Irwin Leclere with his excellent 1917 composition "Triangle Jazz Blues."

Between 1911 and 1920, the Iroquois Theater, a small variety theater at 413–15 S. Rampart St. presented a bill of touring acts and motion pictures for African American audiences, but the entertainment that was listed in the press at the time leaves the impression that the theater lacked the resources to present top-line acts. Like many small variety houses the music was provided by a pianist, or sometimes a pianist and a drummer. The programs were heavy on "ragtime singing, dancing, and coon comics."[2] Among the artists mentioned was Charles Arrant, who played blues trombone with his foot, and a woman artist who was billed as America's "only colored lady yodeler." The pianist and composer Clarence Williams occasionally performed as a solo act, playing his newest compositions and accompanying himself on the piano, and drummer Abbie Foster remembered performing there with a solo number that featured him singing through his snare drum. But perhaps the closest the theater came to a jazz connection was when the very young Louis Armstrong would spend ten cents to sit in the audience to watch a movie, and he once won an amateur contest by dipping his face in a barrel of flour. In February 1919, the lavish two-thousand-seat Lyric Theater opened for African American audiences at Burgundy and Iberville, and the competition from the new theater probably led to the closing of the Iroquois sometime around 1920.

Audiences that were listening to music in the theaters also were entertained with musical ensembles in every restaurant, and the most popular orchestras played a busy schedule of dances and entertainments at the neighborhood dance halls. In the summers there was steady employment at Spanish Fort for the members of Tosso's Uniformed Military Band, which played evening concerts at 6 and 8 p.m. In the summer of 1912 the resort also offered daily performances of the Spanish Fort Opera Company, with its own orchestra, soloists, and a chorus of thirty members. Serious opera productions alternated with popular fare like Gilbert and Sullivan's "Mikado."

At the same time, against this colorful background of entertainment and relaxed pleasure, no one could forget that New Orleans still was part of the South and shared most southern racial attitudes. An editorial in the *Daily Picayune* on June 30, 1910, reacted strongly against an attack by a judge in the New York District Court on the southern attitude toward lynching. The judge pointed out that an estimated 300,000 white southerners had participated in a lynching in the last forty years, "yet no person has ever been convicted of murder for taking part in a lynching." The editorial writer for the newspaper responded with a sarcastic dismissal of the accusation.

> *This judge appears to be one of those who finds no fault with the turning loose of criminals, if only it be done judicially or by regular process of court. The numberless cases in which criminals escape through the almost interminable delays of the law, through the intervention of sheer technicalities, or through influence and favoritism brought to bear on juries, seem to be alright. But such a jurist does not seem to understand that, for the most part, the application of summary punishment by an enraged populace upon the perpetrator of some atrocious crime is simply an emphatic protest against the ineffectiveness and frequent failures of justice on the part of the machinery of the law.*
>
> *If the dealing out of justice by the courts were as prompt, as sure and as reliable in our country as it is in England or Germany for example, there would be no lynching here, any more than there; but, unfortunately such is not the case.*[3]

Within a few days of the editorial's appearance arose the ugly possibility that New Orleans would again be threatened with an outburst of violence similar to the Robert Charles riots of ten years before. The entire country had become tense over the coming prizefight on July 4, 1910, between the black champion Jack Johnson and the white challenger Jim Jeffries. Jeffries, a still popular former champion who had retired undefeated without having ever been knocked down, had been cajoled back into the ring after a seven year layoff to silence the rising clamor against what white Americans saw as the insult of the championship being held by a black boxer. A photograph taken on Canal Street during the fight, which was being announced round by round by telegraph from Reno, Nevada, where the fight was being held, shows the street filled with men staring at the placards. None of the faces were black. With the violence of the 1900 riots still a fresh memory, the city's African Americans had deserted the streets. The large headline across the front of the newspaper the next morning read

RACE RIOTS FOLLOW THE RESULT OF THE FIGHT.

Johnson won easily, taunting his opponent and his seconds, beating Jeffries efficiently and brutally over fifteen rounds. When a bloodied Jeffries lay sprawled half out of the ring after the third knockdown, his seconds leaped into the ring, stopping the fight to deny Johnson the honor of knocking out a white man. The sub-headlines read,

BLOODY CLASHES BETWEEN
WHITE AND NEGROES.

Riots in Nearly All The Large Cities in
the Country

New York, St. Louis Cincinnati and Other
Cities the Scene of Conflicts

Several Negroes and a Few White Men Killed.
Negroes Become Obstreperous When
Johnson's Victory Was Announced

Within a few days the situation was calm, but all of these emotions, attitudes, entertainments, and diversions were woven into the complicated texture of the city. The New Orleans musicians spent their lives within its continual shifts of racial tensions and hostilities. The older group of African American musicians, the Creole in their quiet neighborhoods of the French Quarter, Treme (pronounced tre-MAY), and the 7th Ward continued to cling to some of their old advantages, though they also were forced to respond to the new moods in the city.

Sometimes on winter nights in 1950, when I walked up Bourbon Street listening to the sounds of the bands through the open doorways of the clubs featuring music, I would hear a distinctive, carefully tongued, fluttering performance of the classic clarinet obbligato to the old march "High Society" coming out of the open doors of the Paddock Lounge a few blocks up Bourbon from Canal Street.

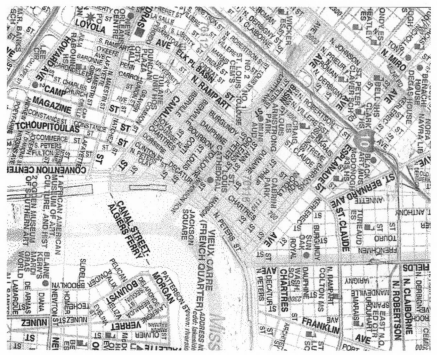

NEW ORLEANS, TREME, "DOWNTOWN," AND THE FRENCH QUARTER, 1970S.

I could usually stand outside long enough to listen to most of the chorus before the club's doorman would insist that I either had to move on or come in and buy a drink.

Standing up on the raised bandstand above the bar was a rumpled, unsteady man with sparse hair, glasses, and fingers that went through the notes of the chorus almost by themselves. I heard many performances of the "High Society" when I hung around Bourbon Street, since it was a piece the tourists all requested, but this was the performance that always drew me to listen. The musician performing it was Alphonse Picou, the Creole clarinetist who had created the chorus more than half a century before. He played it on an old Albert fingering system clarinet that instead of the flaring wooden bell below his fingers, had a small, upturned silver bell. Picou remembered playing his first band rehearsal in 1894, when he was sixteen. He was a figure from those legendary beginnings, when there wasn't even a name for the kind of music they were playing.

Picou was from a light-skinned Creole family, but as a musician he shifted back and forth between the Creole society and the Uptown, more distinctively African American society on the other side of Canal Street and north of Rampart Street. Not only did language, culture, and religion separate the two societies; they also generally stayed in different parts of the city. The Catholic Creoles were Downtown (downstream from Canal) and the Baptist and Methodist African

Americans were Uptown (upstream from Canal). Both neighborhoods were north of Rampart Street and had some of the city between them and the broad crescent of the river. In the city's casual slang, the people of New Orleans were described as living Downtown, Uptown, Back o' Town—the entire extended area of still mostly undeveloped property slowly extending toward the lake—or front o' town, which was the Mississippi and the fringe of older neighborhoods that lined it. In the catastrophe that struck the city in 2005, the front o' town streets suffered the least damage—the French Quarter, the Bywater to the east of it, and the Garden District to the west. Uptown had already been ravaged when large areas were cleared earlier in the century for the railroad lines and industrial areas just west of Canal Street, but the flooding damaged houses in many of the remaining areas.

It is difficult now to get a feeling of the old French Quarter life, when the grid of narrow streets was still a busy neighborhood where an older French-speaking society clung to its old ways—its streets filled with people carrying bundles and baskets, servants out to visit the market, take messages, and bring children back and forth from school. The streets were rutted, unpaved, and covered with filth from the animals and mud after heavy rains. The toilets behind the houses and the open sewers left their mingled odors in the air, and by the turn of the century many of the people were poor. Photographs from the Quarter taken during this period have the atmosphere of other Caribbean port cities—Port of Spain, San Juan, or Panama City. Treme, just across North Rampart Street, still has some of this old character, though none of the stench and the streets are paved. In a handful of streets of old Treme—around St. Augustine's Church on St. Claude Street, and in some of the rows of old wooden houses on the streets just west of Esplanade, between Rampart and North Claiborne—the trees still cast their shade over the wooden porches, and the houses have a quiet solidity. When St. Augustine's Church was still filled on Sundays, there would be the kind of placid neighborhood awareness of each other's families and of the culture and the history that kept them rooted there.

Through most of the nineteenth century and despite so many changes in the city, the heart of Creole culture was still the French Quarter, the same "foreign" section where Walt Whitman had often wandered in 1854. Adding to the mix of the old French families, the Creoles, and their black servants were a small mixture of new immigrants, German and Sicilian, who ran small shops and businesses. Many distinctions were made between the city's different social groups, but in the Downtown neighborhoods it was understood that the French-speaking families were culturally superior to the Anglos who lived across Canal Street. Among the French and the lighter-skinned Creoles—many of whom had been slaveholders in the antebellum years—referred to their servants or the black families moving into the Uptown neighborhoods by the universal southern epithet "niggers."

Although many of the Creoles of Color ran successful businesses and played a prominent role in the cultural life of their society, they couldn't participate in the Anglo-American world that was separated from them by only a few city streets. Within the Creole community there was an emphasis on music, and as the Swedish traveler Fredrika Bremer found in the 1840s, the French Opera on Royal Street maintained the highest musical standards. The seating was arranged with special sections for each social class. Many of the sons—and a few of the daughters—of the Creole families studied with the musicians in the opera orchestra. Both Professor Shaw, who was the orchestra's bassoonist, and Professor Boufant, one of the trombonists, had studios in the French Quarter where they gave lessons. Anthony Page, a regular valve trombonist with the Excelsior Brass Band, one of the two important Creole marching bands, also played occasionally in the opera orchestra.

By the turn of the century, however, despite its position at the mouth of the Mississippi River and its still busy port, New Orleans was sliding into the economic decline that continues to plague the city today. Photographs taken in this same period of black marching bands in other American cities often show as many as forty or fifty musicians. New Orleans brass bands had fifteen pieces at most, and ten or eleven was more common. A brass band with less than a dozen pieces is very small, but after so much experience of playing on the street, the two major Creole marching bands, the Excelsior Brass Band and the Onward Brass Band, developed an instrumental style that enabled them to perform the entire repertoire of marches, concert pieces, and elaborate dirges. They had taken over most of the community's parades and funerals after the Oriental Band, the most important band of the 1860s and 1870s, stopped marching.

The usual instrumentation of the Onward and the Excelsior was three cornets, one a higher E♭ instrument, alto horn—called the peck horn since its role in the arrangements was to play a continual harmony line in a series of small, pecking notes—a baritone horn, tuba, if there were two clarinets one of them the higher pitched E♭, snare drum, and bass drum. The Onward was led by Professor Lainez, and the Excelsior by Professor T. V. Baquet, whose sons George and Achille were both clarinetists. All of the small, skillfully balanced brass bands were said to play with a light, lyric, sweet tone, sounding as though they had twice as many musicians, and they marched down the tree-lined streets in impeccable high-collared uniforms.

Occasionally the bands also had the opportunity to perform in a concert setting. On February 23, 1885, as part of the celebration of the Cotton Festival in New Orleans, the Excelsior Band played a program of light classical pieces for the opening of the African American exhibit, and the *Picayune* described them as "the well known Excelsior Cornet Band of this city," and reported that nearly four thousand people had been present at the ceremonies.

The newspaper of Creole society, the *Weekly Pelican*, often mentioned new brass bands or noted parties and concerts played by the better-known ensembles. A band from across the river in Algiers, the Pickwick Band, often rode the ferry across the river to play for "Calico Balls" in Globe Hall. Among the younger bands were the Pelican Brass Band, which the paper announced had been organized January 23, 1889, and the Alliance Brass Band. The paper reported on April 20, 1889, that the Alliance "are now prepared to fill all orders for music at reasonable rates." The paper noted on May 4, however, "The celebrated Alliance Brass Band, through some unexpected accident, did not receive their new uniforms on the 28th ult., but will be in possession of them by the 6th inst. Strive on, boys." While they waited for their uniforms they played one of their first jobs at a baseball game between the Eclipse Team and the Pinchbacks on April 21. As patriotic gesture, all of the members of the Onward Brass Band enlisted together and served in the Spanish American War in 1898.

The enthusiastic response to balls and dancing was still reflected in the advertisements in the pages of the *Picayune* but, instead of regularly functioning public dance halls, most of the dances in the Creole society were presented by popular social clubs that hired the halls and the musicians and charged an admission at the door that was usually fifteen or twenty cents. Each of the small clubs usually could manage to present only one dance a year, but there were so many of them that sometimes there were three or four dances in a single week. The halls themselves were usually one-story wooden buildings not much larger than the modest frame houses crowded beside them, often in the middle of a block or at the corner of a local neighborhood. Some of the more pretentious halls had tall, wooden pillars to frame the porch and the door, and inside, the dance floor was bare except for tables and chairs pushed close to the walls. In some of the larger halls the bands played on a raised balcony. A few of the old halls were still being used in the 1950s, and had a smell of mould that blended with old odors of food, cigar smoke, and floor polish.

On an outside balcony over the entrance, or on the sidewalk if there was no balcony, the band played a few numbers to let the neighborhood know something was happening, while the members of the social club's entertainment committee waited at the door to sell tickets, take coats and wraps, and lead people inside. Among the most popular halls were Globe Hall at St. Claude and St. Peter; Geddes Hall, Masonic Hall, Veteran's Hall, Union Band Hall, Frans Amis Hall, Economy Hall, and Friends of Hope Hall on Treme Street; Amis Sinceres Hall on Claiborne Avenue; Mississippi River Hall and Longshoreman's Hall on Jackson Avenue; St. Peter's Hall at Cadiz and Coliseum; the Crescent Skating Rink at Washington and Prytania; and the Good Intent Hall in Algiers. The brass bands often were hired for the larger dance halls, and the music was expected to be light and delicately rhythmic, with a full mix of quadrilles, schottisches, waltzes, and Lancers.

For small private parties there were a number of string bands, which in New Orleans usually meant a small ensemble with at least two guitarists, a violin, and a horn, which might be either a cornet or a clarinet. One of the most popular was the Tio-Doublet String Band, a quartet that included one of the Tio brothers, Lorenzo or his older brother Louis, as clarinetists. The Tios had been born in Mexico but were from a Creole family, and had returned to New Orleans in 1877. The Excelsior Brass Band also hired out a string orchestra using its name, under the leadership of violinist Professor Henry Nickerson. Another of the prominent musicians to lead a dance orchestra was Professor J. B. Humphrey, one of the city's popular music teachers and a gifted cornet soloist. His orchestra was named the Crescent City Band, and he often played for evening entertainments as a cornet soloist, usually accompanied by Miss McCarthy or Professor Moret. His grandsons Percy, Willie, and Earl Humphrey all became important musicians themselves.

It was a world of popular musical novelties and the newest dance music, and each ensemble had its own library of printed scores. All of the Creole musicians were expected to read music well and to have had thorough instruction on their instrument. There were a series of attempts to establish a symphony orchestra of Creole musicians; in the symphony orchestra assembled in 1897 by a musical association known as the Lyre Club, the five clarinetists were Louis Tio, his brother Lorenzo Tio Sr., Lorenzo's son Lorenzo Tio Jr., Alphonse Picou, and George Baquet. The three younger instrumentalists, Tio Jr., Picou, and Baquet all went on to become part of the new ragtime era in New Orleans.

For some years it was customary to discuss early New Orleans musical styles in terms of the differences between the Uptown and Downtown ensembles, between the careful musical training of the Creoles and the freer, more spontaneous playing of the Uptown musicians. There have been some attempts at a reevaluation, with writers pointing out that there were musicians like Picou who could fit into either of the two communities of musicians, and emphasizing that, having lost their distinctive position with the legislative act of 1894, the Creoles had little choice but to move closer to the larger African American community.

The changes that had been made by the white legislature in Baton Rouge affected the legal and economic status of the Creoles, but the changes didn't extend to old social patterns. The Creoles insisted on maintaining their special position in what was now a painfully divided black society. In an interview with writer Tom Bethel for the book *George Lewis: A Jazzman from New Orleans*,[4] clarinetist George Lewis, a determinedly proud man himself, spoke freely about the social tension when he talked about the Creole orchestra leader Manuel Perez. "I heard him but never played with him, because there was prejudice among the people—segregation. Some of those Creole bands wouldn't hire a man whose hair wasn't silky. And some of the halls wouldn't accept you in there. There was one on Robertson Street like that, you wasn't accepted there. And they would look at you hard if you was playing in that band. I don't say Manuel Perez ever segregated anybody I know of. But everybody in his band was light-skinned, you know."[5]

Lewis had also been subjected to prejudice in some of his encounters with Downtown Creoles, memories that still left him angry many years later, though he was forced to accept the situation as part of his life as a working musician.

I want to be straight, the majority of the black-skinned musicians stayed together. They stayed together, and so did the light skinned as a rule. Because I can tell you something that happened to me when I was playing with Arnold Depass . . . They hired me to play, and we were working down on Villere Street, two blocks on the other side of Elysian Fields. Picou had been playing with them before me, and he was almost as light as a white man, you know. And when I walked in there, well, whether that lady behind the bar says she Creole or what I don't know, but she talked Creole. Well I understand Creole good, 'cause I done talked it. I'd understand French too, but not as perfect as I understand Creole.

She said, "Where is Mr. Picou?" in that dialect of Creole.

And Arnold says, "He don't play with me no more."

And she say, "Where did you get that?" pointing to me. She didn't say "him," she said "that."

So he say, "Oh, you'll be satisfied."

Lewis went on to play the job. During a break the woman passed around home-brewed malt liquor, and each of the light skinned members of the band was handed a glass, while he was given a jelly glass tumbler. When the woman gathered up the glasses, she told him to hold on to the tumbler. "She told me to keep my glass. And I got mad. Because if she could pick up their glasses—they was Negroes just like I was—she could have picked up mine; but I had to keep mine, so nobody else would use it, because they were light skinned people, you see."

Lewis got up and told the leader of the band that he was going to go out. Depass thought he meant he was going to go around the corner to the bootlegger who was supplying the liquor, but as he left Lewis announced, "'Now if you want to call me a nigger, I'm going to show you what a nigger is like.' And I went out and got drunk. Because I was considered nothing, you see. *They* were all right. They were light-skinned. And they dranked in a fancy glass, and their glass was washed. And Arnold said, 'I believe you,' he said I was right. He didn't fire me. I just come back and didn't play *nothin'*, you see, because I was a bit contrary at that time, and I didn't play nothin'. Because I was hurted, you see, and I know they were colored people."[6]

Although social divisions between the two antagonistic groups had become blurred by the 1950s, there was still a lingering sense of two separate communities, and the Creole musicians often stayed in contact with each other. The second trumpet player in the Eureka Brass Band, Willie Pajeaud, was a light-skinned Creole, and after we became friendly he suggested that I talk to one of the older men who had been part of the rich musical world of the Treme neighborhood, Paul Beaullieu.

When I sat talking with Beaullieu on the porch of his quiet home in the Treme district only a few blocks from Rampart Street, I realized that in many ways he typified the musical ambitions of the men and women who grew up in the Downtown Creole society. He was born on October 20, 1888, on Burgundy

Street in the French Quarter, and his life had been spent within these few downtown blocks. He was ten years younger than Picou, and also light skinned—a thin, pleasant, outgoing man with a gentle, French-tinged accent. Even in his seventies he would suddenly begin talking with a new excitement when we turned to classical music. The operas of Wagner were lifelong favorites. He received his early musical training on the piano from Ellena Meyer and a Miss White, on the cello from Professor Lescar and on the clarinet from Louis Tio. Although when growing up the highest-level job he could hope for was as a mail carrier (because the post office was a Federal agency, and the discriminatory southern controls on employment for African Americans did not extend to federal employment), he stayed in school and graduated from Straight University, a small school for African American students moving beyond the grade school level.

Beaullieu began playing as a boy, and by the time he was thirteen John Robichaux let him rehearse with one of his large orchestras. He was a member of the ambitious Bloom Philharmonic in 1903, and in 1907 he played as a clarinetist with the Melrose Brass Band, a young ensemble that included Joe Oliver and the seventeen-year-old trombonist who would join Oliver in his band in Chicago, Honore Dutrey. During World War I Beaullieu was the pianist for Robichaux's "second" orchestra, and on New Year's Eve in 1915 he took one of Robichaux's jobs at the La Louisianne Restaurant, with cornetist Arnold Metoyer and violinist Wendall MacNeil. In the 1920s he began working for the post office, but he never stopped playing.

Although ragtime was acceptable, someone like Beaullieu would never have considered playing jazz, even if he'd known how to begin playing in a different musical idiom. In these years, however, the Creole community continued to have an active musical life outside of the city's mainstream jazz culture. In December 1932 he organized and conducted a symphonic group called the Crescent City Orchestra for a concert at Xavier University. Even in those tense economic times, he managed to assemble twenty musicians for the concert, many of them from Downtown families with French background. A program of the concert listed the names: Violins, George Carriere, Ferdinand Fortinet, George King, and two students; violas, Ettience Nicholas, Peter Marine; cello, L. Davengnau; bass, Tom Gaspard; piano, Beatrice Stewart Davis; C clarinet, George Kifer; B♭ clarinets, Alphonse Picou, Willie Kerr, Henry Delrose; saxophones, Henry Pritchard, George Humphrey; flutes, Joseph Bloom, George Collins; trumpets, Clyde Kerr, Joseph Ursine; trombone, Oscar Henry.

Although the Creole community found its unique traditions giving way before the continual changes in the city, in the 1950s they still maintained an annual Creole Festival. Beaullieu arranged the music and led the orchestra for a traditional quadrille, danced by sedate couples in nineteenth-century finery. For the celebration in 1954 he used musicians from the Eureka Brass Band, all of whom were excellent readers: Willie Pajeaud, trumpeter; Sonny Henry, trombone; Emanuel Paul and Rueben Roddy, saxophones; and drummer Alfred Williams.

JOHN ROBICHAUX'S ORCHESTRA, ABOUT 1897. FROM LEFT: SEATED, DEE DEE CHANDLER, CHARLEY McCURDY, JOHN ROBICHAUX, WENDALL MacNEIL; STANDING, BAPTISTE DELISLE, JAMES WILSON, JAMES MacNEIL, HENRY KIMBLE SR. COURTESY OF HANNAH ROBICHAUX. SAMUEL CHARTERS COLLECTION.

Beaullieu himself played and conducted from the piano. For the handful of us invited to the very exclusive gathering in a small auditorium in the Treme section, there was a beguiling grace in the swaying white dresses of the women dancers in the softly lit room, and a touching politeness and attentiveness from their cavaliers. Willie Pajeaud's smile as he sat behind his music stand reflected the small community's sense of pride that it still had kept something from its long, complicated, and often unhappy history.

Of all the city's African American musicians, it was probably the Creole orchestra leader John Robichaux who was the best known to dancers at the quadrilles and to patrons of the Lafayette Theater, where he led the pit orchestra. Unfortunately he steadfastly refused to consider recording, referring to it contemptuously as "canned music," so what we have of his career are a handful of photographs and the reminiscences of the many musicians who worked for him. Two early photographs make it clear that Robichaux was taken very seriously as a musician. One, from sometime in the mid-1890s, is the earliest known photo of one of the city's Creole orchestras. His widow insisted that I take it with me when I spent time interviewing her in her small house in the French Quarter in the 1950s. Robichaux's orchestra is posed in their most elegant suits, with stiff collars and carefully knotted ties, and his expression is quietly satisfied.

The other photo was one that the trombone player Vic Gaspard, one of the musicians in the picture, proudly brought out in his living room forty years after

JOHN ROBICHAUX'S ORCHESTRA AT ST. CATHERINE'S HALL, 1913. FROM LEFT: WALTER BRUNDY, VIC GASPARD, ANDREW KIMBLE, CHARLEY MCCURDY, JOHN ROBICHAUX, COOCHIE MARTIN, HENRY KIMBLE SR. COURTESY OF VIC GASPARD.

he'd played in the orchestra. In the photo the orchestra is posed outdoors, sitting in a half circle pretending to play their instruments as though they were at a dance, each of them with their music stands and a piece of music. The photo was taken in 1913, when they were playing for regular dances at St. Catherine's Hall. It's one of only a handful of early photographs of a group actually pretending to play, and the only one I can think of from this period that shows them reading their parts from their stands. Part of Robichaux's reputation resulted from his effort to keep up with the latest music and dance styles from other parts of the country; he was a steady mail-order customer for New York publishing houses. At his feet in the photograph is a large, open suitcase filled with music scores. In the first photo Robichaux shows his pride at leading his first New Orleans orchestra, and in the second he exhibits what he had to offer to anyone thinking of hiring his orchestra. Every time I see the photographs I find myself dreaming that the instruments will begin to move and that I'll hear, faintly, the sound of their sedate music.

John Robichaux grew up outside of the city but, like so many musicians from the outlying areas, he was drawn to New Orleans for its more expansive opportunities. Born on January 16, 1866, in Thibodaux, Louisiana, a rural community southwest of New Orleans on Bayou LaFourche, he was raised by a white family, the Philip La Gardes, and part of his education was a thorough training in music. Although left-handed he was a proficient violinist. In 1891, when he was twenty-five, Robichaux moved to New Orleans, and his first job was as the bass drummer for the Excelsior Brass Band. In 1893 or 1894 he organized the orchestra that posed in their formal suits and ties in the early photograph. The orchestra had two violinists, himself and Wendall MacNeil; two cornetists, James MacNeil (Wendall's brother) and James Williams: Charles McCurdy played clarinets in the keys of B♭, E♭, and A; Baptiste DeLisle, slide trombone (he was one of the first in the city to switch from the valve trombone); Henry Kimble, bass; and the drummer was Dee Dee Chandler.

To live up to his reputation as the man with the newest dance music, Robichaux ordered all of the published dance arrangements from the major New York publishers, and the pile of music grew until it was three or four feet high. Anyone who worked in his orchestras had to be an excellent reader: often they'd spend much of the evening at a dance sight-reading new music. As his reputation grew, his orchestra began playing more and more engagements for white society functions along St. Charles Avenue. Out-of-town visitors were always teased into requesting the newest song they could think of. Most of the time Robichaux would look thoughtful, then say, "I think I have it," smile, and bring out the music. Robichaux's widow still had hundreds of the orchestra's scores when I spoke to her, and the music ultimately found its way to the William Hogan Jazz Archive at Tulane University. The scores have been used by a number of younger musicians as an invaluable source both for the compositions themselves and for their arrangement style—among them Lars Edegran, a pianist and orchestra leader from Sweden who moved to New Orleans in the 1960s and, with clarinetist "Orange" Kellin, founded the New Orleans Ragtime Orchestra.

It was not only Robichaux's determination to have the newest music that gave him an entry into New Orleans's society homes. After his first drummer Dee Dee Chandler, with Robichaux's encouragement, constructed a crude foot pedal so he could play a snare drum and a bass drum at the same time, Robichaux became locally celebrated as the first orchestra leader to introduce the trap drums into his dance arrangements, which made it possible to present the music with a softer, more subtle beat than the insistent sound of the bass drum usually added to the small ensembles. In 1903 another Thibodaux musician, bass drummer Clay Jiles, replaced him in the Excelsior Brass Band, and Robichaux devoted himself exclusively to his orchestra. There were many changes of personnel—even among the Creole orchestras, which insisted on reading skills, there were enough musicians for them to move easily from group to group. Two of the younger players who went on to have jazz careers in the 1920s, guitarist Bud Scott and clarinetist Wade Whaley, remembered occasionally working with the orchestra. During this time Robichaux and his orchestra also played on Sunday afternoons at Lincoln Park, entertaining the crowds with concert numbers and playing during the balloon ascensions that were the feature of the day.

In 1912 or 1913 the Robichaux orchestra began playing for public dancing at St. Catherine's Hall at 1509 Tulane Avenue, and this was the group in the photo that Vic Gaspard had saved. Charles McCurdy, who had been in the earlier group photo, was still the clarinetist, and Andrew Kimble Sr. remained on bass, but all of the others were new: cornetist Andrew Kimble; Vic Gaspard, trombone; Coochie Martin, guitar; and Walter Brundy, drums. By this point in his career Robichaux was probably the best-known orchestra leader in New Orleans, performing for both white and black audiences. The trumpeter Lee Collins remembered that Robichaux, despite his reputation as a legitimate musician, also was curious about the music that was becoming popular among the younger white and black musicians in town. Collins had been working along the coast in cities like Pensacola and Mobile, and he was playing with Jack Carey's band after his return.

So I went back to New Orleans and kept on working with all of the city's great musicians—except for Mr. John Robichaux, who was a very high-class musician. He was the most respected musician among both white and colored, and his orchestra played for the white society dances. But most Negroes didn't care for his music; it was more classical.

Well, Mr. Robichaux came to Francis Amis Hall with some high-class Creole friends of his one night when I was playing there with Jack Carey. I don't think anyone was more surprised than I was when he spoke to me, saying "Hi, little Lee." I didn't think he knew me at that time. But seeing that he did know who I was after all, I went over to him and said, "Mr. Robichaux, I sure wish I could play in your orchestra, if nothin' else but second cornet."

"I would like to have you with me, little Lee," he replied, "but you play such barrelhouse cornet that I don't think you would fit in very well with the places where I work." So I didn't get a job.[7]

At the end of World War I, Robichaux was hired to lead an orchestra at the city's most prestigious African American theater, the Lyric, which opened in February 1919 at Burgundy and Iberville, close to Canal Street. His "orchestra" was in reality a sextet similar to the dance orchestras he'd been leading for several years. In a bit of press agent color, the Chicago *Defender*, on October 20, 1923, gave a useful glimpse into the impressive level of musicianship that Robichaux's group presented.

Prof. John P. Robichaux, violinist, has gotten together five of the best musicians, beside himself, and jazz is their middle name. With Mrs. Margaret Maurice at the piano, they simply walk their way into hearts of a music mad city, the New York of the South. Alphonse Pecon [sic, Picou] does some good work with the clarinet and we all know it is one of the hardest instruments to master, but Alphonse did it. Now we come to the trombone king, John Lindsey [sic], and from the time he picks up his instrument until the baton falls we sit enthralled—some jazz. Arthur Singleton is the drummer and oh boy! He has the spotlight on him so often the performers threaten to give notice. Our boy beats a wicked drum. And last of all we have Mr. Jazz himself, or as he is called

in everyday life, Andrew Kimble, our cornetist. If you've never heard Kimble
you've never heard jazz for he really jazzes a mean cornet.[8]

The drummer was to become better known as "Zutty" Singleton. Although it was a small group, their responsibilities included accompanying vaudeville acts and adding appropriate background music to silent films. Robichaux remained at the theater until 1926, at the same time continuing to play for dancing at private parties and fashionable restaurants.

Whatever the formally trained Creole musicians thought of the new ragtime music, they inevitably found themselves caught between their older, dwindling Creole audience and a new generation of dancers less concerned about the distinctions between legitimate and illegitimate style. As one of the Creole violinists complained testily, "Those Uptown bands turned a violinist, me, into a fiddler." Even in Robichaux's first orchestra at least one of his musicians was already beginning to edge over the line. For many years it was thought that the two MacNeil brothers who played for him were only two among a large group of highly regarded legitimate musicians whose careers were confined to the Creole orchestras. For the older brother, cornetist James, who was born about 1870, that would still be a reasonable description of his musical career. A member of the Onward Brass Band when its members enlisted for the Spanish American War in 1898, he became director of the band, which was expanded and designated as the 9th Immunes Regimental Band in Cuba. He led them down New York's Fifth Avenue in one of the great parades celebrating the Cuban victory when their regiment returned to the United States in 1899.

For his younger brother Wendall, however, born about 1875, the story seems to have been a little more complicated. Since he was a string player, he didn't follow his brother to Cuba, but from two photos that exist of New Orleans string ensembles of the same period it is clear that his musical life in New Orleans was almost as colorful as his brother's with his regiment. In one of the photos, a careful examination of the original print a few years ago revealed that Wendall MacNeil is the previously unidentified mandolin player in a string trio that was working at Tom Anderson's saloon in the Restricted District. The other two musicians in the photo are bassist Albert Glenny and guitarist Youman Jacob. Anderson's was the hub of Storyville and, as many musicians maintained, used only small string groups or pianists in its bar. The violin, MacNeil's instrument with Robichaux, is tuned and fingered identically with the mandolin, and the switch back and forth was common among orchestra musicians of this period.

In the other photo, in which the players have also finally been identified through the original print, Wendall MacNeil is one of a quartet of string players sitting outdoors in the sunlight, playing in front of what looks like a grove of orange trees. The Orange Grove, east of the city, was a favorite New Orleans picnic spot, and the photo probably was taken when the small string band was

THE STRING TRIO AT TOM
ANDERSON'S SALOON IN STORYVILLE,
1890S. FROM LEFT: WENDALL
MACNEIL, YOUMAN JACOB, ALBERT
GLENNY. SAMUEL CHARTERS
COLLECTION.

playing for a party there. The mandolinist sitting next to Jacob could be Coochie Martin, Robichaux's guitarist for the engagement at St. Catherine's Hall, though the guitarist playing for the picnic is smiling much more enthusiastically than the serious musician studying his printed score with Robichaux. Next to the musician who could be Martin is guitarist Youman Jacob, who worked with MacNeil at Tom Anderson's. MacNeil's face and his instruments help identify him, but, despite their scuffed and faded images, in the two photos he also seems to be wearing the same pair of trousers and shoes.

The two faded prints have an importance beyond their glimpse of New Orleans and its musicians at this moment: they also document the diversity of the city's instrumentalists and their casual shifts back and forth between the legitimate and the ragtime musical worlds. MacNeil moved between the saloon world of Storyville, the genteel world of John Robichaux's regularly evening dances, and the loose informality of a country picnic. For most New Orleans musicians this was considered to be part of their working lives. Whatever the job, their comfortable approach to the music they heard around them made it possible to accommodate their talents to it.

Alphonse Picou, whom I heard on Bourbon Street in the cold winter nights of 1950, had one of the longest musical careers of any of the Creole musicians, and he was also one of the early instrumentalists to move back and forth between different musical worlds. Until his death he remained a respected and admired figure in New Orleans music. For many years he continued to play regularly

A NEW ORLEANS STRING BAND, PROBABLY PLAYING FOR A PICNIC, ABOUT 1905. FROM LEFT: YOUMAN JACOB, COOCHIE MARTIN, UNIDENTIFIED, WENDALL MACNEIL. SAMUEL CHARTERS COLLECTION.

with Papa Celestin or with Bill Matthews band at the Paddock Lounge on Bourbon Street. At that time in his seventies, he still added a shining flow of clarinet fills to the hard-pressed band's tourist-style Dixieland music. The clarinet chorus he had created for the march "High Society," based on the piccolo part in the instrumental arrangement, was included in nearly every one of the band's sets. Like Wendall MacNeil, he managed to fit into all the New Orleans musical worlds.

Picou was born on October 19, 1878, and when he was still in his teens he began studying the clarinet with Professor Morand. His recollection of his first band rehearsal in 1894, when he was sixteen years old, is not only an invaluable glimpse into the connections between the worlds of New Orleans music, but also sheds considerable light on the style of music itself. The bandleader interested in his playing was a neighbor, a trombonist named Boo Boo Fortunea, whose barbershop was around the corner from his house. Fortunea heard him practicing, came to the door and said to Picou's mother, "I would like to see that young man who is playing that instrument." When Picou came to the door, Fortunea asked if he was the one playing the clarinet. When Picou said he was, Fortunea told him, "Well, I'd like for you to come to my shop around the corner, because I want to talk to you." When Picou came to the barbershop, the bandleader asked the very young instrumentalist if he'd like to play in a band. Picou said he would like to, and Fortunea told him to come to the rehearsal that night. Years later Picou still had vivid memories of that first night of music. The single rehearsal was on Thursday night. It was for a job the band had playing a "ball" in a dance hall on Liberty Street on Saturday, two nights later.

*So I was invited to the rehearsal that night and I went to the place and I said
to him, "What do you want me to do?" I said, "Do you want me to play my
instrument? Is there any music?" He said, "Music? You don't need none." I
said, "How am I going to play?" He said, "You're going to come in on the choruses." I said, "Alright," and then I tuned up; we all tuned up our instruments.
He said that when I couldn't come in, to just stay out and listen until I could
come in. I did just what he told me and we got into it, and through with it, and
the whole band shook my hand and said I was great.*

*. . . The hall was jam-packed but I thought I would try anyway. I went and
took a few drinks, and the first thing you know I was playing more than them.*

*Every number we played the people just clapped their hands. We had to
play them two or three times, and that's the way I started with a band.*[9]

For his first few jobs Picou still felt uncomfortable playing without written
notes, but he decided that it "seemed a sort of style." He also confirmed what
other musicians had remembered: that to learn a new piece, one of the members of the band who could read music would learn the melody from the printed
arrangement and then teach it to the rest of the band. The Uptown bands usually
learned only the chorus of any new piece, and for dances they played a number
three times, the second repeat played at a softer volume for contrast, a trick they
picked up from marching band arrangements, which usually introduced the trio
section at a lower volume.

Jack Weber, an itinerant musician who was in and out of New Orleans in
these early years, remembered that usually the musician who was reading the
score didn't get it entirely correctly, and as he taught it to the others, it already
had started to drift away from the original. Then, Weber continued, "Other
band leaders stole it in turn, and because they couldn't read either, the tune was
played with many variations. After the leader had shown the trumpet man the
melody (or what he *thought* was the melody), the trumpeter would play it for
the band, and the men would come in, making a complete arrangement."[10]

Both Picou's memories of his first rehearsal and Jack Weber's reminiscences
help to confirm what many musicians later also recalled—that the first style of
playing the new pieces was a unison melody, with all the horns and the violin
playing together. The contrapuntal ensemble style that became characteristic of
the New Orleans style doesn't seem to have developed before World War I, the
period when many young musicians who recorded a few years later first began
playing. The instrumental style on their early recordings reflects the changes.
Picou stayed with the Accordiana Band for the next three years and then became
a leader himself, with his own Independence Band at Hope's Hall. He was also
a member of the Lyre Club Symphony, and in 1899 he worked for some time
with cornetist Oscar Duconge. In 1900 he began marching with the Excelsior
Brass Band, and in 1901 he was also worked occasionally with Freddie Keppard's
Olympia Band.

For most of these early years Picou found himself continually in demand, and as the number of orchestras grew there was steady work for someone like him who could play both Downtown and Uptown music. He was involved in most of the efforts at "serious" music in the Creole community, including the Bloom Philharmonic in 1903, George Moret's concert band at the Fair Grounds in 1913, and Robichaux's "second" dance orchestra. Picou also worked with the marching bands, playing his smaller E♭ clarinet with the Tuxedo Brass Band. At the same time he was playing his ornate, silver bell B♭, clarinet with the orchestra led by trumpeter Wooden Joe Nicholas. He also wrote music, and two of his compositions, "Onzaga Blues" and "Olympia Rag" were recorded by Joe Oliver's Creole Jazz Band as "Chattanooga Stomp" and "New Orleans Stomp." There was less work in the Depression years, and Picou went into semiretirement, though he never stopped playing at any time in his life. He had also purchased a barroom at some point in his career, and he often worked evenings as bartender.

With musicians like Robichaux, Picou, and the other Creole instrumentalists who worked with them in their orchestras, New Orleans music continued to reflect their musical values of lyric restraint and versatility. The Creoles absorbed much from the rougher ensembles of the Uptown musicians, but these musicians playing in their new dance bands probably learned even more from the Creoles' musical sophistication and determination to maintain their world of serious musical achievement.

4

Papa Jack's Boys

Can't truthfully say who had the first white jazz band in New Orleans. Don't know. But I do know Jack Laine had the most popular band at that time. He was more in demand, around 1900, and he developed fellows like Nick La Rocca, Tom Brown, Raymond Lopez. They all played with him. In Laine's own words, he put a horn in their hands! He had two or three bands at that time, so popular that he couldn't fill all the dates. Many times, Bud, my brother, and I subbed for him. Bud is seventy-two now and he played often with Laine. He remembers, too.

ARNOLD LOYOCANO, BASS PLAYER WITH THE FIRST
WHITE BAND TO TRAVEL NORTH TO CHICAGO[1]

Exchange Alley is still there, off of Canal Street. It's more of a commercial thoroughfare than it is an alley, since it's wide and the buildings along it are part of what was the old business district. It doesn't have traffic and doesn't go very far, only from Canal to Conti Street, between Royal and Chartres. In the years before World War I it had a mix of saloons where customers could work on the free lunch while they drank their beer, smoked, and let the time go by on the hot afternoons. You can still buy lunch along its modernized storefronts, and workers from the offices on the other side of Canal Street fill its lunchrooms. Nothing along the street now could be called a saloon, but the air-conditioned lounges do the same job. On any afternoon in 1905 or 1910, the benches along the passageway always had a loose gathering of the new ragtime musicians in bowler hats pushed back on their foreheads, and broad, square-bottomed neckties, who were looking for a job. Since Canal Street was easy to get to, and the streetcars stopped at Exchange, the musicians usually drifted by early in the afternoon and waited for a call. If it rained, they hung out in Blum's Café at 114 Exchange.

Sometimes the afternoons could get a little awkward. It was the period of intense organizing efforts by the American Federation of Musicians, the musicians' union, and most of the ragtime men still hadn't joined up. This continually caused friction with some of the stricter union members, who used the fact that their competitors didn't read music as one way to dismiss their skills. They were conveniently ignoring the reality that for the new style the others were playing, there wasn't any music to read. The offices of the musicians' union were in a room over Martin's saloon, further down the alley. The two groups of musicians couldn't help running into each other, and when jobs were scarce emotions ran high.

What the ragtimers were waiting for was a telephone call for them at the café from a busy bass drum player, orchestra leader, and band manager named Jack Laine. Laine, usually in a band uniform, sometimes with his large parade bass drum, probably shows up in early brass band photographs more than any other musician in New Orleans. If he wasn't leading the band or playing in it, the chances were good that he sent the band for the job. Musicians who spent most of their early New Orleans careers working for him often went out on their first jobs when they were still boys. As he said many times in later years, he had put their instruments in their hands. The trombonist George Brunies, who left to join the New Orleans Rhythm Kings in the early 1920s, played his first marching band job for Papa Jack—on alto horn—when he was eight, and when he was seventeen he still was playing with Jack Laine, though by this time he'd moved up to the trombone and he was playing with Jack's dance orchestras. Arnold Loyocano, who left as the bass player with Tom Brown's Band from Dixie for the first Chicago job by a white New Orleans band in 1915, was hired for a job with Jack when he was eleven.

When I returned to New Orleans several weeks after the disaster of Hurricane Katrina, one of the addresses I hurried to find in the first few days was the severely simple three-story, stucco-front house at 2405 Chartres Street, where Laine had lived from 1903 to 1909, and where sometimes he and his wife had the musicians from half a dozen of his bands using its rooms to catch a few moments of rest at Carnival season. The house is across Esplanade Avenue, outside of the French Quarter, but only a few blocks away from the Quarter and the French Market on Decatur Street, and it had come through the hurricane and flooding. The stucco front looks as though it had been constructed over the more common wooden clapboard. A doorway leads to wooden steps outside the house itself, leading up to balconied galleries of what would have been the servants' quarters. The street outside the house is still quiet, and the trees along the sidewalk cast a mottled shade against the house's windows.

When the first research into the history of New Orleans jazz was begun in the 1930s, as part of the research for *Jazzmen*, one of its writers, Charles Edward Smith, spent considerable time with Laine, who was friendly and comfortable with Smith's questions, and still remembered the early years with undisguised pleasure. He described for Smith the chaotic conditions of their work during the Carnival season. As Smith wrote,

> . . . *there were plenty of jobs in New Orleans and the best of them went to Laine's men, because they were the only white men in the city who knew the jazz vernacular. In the summer at Milneburg, a mecca for New Orleanians from the moist heat that blanketed the city, bands played at houses and on pavilions. At Carnival time jobs piled up, five and six a day. There wasn't time to go home, so they took on a second home and a second mother between jobs. Mother Laine let them sleep wherever there was space, on cots, on chairs, even on the rug. For two hours she saw that they weren't disturbed. Then they went on to another job.*[2]

Of all the musicians from that first generation of ragtimers, Laine lived the longest, and he became part of the efforts to trace early jazz roots in these years before recordings. He was born in New Orleans on September 21, 1873. His father was a contractor and it was a comfortable childhood. He first began playing the drums when he was eleven, when his father brought him a deep toned military snare drum that had been among the things left behind after the Cotton Festival in Audubon Park in 1885. Two or three years later his father bought him a bass drum from the Salvation Army, and it became his main instrument. When he was interviewed by William Russell in 1957 he was remembering back more than seventy years. "I started in music when I was a young kid. I used to play on tin pans until the Cotton and Sugar Exposition were here. That's been seventy-odd years now, and I was about eight years old when they bought me a drum up there, a field drum after they had finished and left from here, see. They closed here and they sold everything they had up there, all kinds of instruments and stuff."[3]

He soon had organized all the children in the neighborhood into a band, and they received some instruction from an older musician who played the piccolo.

> *The other kids had sort of a cane outfit, their daddies used to make 'em cane flutes and stuff like that. And then the boys got to buying the old second hand instruments out here on Rampart Street. You know, it used to be full of all kinds of old instruments, and they'd toot-toot on 'em till finally they begin to make a success. . . . We had a fellow by the name of Meade, a professor, he was a cigar maker, he was a professor of music, real good, real good, he played most any kind of instrument. Well, he came down several times, he used to teach us. I had a nice place where all us kids would hole out for rehearsal. So, long come political parades, one thing or another, you know, I start[ed] to get engagements with them.*[4]

Laine grew up in New Orleans, but over the next decades many of the musicians he hired were from immigrant families. In one of the earliest known photos of a New Orleans band, a white marching band is posed in their uniforms, crowded on the back of a mule-drawn wagon or sitting on the mules, on a visit to Chattanooga in 1894. The band was led by cornetist Siegfried Christensen, who posed standing up on the wagon just behind the mules, with his cornet under his arm. His name certainly suggests a European background. The trombonist standing by the front wheel of the wagon was Angelo Castigliola, one of the flood of Italian musicians into New Orleans, and the band's tuba player, one of a line of musicians standing on the wagon, was usually known as "Joe Alexander" but his name was actually Guiseppe Allesandra. He was born in Italy in 1865. The euphonium player standing against the wagon's back wheel was Dave Perkins, who usually passed as white though he lived close to a black neighborhood and was well known among the African American musicians, both as a music teacher and for his sideline of renting out band instruments.

During this period Laine usually was photographed in a band uniform, but in a less formal photograph from 1898 he is standing in a long apron at the anvil in the shed where he worked his other job, as a blacksmith for the Dennis Sheen Drayage Company. He is in a sleeveless jacket, his muscular arms holding his hammer, his hat pushed back on his head, and with his careful glance, he gives the impression of a man who feels he has his life very much under his control. Beside him, looking slightly abashed, is a skinny twelve-year-old named Frank Christian, who would become one of the most talented trumpet players in Laine's bands.

It was about this time that Laine began to expand his activities, finding bands for almost any occasion. If the people calling couldn't get his own band, he found musicians for them. The lakeside area of Milneburg (which New Orleanians pronounced MIL-nee-burg) was one of his busiest spots.

> *If I had a job somewhere, then they'd have to get another band, you see when they'd pull off some kind of affair or another, a picnic or ball or a dance, or any kind of that sort, if they couldn't engage me, they'd have to engage another band, see, but as I said, I had as high as five bands going and that is the truth and God's truth. . . . I played every, every, every year for the Mardi Gras parades, played balls, picnics, dances, all likes of that you know, weddings and all sorts of stuff like that. Most of my work used to be at Milneburg, used to play out there every, every Sunday. Two, three bands I had engaged out there, every Sunday at Milneburg, then from Milneburg I'd switch over and on to one of those parks, either the Southern Park or the Suburban Park or the Crescent Park. I had jobs like that you know, and I played at night. Come from Milneburg, go right on those other jobs and play, finish out my contract.[5]*

It wasn't only the city's young white musicians who found their way into Laine's bands. He hired lighter-skinned Creole musicians, though he explained to anyone who questioned him that they were "dark skinned," but perhaps Mexican

JACK LAINE'S RELIANCE BRASS BAND, 1906. FROM LEFT: STANDING, DAVE PERKINS, VINCENT BAROCCO, SIDNEY MOORE, PETE PELLEGRINI, FREDDIE NEUROTH, JACK LAINE; SEATED, MANUEL BELASCO AND JOE ALEXANDER.

or Cuban. If he became aware that one of his musicians was passing, however, he quickly dropped him from the roster of names he called. The regular clarinetist in his dance orchestra, Achille Baquet, was Creole, and the trombone player Dave Perkins, also had a Creole background, and when Baquet's father, accomplished string bass player and teacher T. V. Baquet, learned the tuba, he also worked in Laine's bands. From its beginnings, jazz in the city moved steadily, though uneasily, back and forth across the racial barriers.

Two musicians in the photograph of the Siegried Christensen band in 1894, Dave Perkins and Giuseppe Allesandra, were photographed a decade later with a very young and pleased-looking Jack Laine, posed with his eight-piece Reliance Brass Band in dark, high-collared uniforms with visored band caps. The photo was taken in 1906. Among the others in the band were more musicians with Italian American and Latin American names, including Manuel Belasco, Vincent Barocco, and Pete Pellegrini. It sometimes seems that, in a list of the musicians who worked either in Laine's Reliance Brass Band or with one of his dance orchestras, at least half of them had names that indicate Italian roots, and probably for some others their parents had done as Giuseppe Allesandra's and anglicized the family's name.

For many of the bands his wife, Blanche Nunez Laine (clarinetist "Yellow" Nunez was a cousin), sewed their uniforms. "I made every shirt they wore. I made forty-two shirts when they started. Dark red. They had white and black helmets, and I made the ties and I made the Grand Marshal's regalia."[6]

In one of the best-known photographs of Laine from around the turn of the century, he is a handsome, magnetic figure in his marching band uniform; a long, tight, severe jacket buttoned up to his neck, the fabric a dark tone, with a flash of striped ornament on his shoulders. He is tall, square shouldered, his dark hair trimmed short, and his expression is serious, but pleased. By the time the Spanish-American War was declared in 1898 he was twenty-five and already had the reputation of being one of the best drummers in the city. The bands he sent out on his other jobs were known for playing new songs and ragtime numbers along with the waltzes, the formal dances, and the quadrilles that were part of a night's work. His dance groups were usually called The Reliance Orchestra, even if there were five or six bands playing in different places on the same night. Occasionally he varied his offering by presenting himself and his regular ensemble as Jack Laine's Ragtime Band. He also probably played as many street jobs as dance jobs, since New Orleans always seemed to be having a parade somewhere, and the marching group was called the Reliance Brass Band. There is even a brief, silent film clip of one of his brass bands marching in a Mardi Gras parade.

In 1910 Laine's energies led him to set up a circus and minstrel show with the name Laine's Greater Majestic Minstrels in a large tent that was set up at Canal and White Streets behind a streetcar barn. The band posed for a photograph in front of the big tent, with the name BIG SHOW painted above a scalloped dark strip that announced MAIN ENTRANCE. Laine was sitting in front of the others with one hand cocked on his thigh, his hair carefully combed, his face suitably entrepreneurial. Most of the musicians behind him had done their best to look as orderly. The jackets, more flamboyant than his usual marching band uniforms since the band was performing in a show, were hemmed with contrasting piping and cloth stripes on their shoulders in the same lighter shade. Perhaps also part of his pleased expression was the fact that the very young-looking, skinny alto horn player standing just behind his left shoulder was his son, Alfred Laine, who was usually called "Baby" when he first became a member of his father's bands. The serious-faced clarinet player, his jacket neatly buttoned, was Alcide "Yellow" Nunez, whose parents had emigrated from the Canary Islands, and the tuba player, standing stiffly with his large instrument, his eyes staring intently into the camera, was Martin Abraham, who under the name "Chink" Martin was to become the busiest bass player in the city in the 1920s. He was still playing with the same energy and rhythm into the 1960s with a young jazz dance band playing for riverboat excursions, the Crawford-Ferguson Night Owls.

The exceptions to the band's air of sartorial care were the Mello brothers: cornetist Manuel had left his jacket open and a hand in his pocket, and trombonist Leonce had given himself more space by pushing the slide of his trombone out to its furthest extension. His shirt collar was up around his neck above his jacket, his tie askew, and his uniform cap perched on the back of his head. At first glance he looked as though he had just pulled himself out of bed in time for the photo, but in other band pictures from the time he was always as disheveled—cap pushed on an uneven angle on his thick black hair, collar and tie hastily pulled together, his jacket hanging open—so Mello was probably one of the early jazz rebels who was intent on making his own personal statement when it came to band discipline. At the time the photo was taken he was considered to be the

JACK LAINE SEATED IN FRONT OF
HIS MINSTREL SHOW TENT WITH
HIS RELIANCE BRASS BAND, 1910.
FROM LEFT: MANUEL MELLO,
YELLOW NUNEZ, LEONCE MELLO,
BABY LAINE, CHINK MARTIN,
TIM HARRIS.

best ragtime trombonist in New Orleans, with an explosive, boisterous style, so strong and self-assured that when the styles changed about 1913 and 1914 to a more complex ensemble that demanded more subtlety in the trombone's role, he was considered too rough for the new bands that were performing.

Also documented in the photo was another of the crude bass drum pedal attachments that spread to the city's orchestra drummers after Dee Dee Chandler, with John Robichaux's Orchestra, in the 1890s had devised a pedal and chain that was attached to a ball that struck the bass drum head when the drummer stepped on the pedal. The bass drum was turned toward the camera so the ball was visible on the end of the rod, and already there had been a modification since the first attachment that Chandler had constructed.. Attached to the rod, which projected downward down from the top of the drum shell, was a metal arm with a rounded tip that struck a cymbal mounted on the drum head at the same time that the foot pedal swung the pedal against the drum head itself. The sound must have been a booming, metallic clang.

Despite Laine's confident expression in the photograph, a hurricane blew down the tent later in the year and he went back to booking his bands and playing the bass drum.

Although the music of this early period is sometimes called "jazz," the word itself wasn't part of the New Orleans vocabulary. For any of the dance band musicians, what they were playing was called ragtime. As Laine made clear, and as the early recordings by the New Orleans bands also emphasize, the bands didn't improvise on their jobs, beyond casual changes of phrasing or occasional embellishments. Many of the pieces still seem to have been played as a unison melody by all of the horns and the violin, their repertory created in the kind of loose rehearsals that Alphonse Picou described, when all he was asked to do was learn the melody and then join in whenever he thought he had it. This also was reflected in the casualness of the engagements. Anyone who came to play was expected to know the melodies of all the songs they'd be requested to perform. The excitement that their audiences loved grew out of the vigor and strut of their performance.

There is some question about what the bands might have had as musical models, but the obvious predecessors were the ragtime orchestras that were staple novelties for the vaudeville stage, as well as for the touring minstrel companies, and for public dances everywhere in the country. There was also a broad repertory of ragtime novelties that were regularly performed by the concert brass bands that crisscrossed the country on their continual tours. Even more importantly for listeners today, the great concert bands, like Sousa's and Prince's, recorded many of the audience favorites on the new cylinder or flat disc recordings. From these we can hear that what was termed "ragtime" in these decades was generally loud, energetic, and played with considerable humor. For the rest of the repertory, the bands drew on the music of the popular theater. Every traveling minstrel show appeared with an orchestra that was expected to perform cakewalks, slow drags, and the new ragtime successes—along with the accompaniments for the sentimental plantation melodies and the grand walk-around that showed off the entire company. At the same time, the vaudeville houses introduced all the new ballads and sentimental melodies.

The trumpeter Frank Christian, who worked with many Laine's bands, said in an interview that he got most of the late tunes from the young women who came to the bandstand and asked him to play them. He would ask them to bring the piano music with them when they came to the next dance. "Being able to read a little bit, I could produce a rendition shortly."[7]

What Laine described for Charles Edward Smith in their conversations in the late 1930s were long, laborious afternoon rehearsals as the instrumentalists worked out ensemble parts, each of them contributing phrases and harmonies to the developing arrangements. He remembered that one of the clarinetists, "Yellow" Nunez, who often took Achille Baquet's place in the Reliance Orchestra, was particularly inventive, along with the regular cornetist Lawrence Veca. Trombonist Dave Perkins, Laine told Smith, "was wonderful at it." Smith continued, "To prepare for a night's job they got together for rehearsal in the afternoon. In their repertoire were several Uptown rags. *Tiger Rag* they called *Praline*, after the candy made with maple sugar, pecans, and sometimes coconut shreds—because it was a raggy tune. *Livery Stable Blues* was *Meat Ball*. Playing the tunes time after time they stamped them with their own personalities. There were readers in the band, Dave Perkins among them, but you didn't have to read on the rags, since once the tune was set you played it."[8]

Once a band had been collected from the musicians hanging around the saloon in Exchange Alley, where did they go for the jobs? Of all the photographs of the ragtime "fakers" bands from this period, the one that seemed to breathe the most atmosphere was a casually posed picture from an afternoon dance at Quirella's Restaurant, a rambling, ramshackle building built on pilings over the

FRANK CHRISTIAN'S RAGTIME BAND AT QUIRELLA'S PIER, MILNEBURG, 1915. FROM LEFT:
WILLIE GUITAR, MANUEL GOMEZ, HARRY NUNEZ, YELLOW NUNEZ, FRANK CHRISTIAN,
CHARLIE CHRISTIAN, "KID TOTTS" BLAISE.

water at the end of the long pier at Milneburg.[9] Lined up against the railing, looking as though it'd been a long afternoon, were seven of Laine's musicians including bassist Willie Guitar; guitarist Manuel Gomez; two of the Nunez brothers—Harry, a violinist, and clarinetist "Kid Yellow"; two of the Christian brothers—Frank with his early-style trumpet and Charlie, the trombonist; and the drummer, Kid Totts Blaise, who had one foot propped up on the railing. They were all holding their instruments, looking as though they were just about to play. Policemen were standing behind them, with a scattering of dancers studying the camera from behind the band. The band had shown up for the job in their formal dark uniforms, but jackets were unbuttoned, bow ties were wilting, and the uniform caps were jammed on their heads. The smells on the pier would have been the coarse odors of the lake, shallow and dark, just below them, and the kitchen aromas of crab and shrimp. There would have been a sound of the water surging against the wooden pilings, and the dancers would have been able to hear the distant sounds of other music coming from the camps strung out along the water.

During the years that Laine was busiest, most of the cabarets in town that had bands for dancing, like Club Creole or the Pup Club, booked the bands themselves instead of calling Laine. Most of the musicians remembered talking directly with the owners. Laine's contacts were with the hundreds of New Orleanians who hired musicians for everything from company picnics to private birthday parties. A few miles west of Milneburg on the lakefront was the elegant Spanish Fort playground at the mouth of Bayou St. John, with its formal gardens and restaurants that featured brass band concerts and family entertainment. It advertised frequently in the city's newspapers, and was too genteel for most of Laine's ragtimers. For a pleasant afternoon with the children, Spanish Fort was the best the city offered. Its concert brass band, led by Professor Tosso and including many recently arrived Italian musicians, played every afternoon. Because of its swampy shoreline and the uncertainties of the climate, Ponchartrain didn't have any beaches at that time, but this was also the

NEW ORLEANS, FROM A
1917 MOTORIST'S GUIDE TO
THE LAKE FRONT, SHOWING
THE RESORTS AT WEST
END, SPANISH FORT, AND
MILNEBURG. COURTESY OF
THE UNIVERSITY OF TEXAS
LIBRARIES, THE UNIVERSITY
OF TEXAS AT AUSTIN.

era before women generally were comfortable appearing before other people in bathing costumes. The scene at Milneburg was considerably less sedate.

Milneburg was at the end of what is now Elysian Fields Avenue, but at that time people traveled out to the camps on the train. A steam locomotive with a string of cars went back and forth through the overgrown bayou country that lay between the old New Orleans neighborhoods and the lake. There were still soggy stretches of bayou and muddy earth, with a thick tangle of vegetation and flocks of birds. The train was called "Smoky Mary" and the ride out to the lake cost fifteen cents. People in the 1950s still remembered the cars packed with musicians and their instruments on their way out to the jobs, and a flat car with bass drums packed together with picnic baskets and kegs of beer. An aerial photo of Milneburg taken in the early 1920s shows the long pier, extending more than two hundred yards, that went straight out into the lake, with Quirella's at the end. Snaking off from the pier like tentacles were narrower piers leading out to the "camps," small wooden buildings built, like Quirella's, on pilings over the water. In the photo, which only shows the scene along the main pier, there are more than a hundred camps, and on busy days people insist that music was coming from every one of them. Milneburg was one of the few places where the musicians from all parts of the city could hear each other play, and both black and white bands shared the train journey out on Smoky Mary.

In 1954 I recorded hours of music and reminiscences by an elderly businessman named H. J. Boiusseau, who had been one of the "sports" who took the train out to Milneburg every weekend. Quirella's was a popular restaurant and dance hall and it was proper to bring your girlfriend, with a family chaperone, for a fish dinner there, but the camps weren't places where you could take a young woman who was thinking about her reputation. It was the camps, usually

owned or rented for the season by private families or clubs of young businessmen, where Boiusseau and other "blades" from town took shop girls, or girls
who had factory jobs, or somebody who was known to be ready for a good time.
He laughed at the memory of the girls called the "Hernshine Canaries," who
worked at the Hernshine Cigar Factory and who came out with them to their
Bulls and Bears Club camp for Sunday afternoons. He remembered their "baby
doll shoes"—low-heeled black shoes with a strap across the instep that they wore
with white stockings.

Boiusseau was a fine amateur ragtime pianist, and he always spent part of the
afternoon at the camp's piano. One of his specialties was a version of the Spanish-
American War march "Bluebells Goodbye," which he played straight for the first
chorus, then "ragged" in the style he learned at Tom Anderson's saloon for the
final chorus. Out at Milneburg the only thing the girls were expected to do was
dance, laugh, have a good time, and drink a little and pet a little, but, Boiusseau
insisted, with a laugh, "if they didn't want to go along with us we pushed them
in the lake."

Milneburg was immortalized by the tune that some of the members of the
New Orleans Rhythm Kings wrote in its honor, "Milneburg Joys." They had all
spent a lot of time riding out to the lakefront on Smoky Mary to play those jobs
in the camps. Their composition has kept Milneburg's name alive for anyone who
knows the classic jazz repertoire, but in the 1930s it was necessary to construct a
barrier wall to protect the lakeshore from storms and the occasional high water,
and Milneburg disappeared in the new construction.

In the confusions of all the jobs that Jack Laine booked, there could always
be mishaps. One New Year's Eve, a young cornet player named Nick La Rocca
was told to wait on a corner and the rest of a five-piece band would show up.
After two hours the only one who had arrived was the bass player, Willie Guitar,
and the two of them played for six hours at a party as a duet. The personnel of
the Reliance Brass Band also was fluid, but among more or less regular Reliance
musicians were the tuba player Chink Martin, the trombonists Henry Brunies
and Bill Gallaty, the snare drummer Ragbaby Stephens, and Emile Christian,
who played either cornet or trombone, along with cornetists Ray Lopez and
Gus Zimmerman.

The Reliance Brass Band must have played for every fraternal and social organization in white New Orleans, and there is a photo of them—this time with the
band enlarged to twelve pieces—standing along the side of the street as part of
the Mobile, Alabama, Fireman's Day Parade in 1912. Laine, a member of several
volunteer fire departments, remembered that the Mobile job was booked years
in advance. As with the dance orchestra, there was more work than one band
could handle, and there were sometimes two or three Reliance Brass Bands out
on the streets at the same time. Their uniforms were new dark jackets, white
trousers, white shoes, and white crowned band caps. In the summer they came
out in white shirts and ties, the sleeves neatly buttoned. When they lined up on

the street they were neatly dressed like the African American bands, the Onward and the Excelsior, and the formal march music the bands played was probably often very similar.

Laine's activities as a booking agent for the local musicians were more important to the city's musical life than either his bass drum playing or leadership of his bands, but because of the unique situation in New Orleans there was no one among the black musicians who took over a similar role. This had already happened in other cities. James Reese Europe in New York City had so many instrumental groups working as part of his Clef Club organization that he had to have an office to handle the business details. In Detroit, the bandleader Fred Stone also booked jobs for the black instrumentalists everywhere in the city. In New Orleans it could have been the decisive split between the Creole, reading musicians, and the Uptown men who were "fakers" like Laine's men. The respected orchestra leader John Robichaux would been the obvious person to work with a roster of other musicians, since he played for so many society affairs as well dances in the Downtown halls, but he never seems to have been interested in taking on this involved job. The most used arrangement for booking the Uptown musicians was through a barbershop close to Beauregard Square. Anyone looking for a musician left a telephone message and the man's name was entered in a book. If he stopped by to see if anyone needed him and he found his name, he took a dollar deposit that confirmed he was taking the job. Some musicians, however, particularly Bunk Johnson, were notorious for taking the dollar and then not showing up at the job.

Even with all of his energy and his well-known ability to find a band for most occasions, Laine couldn't manage all of the jobs for a city that was hungry for music. Two friends who shifted in and out each other's bands, Happy Schilling and Johnny Fischer, also managed to get their share of the work. Schilling, who was born in 1886, was tall and rawboned with a bluff, open expression, a friendly, popular musician who usually played trombone, though like nearly everyone else he played three or four other instruments. Fischer was older, born in 1877, but he had the same persistence as Schilling, and his face, large nosed and always with a surprised smile, is in several early band photographs. They worked the same kind of jobs as Laine's men, and often performed at the picnic grounds at East End Park on Lake Ponchartrain. In one photograph of a typical outdoor picnic they were posed on a gleaming summer day in the popular white shirts, white trousers, and white shoes, with white uniform caps. The caps had a dark band with the name "Fischers." There were only six of them in the photograph, which would make them the smallest brass band to pose for a camera up to that time.

Fischer, whose name was actually John Henry Phillips, began leading his first street bands at the beginning of the century, and there is a formal photo of his "Ragtime Military Band," in their formal dark uniforms, kneeling before a large marching group, the Big 50 Carnival Club, in front of the new courthouse in the

French Quarter at Royal and Conti.[10] The marching club, in the bright sunlight, were posed incongruously in blackface.

Al Rose and Edmond Souchon, in their affectionate compilation *New Orleans Family Album*, made an effort to list the musicians who worked in Jack Laine's bands. In the orchestra he led himself, there was cornetist Lawrence Veca, clarinetist Achille Baquet, and trombonist Dave Perkins. Among the others who were added to his regular instrumentation as part of the ragtime orchestra were pianists Henry Ragas, Norman Brownlee, Johnny Provenzano, Jules Reiner, and Tom Zimmerman. Guitar and banjo players included Dominick Barocco, Joe Guiffre, "Stalebread" Lacoume, and Jim Ruth; string bass players Joe Brocco, Steve Brown, Jules Cassard, John Guiffre, Willie Guitar, Arnold Loyocano, and Bud Loyocano. Among his drummers were Dave Perkins, Tim Harris, Buster Klein, Anton Lada, Buddy Rogers, Emmet Rogers, Tony Sbarbaro, Johnny Stein, Diddie Stephens, and Ragbaby Stephens.

The optimistic list of musicians who sometimes marched in a Reliance Brass Band uniform that Rose and Souchon also compiled includes almost every white New Orleans musician who was to go on to the cabarets and the dance cafés of New York and Chicago only a few years later. The cornet and trumpet players they list include Manuel Mello, Fred Neuroth, Joe and Johnny Lala, three Brunies brothers, Richard, Merrit, and Albert, Gus Zimmerman, Nick La Rocca, Pete Pellegrini, Frank Christian, Lawrence Veca, George Barth, Harry Shannon, Pete Dietrans, Ray Lopez, and Johnny DeDroit. Trombonists include Leonce Mello, Dave Perkins, Eddie Edwards, two more of the Brunies brothers, Henry and George, Emile Christian, Marcus Kahn, Bill Gallaty Sr., Ricky Toms, Jules Cassard, Tom Brown, and Happy Schilling.

Among the clarinetists were Yellow Nunez, Achille Baquet, Martin Kirsch, Sidney Moore, Clem Camp, Johnny Fischer, Larry Shields, Tony Giardina, Gus Mueller, John Palisier, Red Rowling, and Leon Roppolo, father of the clarinetist with the New Orleans Rhythm Kings.

The brass horn players—alto horn, baritone horn, and tuba—included Jack's son Alfred, Vincent Barocco, Merrit Brunies, and Martin Abraham Sr. Laine usually played the bass drum himself on the street jobs, but other drummers were Tim Harris, Ragbaby Stephens, Johnny Stein, Tony Sbarbaro, Billie Lambert, Diddie Stephens, and Emmet Rogers.

The continual presence of Italian names makes it clear that the beginnings of jazz in New Orleans included a much wider range of music than simply small instrumental ensembles playing ragtime melodies and musicians from one of the city's three racial groups; the Uptown African Americans, the Downtown Creoles, and the different national groups who were lumped together as "white." So much attention has been given to the question of who might have invented jazz that it is forgotten that the racial and social divisions in New Orleans created two jazz styles. One was African American and the other was European American, and reflected the more Italianate instrumental virtuosity and lyric

JACK LAINE'S RELIANCE ORCHESTRA, ABOUT 1917. FROM LEFT: SEATED, CHARLIE CORDILLA, GEORGE BRUNIES, JULES REINER, PIANIST; STANDING (OR LEANING) ALBERT "BABY" LAINE, HERMAN RAGAS, BASSIST, AND JACK LAINE. COMPARING LAINE'S FACE WITH EARLIER PHOTOS, HE MIGHT HAVE SUFFERED FROM SMALLPOX SOMETIME AFTER THE EARLIER PHOTOS WERE TAKEN.

tone of the newly arrived Italian and Sicilian Americans. Each group of musicians was playing for dancers whose rhythms and movements also reflected the social differences between the two societies. After so much time has passed, it seems virtually meaningless to give either of the two musical languages of early New Orleans syncopated ragtime precedence over the other. They were simply different. As Charles Edward Smith concluded after his weeks in New Orleans talking to a wide range of musicians, "It should be emphasized that white New Orleans contributed its own background to jazz, and since this background was different from that of the Negro, 'Dixieland' music was bound to show differences."[11]

It is ironic that even less is known about the musician who was considered the best white cornetist of the period. Lawrence Veca, who played with Laine's Reliance orchestra, is as little known as many of the early black musicians. Smith found that, "Most New Orleans musicians, white or colored, used only superlatives in talking about Veca. Jack Laine described him as 'a master on cornet.' It wasn't simply that he had a warm tone and excellent rhythm, qualities rare enough in themselves. What put him on top with the few really excellent cornet players in the city was that he played creatively, rounding out a tune with original variations and adapting style and tone quality to the tune played. When Veca played cornet there wasn't another white man in the city who could touch him."[12] The New Orleans Family Album notes only that he was born in 1889, died in 1911, at the age of twenty-two, and his name is usually misspelled as "Vega."

Although today Jack Laine sometimes seems to be an almost mythic figure out of the long-forgotten past of the first stirrings of syncopated ragtime bands in New Orleans, he lived until 1966, many years after most of his band members had died. He stopped handling engagements after World War I, and although it isn't certain why he withdrew from his long music career, he once said that so many of his musicians had been killed in World War I that he didn't have the heart to go on, but in reality very few of the Reliance musicians even were picked up by the draft. It could have been that so many of his men were part of the first exodus of New Orleanians out of the city after 1915, when Tom Brown's band played in Chicago, that he couldn't keep his bands together. There is an exuberant photo of him playing drums with a classic jazz band on an excursion to Alexander, Louisiana, in 1919. The trombonist is the seventeen-year-old George Brunies, and sitting on the top of the piano beside him was Laine's son, who has switched from alto horn to cornet, and picked a new nickname, "Pansy." His son led his own band throughout the twenties, and his father might have taken a step back to give Pansy a little room.

Laine was not only a frequent guest of the New Orleans Jazz Society in the 1950s, he continued to be a useful source of information about the older musicians and their world. He even recorded a "greeting" to the jazz world. Although we'll never know what one of those early bass drum pedal attachments sounded like, one afternoon, with drummer and producer Barry Martyn, I was looking through littered shelves in a room in the old building that houses Jazzology Records on Decatur Street. It was after Katrina and we were trying to see if anything had been damaged in the torrential rains that followed the winds. The tapes and test pressings were what was left of the Southland label, the company that had been established by Joe Mares decades before as a way to document the era and the music of his brother, cornetist Paul Mares, of the New Orleans Rhythm Kings. Barry handed me a tape he had picked up, and on the back of the box, from an unissued session in the late 1950s, I saw that Jack Laine's name was listed as the bass drummer.

If anyone could be said to be the "father" of what came to be called the "Dixieland" style of New Orleans jazz that began with recordings by his musicians in 1917 and 1918, and continues resolutely into the modern era, it is certainly Jack Laine.

5

The Other Side of Town

I never do hear "Salty Dog" played the way they used to play it when I was coming up. Of course, some of those men was what you call specialists. "Salty Dog" was the only tune they could play.

Veteran drummer Albert Jiles in an interview in 1954[1]

I t wasn't far to walk from the French Quarter across Canal Street to the other New Orleans world of the Uptown neighborhoods: a few blocks down Burgundy or Rampart Street to Canal, then on along Rampart to Gravier and Poydras, and a few more blocks north to Liberty. The buildings on the Uptown streets didn't look like the rows of old Spanish buildings lining the streets of the French Quarter, but they had their own lines of wooden houses, like the streets around St. Claude and Governor Nicholls where many of the old Creole families lived on the other side of Rampart Street. In the neighborhoods Uptown, the little frame houses—the "shotguns"—were newer, there weren't a lot of trees, and the streets had been laid out in prosaic squares and rectangles. The backyards didn't have space for more than a place to chop wood for the stove and an outhouse as far away from the house as the back fence would allow. The streets were unpaved, mostly unlit, and crowded most of the day or night. It was only a short distance from one neighborhood to the other, but for most Creoles Uptown was a part of town they never saw.

George Foster, the bass player who picked up the nickname "Pops" from Louis Armstrong in the 1930s and was known as "Pops" Foster for the rest of his life, moved from a backcountry plantation to Uptown New Orleans about 1900. He still had vivid memories of the neighborhood when he dictated his detailed and invaluable autobiography to writer Tom Stoddard in San Francisco in the late 1960s.

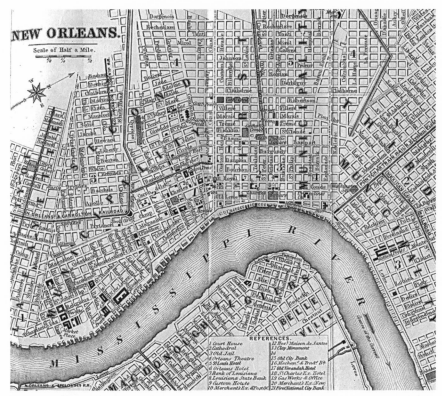

NEW ORLEANS, "UPTOWN" IN 1869. MOST OF THIS AREA WAS CLEARED ORIGINALLY FOR
THE RAILROAD TERMINAL AT THE UNION STATION, AND THEN IN THE 1960S FOR THE CIVIC
CENTER AND THE SUPERDOME. COURTESY OF THE UNIVERSITY OF TEXAS LIBRARIES, THE
UNIVERSITY OF TEXAS AT AUSTIN.

*On the plantation you didn't see anything but sugarcane and corn. When I
first got to New Orleans, I saw everybody going everywhere delivering coal,
selling vegetables, and doing different things. In those days the markets opened
at three or four in the morning and stayed open till noon. They sold everything
you wanted to eat at the outdoor markets.... In the heart of town they had a
big dump, and if you lived near you sure could smell the rotten garbage and
stuff. Later they started carrying the garbage out in the Gulf in big barges.
We used to have backyard toilets in those days, and colored guys used to come
around and clean them out. They'd put the crap in barrels, roll them out to the
aggravatin' wagon, then haul them down to the docks and load them on boats,
and they'd carry them off down the river.... Those outdoor toilets caused
some of the biggest roaches you ever saw. They were big red flying ones and it
really hurt when they bit you. The mosquitoes were terrible too. It was so bad
in one place we played named Howard's Canal, we had to wear nets over our
heads. New Orleans in those days was a mess, very few streets had gravel, and
only the ones like Canal Street had cobbles, most were just mud.[2]*

Louis Armstrong, who was ten years younger than Foster, was born into the same Uptown neighborhoods, and in his various autobiographies he returned to the streets and the life that filled them. In 1954, in *Satchmo*, he reminisced with what seems to be a little editorial help with sentence structure:

When I was born in 1900 my father, Willie Armstrong, and my mother, May Ann—or Mayann as she was called—were living on a little street called James Alley. Only one block long, James Alley is located in the crowded section of New Orleans known as Back o' Town. It is one of the four great sections into which the city is divided. The others are Uptown, Downtown and Front o' Town, and each of these quarters has its own little traits.

    James Alley—not Jane Alley as some people call it—lies in the very heart of what is called The Battlefield because the roughest characters in town used to live there, and would fight and shoot so much. In that one block between Gravier and Perdido Streets more people were crowded than you ever saw in your life. There were church people, gamblers, hustlers, cheap pimps, thieves, prostitutes, and lots of children. There were bars, honky-tonks and saloons, and lots of women walking the streets for tricks to take to their "pads" as they called their rooms.[3]

Armstrong's early years were chaotic: his mother moved out and left him with his grandmother; then, when he was four or five he went to live with his mother again a few blocks away in the notorious neighborhood around Liberty and Perdido in the middle of what sometimes was called "Black Storyville." What he noticed after a few days was that there was music everywhere. The little barrooms he was used to around Jane Alley (as the street sign at the corner identified it) just had pianos, but in the honky-tonks that he remembered on every corner, there was every kind of musical instrument he could think of. Most of the balls and dances in the more staid Creole neighborhoods only a half-mile away were held in the roomy, wood-framed social halls scattered through the neighborhood. Even in the Restricted District, which lay between Downtown's gentility and Uptown's roughness, the bands played in popular cabarets and the two large dance halls, entertaining a crowd that had as many local businessmen out for an evening as it did tourists and the local sports. Every musician who played in the district remembered that this carefully delineated section of the city was continually patrolled by the police, who were vigilant about keeping anyone underage off its streets—and certainly off its bandstands. On the streets where Armstrong grew up, however, if one of the boys from the neighborhood started playing an instrument in one of the rough dives, nobody paid much attention.

Within certain broad dimensions, history is whatever we choose to make it. In 1939, after a letter written by the cornetist Willie "Bunk" Johnson, was quoted as the epigraph of the first book about New Orleans music, *Jazzmen*, Uptown cornetist Buddy Bolden came to symbolize the beginnings of jazz in the city. The epigraph read:

> *Now here is the list about that Jazz playing. King Bolden and myself were the first men that began playing Jazz in the city of dear old New Orleans and his band had the whole of New Orleans Real Crazy and Running Wild behind it. Now that was all you could hear in New Orleans, that King Bolden's Band, and I was with him and that was between 1895 and 1896 and they did not have any Dixie land Jazz Band in those days. Now here are the Bands that were in their prime in them days: Adam Olivier Band, John Robichaux, old Golden Rule, Bob Russell Band. Now that was all. And here is the thing that made King Bolden Band be the First Band that played Jazz. It was because it did not Read at all. I could fake like 500 myself; so you tell them that Bunk and King Bolden's Band was the first ones that started Jazz in the City or any place else. And now you are able to go ahead now with your book.[4]*

Buddy Bolden is the figure of legend and colorful story on whom the entire façade of early New Orleans black musical styles has been erected, but despite years of patient research there still is not much known about him beyond a few tantalizing scraps of information and a collection of colorful stories. Many of the stories were without substance, but they grew more and more colorful as the years passed. It was Bunk Johnson who precipitated the flood by telling the first young writers and jazz enthusiasts who wrote to him, among them William Russell, Frederic Ramsey Jr., and Charles Edward Smith, that Bolden was the first person to play what was later to be called jazz, that Bunk had been there with him on second cornet when it happened, and that Bolden was the man who invented the city's "blues music." In an unconscious shaping of the myth, when Smith went to New Orleans himself to do research for *Jazzmen* he approached older musicians with Bolden and his music among his first questions.

Johnson's claims that Bolden played something that could be called the first orchestral blues became the starting point for much writing about early jazz. Smith, in his research, found the only known photo of the Bolden band, which has been widely reprinted. The term "blues" was also used casually, without any attempt to define what the term meant. It certainly didn't mean the twelve-bar, three-chord harmonic sequence that became standardized later among orchestral musicians. What it seems to have meant in New Orleans at this time was any kind of melody that wasn't orchestrated, and that had some of the vocalized style of the new ragtime songs popular on the vaudeville and minstrel stages.

Little was added to the romanticized portrait of Bolden presented in *Jazzmen* until an indefatigable New Orleans researcher named Don Marquis located the surviving members of Bolden's family in the 1970s. Marquis was able to fill in a few of the gaps in the knowledge we had of Bolden, and he also found that the

THE BUDDY BOLDEN ORCHESTRA,
PROBABLY ABOUT 1900. FROM
LEFT: STANDING, WILLIE WARNER,
WILLIE CORNISH, BUDDY BOLDEN,
JIMMY JOHNSON; SEATED, FRANK
LEWIS, BROC MUMFORD.

family had an additional photograph, a heavily retouched photographer's studio portrait that Marquis presented in his essential book, *In Search of Buddy Bolden*.[5] Marquis was able to confirm a few dates, although he also found much of what is known about Bolden to be extravagantly embellished hearsay.

From the family and from city records, Marquis learned that Bolden had been born on September 6, 1877, the second child of a domestic servant named Wentmore "West" Bolden and Alice Harrison Bolden. At that time they were living at what was 319 Howard Street under the city's old system of house numbering. Six years later his father died; the next year, now a young boy, he was baptized on March 6. In 1887, when Bolden was ten, his mother moved to 2309 First Street (in the modern numbering system), and they lived there until about the time he was committed to a mental hospital nineteen years later.

Although there was considerable wind damage to the neighborhood in the hurricane in 2005, there was no serious flooding, and the house on First Street is still there. The area around it has been on a downward spiral for many years, and although the streets have scraggly trees, and the downtown business section isn't far away, it is one of the city's high-crime-rate neighborhoods. The one-story frame house is a divided shotgun, solidly constructed, and Bolden's doorway—up three concrete steps—was the one on the right as you stand in the street looking at the house. The house was once in very poor condition but was recently painted, and doesn't show signs of deterioration.

In 1894 a man named Louis Jones, who became a close friend of Bolden's, moved to the same block. Jones was to be one of the only sources of information for the meager details that are known about Bolden's everyday life. Certainly for the next ten years Bolden was an almost unseen presence among the city's active band musicians. On May 2, 1897, a Charles Bolden and Hattie Oliver became the parents of Charles Joseph Bolden Jr.; Bolden's profession was listed in the New Orleans city directory for the year as a plasterer. Like most New Orleans musicians, he had a day job, since music paid so poorly. In some stories of the

THE "DOUBLE SHOTGUN" HOUSE WHERE BUDDY BOLDEN LIVED UNTIL HE WAS CONFINED TO AN ASYLUM IN 1906. BOLDEN'S DOORWAY WAS ON THE RIGHT. PHOTOGRAPH BY SAMUEL CHARTERS.

night of the Robert Charles riot in the summer of 1900, Bolden was playing with accordionist Henry Peyton's orchestra, and the group also included Jib Gibson on guitar, Octave Brown on trombone, and Louis Nelson DeLisle was described as the band's bassist, though his usual instrument was the clarinet. According to the stories, the mob of angry whites surged into Storyville and the streets around it, and the cornetist lost his coat and his watch, which he'd left on the bandstand. Different musicians, however, among them cornetist Oscar Celestin, have been named as members of Peyton's orchestra on the night of the riot. Louis DeLisle, the most probable source for the story, was only fifteen at the time, and even in the Restricted District a fifteen-year-old was a little young to be playing in an orchestra.

Bolden was listed as a music teacher in the city directory in 1901, and he continued to be listed in its pages for the next five years as a musician. In April 1902 Johnson Park, the baseball field where he was remembered playing, opened near Carrollton Avenue; in July another baseball field, Lincoln Park, opened on the block in front of the first. That same year he married Nora Bass, who was twenty-two, and the next year a daughter, Bernadine, was born. The only known confirmation of a job played by Bolden's orchestra is a Carnival Ball invitation from 1903, now in the collection of the William Hogan Jazz Archive at Tulane University.

LOUIS JONES'S CORNER BARBER SHOP WHERE BOLDEN FREQUENTLY SPENT HIS AFTERNOONS. PHOTOGRAPH BY SAMUEL CHARTERS.

The Knights of Pleasure Club
Requests the presence of your company
at their
First Grand Soiree
at the Ladie's Providence Hall
Cor. of Phillip and Liberty Sts,
Wednesday Evening Feby 18, 03
Music by Professor Bolden's Orchestra
Dancing from 8PM to 2:30 AM
Subsc. 15c

Bolden emerges from obscurity again in 1906, when New Orleans newspapers included a police report that he had been arrested on March 26 for hitting his mother-in-law with a pitcher, and that three days before had spent the day at home with a violent headache. Another of the elusive stories told about him also referred to his mental illness. He was said to have been marching with the Allen Brass Band for a Labor Day parade, but he was unable to continue and dropped out before the parade had ended. There might be a germ of truth in the story, but it would have to have occurred sometime earlier, since researcher Marquis found that at the time of his commitment to the institution a few months later, he was entered in the court ledger as "destitute, incoherent, and listed as a laborer."

The increasing bouts of mental instability, which were documented in the police records of his arrests, have been attributed to a syphilis infection. But he lived on for almost three more decades, which probably means that his mental illness had some other cause, since tertiary syphilis, the stage of the disease in which mental instability is noticeable, was virtually untreatable at that time. On September 9, 1906, he was briefly arrested for "insanity." On March 13, 1907 he was arrested again for insanity, and on April 4 he was declared legally insane. He was twenty-nine years old. On June 5, he was assigned to the Insane Asylum at Jackson, Louisiana, where he was remembered as a quiet patient, and there was some recollection of his playing the cornet in the institution's musical group. He died there twenty-four years later, on November 4, 1931.

Against this meager record of Bolden's life must be set the mantle of anecdote and supposition that has been woven around his life. Most of what has been written has to be taken with considerable reservations. Many of the anecdotes, and certainly the whole shape of the legend, seem to have originated first with Bunk Johnson, and then to have been embellished by Jelly Roll Morton. In part, their credibility hinges on their ages at the time when Bolden was playing, and both of them were considerably younger than the image they tried to project. They were born in 1889 and 1890, respectively, which would mean that they were only thirteen or fourteen years old at the time of Bolden's one confirmed engagement. Each of them also traveled, Johnson generally with circuses and shows. Morton remained in New Orleans until about 1907, but he was also an adolescent at the time of Bolden's commitment, and there is no confirmed record of Morton returning to the city to work as an orchestral musician, though he may have passed through as a vaudeville entertainer or Storyville pianist.

More colorful anecdotes about Bolden's life and career that were recounted for researchers later may have filled in some details of the little that is known. But as they talked with their sources, the younger researchers asked continually about Bolden, so he increasingly became the central figure in an emotional and psychological construct. The reminiscences of a musician like trumpeter Lee Collins, who was six years old when Bolden was institutionalized, certainly stem from the researchers' enthusiasm, and the writings of guitarist Danny Barker, who played in Collins's band in the late 1920s before he left New Orleans, reflect this process of what is essentially legend building. Barker was not born until 1909, two years after Bolden entered the asylum.

The image of Bolden that was created in this search for any kind of biographical verification filled an emotional need to create a narrative about the early jazz decades around a figure larger than the little information that existed about him could actually support. In the collection of stories and memories that slowly accumulated, however, there were some small bits of hopefully useful information. Bolden's first orchestra was remembered as a quartet, which included three musicians present in the photo taken of the band: Frank Lewis was the clarinetist, Jimmy Johnson the bassist, and "Broc" Mumford the guitarist. In the first accounts of the band Mumford's name was spelled "Brock," but one of the editors of *Jazzmen*, Frederic Ramsey Jr., in later research learned that he had suffered from a skin disease, which left his face splotched, and the nickname "Broc" was an unkind comparison to the look and texture of broccoli. Both Johnson and Lewis were considered to be good reading musicians, and Bolden would also have had some music reading skills, if his listing in the city directory as a music teacher, as well as the orchestra's engagement for a Carnival Ball in 1903, can be taken as evidence. In the one photograph of the band, which can't be accurately dated but is probably from the late 1890s, there are two additional musicians, clarinetist Willie Warner and trombonist Willie Cornish. Little is known about Cornish. He enlisted in the Army during the Spanish-American War, shortly after he'd joined the band; he returned to the orchestra following his discharge and stayed with the group until about 1903 or 1905, when he was replaced by Frankie Duson. Cornish played a valve trombone, which was beginning to go out of fashion, and Duson may have replaced him because he played the newer slide trombone, but that can only be a guess.

Another musician who lived Uptown is sometimes included with Bolden as sharing the credit for creating the new syncopated style: Charlie Galloway, who played the guitar, was a cripple who got around on crutches and was probably two years older than Bolden. He lived on St. Mary Street, and Bolden's house on First Street wasn't far away. The dance orchestra Galloway was leading about 1894 included two musicians who were later associated with Bolden—bassist Bob Lyons and the clarinetist Willie Warner, who is standing beside Cornish in the Bolden band's photo. Warner looks young and diffident, almost as though he doesn't feel entirely comfortable being in the photo. Galloway's regular cornetist, Edward Clem, who had moved to New Orleans from St. Joseph, a small town on the Mississippi north of New Orleans, sometimes substituted for Bolden. Again, guessing from what little is known, Galloway and Bolden could have even played together at some point—Bolden working out the melodies for some of the local ragtime favorites, and Galloway supplying harmonies on the guitar.

The photograph of the band does reveal something about them. Although the background seems to be a rough studio backdrop, the band made an effort to present themselves well. They were all in dark coats with buttoned white shirts. Mumford and Lewis, seated in the front, can be seen wearing matching striped dark trousers. Four of them were wearing identical small, dark bow ties, and the fact that Warner was wearing a straight white tie may confirm that he was only occasionally with the band. There is no indication in the photograph that they were anything other than a group who took themselves seriously, even though they must have come from a poor neighborhood, which would account for the rough backdrop and the sparse setting. Bolden himself projected an air of bluff confidence, a handsome man with a broad, strong face. His orchestra wasn't as elegantly dressed or as sumptuously posed as the photograph taken about the same time of the orchestra led by John Robichaux, the most successful of the Downtown Creole orchestras, but they were also clearly not a band to be casually ignored. If nothing else, the fact that they posed for the photograph without a violinist is making a statement that they were a different kind of dance band.

The band was sometimes said to have appeared at the two new baseball fields, Lincoln Park and Johnson Park. The fields were fenced-in city blocks with wooden bleachers, and they were used for everything from baseball games to political gatherings. The group was sometimes also remembered as playing for the popular hot air balloon ascensions of a daredevil aerialist named Buddy Bottle, but a program from one of his Sunday afternoon shows included music to accompany variety acts, as well as a concert by the band before Bottle made his appearance. The orchestra named on the program is Robichaux's. If Bolden played for one of the afternoons, then the band was much more sophisticated than the accounts of Bunk Johnson or Jelly Roll Morton suggested. There were many descriptions of the sound of Bolden's cornet carrying across the quiet streets when the band played for a night's dancing at either of the baseball fields, which sounds much closer to the kind of music they were supposed to have played.

Bolden's Orchestra often performed at Incorporator's Hall, beginning the evening by playing a few numbers outside about 7 p.m. to attract crowds. It was a memory of the band playing in front of "Funky Butts Hall"—as Kenna's Hall, on Perdido Street between Liberty and Franklin, was always known—that the very young Louis Armstrong might have recalled. Admission to the dances could be anywhere from fifteen to fifty cents, with ten cents for a glass of beer. They played from 8 p.m. to 4 a.m., and were said to have earned $3 for the advertising and $5 for the job—a substantial salary for the period, but probably not an accurate figure unless it included tips. The band diaries trombonist kept by Emile Barnes when he was a member of Chris Kelly's band between 1920 and 1923 list their pay as just about the same amounts, but that is many years later. In those late hours, according to the legends, the dancing got meaner and the music got dirtier. At this time of night the musicians would have been playing without a break for six or seven hours and typically drinking as they played, so the music certainly could have gotten a little less organized, and simple melodies would have worked more successfully than anything too complicated.

One of the handful of descriptions of the band and its playing style comes from this period. As he reminisced, the Creole clarinetist George Baquet was referring to something he remembered from nearly half a century before, and had often been asked about Bolden. It is difficult to reconcile his memory of Bolden holding a trumpet as he catches the band's attention, then lifting a cornet to his lips, and the composition Baquet remembered, "Make Me A Pallet On Your Floor," wasn't a melody that other musicians remembered from Bolden's repertory.

I was out celebrating with some of my friends, when we went to a ball at the Odd Fellow's Hall, where Buddy Bolden worked. I remember thinking it was a funny place, nobody took their hats off. It was plenty tough. You paid fifteen cents and walked in. When we came in, we saw the band, six of them, on a low stand. They had their hats on, too, and were resting—pretty sleepy.

We stood behind a column. All of a sudden, Buddy stomps, knocks on the floor with his trumpet to give the beat, and they all sit up straight, wide awake. Buddy held up his cornet, paused to be sure of his embrouchure, then they played Make Me a Pallet on the Floor. *Everybody got up quick, the whole place rose and yelled out, "Oh, Mr. Bolden, play it for us, Buddy, play it!"*

I'd never heard anything like that before. I'd played "legitimate" stuff. But this! It was somethin' that pulled me! They got me up on the stand that night, and I was playin' with 'em. After that, I didn't play "legitimate" so much.[6]

Baquet, who was born in 1883, was certainly old enough to have heard the band, though by the time this reminiscence was published in *Down Beat* magazine he could just as well have read one of the jazz histories that had appeared in the wake of *Jazzmen*.

Pops Foster heard the Bolden band in one of the outdoor parks where they often played, but his impression was more laconic. "I only saw Buddy Bolden's band play once at Johnson's Park. That's where the rough people went. I knew all the guys in the band and later on played with them. Buddy played very good for that style of stuff he was doing. He played nothing but blues and all that stink music, and he played it very loud."[7]

Louis Armstrong, in *Satchmo*, also said that Bolden had played "loud," and suggested that he maybe played "too hard . . . In any case he finally went crazy. You can figure that out for yourself."[8] Although he mentions Bolden in his *Swing That Music* in 1936, Armstrong, by the time he wrote the later autobiography, had been asked about Bolden for nearly two decades, which meant that he'd finally come up with a story; but his own birth date has been established as 1901, which means he was five years old when Bolden was last known to have played, so his reminiscence has to be taken with considerable reservation.

If all the conflicting evidence is sorted out, however, it still seems clear that Bolden and his band did have an enthusiastic audience for their new ragtime. In the 1950s, the musicians I talked with who had heard them insisted that there was something different about them, but they always were just as insistent that the band had only a small repertoire of their special syncopated pieces—perhaps three or four numbers. For the rest of a dance they played the usual assortment of quadrilles, Lancers, polkas, and waltzes. It was their way of playing these numbers with a looser swing and the headier excitement that brought them their audiences. The most tantalizing question of all that hangs over the band and their legend is obviously, What did they sound like? The immediate answer is that because they didn't leave a recording behind, writers can project whatever they want on to what they conceive as Bolden's style. He will always be an elusive figure of legend.

For the musicians who had heard the band, the first point they made was that the band played its special numbers in a melodic unison. Charlie Love, a trumpeter, came over from neighboring Plaquemine to listen to the bands in

THE BIRTHPLACE OF LOUIS ARMSTRONG, ON JANE ALLEY, CLOSE TO PERDIDO STREET, 1950S. PHOTOGRAPH BY SAMUEL CHARTERS.

the city when he was in his late teens or early twenties, and he agreed with other accounts that Bolden played in the middle range of the cornet, seldom playing in a higher register, and that for the specialty numbers the others played in unison with him, though the trombone was pitched an octave lower.

Considering the instruments in the group, the sound had to be considerably lighter in texture than later bands in the city. There was no drummer; the rhythm was a soft-toned, gut-string guitar, which Mumford played in a steady chorded rhythm of four beats to the measure. The bass was played with a bow, and it accented the first and third beats of the of the measure, just as in the published arrangements for dance orchestras in the period. I asked several musicians who'd heard the band to hum or sing what would have been their own part in the ensemble, as they remembered it. When I put together a group to recreate the sound through the notes I'd transcribed, I found that the *feel* of the band was much closer to the surviving recordings of dance orchestras in Cuba and Venezuela from this same period—the textures more reminiscent of the Cuban *danzon* or the Venezuelan *paseo*, with their lighter, more fluid rhythmic pulse, than to the march-oriented music of other American cities. Havana, at that time, was only a short excursion boat ride away across the Gulf. The musicians who thought back to those first years also agreed that Bolden's band didn't improvise. The instrumental parts for their general repertoire, as well as for their specialty pieces, were worked out in rehearsals and each player played from memory.

A hundred years after Bolden disappeared into a mental institution, and seventy years after he first took a place in the emerging historical narrative of the emergence of jazz in New Orleans, there seems to be almost no agreement about anything relating to his life and his music beyond the handful of established dates and official notices—and even the picture they present has large gaps and inconsistencies.

The romanticized account of his life in *Jazzmen* created his image as a jazz icon, but an earlier article by a New Orleans Creole writer was actually the first place in which his name appeared, and the account is considerably less romantic. The band's popularity was described as resulting from the obscene lyrics the trombonist had written to go with a well-known popular melody. On April 22, 1933, an article appeared in the New Orleans black newspaper *The Louisiana Weekly*. It was entitled "Excavating Local Jazz, Part One," and it was written by an African American high school art teacher and enthusiastic promoter of the local music scene named E. Belfield Spriggins. The article was discovered by researcher Don Marquis when he was doing the basic work for *In Search of Buddy Bolden*. He introduced the article and quoted the paragraphs relating to Bolden. The background for the article was an interview with Bolden's trombonist, Willie Cornish, whom Spriggins had interviewed. The article also documented the origin of the words to "Funky Butt," a song closely associated with Bolden.

> *Many years ago jazz tunes in their original form were heard in the Crescent City. Probably one of the earliest heard was one played by King Bolden's band. It seems that one night while playing at Odd Fellow's Hall, Perdido near Rampart, it became very hot and stuffy and a discussion among members of Bolden's band arose about the foul air. The next day William Cornish, the trombonist with the band, composed a "tune" to be played by the band. The real words are unprintable but these will answer:*
>
> > *"I thought I heard Old Bolden say*
> > *Rotten gut, rotten gut*
> > *Take it away."*
>
> *The rendition of this number became an overnight sensation and the reputation of Bolden's band became a household word with the patrons of Odd Fellows Hall, Lincoln and Johnson Parks and several other popular dance halls around the city.*[9]

(The melody of the song Cornish remembered was a folk tune known up and down the Mississippi by several names, and popular at this time as one of the themes of the rag "St. Louis Tickle," by Theron C. Bennet. It was recorded in 1906 on a very successful Victor Records single by a trio led by banjoist Vess Ossman.)

The only information Spriggins presented about Bolden was this anecdote about the words that Cornish had written for "King" Bolden's band. Obviously either Cornish or Spriggins had been influenced by the use of "King" by cornetist Joe Oliver, since other musicians generally agreed that the term was never used in New Orleans before Oliver traveled to Chicago. The next week, in his

April 29, 1933, column, "Excavating Jazz Part Two," Spriggins again mentioned Bolden but continued in his article to praise two other early cornetists, Arnold Metoyer, whom he credits with being "one of the first persons here to play the jazz cornet," and Manuel Perez. "Following close upon the heels of the Bolden Band, which was increasingly popular in the upper section of the city we find that Manuel Perez, another famous musician of the old school, [was] organizing a band in the down town sections of the city that was destined to outshine the Bolden band in this free style of music."[10]

When Bolden was committed to the asylum, his band continued under the leadership of the trombonist Frankie Duson, who renamed it the Eagle Band. Duson was from Algiers, across the river, but the others in the new band were from the city. The clarinetist Frank Lewis and guitarist Broc Mumford stayed on, while for a few months cornetist Tig Chambers took over Bolden's lead. The bass player was now Bob Lyons, and a drummer had been added, Henry Zeno. The band continued to play the Bolden specialties, and with the usual casual shifts of personnel Duson kept the band together until 1917.

There was steady work for all of the Uptown bands, enough jobs in the dance halls and for clubs and street advertising, that a continuing stream of young musicians followed along in the wake, even if no one was paid very much. This rough and ready apprenticeship created a generation of New Orleans musicians technically skilled enough to play almost any kind of a job. Most of the bands had only two or three musicians who read much music, but that was enough for them to keep up with requests for the new popular songs. Despite the narrowness of the New Orleans repertoire as it's presented today, in that early period there was the expected effort to please everyone's requests, which could include almost anything that had been a hit on one of the local vaudeville stages.

The autobiography by George Foster, *The Autobiography of a New Orleans Jazzman*, caught some of the flavor of these years. Since he was quickly recognized as one of the best of the young bassists, Foster was in the middle of the new music that was developing all around him. He was born in 1892 in McCall, Louisiana, not far from New Orleans, and grew up playing cello in a family orchestra that included his brother on guitar and his sister on mandolin. Their trio played for entertainments in their neighborhood in Donaldsonville, where they moved when he was still a boy. When Foster was about ten, his family moved into New Orleans during the Carnival season, and he began taking lessons on the bass. As a teenager he played with a string trio called the Roseals Orchestra; two years later, in 1908, he was already experienced enough to work occasionally with the Olympia Orchestra, which had been together since about 1901. When he joined the orchestra, guitarist Louis Keppard, the brother of the cornetist Freddie Keppard, was the leader and manager. The orchestra had a job playing a house party and they couldn't find a bassist, so Keppard called the sixteen-year-old for the job. Foster was a tall and gangling adolescent, but already with the assured expression and watchful eyes that he kept through his life.

For the next ten years Foster worked with most of the African American bands in the city, including Duson's Eagle Band, and the orchestras led by Kid Ory, Joe Oliver, Jack Carey, and Armand J. Piron. He also knew most of the white musicians who were playing in the new ragtime style, and often for large gatherings there would be both a white band and one of the bands Foster worked with playing for the same crowd of dancers. He mentioned white instrumentalists like Larry Shields, Tom Brown, Johnny Fisher, and Leon Roppolo, and remembered a picnic he played with the Brunies brothers' orchestra. "The Brunies and their band played very good."[11]

In 1918, when Foster was twenty-six, Peter Bocage, a violinist and cornetist from Algiers who played throughout his career with both Uptown and Downtown bands, helped him find a steady job with the orchestra on the SS *Capitol* excursions steamboat, led by Fate Marable. With Marable's ensemble—often described as a musical apprenticeship for younger musicians, since Marable insisted that they improve their reading skills—Foster developed into an accomplished orchestra musician. When he left the boat in 1921, it was to join Charlie Creath's popular orchestra in St. Louis. His richly detailed autobiography described the unsteady economic realities that were part of a New Orleans musician's life.

> *When I first started with the Magnolia Band, we made most of our money on Saturday, Sunday, and Wednesday. Sunday was the biggest day and we made little money on Monday. I used to do longshore work, drive a cotton wagon or coal wagon, and so; Monday was your roughest day. On Sunday you might have an afternoon job at the lake playing a picnic till six o'clock. Then you'd get on a streetcar and go way over to Gretna to play a night job at the Come Clean Hall.... You'd go home then, hang up your tuxedo, put on your overalls and leave about 5: a.m. and catch the streetcar to the stables. There you'd pick up your mule team at 6:00 a.m. and start out for the docks to pick up a load at 7:00 a.m. Once you got your team hooked up and started toward the docks, you could sleep because your mules would follow the wagon in front. Sometimes you'd have a helper; he'd drive the wagon where you were going and you'd sleep. He'd wake you up to load and deliver. If you had a Monday night job you'd go home, get a little shuteye, and start playing at eight o'clock.*[12]

Foster made careful distinctions between the three styles of bands that were part of the New Orleans musical life, and the styles of music and dances where they played.

> *From about 1900 on, there were three types of bands around New Orleans. You had bands that played ragtime, ones that played sweet music, and the ones that played nothing but blues. A band like John Robichaux's played nothing but sweet music and played the dicty affairs. On a Saturday night*

Frankie Dusen's [sic] Eagle Band would play the Masonic Hall because he played a whole lot of blues. A band like the Magnolia Band would play ragtime and work the District. They would play Bag of Rags, Frog Leg Rag, Maple Leaf Rag, Champagne Rag, *and ones like that; they were all dance numbers. All the bands around New Orleans would play quadrilles starting about midnight. When you did that nice people would know it was time to go home because things got rough after that. The rough guys would come about midnight. They were pimps, whores, hustlers, and that bunch. They'd dance with no coats and their suspenders down. They'd jump around and have a bunch of fun. They wanted you to play slow blues and dirty songs so they could dance rough and dirty. On the boats when they got to dancing that way you had to shoot a waltz in. Sometimes it was so rough you played waltzes back to back.*[13]

Most nights of the week there was a formal ball or a picnic or dancing in one of the cabarets that occupied the corners of the Uptown neighborhood, so there was work for dozens of musicians. The pay was so small—sometimes as little as seventy-five cents for a job—that only somebody who had a part-time job could work more than an occasional weekend. All of the musicians who worked more steadily heard each other's playing, drifted in and out of each other's bands, and when they weren't playing they were usually with a friend from another band who also played the same jobs.

Bunk Johnson was one of the musicians Foster remembered from this early period. One of the conflicting aspects of the stories that Johnson told in his letters was his birthdate. He claimed that he had been born on December 27, 1879, which would have made him only eleven years younger than Buddy Bolden, and his stories of playing with Bolden's band before 1898 would have some credibility. Researcher Lawrence Gushee, however, has spent considerable time tracing early New Orleans jazz dates and has found documentation that Johnson was born in 1889, which mean that he was ten years younger than he claimed. In the only known photograph of Johnson from this period, as a member of the Superior Orchestra, taken about 1910, when he was twenty or twenty-one, his face is clearly that of a very young man. It seems that many of Johnson's stories are elaborations, and as clarinetist Wade Whaley, who knew him during this period, commented one night when he was talking on the bandstand with banjoist Dick Oxtot in California in the 1950s, "In New Orleans, we didn't call him 'Bunk' for nothing."

Johnson began studying the cornet with Adam Oleavia (whose name is commonly spelled Olivier) and played his first professional engagements with Oleavia's orchestra. Oleavia, born about 1865, was a barber as well as a part-time musician. He also must have taught Johnson to read music, since Johnson recalled that his first full-time job, in 1905, when he was sixteen, was touring with the P. G. Loral Circus, which traveled through Texas and, Johnson claimed, took him to California. He returned to New Orleans a year or so later and began working with the Superior Orchestra, led by Billy Marrero; the violinist, Peter Bocage, remembered that he had to help Johnson with his reading. Before Johnson left with the circus he certainly could have heard Bolden's band playing one of their outdoor jobs or a ball in one of the dance halls, even if he still was a little young to get into the late-night cabarets. He could even have joined them as an adolescent musician for part of an engagement, though his own claims for himself as a regular second cornetist with the band are difficult to credit. By the time Johnson returned from his travels with the circus, Bolden had been confined to the mental institution.

Although Johnson was to spend three or four more years working sporadically in New Orleans, he continually went back to the circuses, and never was considered on the same musical level as Manuel Perez among the Downtown cornetists, or Freddie Keppard, who was considered the most exciting of the new Uptown performers. Joe Oliver, the cornetist usually remembered as the one rival for Keppard, had started a few years behind Keppard in his local career but had already begun to play with the variety of mutes and tones that later would become his trademark. Also, by Johnson's own admission, he was already drinking heavily, something that was to be a serious stumbling block to his success, even in his last years when he had become an icon of the New Orleans revival. George Foster heard him with the Superior Orchestra and he liked his playing, but he also remembered the problems with drinking.

> The first time I saw Bunk was at the Fairgrounds at a big picnic in 1908. There were three bands playing dance music outside; and the Superior Band was out on the racetrack and were playing for people to dance on the grass. The Superior Band was a ragtime band. They had Bunk, Buddy Johnson, trombone; Peter Bocage, violin; Rene Baptiste, guitar; Billy Moran, [sic], bass; Big Eye Louis, clarinet; and Walter Brundy, drums. Bunk played a beautiful horn and nobody else around New Orleans played the same style Bunk did. He played the most beautiful tones. After a while Bunk got to drinking so bad they fired him and then he went with Frankie Dusen's [sic] band.
>
> Frankie Dusen was the only guy that Bunk was afraid of and who could make Bunk listen. Bunk would show up to play so drunk he'd be draggin' his coat across the floor and couldn't find the bandstand. He'd try to put his horn up to his mouth and hit his nose or chin, and couldn't even find his mouth. When he was like that or just passed out, the guys would say to him, "Hey Bunk, here comes Frankie." Bunk would straighten right up. The reason was Frankie used to beat Bunk just like you beat a kid. He'd get a razor strap or his belt and whip him.[14]

Foster remembered that Johnson finally was fired by the Eagle band, and left town with a minstrel show. Johnson certainly disappeared from the New Orleans scene about this time, and it was almost thirty years before he played in the city again. His own memories from this time were that after he left the Eagle Band he played pick-up jobs around the District, with occasional steady work at Pete Lala's, at Custom House and Marais, across the street from Manuel Perez, though Lala employed a series of bands and both Keppard and Oliver were playing there from time to time. Johnson also said he sometimes let boys sit behind the bandstand to listen to him, and one of the boys was Louis Armstrong, who would have been about ten years old when Johnson was with the bands at Lala's. Johnson usually bought a cheap wine named for the prizefighter Jack Johnson, which he gave to the small boys who entertained in the sidewalk street bands.

Jack Carey, a popular trombonist, and his younger brother Thomas "Mutt" Carey, who played the cornet, were also an established presence in the Uptown music scene. Their version of an old French quadrille melody that Mutt found in a music album, with Jack's added trombone roars, was perhaps one of the first versions of what later was turned into the multi-strained piece that was eventually titled "Tiger Rag," although a dozen other New Orleans musicians also claimed that it was their composition. For some years one of its titles was "Jack Carey." Among white musicians it was usually called "Number 2." Mutt's playing was later of considerable historical importance, because he was the earliest of the Uptown cornetists to record (in California in 1922), when his style still had the characteristic New Orleans brightness and subtlety.

George Foster worked with the Carey brothers for two years, and Jack was a colorful presence in his reminiscences. Like most New Orleans bass players, Foster played both string bass and tuba, and when he marched on the streets he was carrying his brass instrument.

Jack Carey played trombone and got the Jack Carey Crescent Band together. Jack was a guy who had kids all around New Orleans. We'd be playing a place and someone would come around saying one of Jack's kids had died. Sometimes we'd play two or three funerals and find out they were all for Jack's kids. I played with Jack's band in about 1914 and 1915. . . . Jack's band was out at the lake playing a picnic one Sunday. Everybody had brought a big picnic basket and put them up on the bandstand then went to stroll around. Jack started snooping around through the baskets tasting the wine. He reached over a mud puddle to get one bottle and fell in with his white suit on. After we quit laughing, we went off and stole a table cloth and wrapped him up in it. He played all afternoon standing up there wrapped in that tablecloth.[15]

The streets and the sounds of the Uptown neighborhoods were woven into the fiber of New Orleans and its music—a world farther away from the quieter streets of the Quarter than the few blocks between them would suggest. A decade later its musicians would be part of a wave of traveling performers who brought their new jazz style out of the city to a larger audience.

6

On the Circuit

THAT CREOLE BAND of six pieces, cornet, guitar, clarinet, fiddle, and bass viol played a rather ragged selection for a starter, the clarinet being particularly strong for comedy effect.

The old darkey whom they were serenading responded by singing "Old Black Joe" and the band chimed in with fine harmony both instrumentally and vocally. The playing of some ragtime melodies worked the old darkey to dancing pitch, and he did pound those boards until the kinks in his knees reminded him of his age. Lots of bows, an encore, more bows and another encore stamped this offering O.K.

THE NEW YORK CLIPPER REVIEWING THE VAUDEVILLE ACT OF FREDDIE
KEPPARD AND THE CREOLE BAND, DECEMBER 11, 1915[1]

In New Orleans there was a looser interpretation of questions of racial identity, because the city was accustomed to the designation of Creoles of Color, which implied some acceptance of racial mixing. New Orleans, however was a Southern city, and on virtually every other level it accepted the racial attitudes of the rest of the South. In the years before World War I, white Southerners, and to a greater or lesser degree most Americans, had very decided views about what they wanted African Americans to do for them. They wanted them to do jobs like cleaning the streets, taking care of the washing and cleaning in their homes, nursing their children, emptying the toilets behind their houses, meeting trains to carry their luggage, digging ditches, and emptying the garbage. The same Southerners and most white Americans also had very decided ideas about what they *didn't* want African Americans to do for them. They didn't want them to do things like work as tellers in banks, sell them ladies' undergarments, occupy jobs in offices that could be done by white people, teach their children how to read and write, operate steam locomotives, plan for a university education, or play lawn tennis. They did agree, however, that there was one thing African Americans did well, and they encouraged them to take it up as a line of work. The average white perception was that African Americans had found their niche as entertainers; as singers, dancers, and low comedians; and entertainers they became.

With so few avenues open for any kind of economic advancement, it wasn't surprising that there were so many African American musicians in New Orleans. It was just as surprising, because the jobs paid so poorly, that there were so many white musicians, though most of them were first-generation Italian immigrants. For black instrumentalists, the jobs paid a little better than the kind of physical labor that was all they could expect to find, and also offered a chance to leave, to travel, to get out of town, even if only for a season or a few months. In the era before even the phonograph record had come into most homes, if there was music there had to be someone playing it.

New Orleans band musicians had many opportunities to travel, since the country was crisscrossed by the traveling circuses and touring minstrel show companies that provided entertainment for every level of society. Most of the large circuses had two bands and two shows, one for their black customers and the other for their white. If, however, they chose to employ a black band for the main show, there were no protests; the black faces were only in the background, and the only thing they were doing was playing their instruments. Some New Orleans musicians, like cornetist Bunk Johnson, never got back home once they'd left. A road show, a circus, a medicine show became as much of a home as they had.

Some of the finest of the young musicians spent time on the road during these years. Clarinetist Sidney Bechet toured Texas with a road show put together by pianist Clarence Williams. Another clarinetist, Johnny Dodds, left with his brother "Baby" to tour with Billy Mack's vaudeville troupe. Clarinetist George Baquet left when he was a boy to appear with the "pickanniny" band of P. T. Wright's Georgia Minstrels. The trumpeter Punch Miller was still on the road with traveling circuses into the 1940s. There were also opportunities for the city's musical virtuosos. The Creole concert cornetist Arnold Metoyer spent most of his musical career as a featured virtuoso soloist with a series of tent shows. He was light-skinned and often passed, but as a black entertainer he also would have been encouraged to perform—though his salary would have been considerably smaller. The virtuoso cornetist George McCullum led the black brass band with the widely known Barnum and Bailey circus in 1909.

Even if New Orleans hadn't been so poor, there still would have been the same intense restrictions over the jobs that were available for African Americans. In the chaotic months of the spring of 1917, when New Orleans was joining the mobilization for the war in Europe, there were large ads in the city's papers offering jobs for the military construction that was planned. The ads, in large letters, asked for

WHITE CARPENTERS
COLORED LABORERS

The first New Orleans band to leave the city wasn't organized as a group when they left, and the musicians had no intention of staying away for so many years. The band, which became known as "The Creole Band," was the first to travel throughout the country, and much of what they presented to their audiences was New Orleans–style music, but they probably wouldn't have played such a visible role in jazz history had it not been for the presence of their cornet player, Freddie Keppard, one of the figures who became jazz legends in the pages of *Jazzmen*. In their chapter on New Orleans beginnings, writers William Russell and Stephen W. Smith described Keppard's musical role in the Creole Band and presented him in his New Orleans setting.

> *Since he was the only one able to read music in the Creole Band, Baquet usually had to carry the melody in a fairly straight manner, low down. Keppard, meanwhile, embellished the tune with intricate passage work, utilizing his remarkable range. Keppard, without having too perfect an execution, did have the greatest range of any cornetist of his time. He had such imagination in invention that other cornetists found his figurations impossible to copy. At times Keppard played so low he sounded like a trombone. On the other hand, he was the first to exploit the high range, going even above high E. As strong as Samson, he was noted for his powerful tone. When he was on tour with the Creole Band, the patrons in the front rows of the theatres always got up after the first number and moved back. But at times Keppard played so softly he could be heard only a few feet away.*[2]

The younger Uptown cornetist Mutt Carey also described Keppard's playing enthusiastically in a later interview: "Keppard was the first man I ran into in a band battle, and it was just my luck to run into the king. We had a big audience on the street. It was on Howard and Villere Streets in New Orleans. The crowd knew I was a younger musician and they gave me a big hand mostly to encourage me. It certainly was an experience for me I'll never forget. Freddie had a lot of ideas and a big tone too. When he hit a note you knew it was hit. . . . He didn't have much formal musical education, but he sure was a natural musician. All you had to do was play a number for him once and he had it—he was a natural!"[3]

George "Pops" Foster occasionally played for casual pick-up jobs with Keppard in New Orleans, and his memories of Keppard's style of playing were more precise. He remembered that Keppard played what he called a "walking trumpet. It was Ta-Ta-Ta-Ta-Ta. They were straight clear notes."[4] Foster's description of Keppard's playing makes it clear that the bright staccato attack Keppard displayed in his later recordings was a characteristic of his style before he left the city. At that point Keppard was in his early twenties, pudgy faced and burly, already with a conscious strut and a weakness for alcohol. He was twenty-four when he traveled to Los Angeles in May 1914, and although he might have returned for visits he doesn't seem to have played in New Orleans again.

Keppard was born on February 17, 1890, at 427 N. Villere Street, at the edge of Storyville. His older brother Louis, was born in February 1888, but he lived a long life and it was still possible to interview him in the 1950s. With Storyville so close, Louis described the two brothers sneaking into the district and shining shoes for five cents. As others have also recalled, the police were a continual presence in the district, and the two of them wore long pants to make them look a little older. Freddie was soon taking lessons on the accordion, mandolin, and violin, while Louis played the guitar. Their mother sometimes took them to neighbor's houses where they entertained the adults playing mandolin and guitar duets. Louis recalled that they knew two tunes, "My Tiger Lily" and "Just Because She Made Them Goo Goo Eyes." Freddie was ten and his brother was twelve.

Louis also recalled that Freddie became impatient playing the mandolin because he couldn't play loud enough, and when he was sixteen he began taking lessons on the cornet from Adolph Alexander, who played cornet and baritone horn with many orchestras, including the Superior Orchestra and Manuel Perez's Imperial Orchestra, at the same time marching with the Onward and Excelsior Brass Bands. Keppard played his first job, only a few months after he began lessons, with the band of clarinetist Johnny Brown at the Lucien Pavilion at Spanish Fort. Perhaps because of information from Bunk Johnson, Keppard is thought to have organized the Olympia Band about 1907, a group, however, that also included valve trombonist Joseph Petit, who was older and more experienced and probably handled the band's affairs. The others in the band were clarinetist Alphonse Picou, drummer Jean Vigne, and Freddie's older brother Louis as guitarist. As they were described in *Jazz: New Orleans*, "It was a legitimate orchestra, playing society jobs. By 1910 Ernest Trepagnier had replaced Vigne, Eddie Vinson [sic] had replaced Petit, and the band was playing in the Uptown dance halls. Freddie played occasional jobs with the Eagle Band, then in 1911 went into Hanan's Saloon, at the corner of Liberty and Custom House, with Johnny and Herb Lindsay and their father, a guitar player. The band sat on ordinary chairs right near the door, playing for dancing. Freddie was highly regarded in the district, and made most of his tips imitating a horse on his cornet."[5]

Herb Lindsay played the violin and his brother Johnny—one of the New Orleans men whose name is still remembered because of his later recordings with Jelly Roll Morton's Red Hot Peppers—played the bass. As bands were categorized at this time, the group would have been called a string band, since there were three string instruments with an added horn.

It was Keppard's background in the cabarets that led to the train journey out to California. Lawrence Gushee has determined, in his excellent study of the band's journeys, *Pioneers of Jazz*,[6] that Keppard didn't leave with a band. He took the long train ride to Los Angeles with clarinetist George Baquet and trombonist Eddie Vincent in May 1914 to join the other members of the group, who were already waiting in Los Angeles. The organizer and leader of the band was a bass player named Bill Johnson, who had taken the first band to play in California as early as 1907. Johnson is usually considered a New Orleans musician, but Gushee's conscientious efforts to sort out what details are known of Johnson's life confirm that he was born in Montgomery, Alabama, probably in 1874; and although Johnson in later interviews recalled that when he was younger he worked for a grocery business delivering food to the Storyville brothels, by 1900 the family had moved again and were living in Biloxi. Before the move he had begun to spend time in a barbershop at the corner of Gasquet and Liberty, where he was learning the bass and the mandolin. Although he came from the heart of the South, Johnson was light skinned and, perhaps because of his years in New Orleans, he spoke with what some considered to be a light accent. William Russell, who interviewed him in 1972 before his death at the age of one hundred in a nursing facility in New Braunfels, Texas, felt that at some points in his career Johnson had passed as white.

The information about Bill Johnson's life and career that I was able to glean in the 1950s, when I wrote about the musicians working in New Orleans in this early period, was that he had been born on August 10, 1872, began playing the guitar in 1887 but about 1900 started playing the bass, and soon was playing in the trio at Anderson's. From time to time he played with Bab Frank's Peerless Orchestra or with Frankie Duson's Eagle Band. I was told by some informants that he played the tuba as well, and marched with the Excelsior Brass Band during the Mardi Gras seasons. What is certain is that in 1904, when he was in his early thirties, he decided he would have more opportunities for the business ventures that interested him if he moved to California, and he had a cousin there whom he felt could introduce him to the new city. When he traveled there by train with a New Orleans band it was to see what the new city of Los Angeles had to offer him.

Bill Johnson was not alone in his curiosity about the city on California's golden coast. In the ten years between 1900 and 1910, the population of Los Angeles grew from 160,000 to 320,000; the city was given an additional economic push in 1906 when San Francisco, its older and better established rival five hundred miles to the north, was destroyed by an earthquake and the fires that raged after the earth shocks had subsided. Although the racial situation was also difficult in Los Angeles, it had different dimensions. At the time of its founding as part of northern Mexico in 1781, the city had forty-four original settlers, twenty-six of them with African ancestry. In 1845, when the United States army seized California as part of the invasion of Mexico that annexed the northern third of the country, Los Angeles was still only a small trading center.

The discovery of gold in the Sierra foothills in central California in 1848 irrevocably changed the character of California, but because Los Angeles had been a part of Mexico it had a large Mexican population, which continued to grow. There were close ties to the Mexican border city of Ti Juana, an easy trip down the coast, and by 1900 it had become an integral part of southern California's amusement scene. The Ti Juana horse-racing track was especially popular, and special trains made excursion trips down for the races. Although Los Angeles was at the western edge of one of the world's most extensive deserts and separated from the central American continent by two ranges of mountains, Los Angeles, because of its port facilities that opened it to trade in the Pacific, had already become a transportation hub for the southwestern states. The Southern Pacific Railroad reached it in 1876, and the Santa Fe Railroad followed in 1885. With the opening of the Panama Canal in 1914, Los Angeles became a world city— still relatively modest when measured against New York or Havana, but growing with feverish enthusiasm.

With the city's growth there was a steady expansion of its African American population, centered then, as it is now, around Central Avenue. When Bill Johnson decided to make the train journey in 1904 he was uncertain about what awaited him, but he seems to have found it a congenial climate for his business ventures, and when he returned in 1907 or 1908 he brought a small string orchestra with him. The band made a nomadic, gypsylike journey, playing as they went. Johnson played the mandolin; the guitarist was a man named C. C. Washington; Alphonse Ferzand from Biloxi played the bass; and there were two horns, valve trombonist Harold Patio and cornetist Ernest Coycault (pronounced CWAH-CO). Coycault was the most significant member of the group: after their trip he returned to New Orleans, then left again for Los Angeles to join Sonny Clay's Plantation Orchestra, and recorded with that band in the 1920s. Sorting through various interviews that were done with Johnson by a number of researchers, Gushee was able to confirm some of the details of this first trip. "They left New Orleans with a ticket taking them as far as Morgan City, Louisiana, 80 miles west on the Southern Pacific line, paying the conductors cash bribes for their further progress west. Next came Lafayette still in Louisiana, then the Texas cities of Houston, Dallas, Fort Worth, Hutchins (assuming this is the reality lurking behind 'Hudgin'), Waco, and Galveston, followed by Phoenix, Yuma, and possible Bisbee in Arizona. . . . How long such a trip might have taken obviously depends on how often the band left the train to play."[7]

Very little is known about what the band did after their long journey. Johnson remembered playing in local cabarets, which with their ensemble wouldn't have been surprising, and they traveled some distance out of Los Angeles, perhaps as far north as Oakland. The importance of this first trip by a New Orleans band was that Johnson became certain that future trips could be even more successful, though even on this trip he claimed that the members of his band returned to New Orleans with "pockets full of money."[8] There is some question whether

Nenny Coycault returned with them or remained in California, but musicians interviewed in New Orleans in the 1950s remembered him taking over as cornetist with the Superior Band about 1910, when Bunk Johnson left, and also playing with Bab Frank's Peerless Orchestra. In 1914 he seems to have returned to Los Angeles, where he ultimately joined Sonny Clay's band. Coycault's playing on the band's singles in 1922 has such a distinct New Orleans flavor that it's difficult to imagine he could have left in 1907 and not returned to the city again for a lengthy period.

Bill Johnson also returned, perhaps within a year, and eventually opened a pool parlor and cigar store in Oakland, where there was a large African American population. By 1912 or 1913 he was back in Los Angeles, joining his mother and his sister Bessie, and once again operating a cigar store with a poolroom on Central Avenue. Johnson wasn't physically prepossessing; he was about the same height as the others in the band he led. But in his photos he projects a calm solemnity. With his Caucasian features and his reserved air he looks more like a banker than a ragtime band bassist. His brother Ollie "Dink" Johnson, a drummer, had been helping Bessie run a saloon in Las Vegas before he joined his family in Los Angeles. They weren't the only New Orleanians who found their way to California's sunny southland, but they were among the first to make the journey. A small colony of Crescent City musicians and entertainers steadily established themselves there, and it became the setting for significant periods in the musical careers of, among others, pianist and itinerant vaudeville performer Jelly Roll Morton and the ambitious Uptown trombonist Kid Ory. Bessie Johnson, who was now called Anita Gonzalez, entered Jelly Roll Morton's life as lover, sometimes companion, and common-law wife.

When Johnson decided to bring a second group of New Orleans musicians out to California in 1914, he doesn't seem to have had anything in mind except to play for dances in the growing African American communities of Los Angeles and Oakland. He was to be the manager of the band as well as the bass player; his brother Dink would play the drums, there was a guitarist named Norwood Williams, and the violinist and musical leader would be Jimmy Palao (pronounced Pah-LAW-o). Palao was born across the river in Algiers, and at the time he joined Johnson he had been working steadily in the dance halls and the clubs close to Storyville. He was light-skinned, with wavy hair, a good-looking man and one of New Orleans's accomplished violinists and leaders. He is pictured in three early photographs in the New Orleans Family Album.[9] The first, taken early in the century, shows him with an orchestra, and although the setting is informal—in a backyard sitting on kitchen chairs—the musicians are stylishly dressed, with hats set at a jaunty angle. A few years later he is in a high-necked band uniform with the Imperial Orchestra, a "legitimate" group led by cornetist Manuel Perez and including trombonist George Filhe and clarinetist Big Eye Louis Nelson DeLisle.

Palao also had ambitions as a composer, and in his book Gushee included the score of Palao's "O You Sweet Rag," an instrumental ragtime piece published in Washington, D.C., by H. Kirkus Dugdale in 1911.[10] Palao's marriage in New Orleans began to show strains that reflected his casual life style as a musician, and his wife left him in 1912. She moved to Los Angeles, where by chance she met Bill Johnson, whom she'd known in New Orleans. For several months Palao remained in New Orleans, then finally joined her about the middle of 1913. In the meantime, through Johnson, she had met many of the New Orleanians who had settled in the city. It would be an oversimplification to say that the musicians like Johnson and Palao made the move to Los Angeles to escape the racism that controlled so much of their lives in Louisiana, since they couldn't leave behind what was a larger American problem simply by changing states. California, however, presented economic opportunities and a less heightened racial tension, and it increasingly became a magnet for African Americans hoping to leave the South.

Palao, who by all accounts was an experienced, professional violinist, was soon working in a string trio with Norwood Williams and Johnson playing the bass. When Johnson decided to bring a band from New Orleans, it was probably Palao who suggested the personnel that joined them, since Keppard had begun playing after Johnson had left for California several years before. The trombonist Palao suggested, Eddie Vincent, was a friend and fellow musician from Algiers. The clarinetist Baquet, who was older and had been very active before Johnson left, would have probably been the only one who was known to him. Baquet's brother Achille, also a clarinetist, had played for several years with Jack Laine's Reliance Orchestra, passing as white.

When the three new musicians arrived, the band rehearsed daily at the Clark Hotel, which like the cigar store and billiard parlor Johnson had opened sometime before, was close to the railroad depot on Central Avenue. It was probably Johnson who arranged for business cards to be printed, with the names of each of the musicians and the slogans, "Let Us Do Your Playing, the famous CREOLE ORCHESTRA from NEW ORLEANS, La, For Balls, Parties, and Picnics, Reasonable Prices to Everyone, Give Us Two Days' Notice." The only copy of the business card ever to surface was lent by Johnson to the editors of *Jazzmen*. Presumably at the same time, they posed for a formal band portrait, which has been widely reprinted. It was certainly intended to be a promotional tool for the band, since the bass drum head was painted with the name The Original Creole Orchestra and their phone number. To make the best impression possible, they are in white tie and tuxedo, holding their instruments with what was probably meant as Creole hauteur.

Whatever ideas they had about becoming a successful dance orchestra were very quickly transformed into something more ambitious. They were working any kind of job they could find to earn a little money, and they were playing a street advertising job for a dollar a man when they were heard by a dapper young singer and entertainer named Morgan Prince, who had been touring with larger shows for some time but was now working as a singer in one of the local cabarets. It will probably never be possible to sort out the details of what happened

THE ORIGINAL CREOLE ORCHESTRA, SHORTLY AFTER THEY ORGANIZED IN LOS ANGELES IN 1914. FROM LEFT: STANDING, EDDIE VINCENT, FREDDIE KEPPARD, GEORGE BAQUET, BILL JOHNSON; SEATED, DINK JOHNSON, JIMMY PALAO, NORWOOD WILLIAMS.

in the next few weeks, but it seems that Prince became involved enough with them to approach a Los Angeles businessman named Jack Doyle, who was operating a successful outdoor fight club and gymnasium, and ask if this new ragtime band could play between bouts at a fight between Mexican Joe Rivers and Leach Cross. The fight, and the band's appearance, took place on August 11, 1914. In 1948, for a lecture for the New Orleans Jazz Club, the band's clarinetist prepared a memoir of the event. "The arena took up a whole square block and was packed. After every bout we played, and when we played the then popular number *In Mandalay*, Freddie Keppard, our cornetist, stood up with his egg mute and old derby hat on the bell of the instrument. The crowd stood up as one man, and shouted for us to get in the ring, and screamed and screamed. That was just before the main bout. When we got down, Mr. Carl Walker (Mr. Alec Pantages' manager) stepped up asking for our card, and asked if Mr. Pantages sent for us, would we come to the theater?"[11]

Since the band had also had some favorable press notices reviewing their appearances in a local cabaret, Prince may have gotten in touch with someone from the office of the vaudeville theater owner Alex Pantages, whose theaters covered most of the Pacific Northwest and as far south as Los Angeles. On

August 17, less than a week later, the *Los Angeles Tribune* included a small article: "Last week at Vernon, during the progress of the Cross-Rivers engagement, Alex Pantages discovered a new vaudeville attraction, a colored ragtime band with a style of comedy-music all their own. The vaudeville magnate believes he has secured a unique attraction, and to try the public opinion of the act before sending it over the circuit, will present the band here as an added attraction with this week's shows."[12]

Whether the band hurriedly put together the idea for their sketch, or whether it was something that Morgan Prince had already been rehearsing with them, their vaudeville turn satisfied Pantages when they went to his office—though he later had them appear for a tryout as an added feature in one of his less important theaters in Los Angeles. Although some writers have described the band's appearances as an early presentation of New Orleans jazz, the reality was that they were working in black face, with "plantation" costumes, and their act included more singing and dancing than it did instrumental music. It was in many ways a typical "darkey" stage piece, lasting about fifteen minutes, though often during their shows their audiences noisily requested encores. Gushee, using notes from interviews with Bill Johnson and Morgan Prince, conjectured what audiences saw and heard for the next nearly four years:

> When the curtain was drawn, Baquet, the clarinetist played a solo rendition of Abe Olman's intermezzo "Egyptia," which Johnson remembered as "the Gypsy." The moon and stars rose, then with a whistle from the wings the steamboat appeared and the band unloaded the boat, humming "Old Folks At Home."
>
> An old man in black face—Uncle Joe—came out of his cabin; it was his birthday and the band serenaded him. This warmed his old bones to the point that he danced a vigorous buck and wing. There was a chicken involved with the act, which sometimes escaped into the audience.[13]

It is instructive to find that Morgan Prince's memories of the act, which they performed more or less unchanged in hundreds of theaters, were considerably different from Johnson's, which could simply mean that the act changed over the years. Prince's memory was that as the curtain came up, the band entered in a car while the moon rose and they played "some tune from New Orleans" while a boat passed in the background. "Bill Johnson would ask loudly for 'Uncle Joe.' After much commotion, old Uncle Joe came out of the log cabin and said 'What's all this noise?' Bill Johnson answered that the band was looking for Uncle Joe so that they could serenade him on his birthday. Then they sang and played 'Old Black Joe.' The old man, wearing a Prince Albert coat—no doubt somewhat tattered—wept with emotion, and the rooster crowed. At this point, Morgan Prince would dance to a wild band rendition of 'Ballin' the Jack.' Prince remembered that the trombone player—not recalling his name, apparently—moved the slide with his foot."[14]

The live rooster was part of the act, and everyone agreed that occasionally it would slip out of Prince's grasp and have to be captured, which audiences always enjoyed. The energetic dance ended when Prince felt his old knees beginning to give out and he had to turn to singing to thank the band for coming to wish him well. As some reviewers pointed out, the sketch was similar to many others that had appeared on vaudeville stages for several decades, but the writers also felt that the comedy and the harmony singing by the band were better than usual, and the popular ragtime tunes they introduced were played with a lively style that often left the audiences demanding encores. The band also joined Prince in other minstrel show favorites. "Massa's in the Cold Cold Ground" and "Old Folks at Home," were often mentioned by reviewers.

As for so much New Orleans music from this period, the question is, What would the band have sounded like? None of the first New Orleans bands that recorded performed anything like the music the reviewers described, however other bands who presented similar acts did record, and their music is perhaps useful in putting a sound to the visual descriptions of their act. Following the overnight success of the first New Orleans band to record, the Original Dixieland Jass Band in February 1917, a number of record companies rushed to follow their lead with music and bands that they thought might have some of the new sound. In the rush, the recording directors sometimes turned to older styled arrangements, which went back to the period two or three years before, when the Creole Band was touring the theaters. Late in the spring of 1917 there was a recording by a hurriedly assembled band, Earl Fuller's Famous Jazz Band, that was unlike their other efforts to imitate the New Orleans group. Their lively recording of "L'il Liza Jane" has all the trademarks of a ragtime band's stage novelty. They played a unison melody by the trumpet and clarinet, with trombone fills, the ragtime style that was probably common everywhere , then the band put down the instruments for alternate choruses to sing the words in the classic minstrel show "walk around" manner. The single was also a helpful example of how a unison melody could still have an individual excitement. Fuller's trumpet player added embellishments and flourishes, turning the melody into a flashy, virtuosic display with an array of tricks that sound similar to the descriptions of Keppard's playing. Perhaps some of the musical effect of the Creole Band's appearances was reflected in the Fuller single.

Although the Pantages circuit of theaters was not one of the most extensive or highly regarded of the vaudeville circuits, the chain of theaters—mostly centered in the Pacific Northwest and western Canada—had strong local audiences and the acts were often enthusiastically received. Since distances were long between stops, the managers of the circuit usually sent out a package of acts that traveled together, mostly by train, from theater to theater. The Creole Band spent their first season traveling with an elaborate act titled "Yesterdays," with six chorus girls, an Irish monologist named Arthur Whitlaw, a couple who danced on roller skates, and a song and dance act with a "strong" baseball finale by McConnell and Niemeyer.

Over their three seasons on the vaudeville stage, the band was reviewed at many of the theaters where they appeared. The reviewers in the small cities were generally enthusiastic; in the larger cities the comments tended to be less positive, sometimes suggesting that the act needed some trimming or reshaping. The audiences seemed to be impressed with the stage set that traveled with them, and there was often as much positive response to the band's quartet singing, Prince's dancing and his solo singing, and their comedy as there was to the ragtime numbers, though there was general agreement that the ragtime numbers were something special and no audiences could keep from tapping their feet to the wild musical strains. They had about fifteen minutes on stage, to crowd in the opening instrumental number, the comedy exchanges with the "old darkey" and the chicken, his lively dance, then his rendition of generally two Stephen Foster favorites, with the band adding their vocal harmonies, and presumably an uptempo finish by the entire troupe, in which Prince would dance, Bill Johnson would twirl his bass, and the band would strut as they went through the usual vaudeville posturing. Although the reviews often spoke of encores, there was never any specific description of which part of the act was encored, though the mention of additional Stephen Foster songs could mean that it was Prince, as well as the band, who gave the audiences something more.

Their continual traveling brought them to Chicago and to the Northeast, and they occasionally filled in down time with a cabaret engagement. The "Creole Ragtime Band" made it to New York to appear in an elaborate review titled *Town Topics*, which toured steadily through December 1915, and continued until May 1916 despite mounting losses for a production that was top-heavy with stars and expensive staging. Their role in the elaborate show was to accompany a new performer, a young white tap and buck and wing dancer named Mabel Elaine, who performed in blackface. Initially she only did one dance number with the band, but though her act was given more time, the band seems to have continued on the tour, making their appearance only in a single number. The act generally received enthusiastic reviews. The Boston *Herald*'s critic wrote on January 25, 1916: "Of the newcomers, the feature that aroused the audience to the utmost enthusiasm was the Creole Ragtime Band, a group of colored musicians who played their instruments as if they were trying to express Richard Strauss in his most extravagant moods. Miss Mabel Elaine, who danced to their wild music, performed with such frenzy that she appeared to have swallowed a corkscrew or a spring mattress."[15] The reference to European composer Richard Strauss was intended to compare his music, which was considered wildly frenzied and advanced, with the "wild" music of the band.

It perhaps seemed to the musicians that at the end of the spring season in 1916, after months with an expensive, star-studded review, they were poised for a step up to more advantageous bookings, but when they looked back later they probably realized that it had been the high point of their vaudeville career. Things began to fray at the edges as they went out on the road again in the fall. Baquet had already left the group in Philadelphia to get married, and he was touring on his own as a solo novelty act with his new wife, who was a dancer. The others sent back to New Orleans for a replacement, a clarinetist that Palao, Keppard, and Vincent knew, Louis Nelson DeLisle. He received the telegram on June 8, 1916, and took the train north to join the band. As I wrote in *Jazz: New Orleans*, drawing on a number of sources that confused this first mishap with the band's final breakup a year later: "Nelson left to join the Original Creole Orchestra feeling that this was his big chance. A few weeks after he joined the group there was a mix-up with trains in Boston and he lost track of the others. He never did find them. In New York he got a room with Scott Joplin's widow, and went into Harlem to see if he could find out where the others where. The first person he ran into was Keppard, who announced he didn't know what had happened to the others either, and guessed that he just couldn't keep a bunch together. Nelson returned to New Orleans bitterly disappointed."[16]

DeLisle, in fact, was with the band when they went out on tour again in the fall. Morgan Prince was the next to leave, sometime in the winter. He became ill and finally was replaced by a friend of Bill Johnson's from Los Angeles, who didn't go over as well with the audiences. Keppard had always been difficult because of his continual drunkenness, and often they couldn't be certain where he was when it was time to go on stage. They spent much of the winter season of 1916 and 1917 in a series of appearances in theaters spread over a wide area of the Northeast. In March 1917 they played for two weeks in New York at the same time that the New Orleans band led by Nick La Rocca, the Original Dixieland Jass Band, was playing at Reisenweber's Restaurant. "Jass" had become New York's latest entertainment novelty, and a reviewer went to listen to the new sensation for himself in two different places in one evening: at the Monmartre, a late-night supper club at Broadway and 50th Street where the Creole Band was appearing, and Reisenweber's Restaurant, where the second group of Jack Laine's musicians to leave for the North was playing. After hearing the two bands, the reviewer concluded that "jass" meant that, "One carries the melody and the others do as they please."[17]

The band remained for only ten days at the Monmartre, but Gushee makes a plausible suggestion that they had been engaged only for these weeks, because they appeared in vaudeville again shortly afterwards. They were replaced in the club by a "jazz" group from San Francisco, which featured the saxophonist Rudy Weidoeft. Morgan Prince had already clashed with Keppard over the alcohol problem before he became ill, once hitting him on the back with a stick during a rehearsal; when he recovered after three months of convalescence, Prince took a factory job instead of rejoining the group, and finally returned to California.

Finally, in April 1917 Keppard failed to show up in time at the depot in Boston for the musicians to get their train to a job in Portland, Maine, and Bill

Johnson, who had had enough, broke up the band. There are a number of stories that, sometime when they were appearing in New York, they were approached by the Victor Talking Machine Company about making a record. The point of the story, which was repeated in *Jazzmen*, is that Keppard refused, saying that he didn't want other musicians to "steal their stuff." The stories usually emphasize that this would have been a year before the Original Dixieland Jazz Band did their first recording, with the implication that if the Creole Band had been the first to record, they would have achieved the success of the later group. All of this remains speculation and, as other writers have also questioned, could have been just a story they presented to assuage their feelings at *not* having been approached for a recording. Gushee's conclusion is that the story was apocryphal.

Although the ending of their vaudeville career was an anticlimax after they'd achieved so much, the band clearly did bring the excitement of the emerging New Orleans ragtime style to audiences everywhere in the United States, even if the bright sheen of the music had to be wrapped in the costumes and the racist cliches of a plantation act. After what began as an unscheduled appearance in the ring between the bouts of a Los Angeles boxing arena only a few years before, playing for coins thrown up into onto the canvas, their successful vaudeville years and the surprised, genuine response to their music must have seemed difficult for them to believe.

7

"Jass"

*Now just remember that there had been a string ensemble playing there, and
WE had been playing on the back of a wagon. We couldn't play soft. Didn't
know what soft was! Here we come in with a trombone, clarinet, and cornet.
People held their ears and yelled, "Too Loud." Well, why not? We'd followed
strings! And there was a tile floor in the place and what looked like a tin ceiling.*

BASS PLAYER ARNOLD LOYOCANO DESCRIBING THE FIRST NIGHT AT LAMB'S
CAFÉ IN CHICAGO WITH TOM BROWN'S BAND FROM DIXIELAND, APRIL, 1915[1]

I t might have taken a little longer to get to New Orleans than it did to get to
other cities, but every kind of popular entertainment that was on the road
in the United States made its way to the city some time or other. As well as
the shows and vaudeville acts and touring concert bands, it sometimes seemed
as though there were as many touring musicians and entertainers in and out
of town as there were bands and singers in New Orleans itself. It was this informal network of traveling performers who spread the word of the New Orleans
style of ragtime. The accounts of these first encounters between the vaudevil-
lians and the local instrumentalists often contradict themselves and just as often
present unlikely scenarios, but they breathe the infectious enthusiasm of the
period, when the music was new and everyone seemed to be at the beginning of
their careers.

Of all the stories that have been passed on about these Columbus-like journeys of discovery, none is more colorful than the account that dancer and
comedian Joe Frisco dictated to friends late in his life.[2] Frisco's name has been
mentioned often in discussions of New Orleans jazz beginnings, but invariably
he is assumed to have been the well-known eccentric jazz dancer who had a surprise success in the Ziegfeld Follies three years later. It was the same person, but

in the winter of 1914–15, when he first turned up in New Orleans as a nervous stage beginner, his appearance didn't attract any headlines.

In the last months of 1914, Frisco was only one of hundreds of young dancers in Chicago with fiery ambitions and no prospects. He was doing any odd jobs he could find, trying to convince theater managers to hire him to dance. One afternoon, when he was making a delivery to one of the "dancing schools"—the establishments were actually taxi dance halls, providing music and women dancing partners for anyone who came in the door with the money for a dance ticket—he saw a pretty young woman named Loretta McDermott, working as a dancer. She was even less experienced than he was, but she had the same ambitions. After they practiced together a few times, he went to a booking agent and talked him into giving them an engagement, although it turned out that the only booking he could provide was at a small vaudeville house in New Orleans. Theater managers at that time had no way to know what a new act they were sent could do, so they generally retained the contractual right to let the performers go if they didn't "go over" with the public. The new dancing team of Frisco and McDermott didn't make it past the first night, and in classic vaudeville style they were stranded in New Orleans.

As they walked the streets after they left the theater, trying to think of some way out of their predicament, Frisco remembered that they heard music as they were passing a place called the Club Creole. Trombonist Tom Brown was leading the band. Loretta supposedly exclaimed, "Boy, listen to that music; what a band. C'mon Joe, let's go. What rhythm!" When they slipped inside the door, they didn't have enough money to sit down at a table and order dinner, so they started dancing, and found that the band's rhythm was new to them—it was the looser New Orleans dance tempo, with a springy down beat. With all the noisy response that followed the bands as they went north, it's often forgotten that what "went over" was a "peppier" rhythm for dancing. The New Orleans bands broke through to new audiences when they took extended engagements in northern cabarets with their new dance beat.

Frisco and his partner went to the telegraph office the next morning and somehow convinced the agent that they'd done well enough that they should get another booking. The agent found them an engagement in Baton Rouge in a theater that was as unresponsive as their first audience, but they managed to last out the week, and returned to New Orleans with a little money and another booking, this time at the Nemo Theater, across the river in Algiers. For once, the audiences seemed to like them, and they also had a little more experience presenting their act. Frisco remembered that they couldn't stay away from the Club Creole, and every night when they finished at the Nemo, they hurried to the ferry to cross the river so they could dance to the rhythm of Brown's band. By the second night, the other dancers were beginning to watch them, and on the third night, their last before they had to take the train back to Chicago, they met the members of the band, had some rounds of drinks together, and this time when he and Loretta went to the dance floor, the other customers let them have it to themselves. When they finished, the crowd began applauding enthusiastically but Frisco—who suffered from a stammer—held up a hand and shouted "D-D-Don't applaud, folks, just throw m-m-money." When the coins stopped clattering down on the floor around them, they saw that they'd earned more for a few moments of dancing to Brown's band than they'd earned for their appearances at the Nemo.

When they returned to Chicago, they had to start again at the bottom of the agent's list, and Loretta McDermott drifted off with another partner, leaving Frisco to put some kind of career together. He found a job as an entertainer at a restaurant called Lamb's Café, at the corner of Clark and Randolph in the Chicago Loop district, and the manager asked him to find some more entertainment for the customers. Lamb's was downstairs in the basement of the Olympic Theater building, a large, boomy cellar space. The café already had a string ensemble, but they were always looking for novelties, and Frisco began talking about the new kind of dance music he'd heard in New Orleans. Finally the café's owner, Smiley Corbett, agreed to bring the band north so his entertainer would have something to dance to.

As nostalgic and as plausible as the story might be, the recollection of the band's pianist and bass player, Arnold Loyocano, was considerably less romantic, although it is possible that Frisco did talk to the owner of Lamb's Café about the band, and his enthusiasm helped build up interest in the new dance music. Loyocano remembered that a dancer named Myrtle Howard, who was appearing in the vaudeville show at the West End resort on Lake Ponchartrain, told her agent Joe Gorham about the band. Gorham went to hear them play and recommended them for the job in the north. In an article in the English jazz magazine *Storyville* in 1976, based on letters from the band's cornetist, Ray Lopez, to Richard Hadlock, two telegrams from the manager of the cabaret in Chicago to Gorham were reproduced, confirming Gorham's role in bringing the band north.[3] The first read,

Chicago, March 27, 1915

Joe Gorham,
Hotel Grunewald, Neworleans

Have given musicians notice finish April seventh are you sure Brown band right for our place answer me if you can have them come on. What price wire me

John Wilmes.

The "musicians notice" probably meant that Wilmes had already decided to bring the band north and he was dismissing the band he was presently employing. The second telegram, after the negotiations with the band, is dated six weeks later.

THE TELEGRAMS, MARCH 27 AND MAY 12, 1915, THAT BROUGHT TOM BROWN'S BAND TO CHICAGO, THE FIRST NEW ORLEANS RAGTIME BAND TO OPEN IN A CHICAGO CAFÉ. RAY LOPEZ, THE BAND'S CORNETIST AND MANAGER, ADDED THE NOTE: "6 WEEKS. WITH OPTION OF RENEWAL RENEWAL [SIC] TO BE MADE BEFORE FIFTH WEEK IS PLAYED."

Chicago, Ill. ?May 12/15

Joe Gorham
Hotel Grunewald
N. O., La

Will wire tickets contract band for six weeks with option to open monday May seventeenth

John Wilmes

A handwritten note on the bottom of the second telegram reads, "6 weeks. With option of renewal to be made before fifth week is played."

The band that Tom Brown was leading at the Club Creole took the train north and opened on May 17th, 1915, at Lamb's Café on a six-week contract. The café had an option to renew the contract at the end of the fourth week. When the band finally took a break in August, it was to do renovations to the room so the café could accommodate more customers. With Brown, who played trombone, were cornetist Lopez, who was also the band's business manager, clarinetist

Gussie Mueller, drummer Billy Lambert, and Arnold Loyocano, who played the piano in the restaurant but also doubled on string bass. They arrived to an unfamiliar landscape that even in spring was colder than they, the first New Orleans ragtime band to play in the northern city, were used to. They were as unfamiliar to their new audiences as the weather was to them, and the first reaction was mixed. As Loyocano remembered, there was an initial problem with the band's volume, and he also remembered that the band had left New Orleans with some uncertainty about what was waiting for them.

> No one knew we were leaving [New Orleans] because if we didn't make good and had to come back, that'd look pretty bad. So we kept it a secret. When we got to Chicago it was snowing and very cold. We stayed at the first hotel we saw, the Commercial, on Wabash and Harrison Streets. We didn't even have an audition. We began playing at eight o'clock that night.
>
> Now just remember that there had been a string ensemble playing there, and WE had been playing on the back of a wagon. We couldn't play soft. Didn't know what soft was! Here we come in with trombone, clarinet, and cornet. People held their ears and yelled "Too loud." Well, why not? We'd followed strings! And there was a tile floor in the place, and what looked like a tin ceiling.
>
> The first piece we played was No. 2. It was popular [in New Orleans] but no one knew the name of it. We just called it No. 2.[4]

Loyocano was being a little disingenuous. "Number 2," the first piece they played, was the New Orleans dance hall favorite "Tiger Rag," and it was generally played as loudly as the bands could manage. What was most important to him was that for once he was earning some money. "They paid us twenty-five dollars a week in Chicago—the salary was the big thing. We'd been making a dollar a night down in New Orleans."[5]

Lopez remembered that when they came into the café for an audition the manager, confused, asked them where their music was. They answered that it was in their heads.

> He wanted to hear a sample . . . We played "Memphis Blues." We kicked off, and twisted that number every way but loose. We worked it up to the pitch that used to kill folks back home—and found our way back smooth as glass. We were right in there. It sounded fine.
>
> But Corbett was white as a ghost. He roared: "What kind of noise is that! You guys crazy—or drunk?" Well, we played our novelty tune, "Livery Stable Blues." The cashier made faces and held her ears.[6]

It was at this point that the word "jass" made its appearance. As with everything else about the new musical style in these early years, there are conflicting

Tom Brown's Ragtime Band, lined up for their appearance at Lamb's Café in Chicago, May 17, 1915. From left: Ray Lopez, Arnold Loyocano, Billy Lambert, Tom Brown, Larry Shields.

stories about how the New Orleans musicians, who always thought of their music as ragtime, suddenly discovered that what they were playing had been given a new name. What is clear is that there was considerable controversy among the Chicago musicians themselves. During this period the musicians' union was actively expanding its role in the restaurants and cabarets, and the musicians with Brown were not union members. As far as the Chicago musicians were concerned, they were simply scabs. One of the often repeated stories is that there were demonstrations outside the café, and one of the demonstrators carried a placard that Brown remembered as reading, "Don't Patronize This Jass Music," implying that the band's style was somehow disreputable. Others remembered that it was the union musicians in the string ensemble who were also employed at Lamb's who first used the word, calling it across the restaurant to taunt the New Orleanians. The legitimate musicians could, however, have read the placard when they came to work.

Perhaps the most interesting of the various accounts is Lopez's recollection. Lawrence Gushee summarized the account Lopez gave in one of his letters.

> . . . *they had just finished a "beautiful" number,* Hawaiian Butterfly, *when a South Side grifter named Darby Kelly shouted, "Jazz it up, Ray" and the band played the up-tempo "Banana Peel Rag." Two "big wheels" from Lyon & Healy— the most important music store in Chicago—were intrigued by the music and the word "jazz." Smiley Corbett, the owner of Lamb's, had his waiter bring over a dictionary from the hotel across the street he also owned. Corbett and the two men from Lyon and Healy tried in vain to find the word "jazz" in the dictionary, but found what seemed to them to be close: "jade, a wild and vicious woman."*[7]

Whoever first used it as a derisive description of the band's music, the unfamiliar word "jass" only heightened the confusion—and the dancing public's interest—since nobody knew what it meant. Almost a century later, there is still no agreement about either the source of the word or its meaning. There was certainly some awareness in Chicago that the word was already being used in San Francisco, where sports writers had for some time been employing it to describe the pep and energy of the players on the San Francisco Seals baseball team. In an April, 1912 edition of the *Los Angeles Times* it was used by pitcher Ben Henderson to describe his "jazz curve," "I call it the Jazz Ball because it wobbles and you simply can't do anything with it."[8] This would substantiate the use of the word in an advertisement in the New Orleans *Picayune* in 1918, in which "jazzed" meant to be completely confused. When a San Francisco dance band led by Art Hickman went to the Seals training camp to play in the training season of 1913, they were described as a "jazz band"—the earliest known use of the term to describe a way of playing music. Lopez, in his letters to Hadlock, wrote that he remembered first hearing the term sometime before June 1912, at a rehearsal in the Orpheum Theatre. "I was an assistant property man. I remember watching a comedy act rehearsing. This Bill Demarest was explaining a music cue, such as: 'When I kick the old lady in the belly, go into *When the Midnight Choo-Choo Leaves For Alabam*,' to the leader, and then said: 'You know, Jazz it up—loud and snappy.' . . . That was the first time I had heard the word used in connection with music until I heard Darby Kelly shout it across the dance floor of the Lambs Café in Chicago in 1915."[9]

Lopez also made it clear that it wasn't a word in circulation in New Orleans. In 1914 or 1915 the Brown band was playing for an advertising ballyhoo at the corner of Canal and Royal and two touring black-face comedians, Johnny Swor and Charlie Mack, heard them playing.

> They were standing in the crowd and Big Charlie started to do his shuffle dance that he did in their act. He came over to the wagon. Tom, playing trombone, was sitting on the tailgate of the wagon so as to have room to work his slide. Mack shouted out: "Boys, y'all got steppin' music, you hear me?" Well, they followed us for about three blocks. "What do you boys call this music?", Mack asked. Tom Brown said: "We call it blues or ragtime. This is New Orleans music." Swor said: "This music has got to travel, man! How about coming north with us?" . . . I gave him our card which read: "Brown's Band. Music for all Occasions. Parades, Parties, Picnics and Balls."[10]

The word would certainly have been familiar to a drummer named Bert Kelly, who was playing in San Francisco at the time. He then moved to Chicago, where he became one of the important figures in introducing Chicago audiences to the New Orleans musicians. He also insisted that he had been the first to use the word for a band himself, though so far there is no way to document his claims.

The various later proposals, that the word has some sexual connotations—never defined—or that it is derived from one of several African words—there is no agreement as to which words—leave the confusion about where it was in the spring of 1915. Ray Lopez noticed that in some of the advertisements in the newspapers the word was spelled "Jab" or "Jad," and his assumption was that the publicists were staying away from "Jass" became of some moral implications, which he also was uncertain about. The spelling "Jad" was employed in the first advertisements for the band that appeared the weekend after their opening.

Brown himself didn't mind the new advertisements, which described them on a sign outside as "Brown's Dixieland Jass Band, Direct from New Orleans, Best Dance Music in Chicago." The band didn't know what the word meant either, but since it seemed to be drawing customers, they went along with the excitement. Four of them, without Brown, posed for a photo that they sent home, all of them with their coats unbuttoned, their bow ties managing to look casual, and the three who were wearing caps had them pushed back at a jaunty angle. Even in the tones of the old photograph, there was a suggestion of the old New Orleans swagger.

In the early 1890s cylinder recordings were made in New Orleans by a Creole performer named Louis "Bebe" Vasnier, who recited minstrel show–style plantation sermons as "Brudder Rasmus." The rare recordings—only one of the cylinders has been found—were made for a new local company called the Louisiana Phonograph Company, and intended for play in new coin-slot phonographs in local amusement places.[11] However, despite rumors of cylinders made by other musicians, among them Buddy Bolden, New Orleans doesn't seem to have been the scene of further recording activity until the 1920s. When New Orleans bands began recording after they'd spent some months in the cabarets in Chicago and New York, it was clear that their arrangements and repertoire were shaped entirely to the needs of the couples on the dance floor. The arrangements didn't leave room for solos. Since the bands were playing without any kind of amplification, every musician in a small group of only five pieces had to be playing steadily to fill out the ensemble sound. This was such an established policy that if anyone stopped playing for more than a few measures, a quick suggestion would come from the cabaret owner that he'd hired them all to play music, not sit around. There was little fluctuation away from the initial dance rhythm, and drummers were hired for their ability to hold a tempo. Even if there were breaks or sections in the arrangements where one instrument had a more prominent role, a supporting rhythmic background was played by the others.

Today the early bands are also sometimes criticized for not straying far from the melodies, but for ordinary dancers, who consciously danced to the melody, it was more helpful to them if the melodies were repeated continuously. The tempos of those first recordings mirror the dance fashions of the period, including the newly introduced one-step, which was danced as a nimble, rocking glide and played at reckless speed, and fox-trot, which slowed the tempo for more elaborate footwork. The New Orleans bands also introduced an even slower fox-trot, which they generally called a blues even though there was no concern about using the twelve-bar blues harmonic forms with any consistency. Their early band blues were closer to what was printed in sheet music and advertised on piano rolls as a "slow drag." Whatever they called it, their springy slow drag brought everyone out on the floor. Occasionally the bands recorded larger 12-inch discs—the standard was 10-inch—which gave them as much as a minute more time for their rendition; but they made no effort to change the arrangements or alter the style of playing—they just let people dance to the melody for an extra two or three choruses.

Tom Brown, who led the band at Lamb's, was born in 1888, so he was just twenty-seven when he left New Orleans. Like the other musicians in the band, he had worked steadily in Jack Laine's Reliance orchestras and brass bands, first joining the bands when he was a teenager. After 1910, however, when he was in his twenties, he usually led his own ragtime orchestra at places like the Poodle Dog Cabaret at Liberty and Bienville, or the Club Creole, where Frisco and his partner heard them, or led a small society dance orchestra with cornetist Lopez. Brown's younger brother Steve, who was two years younger and played both brass bass and string bass, often was a member of the bands. In the 1920s he matured into one of the most important and distinctive of a new group of string bass musicians who modernized the jazz bass style.

Tom was short and slight, with a square-jawed face. His usual expression was guarded, even distrustful. His hair color gave him his nickname of "Red." In a comic studio photo that the family of clarinetist Yellow Nunez has preserved, Brown was standing in what was mocked up to be the wicker basket of an ascension balloon drifting above Canal Street. He was squeezed between Nunez, who looked comfortably casual, and trumpeter Frank Christian, who was smiling. Their hats had been pushed back and their hands were dangling over the railing of the basket in a relaxed pose. The only dissonant note in the photo was the troubled expression on Brown's face. He looked as uncomfortably apprehensive as if the balloon actually were hanging over the New Orleans streets.

In the 1950s Brown occasionally played the trombone and doubled on bass for trio and quartet jobs with clarinetist Ray Burke in a small lounge on Esplanade Avenue. Brown still was as thin, his clothes as rumpled, and his expression as watchful as it had been in his old photographs. His face was always tired, and toward the end of the evening his shoulders slumped a little, but his eyes still followed everything that was happening on the dance floor. When I tried asking him questions about that first trip north, it didn't seem to be something that interested him.

Ray Lopez, Brown's cornetist in Chicago, was a slim, serious musician who had worked with Brown in the Laine bands. He never learned to read music, but like most of the musicians he worked with he could remember any music that he heard. He was born in the French Quarter, on Orleans Street between Bourbon and Dauphine, in 1889. He remembered his father as an accomplished cornetist who played at the Opera, though his father left the family when Lopez was eight. Lopez taught himself to play the cornet from an instruction book he bought, and played his first jobs when he was in his teens. In a 1911 photo of the Reliance Brass Band, taken on a bright sunny day, all of the band were in their white summer shirts, with straight ties, and white trousers. Lopez, holding a small cornet, and with his white uniform cap sitting straight on his head, looked directly into the camera, his expression careful and consciously serious. When he and Brown led an orchestra together, they usually played legitimate dance music.

The clarinetist for the northern adventure was Gussie Mueller, round faced and a little pudgy, another of the Laine regulars who was a year younger than Lopez. The pianist Arnold "Deacon" Loyocano, who also took his string bass north with him, was one of a large musical family. The same age as Lopez, he had been a precocious learner, and he began playing at Spanish Fort and Milneburg when he was nine. The drummer, Billy Lambert, was the youngest, and he is the one in the band about whom the least has been written.

Some of the musicians who followed them to Chicago insisted that Brown's band shouldn't have been the one that was hired for the job, since they relied on standard ragtime novelties for some of their effect, pieces like "Turkey in the Straw" and "The Old Gray Mare" that the vaudeville ragtime acts often featured. From the recollection of members of the band, however, it is clear that they played an extensive repertoire of popular songs, as well as ragtime numbers popular in New Orleans. They had, after all, been working as cabaret musicians in New Orleans for most of their careers, and those bands lived on tips for playing requests. Since they'd opened the first night with "No. 2," however, they obviously were used to the familiar New Orleans pieces. They were also playing with the dance beat that Joe Frisco found so irresistible, but it was two or three weeks before crowds discovered them, and the manager of Lamb's was initially upset with everyone who had advised him to hire the band. Word spread, however, and with new signs outside advertising they were a dance band, they soon were pulling in such large crowds—some drawn to the restaurant simply by the novelty of the name jass—that other cabaret owners began to think about bands that might still be in New Orleans.

The first club manager to make a move was Bert Kelly, who also played the drums with his groups, and at that point was managing the White City Cabaret, which may have been an early name for his later and better known establishment, Bert Kelly's Stables at 431 N. Rush Street. He was already familiar with what he thought of as "jass" from San Francisco, so he decided to make up a jass band by adding New Orleans musicians to the band that was already working in his cabaret, and he asked Brown for names of people to contact. Brown told him to get in touch with clarinetist Larry Shields, who in New Orleans was already considered one of the most polished of the new ragtimers. With an exchange of telegrams, Shields agreed to join Kelly's band, and after the trip north he found a room in the Commercial Hotel with the musicians from Brown's band.

A few days after Shields arrived, Brown ran into him in the hotel hallway in the middle of the night, when they'd both gotten off the job. Shields complained unhappily that he was having trouble with the music the other band was play-ing. It seems to have been a reading band, and he wasn't a strong reader. He complained that his style "just didn't fit in." Brown's clarinetist, Gussie Mueller, wasn't satisfied with where he was and had been talking about playing with some other band, so in an easy move Brown and Kelly switched clarinetists. Shields went to Tom Brown's Band from Dixieland and Mueller joined Kelly's jass band. The San Francisco bands Kelly was familiar with had already begun using the newly popular saxophone—"hot" saxophone soloist Rudy Weidoeft, who was to turn the jazz world upside down two or three years later, had begun his career in San Francisco—so the first week Mueller was with the band, Kelly took him to a music store and they bought a saxophone for him. It could have been Shields's unwillingness to learn the new instrument that led to his unhappiness with Kelly. His first night with Brown's band at Lamb's was August 4, 1915.

One of the most startling photographs from these first years of jazz is a crowd scene taken on a street in Chicago a few weeks later.[12] In the center of the scene was the diminutive Joe Frisco, resplendent in a pinstriped suit, spats, waistcoat, cigar, and light fedora perched on the back of his head. His arms were outstretched as though he were conducting the events of the afternoon. Behind him in the front of a circle of faces were a handful of musicians playing their instruments. The musicians are the members of Tom Brown's band. By this time they had been working steadily at the Café for more than three months, and the crowds had continued to grow. Finally the owner closed the room on August 28 to expand the space, asking the band for an assurance that they wouldn't play in another Chicago café until he reopened. The band also assumed that if Frisco did any dancing, it would be with their accompaniment.

The musicians standing together in a line behind Frisco's outstretched left arm were Tom Brown, Ray Lopez, and Larry Shields (which means the photo-graph had to be taken after August 4). Beside him the broadly grinning string bass player, Deacon Loyocano, squeezed against the crowd. The drummer Billy Lambert was on the other side of Frisco, his face hidden by the Frisco's hand. Everything was considerably more formal in the early days of jazz: all of the musicians were in suits and ties, Shields and Lopez were wearing cloth caps, Brown and Loyocano were in fedoras, and only Lambert was "sporting" a little, with a Scottish plaid cap. The crowd looked more like the usual gathering of men trying to get into a prize fight; there wasn't a woman anywhere in sight. Giving the scene a more obvious Chicago flavor, standing beside Lambert was a young, strong-faced Chicagoan in a suit and a cloth cap, his hand resting on Brown's upturned trombone case. The young man was Al Capone, who in a few years was to become one of Chicago's best-known citizens. (See p. 8.)

The photograph was probably taken when the band began a vaudeville tour with Frisco, or were appearing by themselves, first as the "Kings of Ragtime," then as "Five Musical Rubes," for the next six months. Despite their informal agreement with Smiley Corbett, they also seem to have played together at the Arsonia Café at 1654 Madison Street, which was run by Mike Fritzel. Frisco's jazz dancing was beginning to attract crowds for its own unique novelty and style. He was doing a kind of "snake hips" shimmy that didn't use much space on the dance floor; the eccentric bends to his body and his arms gave what he was doing its comic effect. In a photo of him performing with them, his feet and legs were pressed tightly together. According to Frisco, their act was so popular that Fritzel began moving tables onto the dance floor to make room for more customers. Finally Frisco complained that if they kept adding tables to the space, he'd have to begin dancing without using his feet. Fritzel just shrugged and said that he was the only dancer who could.

In his letters to Hadlock, Lopez remembered that they did three split weeks in nearby theaters, and went as far east as Hammond, Indiana, for a single night at the Palace Theater there. An agent working out of New York named Harry Fitzgerald saw them perform and offered them a booking in a new review, *Dancing Around*, scheduled to open with Al Jolson as its major star. They arrived in New York a month after their last night at Lamb's, on September 27, only to find that because of a disagreement between Jolson and the producers the show had been cancelled. Fitzgerald was able to book them into a new show, *Town Topics*, where they provided their new dance music in a lobby foyer before and after the show. The show, however, closed after two weeks, and both Brown and Lopez remembered they were never paid. A new agent picked them up, and they spent most of the winter doing vaudeville dates around New York. What is most significant about their months in New York is that they introduced audiences to the New Orleans ragtime style. Along with the Creole Band, who also were doing theater engagements with their novelty ragtime entertainment, they laid some of the groundwork for what would be the major breakthrough of the second white band to leave New Orleans for the north, the group that drummer Johnny Stein brought into another Chicago café in the spring of 1916.

By this time the members of Brown's band had been traveling and playing for almost a year, and for some of the musicians it was time either to return to New Orleans or to go on to something else. Mueller had already left and was still playing in Chicago, but he was drafted when the United States joined the war in Europe in the spring of 1917. When he was discharged he eventually moved to California, where he joined the new orchestra led by a young violinist named Paul Whiteman. Shields had become discouraged over the band's financial difficulties in New York and he was already back in New Orleans. Lopez doesn't seem ever to have returned to New Orleans, at least not as a musician, but of all of them he immediately became one of the most widely known.

Lopez had started out in New Orleans as a worker in a railroad repair shop for a dollar a day, and the realization that by playing the cornet he could make much more than that and not have to get up early held a strong appeal for him. He was also ambitious and was known for always having a music job somewhere. When Brown's band broke up after their long vaudeville run, Lopez returned to Chicago and began working as part of a band accompanying a vaudeville trio that doubled at a café and at the Majestic Theater, where he was featured from the orchestra pit. He stood on a chair for the last number, "Darktown Strutters Ball," and played New Orleans–style jazz choruses, using a derby hat for a mute. It caused such a sensation that the featured act of the show, a woman singer named Blossom Seeley, hurried from her dressing room to see what was happening. She immediately signed a contract with Lopez, and for the next three years he was on the road with her act, featured in a specialty number as "Mister Jazz Himself." Richard Sudhalter suggests that on this tour, Lopez "may have been the very first jazz *star*—that is, the first hot player accorded a featured role in vaudeville outside an organized band, and singled out as such by the press."[13]

In December 1920 Lopez was back in Chicago, working in a trio and finding the weather as miserable as he remembered from his first weeks there five years before. In the middle of a snowstorm one night, a man called to him on the street and introduced himself as the brother of California bandleader Abe Lyman. He bought Lopez a cup of coffee and asked him if he wouldn't rather be in California. The offer was $150 a week plus tips to join his brother's orchestra. Lopez was on a train to California a week later.

If, as is often said, jazz is a musical style that lives through recordings, then it is with the music of those first musicians who left in February 1915 that our knowledge of the early New Orleans ragtime style begins. From this point we have recordings by nearly all of the musicians who were part of this first northern exodus. Unfortunately, Tom Brown's band, like Bill Johnson's Creole Band, didn't record as a group, but its three lead musicians recorded within a relatively brief period after the band broke up, and their individual styles on the recordings certainly still contained most of the elements of the music they had performed as a New Orleans group.

Brown himself became the most active in the recording "laboratories," as they were called then. Around 1919 he signed a contract with Harry Yerkes, a New York music producer who had been an early ragtime drummer and marimba virtuoso. As the record business began to expand after the war, Yerkes was in demand as an organizer of pick-up sessions for nearly every record company that had recording facilities in the city. Brown's contract with Yerkes guaranteed him $50 per recorded side, with a minimum of four sides to be recorded each week. Between his work with Ray Miller's orchestra and the studio sessions, Brown was earning more money than he ever could have made in New Orleans. He remained on Yerkes's payroll into the twenties, but finally returned home to resume his local career working and recording with the new bands led by old friends.

Yerkes had no serious interest in jazz, but it was one of the styles of music he could bring into the studio, and occasionally one of his sessions caught fire. Yerkes generally attached his name to the final product, whether or not he'd done anything more than set up the sessions and bring in the musicians. Brown made so many different recordings, with so many groups using so many different arrangements, that it's obvious he was a more than capable reader. Despite the short times the bands had to rehearse and record a new piece, he never sounded uncertain in his attack or phrasing. He was an ideal studio musician. Often, however, in the poorly balanced, faintly recorded acoustic sessions, it was difficult to hear him at all. A strong example of his style, that for once was well recorded, was a single released as Yerkes' Southern Five, with Brown teamed alongside his old friend from the Jack Laine bands, clarinetist Yellow Nunez, and a small rhythm section, with a busy banjoist sometimes filling the breaks for a Luckey Roberts composition titled "Railroad Blues." The session was held on March 5, 1920, in New York. Without a cornet or saxophone lead, the two horns could stretch out against each other's melodies, and it's possible to hear the essential elements of the New Orleans ensemble style in Brown's playing. Often he limited himself to punching out the harmonies, but there were smoother legato passages where he countered Nunez's lead with flowing phrases of his own, and he had his own repertoire of loose, smeared breaks. It was a minimalist New Orleans trombone style, remarkable for its precision and its gruff ballyhoo band muscularity.

Gussie Mueller returned to New York with Paul Whiteman's Orchestra in 1920, after his discharge from the Army, and he was featured on Whiteman's first success, a composition with Mueller listed as a co-composer, the popular "Wang-Wang Blues" recorded on August 9, 1920, for Victor Records. His supple breaks gave the arrangement a lilting swing and it was obvious that he was one of the most talented of the new generation of New Orleans clarinetists. His tone was assured and focused, without the intrusive glissandi that were already being passed off as the New Orleans idiom by uneasy musicians from other cities who were suddenly being asked to play in the new style. In the breaks that were at the heart of the single release, his rhythmic sense was impeccable. Although Whiteman had larger ambitions, at this point his orchestra was still small, only seven pieces, with the classic trumpet, clarinet, trombone ensemble sharing the arrangement. Mueller left the orchestra as it grew in size and began to experiment with a more "symphonic" jazz style. Within a few years the orchestra had grown to fifteen musicians who played an array of instruments, and the arrangements reflected Whiteman's interests in a more elaborate, and eclectic, musical palette. Mueller never was comfortable with the arrangement parts he was supposed to read, and he left the orchestra not long after recording his featured composition. In his autobiography Whiteman remembered Mueller's unhappiness, though he also still remembered him with fondness.

Gus Mueller . . . was wonderful on the clarinet and saxophone, but he couldn't read a line of music. I tried to teach him, but he wouldn't try to learn, so I had to play everything for him and let him get it by ear. I couldn't understand why he was so lazy or stubborn or both. He said he was neither.

"It's like this," he confided one day. "I knew a boy once down in N'Awleens that was a hot player, but he learned to read music and then he couldn't play jazz any more. I don't want to be like that."

A little later, Gus came to say he was quitting. I was sorry and asked him what was the matter. He stalled around awhile and then burst out:

"Nuh, suh, I jes' can't play that 'pretty music' that you all play. And you fellers can't never play blues worth a damn!"[14]

When he reached California Ray Lopez joined Abe Lyman's Ambassador Hotel Orchestra in Los Angeles. He stayed with the orchestra throughout its most prolific period of recording, and although much of the work they did in the studio was limited to commercial dance music, his hotter cornet style could be heard on a number of arrangements. In 1923 he convinced Mueller that he should leave New York and join the band, and in July they were both on sessions that produced "California Blues" and "Bugle Call Rag." In Lopez's earliest recordings with Lyman the exaggerated muted effects in his breaks and solo choruses veered close to the near-parody comedy style that was a feature of a number of arrangements for early bands who were still struggling with the idea of "jazz." Probably what he played in his period as "Mister Jazz" were these throttled effects with the mute. On a recording made some time later with Lyman, however, "Shake That Thing," his playing shook off the raucous overlay of comedy and his solo passages sparked the ensemble with the lyric melodic line and warm tone characteristic of the New Orleans cornet sound. The sound of the three horns that can be heard on their recordings—Lopez's lead, assertive and confident; Mueller's warm-toned clarinet; and Brown's pungent trombone— would have given the band that came to Lamb's Café, only a few years before, the lyric drive that the dancers found irresistible in their music. Their identification with this distinctive New Orleans band idiom helped lead to long and productive careers for each of them.

Individual recordings by the musicians who had taken the train north with Tom Brown's band in 1915 make it possible to hear some of the raggy characteristics of the ensemble style they brought with them. But the groundbreaking recordings of the next New Orleans band that made the journey a few months later finally let curious audiences hear what the new ragtime dance music sounded like played by a genuine New Orleans "jass" band. For the first time, also, along with all of the excitement that their music stirred up, it was possible to come a little closer to the musicians themselves, and begin to know them as individuals. Getting to know them better, however, didn't necessarily mean that later critics liked all of them better.

8

The First Sensational Musical Novelty of 1917!

This is the band that clean up Chi. Ill. And run all the other boys back home. Jack, you no [sic] that, what [sic] the use of bringing it up again?

YELLOW NUNEZ, WRITING TO JACK LAINE WITH A PHOTO OF
STEIN'S BAND AT SCHILLER'S CAFÉ IN CHICAGO, 1916[1]

It is all done in correct time—there is no fault to be found in the rhythm of it. Even though the cornetist is constantly throwing in flourishes of his own and every once in a while the trombonist gets excited about something and takes it out on his instrument, their tapping feet never miss (a) step.

F. T. VREELAND REVIEWING THE ORIGINAL DIXIELAND JASS
BAND IN THE NEW YORK *SUN*, NOVEMBER 4, 1917

In a letter to critic Leonard Feather in 1959, Nick La Rocca blustered, "Many of the so-called historians pass on me as if I never existed, and the ones who do write about me have twisted . . . history."[2] Of all the anomalies of jazz history, one of the most problematic is the difficulty of many writers to deal with La Rocca and the Original Dixieland Jass Band. He may not have been "The most lied about person in history since Jesus Christ," as he railed in another letter, but the insistence on the part of many modern critics that the white musicians in New Orleans played no role in the development of the city's ragtime idiom upset many of New Orleans's veteran musicians, not only La Rocca. When someone like English jazz writer and discographer Brian Rust, who admired the band and what they'd accomplished, spent time with La Rocca, however, he found him less bristly. La Rocca readily confirmed that in those first years, the new rag-time style was handed back and forth so many times between the musicians of the two races that it was difficult even then to tell who had originally created the repertoire they shared and the new band style. Although La Rocca was often vituperative in his judgments, and some of his statements were both racist and anti-Semitic (especially in notes and papers that he turned over to the William S. Hogan Jazz Archive at Tulane University), Rust insists that La Rocca's personal memories were considerably more balanced.

Others who met him during these last years, when he was living quietly on Constance Street in New Orleans, felt that he wasn't well and that his poor health was a contributing factor to his outbursts. When Jelly Roll Morton made substantially the same claims, with much the same bluster, and said some of the same things about his critics, as well as made racist comments in his letters, it was generally accepted as the disappointment of someone who, despite every-thing, *had* played a role in the early days of jazz, even though it became clear in later years that Morton had left New Orleans as a teenager and his experience had been limited to jobs as a parlor pianist in Storyville, and evenings playing the guitar with friends. Even though La Rocca had certainly been part of the excitement in the city's dance halls before World War I, and had played a crucial role in the first years of the worldwide spread of jazz, his outbursts seemed to set everyone's teeth on edge.

Virtually everything about the band has upset many of the new generation of jazz writers. In his *A New History of Jazz* in 2001, Alyn Shipton complained about one of illustrations the band used for advertising, which depicted them clowning with their instruments. He described the photo, which they used as a letterhead on their printed stationery, as "a revealing insight into the group's self-image. Sbarbaro's giant bass drum booms as he waves castanets and bells above his head. Edwards and Shields point to left and right respectively, while La Rocca sits atop the back of his chair, feet in the seat, aiming his cornet at the ceiling. Ragas appears simultaneously to be dancing a kind of Charleston and pressing his nose against the keyboard, while a terpsichorean couple spin around the dance floor."[3]

The reality is that from about 1918 to the mid-1920s virtually every jazz group in the country posed clowning with their instruments. In the photo of the Fate Marable riverboat orchestra from about 1919 or 1920, Louis Armstrong has thrust his face forward with an exaggerated grimace and one hand is held behind his head as he lunges toward the photographer. In a photo of Mamie Smith's Jazz Hounds about 1923, the tenor saxophone player crouched on the floor, looking ready to spring, grinning broadly as he plays, is Coleman Hawkins. In a photo-graph of Wilbur Sweatman's orchestra on stage at a New York theater in 1925, the pianist wearing a cummerbund, standing at the piano and waving with a sly smile, is Duke Ellington.

Shipton, at least, did give La Rocca an opportunity to contradict some of the attacks on what were termed their "stage antics": "We had to play up over the heads of the dancers, for if we played at them, or down at the floor, we wouldn't have been heard in a large ballroom. . . . We used the top hats to show who we were, that's all. As for the dancing I did, I was always supposed to be a good dancer, and when I started doing it on the stand and it brought rounds of applause, I kept doing it."[4]

This musician who upset so many people was a short, nervous Sicilian American, one of the many New Orleans musicians of Italian background who gave early jazz its heightened sense of musical drama. The new arrivals made their way to New Orleans in the wave of immigration in the 1880s and 1890s that filled America's slums as they struggled for a footing in the new society. Dominick J. La Rocca was born in New Orleans on April 11, 1889. La Rocca's family, like that of another young Italian musician in the neighborhood, Leon Roppolo, was against his becoming a musician. Despite his own love of music, La Rocca's father, Giarolamo La Rocca, didn't consider it to be a suitable profession for any of his children and insisted that his son would become a doctor.

Giarolamo La Rocca emigrated from Sicily in 1876 and found work in New Orleans as a shoemaker. He was an enthusiastic amateur cornetist, and the family, with his son, would follow him to dances or out to Spanish Fort to listen to his playing. He was so adamant, however, about his son not becoming a musician that when Dominick managed to teach himself enough to play a simple melody and performed it for his father on his father's cornet, the elder La Rocca took an axe and smashed the instrument. He gave up music himself, despairing that he'd been a bad influence. When he found that his son had saved money from small jobs and bought another battered instrument that he was practicing on out of the house, his father seized his axe and destroyed this one as well.

His son, now in his early teens, recognized that his father was justified in his opposition to the uncertainties of a musician's life, since their work was so irregular, they were so poorly paid, and musicians were far down the scale of social achievement. Like virtually every other New Orleans musician, Dominick needed a trade to get by. He apprenticed as an electrician and then general contractor, and for a few years music was a sideline, though his experience as an electrician was to be useful to him later in New York. He organized his first band in 1908, when he was nineteen, and the clarinetist was a fifteen-year-old Larry Shields, who was to be associated with La Rocca for almost all of his musical career. Like virtually every other white musician in New Orleans, La Rocca played regularly with the Jack Laine orchestras. He wasn't considered as showy as Lawrence Veca or Frank Christian, two of Laine's stars, but even though he was self-taught he had developed a strong embrouchure and could play steadily for hours without tiring. Among the city's other "fakers" he was considered to be strong but limited in his musical ideas, and according to trombonist Eddie Edwards, he wasn't the first choice to go north with the band that was being organized by drummer Johnny Stein and Edwards early in 1916.

An agent named Harry James booked that band into Schiller's Café, at 318 E. 31st Street at South Calumet in Chicago. The café was in a seedy neighborhood, but it was still popular with dancers. According to one version of the story of when James first heard the band in New Orleans, he came into the 102 Ranch on Franklin Street, where a trio led by drummer Johnny Hountha, who went under the name Johnny Stein, was playing. The clarinetist was Alcide "Yellow" Nunez, and the pianist was Henry Ragas, one of the best of the young ragtimers who were introducing pianos into the bands. With the success the spring before of Brown's band in his mind, James wanted to hire them for an extended engagement, and he also insisted that they have the same instrumentation as Brown's group, which meant adding a cornet and trombone to the trio.

Nunez and Stein remembered that they immediately asked Edwards to join them as trombonist, and after some discussion the three of them decided to ask La Rocca. However, in the biography of La Rocca written by H. O. Brunn after years of friendship with La Rocca and other members of the band, the story is considerably different. Brunn also located the agent, Harry James, who in 1957 was living in New Orleans, and James still remembered his excitement at hearing the band for the first time. Brunn wove together the versions of the story from both men, La Rocca and James, for his own account of the first meeting.

> On December 13, 1915, one of Laine's ballyhoo bands was playing on the corner of Canal and Royal Streets advertising a coming prize fight between Eddie Coulon and the popular New Orleans featherweight Pete Herman, and receiving a total of $7.25 for their services. Standing in the crowd was a dapper young man named Harry James, a Chicago café owner who had come to New Orleans to witness the very same prize fight now being loudly heralded by Laine's band. James, who had been passing down Canal Street, had been attracted first by this unusually loud and unconventionally fast combination. La Rocca, pointing his cornet skyward and blowing to the point of apoplexy, ripped off polyphonic phrases of his own original melodies, as trombonist Leonce Mello, seated on the tailgate of the horse-drawn wagon, answered in powerful blatting tones that rattled the plate glass windows across the street. Over this pair rode the screaming clarinet of Alcide Nunez, and behind it the booming of Jack Laine's big parade drum.[5]

James described for Brunn how he stood for an hour listening to the band. When Laine took a break and climbed down from the wagon, James asked him if he would bring the band north to Chicago. Laine said he was too busy, but that James should talk to La Rocca, who told him to come and hear the band that night at the Haymarket Café. The Haymarket was a rundown restaurant on Iberville Street between Burgundy and North Rampart Streets. The dining room itself was a large, high-ceilinged space with a tile floor, filled with tables and chairs, and there was an annex for dancing. La Rocca's memory of the evening was that James heard the entire band there, led by drummer Johnny Stein, with himself and Mello.

In still another version of the story, in Tom Gracyk's *Popular Pioneer Recording Artists*, trombonist Edwards's memory of the events was that Stein's band was playing at the Pup Café at 1017 Iberville Street, and an actor named Gus Chandler who was passing through town told Stein that he should take the band to Chicago. This doesn't necessarily contradict La Rocca's memory of what happened, since the two encounters could have occurred at different times. The "Christian" who was first asked to join them on cornet was Emile, Frank's younger brother, since Frank already had too many jobs booked. Emile, however, decided to stay as trombonist with his brother's band. La Rocca was next on the list to be approached.

Although there is considerable divergence among the various stories, there is agreement that Mello was not considered as trombonist for the job despite his flamboyance and his local popularity. The impetuous Mello probably blew too loudly for the other two horns. La Rocca would have preferred to have Larry Shields with him as clarinetist, but Shields was touring with Tom Brown's band, so Nunez made the trip instead. According to Brunn, Edwards also had some initial misgivings about taking a job that would keep him away from New Orleans for such a long period, because he was also a semiprofessional baseball player and had a chance to move up to the Cotton States League as third baseman for the team in Hattiesburg, Mississippi. There is no way of knowing which of the stories is the closest to what actually happened when Harry James came down from Chicago to watch a boxing match, but Stein received a serious offer from James in February 1916 to open the Booster's Club, which James was managing, and Stein agreed to bring the band.

The addition of pianist Ragas was a sign of the new styles then evolving in New Orleans. Most of the dance halls and cabarets where the bands worked didn't have pianos, but there were jobs for solo pianists in the District and in some of the smaller clubs around it. Born in 1897, Ragas was only nineteen when he joined the band. His brother Herman played string bass with Laine's orchestra groups. Henry probably began working with drummer Johnny Stein about 1913, and in 1916 he was performing in the trio with Stein and Yellow Nunez at the 102 Ranch when Harry James approached them about the job at Schiller's Café. With the new members added to the group, they rehearsed for two weeks at Stein's house, and left for Chicago on March 1, 1916.

A few weeks later Jack Laine received a postcard from Yellow Nunez. The message on the card was proud and excited, which could account for some of the struggles with spelling and syntax. On the card was a photo of the five members of Stein's band posed on the bandstand in Chicago. "This is the band that clean up Chi. Ill. And run all the other boys back home. Jack, you no that, what the use of bringing it up again? And when we come back home this band will be Jack Laine's Band, that what all us boys say to each other. All saying that the old man was good to all us boys and they can't forget you. Well Jack, I heard that you are big and fat as ever and was good to hear that. From Kid Yellow. Best wishes to family."

It had still been cold when the band got off the train in Chicago, and they didn't have anything warm to wear—or anything to wear on the bandstand. James took them to a cheap clothing store and bought them long dusters, the ankle-length covering that early automobilists wore in this period when many automobiles were still without roofs or windscreens. James's memory of them in their outfits was that they looked like "five undertakers." Before they arrived, however, the Booster's Club had been closed by a police order, so James arranged for them to audition at Schiller's Café. For the opening on March 3 they were billed as Stein's Dixie Jass Band. They were photographed on the bandstand at Schiller's wearing their dusters as a band uniform, and all of them, except for the usually thoughtful Ragas, smiled broadly. It was one of these photos from Schiller's that Nunez sent back to Papa Jack.

Whoever tells the story, the band was a genuine success in their first nights—helped, perhaps, as Nunez had noticed, that they were the only New Orleans ragtime band in town. Tom Brown was back in New Orleans, taking a break from his long months on the road while he put a new band together, and though Bill Johnson's Creole Band often passed through Chicago on their perpetual tours, occasionally playing cabaret jobs, they apparently were not working in the Windy City during those first weeks. During these same months a classically trained New Orleans Creole violinist named Charles Elgar, who had moved to Chicago in 1913, brought up an orchestra led by trombonist George Filhe to play at the Fountain Inn at 63rd and Halsted sometime in 1915 and 1916. There is a possibility that Elgar also played with another New Orleans orchestra at Mike Fritzel's Arsonia Café, at Madison Street, where Joe Frisco had drawn large crowds with Tom Brown's band. The orchestra was possibly led by cornetist Manuel Perez, and included clarinetist Lorenzo Tio Jr., trombonist Ed Atkins, who had dropped out of the vaudeville tour with the Creole Band, and drummer Louis Cottrell Sr. If they were playing in Chicago, however, they were among the elite of New Orleans legitimate Creole musicians, and the new ragtime was not part of their repertoire. For the moment, Stein's band had the young Chicago dancers to themselves.

Although Tom Brown's band had been advertised as a "jass band" in the Chicago press as early as May 1915, and Stein's band opened less than a year later already labeled as a jass group, William Howland Kenney, in his book *Chicago Jazz*, noted that the word wasn't used in the Chicago African American press until September, 30, 1916, almost a year and a half after the word came into common use as a description of the white New Orleans bands.[6] The most probable reason is that Chicago in 1915 still had a small black population, and the community's leaders placed a strong emphasis on cultural assimilation as the most hopeful response to the widespread discrimination in the city. Before the hotter New Orleans Uptown black musicians would make the trip north, Chicago itself would have to change.

The first months in Chicago often involved almost continual changes in personnel for the New Orleans bands, and Stein's group went through the familiar process.

With materials in the possession of Eddie Edwards's grandson, Gary Edwards, it is possible to follow what happened. With crowds filling Schiller's every night, the band became dissatisfied with the salary they'd agreed on, and when Stein insisted that he felt he had to honor the terms of the contract he'd signed, the other four walked away from the job, sending a formal letter of resignation to the management of Schiller's on May 25, 1916. Their letter read, "Gentlemen: We beg to hand you herewith our resignation, to take effect two weeks from this date (5/25/16)." Edwards was acting as the band's business manager, and his archive of letters and scrapbooks offer an invaluable glimpse into the complicated world of the small band's burgeoning career.

With so many New Orleans musicians in and out of the Chicago cabarets, it's difficult to follow all the changes. While Stein's former band members were putting their own group together, he was left with a contract and no musicians. He was able to get in touch with Larry Shields, who was still in New Orleans, and hired another New Orleans cornetist, Bernard "Doc" Berendson, and trombonist Jule Cassard, who, like Shields, had been a member of La Rocca's first band. A pianist named Ernie Erdman had also worked occasionally at Schiller's during their engagement, so Stein hired him to replace Ragas.

The four former band members who had left to form their new group had to replace only the drummer Stein, and they brought up eighteen-year-old Tony Sbarbaro, who had played with Edwards in an earlier ragtime ensemble. He arrived in Chicago in June. They had a meeting to decide on a name for the band and Edwards remembered that he suggested they call themselves a "Dixieland" band, since the other names they talked about, "New Orleans" or "Louisiana" were too "sectional."[7] The group was photographed on the bandstand of their first job at Del'Abe's Café, in the Hotel Normandie at Clark and Randolph, wearing comfortable, light-colored business suits, in one pose sitting sedately with their instruments, in another pretending to play. The band name they had given themselves was The Original Dixieland Jass Band.

Within a few weeks they were playing to large and enthusiastic crowds of dancers. The agent Harry James, their original supporter, had now acquired a half interest in the Casino Gardens, at the corner of Kinzie and North Clark, and he talked the band into leaving Del'Abe's. They opened at the Gardens on July 6, 1916, and soon settled in, drawing increasingly large crowds. However, there was continual friction between La Rocca and Nunez. Nunez had been a member of Jack Laine's busiest groups, had learned his skills by playing in the old unison melody style of band ragtime, and continued playing along with La Rocca's lead melody, his C-clarinet high-pitched and very loud. He also began to drift back into old New Orleans habits of showing up on the bandstand late and running up a heavy bar tab. After a final quarrel Nunez was fired, and in an exchange of clarinetists, he went back to Stein's band at Schiller's and Larry Shields joined the other four at the Casino Gardens. With this final switch, they became the band that within a few months would bring the New Orleans dance rhythms to New York City.

The Original Dixieland Jazz Band, spring 1916, the first personnel. From left: Tony Sbarbaro, Eddie Edwards, Nick La Rocca, Yellow Nunez, Henry Ragas.

In the last months that the Original Dixieland Jass Band worked in their Chicago cabaret they continued to extend and adapt their New Orleans repertoire, and also to polish their ensemble playing until they were—certainly on their early recordings—the most musical and rhythmically the tightest of any of the early groups calling themselves a jass band. In the years that followed, the compositions they created, either those by the band members or their adaptations of the common pool of New Orleans melodies, were to have as much of an impact on the new jazz idiom as their playing itself.

The story of early New Orleans jazz is often centered either in its Italian American or its African American musicians, but the city's ethnic blend was a broad spectrum, including someone like the trombonist Eddie Edwards, whose father was a recent arrival from England. Edwin Branford Edwards was born in New Orleans on May 22, 1891. He was two years younger than La Rocca, who was the oldest of the band. He had a more formal musical education than the others, and his first job was as a violinist in an early silent movie theater. He turned to the trombone in 1914 to join the parade bands, and was soon one of the many musicians that Laine picked up for his jobs.

He also decided that some other trade was necessary to give him a steady income, so like La Rocca he became an electrician, and they entered into a business partnership rewiring houses. Many people were moving in this period from gas to electricity, and the partners were steadily employed. Since neither of them had a place to practice, they began bringing their instruments with them, and they would sit out the heat of the afternoon in one of the empty houses improvising duets. These informal sessions may have led to the tightly woven instrumental lines they played in the later recordings. It was also Edwards who sent the telegram to teenage drummer Tony Sbarbaro, who had worked with him in another band a year or so earlier. Like La Rocca, Sbarbaro was Sicilian, but he didn't have the cornetist's fiery temperament.

Shields had already done a vaudeville tour with Joe Frisco as one of the Five Rubes when he was playing with Tom Brown's band, but work in the theaters was new for the other four. At the end of the summer, they added to their nightly performances at the Casino Garden a short vaudeville run as the accompaniment for a dancing troupe of three couples and two solo dancers assembled by a veteran named Johnny Fogarty for MacVicker's Theatre. Like the appearances of the Creole Band, who had been touring the vaudeville circuits the summer before, the appearances of the Original Dixieland Jass Band were immediately reviewed in the professional press. The most colorful notice appeared in *Vaudeville* on August 31: "Fogarty's Dance Revue and Jass Band hit it off like a whirlwind in next place. The Jass band was a hit from the start and offered the wildest kind of music ever heard outside of a Commanche massacre." The Chicago *Breeze* the next day also singled out the band. "Johnny Fogarty, who has been prominent as a dancer for many years, and has had big acts with society dancers for the last few years, has seen the popularity of 'The Jass Band' and turned it into vaudeville." Their act was designed to show the dancers stepping to the new rhythms, and the band also had a number of their own. The reviewer noted, "The band took big applause Monday night at the first show." *Billboard* reviewed the act on September 1 and again singled out the band, saying it was something new to vaudeville. The Revue "incidentally introduces vaudeville's newest craze, 'The Jass Band,' and the way the five of them tear away at their instruments brought down the house. Each member is an artist."[8]

It had been a long journey north on the L&N coaches for the New Orleans ragtime bands to open up Chicago to their "jass" style, but beyond Chicago there was still a further challenge. Edwards soon began to negotiate with booking agents who wanted to bring the band to New York. By this time New Orleans bands had been playing in Chicago to growing crowds for two years, and were beginning to appear in vaudeville either as musical novelty acts or accompanying dancers. The first of the New Orleans bands to leave, the Creole Band, was crisscrossing the country with their own syncopated ragtime, and the word "jass" or "jazz," which had been used to describe the new sounds as early as 1914, was appearing regularly in the music press, although there was no agreement about the spelling. So much about these first years of the musical exodus from New Orleans is still a confused blend of uncertain memories and scanty documentation, but thanks to Edwards's archive, much of the story of the band's odyssey can be pieced together.

They were first approached by a New York agent named Max Hart, whose son Lorenz Hart was to achieve considerable success as the lyricist for composer Richard Rodgers. In his chapter on the band in his book *Popular American Recording Pioneers*, Tim Gracyk quotes one of the letters Edward received from a booking agent named J. B. Grenblen, who expressed an interest in the band but didn't seem to know much about them.

THE ORIGINAL DIXIELAND JAZZ BAND, SPRING 1917, THE CLASSIC LINE-UP. FROM LEFT: SBARBARO, EDWARDS, LA ROCCA, LARRY SHIELDS, RAGAS.

"Mr. Jo Termini, violinist with the Bessie Clayton Sextette, gave me your name and address. I can use a Jass Band here in New York on a steady engagement, so will you please let me know just what instrumentation is included in your combination—whether the boys sing or not, and how much money you will expect on a café job, say four to five hours a night. I might add that there is no Jass Band here in New York, and it look [sic] as if there will be quite a big demand for it. Kindly hurry the information asked for in this letter, as I must give my party an immediate reply."[9]

Finally Max Hart arranged with Edwards for the band to appear at the 400 Club Room, a smaller ballroom in the newly opened Reisenweber's Restaurant building on Columbus Circle on Manhattan's Upper West Side in January 1917. Edwards negotiated a contract for several weeks at a salary for the band of close to three hundred dollars a week—a very respectable paycheck for an unknown group—plus transportation from Chicago.

The band's opening in New York was confused by delays in the decorations of the room where they were supposed to play, though it was advertised in the *New York Times* on January 15 that they would be opening in another dance venue in the Reisenweber building, the Paradise Ballroom. Since there was still no agreement on how the word was spelled, the copywriter did his best to come up with a compromise for the advertisement.

The First Sensational Amusement Novelty of 1917
"THE JASZ BAND"
Direct from its amazing success in Chicago,
where it has given modern dancing new life and a new thrill.

The Jasz Band is the latest craze that is sweeping
the nation like a musical thunderstorm.
"THE JASZ BAND"
comes exclusively to "Paradise," First of all New York
Ballrooms,
and will open for a run TONIGHT (Monday).
You've Just Got To Dance When You Hear It.

Telegrams to Edwards in Chicago, however, make it clear that the band was still waiting there as late as January 23. They finally reached New York in time to have themselves fitted for tuxedos before they opened at the 400 Room on Saturday, January 27. Still another setback faced them when they arrived in the evening: there was a problem with the new wiring that had been installed as part of the decorating, and hence no electricity. The room where they were supposed to play was dark. For any other band this would have been a problem, but La Rocca and Edwards had worked for years as electricians. Once they'd helped Sbarbaro set up the drums in the semi-darkness they went down to the basement and La Rocca found that during the renovations the wiring to the main fuse box had been done incorrectly. Once he'd reversed the wiring the lights in the room came back on.

The band's style was so different from anything that the audience expected that despite an opening announcement by the manager of the 400 Room that it would be an evening of dancing, the first piece they played—La Rocca remembered it was "Tiger Rag"—so stunned the people at the tables that they stayed where they were, unsure if this was a kind of novelty show or if they were expected to dance to the music. When they finished, the manager repeated that the music was for dancing, and the second number they played was at a slower tempo, and the first couples came on to the floor. Within an hour the dance floor was filled, and by the end of the first week the customers were lined out the door, waiting for a table to become empty.

The band literally took New York by storm. Usually advertisements, in themselves, don't really reflect the effect of a musical event, but for once the series of ads that Reisenweber's placed in the *New York Times* over the rest of the week told the story. In the ad for Tuesday, January 23, the featured entertainment, outlined in a large, separate box, was Gus Edwards's new revue, "Round the Circle." The top of the ad announced that there were special dinners for $1.25, or "an exceptional beefsteak dinner" for $1.50 at the 400 Room, and there would also be entertainment. A small line of type added,

Including THE JASS BAND First Eastern Appearance.

When the restaurant advertised again on Friday, January 26, the layout of the ad was the same, but the line about the band had been changed. They were now becoming more noticed, and there was some confusion over the word describing what they were playing.

Including THE JASZ BAND the Latest Western Rage.

The next day the ad was changed, and Gus Edwards's revue had been dropped to a small notice. The restaurant now announced:

Including the First Eastern Appearance of
THE ONLY ORIGINAL DIXIELAND
"JASS" BAND
Untuneful Harmonists in "Peppery" Melodies

On Sunday, January 27, the add was changed again to read

Including the first Eastern Appearance of the
FAMOUS DIXIELAND
"JASS" BAND

In five days in New York they had moved from being added to the entertainment in their first Eastern appearance to being the "Only Original" and then the "Famous" Original Dixieland Jass Band. A later newspaper advertisement repeated the description of them as "The First Sensational Musical Novelty of 1917!"

The success and the crowds, however didn't mean that everyone was won over to the new dance craze. A review by F. T. Vreeland in the New York *Sun*, written a few months later, managed at the same time to be both impressed by the band and appalled by the music they were performing, but one paragraph makes it clear that he was listening hard—he just wasn't able to make sense of what he was hearing. "It is all done in correct time—there is no fault to be found in the rhythm of it. Even though the cornetist is constantly throwing in flourishes of his own and every once in a while the trombonist gets excited about something and takes it out on the instrument, their tapping feet never miss [a] step. The notes may blat and collide with a jar, but their pulses blend perfectly. In fact, they frequently inject beats of their own between the main thumps just to make it harder for themselves, yet they're always on time to the dot when the moment arrives for the emphatic crash of notes."[10]

Within a few days, Edwards was negotiating with the two major American record companies, the Columbia Graphophone Company and the Victor Talking Machine Company, about a contract for a recording.

In some of the Dixieland clubs along Bourbon Street in New Orleans in December 1950, it wasn't a problem to go back to the dressing room and talk with the musicians while they smoked a cigarette and sipped a drink between sets. One night I sat out a set at the Famous Door to listen to clarinetist Harry Shields and

REISENWEBER'S RESTAURANT INTRODUCES THE JASS BAND'S "FIRST EASTERN APPEARANCE,"
TUESDAY, JANUARY 23, 1917, AND THE ADVERTISEMENT FOR THE FOLLOWING SUNDAY'S
DINNER SPECIAL, NOW FEATURING THE "FAMOUS ORIGINAL DIXIELAND 'JASS BAND.'"
COLLAGE BY THE AUTHOR.

trumpeter Sharkey Bonano, then I went to the dressing room, hoping shyly that I
might meet them. Inside the small room Harry was talking to a tall, white-haired
man I hadn't noticed before. Then Harry introduced me. It was his brother Larry,
the clarinetist with the Original Dixieland Jazz Band, whose playing on those early
recordings had been one of the things that helped me get through adolescence.

As I shook his hand, too overwhelmed to say a word, I had the feeling that I was meeting one of the most important people I'd ever encounter in my life.

For most of their new audiences, and certainly for most of the people who bought their first recordings, much of the band's excitement centered around Shields, and he left his stamp on the style of virtually every clarinet player who followed him in the New Orleans jazz idiom. Even Johnny Dodds, the great Uptown clarinetist who was to be one of the dominant figures of the next decade in Chicago, echoed phrases from Shields's ensemble figures in his early recordings. Shields was given breaks or solos with riffed backgrounds from the other horns on virtually every arrangement, and in one of the pieces, "Clarinet Marmalade," which was set up to feature him, he played fifty-one short breaks in the three minutes they had for the piece on the 78 r.p.m. disc. Although many clarinetists have tried to follow the ensemble style he developed for the band's arrangements, what is almost always lacking is his powerful tone and fierce attack. He is as close to being a legend as any of that first group of New Orleanians who came north at the same time.

Of all the apprentice musicians who came up through Jack Laine's bands, Shields was one of the most talented. When he was born, on September 13, 1893, New Orleans wasn't as strictly segregated as it became later, and he and his brothers—all of whom became musicians for at least some of their lives—grew up on First Street, not far from where the colorful black cornetist Buddy Bolden lived. His family was part of the Irish immigration of the post–Civil War era. Shields was playing professionally with Jack Laine's bands while still a teen-ager, but his brother had in his collection an even earlier photo of him when he was a school musician. In the stiffly posed photograph of the St. Francis De Sales Military Band in front of their school building, he is serious faced, his white uni-form cap set squarely on his head. There is no way of knowing what the band sounded like but, in their uniforms of white shirts and ties, dark suit jackets, and white pants tucked into canvas puttees, they were certainly one of New Orleans's best-dressed musical ensembles.

At the same time, Shields had already started playing the city's other style of music. He had taught himself to play the clarinet and later other musicians won-dered if he'd learned to finger it properly, since he got sounds out of it unlike anyone else's. The first band he played in, about 1908, when he was fifteen, was the first led by another self-taught instrumentalist, the nineteen-year-old cornet-ist Nick La Rocca. Over the next few years Shields was one of the clarinetists on Jack Laine's list of available musicians, and he had the kind of rough apprentice-ship that made it natural for him to play any kind of job that turned up. Although he wasn't with the first band that went to Chicago, Tom Brown's Band from Dixie, he had been part of the earlier switch of clarinetists, when Gussie Mueller left Brown's band and Shields left Bert Kelly's reading band to join Brown.

It was only a month after they opened at Reisenweber's that the band recorded their historic single for the Victor Talking Machine Company in New York City, and it's obvious that many of the musical changes that made their ensemble style so unique had already been shaped in the months they played together in Chicago. Some of their distinctive style of arrangement was probably developed in the opening months at Schiller's—with Yellow Nunez, who had always been considered good in idea sessions, adding his part to the changes. After their first success in New York, they rehearsed early in the afternoons through the spring months at Reisenweber's, continuing to develop their dance repertory. This group of arrangements, which they went on to record over the next year, clarified the musical outlines and emphasized the direction of the steadily evolving style.

The release of the first single by the Original Dixieland Jass Band in March 1917 marked the beginning of a legacy of recordings that contain most of the elements of the music that was to be given the name of New Orleans jazz. Their long sessions in the recording laboratories—as well as recordings by the other New Orleans band who quickly followed them—constituted a musical document that still somehow manages to arouse controversy, even if at the time, no one thought of doing anything with the music they listened to on the noisy, primitively recorded discs except dance to it.

9

Some Record!

. . . only with the greatest effort were we able to make the Original Dixieland Jass Band stand still long enough to make a record. That's the difficulty with a Jass band. You never know what it's going to do next, but you can always tell what those who hear it are going to do—they're going to "shake a leg."

FROM THE *VICTOR RECORD REVIEW* OF MARCH 7, 1917, ANNOUNCING THE FIRST RECORDING BY THE ORIGINAL DIXIELAND JASS BAND

Only two days after their opening at Reisenweber's on Saturday night, January 27, 1917, the first record company was already showing an interest in the Original Dixieland Jass Band and their new dance music. A letter dated January 29, delivered to "Jass Band, c/o Reisenweber's Restaurant, 58th Street and Columbus Circle, New York City,"[1] said that the band should call on an executive of the Columbia Graphophone Company ". . . to discuss a matter which may prove of mutual benefit and interest." The letter was signed by A. E. Donovan, the manager of Columbia's record departments at 59th Street and Broadway, a short distance from Reisenweber's. Edward's noted on the letter was "Forbish—Wednesday afternoon, 2:00 P.M." "Forbish" was Walter Forbush, a recording manager for Columbia.

Edwards and La Rocca both remembered the meeting at Columbia's offices on January 31, but what actually happened there still is unclear. The only thing that is certain is that they didn't do any recording. Edwards remembered that while they were playing, carpenters were noisily building some shelves in the studio. What seems to have happened is that the band took their instruments to the Columbia offices and played an audition; from the vague address of the letter, the Columbia executives may not even have been at the restaurant for the opening. Why the band wasn't offered a contract to return and do a single for Columbia is unclear, but Columbia's much larger rival, the Victor Talking Machine Company, the most successful and ambitious record company in the United States, had contacted the band almost as quickly. A contract was signed through their agent Max Hart, who had brought them from Chicago and taken over some of band's business affairs, and on February 26, only a month after their New York opening, they recorded two selections at Victor's recording laboratory. The single was announced on March 3, only a week after the recording.

The New Orleans musicians played louder than the usual studio players, and Charles Souey, Victor's recording engineer, had difficulty with echoes bouncing off the room's walls and ceiling and back into the large acoustical horns that carried the sound to the cutting needle on the wax master. La Rocca's memories of their first session were still vivid when H. O. Brunn talked with him forty years later. "First we made a test record, and then they played it back for us. This is when they started shifting us around in different positions. After the first test record, four men were rushed in with ladders and started stringing wires near the ceiling. I asked them what all these wires were for, and one of the men told me it was to sop up the overtone that was coming back into the horn. The recording engineer at Victor had the patience of a saint. He played back our music until it sounded right."[2]

The final balance placed La Rocca about twenty feet from the horn, and Sbarbaro's drums even further, five feet behind La Rocca. Pianos recorded poorly under the best of circumstances, so Ragas was the closest to the recording horn—only a few feet away. Souey also made some of his decisions based on the musical arrangements of the two pieces they were recording. He brought Ragas forward enough so that his playing is audible in the ensemble, and at the other end of the sound spectrum he allowed Sbarbaro to thump on his large bass drum. The sound emphasized the tightness of their tonal balance, and although La Rocca's lead was less prominent than he was on the bandstand, the interplay between his cornet and Edwards's trombone made it clear that the long afternoons they spent playing duets on their house wiring jobs had given them an instinctive response to each other's musical ideas. La Rocca also thought that some of the balance problems were caused by everyone's nervousness. They couldn't count off the rhythm because it would be heard on the master disc, which meant they had to wait until the studio's red light went on, count to two, and begin playing—so when the piece did start, they played louder than they had in the repeated tests.

The patient care Souey spent on the balance is most evident in the "animal" sounds of "Livery Stable Blues." Shields imitates a rooster, La Rocca follows with a horse's whinny, and Edwards ends with a desolate cow's moo. The story was that La Rocca imitated a horse's whinny one night when they were clowning on the stand in Chicago and it went over with the crowd, so they added it to one of the compositions he'd brought with him from New Orleans. The three instruments have different tone levels, but with Souey's placement the comic effects flow with a consistency of sound which helped make that the selling point that brought the record into a million American homes. On the other side of the single, the uptempo "Dixie Jass Band One Step," Shields had a series of slashing breaks, so it was obvious that his playing would have to be emphasized. Since Shields was considered the band's "star," many of the arrangements featured his playing, so the balance on many of the recordings they did for Victor was weighted toward the clarinet. Perhaps most important about the work Souey did is that he caught the band's raw energy and their primal strut. Overnight they became one of the most imitated ensembles in the United States.

But how did the two new "jass band" selections sound to Victor Records customers? Like many of those early listeners who heard the record for the first time, I had no idea what to expect. In the mid-1940s, as a teenager in Sacramento, California, I'd gotten interested enough in jazz to read the three or four books about it in the City Library. I tried to get to the Salvation Army Thrift Shop in the downtown "Skid Row" at least once a week to go through their piles of worn 78 r.p.m. singles in a search for some of the music the books so poignantly described. In those years there were no reissues to be found in local record stores, and no jazz that I knew of on our local radio. Something like a 1917 jass record was as far outside the parameters of my California teenage experience as life on the French Riviera. After two or three months without finding any of the music I was reading about, one afternoon, with grubby fingers and a stiff back, I found myself holding a much-worn copy of Victor 18255, that first single by the ODJB. It was the only catalog number of a single that I knew by heart, and I still remember it sixty years later.

When I took the record home, scrubbed off some of the dust in the bathroom sink, and played it on the little phonograph in my bedroom, I had the same stunned response that most of the record's first listeners must have had. It was the sheer energy of it that I heard first—the rushing tempo of the one-step and the insouciant comedy of the blues. I had already started to play clarinet in what I thought was a jazz style, and Shields's breaks and the flying interweave of his obbligato phrases with the insistent instrumental lead burned their way into my consciousness. Even many years later, when I hear the record again—usually now in reissue collections with much cleaner sound than my worn 78—I still experience some of the same emotions.

At the time that I first listened to the record, and as late as the 1970s, it was still generally considered that the Victor release was the first jazz record, and that the history of jazz, and what we knew of the historical development of the music, began there. But the picture has become much less clear since that time, and it has become a sensitive issue that something termed the "first" jazz recording was done by white musicians. It is certainly the first release on record of anything that was called "jass," but the term had already been used to describe the music that Tom Brown's band brought to Chicago in the spring of 1915. Piano rolls using the word "jazz" to describe the style of music had already been advertised in New Orleans newspapers before the Victor release. The Victor executives themselves were uncertain about the spelling. At least five variants were in circulation: Jad, Jass, Jas, Jasz, and Jazz. They finally decided that, since the band's business card read "jass," they would use that spelling, but within a few months the modern spelling had become standard and they went with the change.

Recordings by a number of earlier groups were certainly on the cusp of a nascent jazz style, including Victor releases by the ragtime orchestra that James Reese Europe led to accompany the dancing of Irene and Vernon Castle in 1914 and 1915, which had the lead melody played by an enthusiastic duet of mandolinists. A few weeks before the Victor session by the ODJB, the African American clarinetist Wilbur Sweatman, who had been successfully touring vaudeville for some years as a ragtime clarinet soloist, recorded a quartet version of his own "Down Home Rag" with three white studio musicians, including saxophonist Nathan Glantz, for a little-known company that released their short instrumentals as 7-inch singles (the usual format for singles was either 10- or 12-inch) on the Little Wonder label. The performance had a tense swing, and Sweatman edged close to what some listeners consider a jazz feeling, though for the audience at the time the performance would have inevitably been classified as a "novelty ragtime." The group's playing offered the familiar sound of syncopated instrumental rhythms, and novelty ragtime was a vaudeville staple.

For many modern listeners the music of the ODJB also comes too close to what they consider novelty ragtime. But with their recordings it is possible to trace some strands of the New Orleans band idiom that have come down to our modern era. The recordings are a decisive historical development that enables us to move beyond the romanticizing about how jazz might have sounded earlier. We can imagine rhythms and melodies before these first recorded examples, but all we have with any certainty is these first recordings. In his discerning study *Early Jazz*, composer and musicologist Gunther Schuller was ambivalent about the band's musical intentions and found the rhythms often "frantic." Writer William Kenney, in *Chicago Jazz*, labeled all of the sounds of the early white musicians as "nut jazz"—at least conceding that it was jazz, though a style he also dismissed. The difficulty for writers who chose to ignore the white musicians was that their early recordings didn't fit with any preconceptions of what a music based on African American church music or field song would sound like. These writers ignored the European elements of early jazz: the melodic, harmonic, and structural forms of marches, ragtime, dance pieces, and minstrel songs that played as decisive a role in the development of the new musical style. A number of African American ensembles also recorded syncopated dance music before the first ODJB sessions, or at roughly the same time—among them New York orchestras, W. C. Handy's orchestra from Memphis, and Wilbur Sweatman's orchestras combining musicians from several cities—and their music was generally in a similarly strenuous ragtime style with considerable emphasis on comedy and novelty effects. One of the veteran New Orleans African American musicians included in the book *Bourbon Street Black*, by Jack V. Beurkle and Danny Barker, discussed the relationship between the city's black and white jazz musicians in these early years. (The writers did not identify the speaker in the text or the notes.)

> *Some of the bands—they call 'em Dixieland. They play little pieces, and some of 'em have been listening to the Negro musicians—and they put it together. And it was just a little bit more organized. La Rocca. He went up there [to the North]. He wasn't no great musician. He just played a little straight horn, and I don't think he could read much. But, some of the guys, like Edwards, I think he was a fair musician. Larry Shields, he couldn't read much, but he had a nice tone. Ragas was one of them. They were a little bit organized. They got their harmonizin' voices—they got together. And, they're the ones who put this stuff together, but it's not the way we play it. We just play.*[3]

Regardless of how the first recordings sound to us today, other musicians in 1917, as well as their audiences, heard the first singles as something new and decidedly different, and within a few weeks other groups, white and black, were hurried into recording laboratories by competing companies to catch on to the new craze. I asked a number of older New Orleans musicians what they thought of the music when they heard the first singles, and they agreed that it was something like what they'd all been playing, but considerably more organized and rehearsed, and they had to learn the new repertory from the recordings, since even the occasional strains they recognized had been changed and reshaped by the band's arrangements. Joe Oliver paid the ODJB the ultimate compliment of firing one of the musicians in his band so that he could also present his band as a quintet. All of the recordings were sold as dance music. The labels on the record indicated that all of the performances were dance pieces, with the name of the dance step often included on the label. Even the often-criticized blistering tempo of their one-step was simply the "peppy rhythm" as couples swept out over the Reisenweber dance floor in an attempt to match the effortless glide of the popular dancers Vernon and Irene Castle.

What was significant about the Original Dixieland Jazz Band's recordings was that they presented a style of syncopated music different enough for other musicians to be forced to try to learn it as a distinct genre. The New Orleans bands shifted the melodic lead from the violins or flutes of earlier syncopated orchestras to the cornet or trumpet, which in New Orleans was played with a distinctly Italianate brilliance and articulation. Accompanying this assertive melodic lead was a looser rhythm, an accent that fell a little off the beat, and the groups slowly created a contrapuntal ensemble arrangement that had its source in published arrangements for small orchestra ensembles that were popular everywhere.

The early recordings certainly included ragtime pieces and ragtime melodies, but even these had been rephrased to allow more freedom for the lead instrument.

The basic pulse was cleanly articulated, and the rhythms were often in a definite four-beat meter, unlike faster ragtime, which was played in two-beat march time. At the same time, the New Orleans lead players allowed themselves continual shifts in the entering notes of a phrase, to give a decisive propulsion to the rhythm. The style had a strong thrust, and for dancers at the time the music had an irresistible strut. For the next two or three years the local *Times-Picayune* editors chose to attack the "cacophony" of the new recordings, but when the first release came on sale in March 1917, an advertisement by one of their important business customers, the Maison Blanche department store on Canal Street, was prominently featured, and the story of the advertisement more accurately reflected the local attitude toward the band. Under a photograph of the ODJB as they performed, the text read:

> *Here is positively the greatest dance record ever issued. Made by New Orleans musicians for New Orleans people.*
>
> *We say "the greatest dance record ever issued" without reserve, remembering the hundreds that have been issued previously; and you'll quite agree with us when you hear it. Some folks claim phonograph music is not suitable for dancing and to these, especially, we direct this.*
>
> *The record was made by a half dozen [sic] New Orleans musicians, formerly playing in local restaurants and cabarets, who journeyed to the Victor laboratory for the purpose.*
>
> *It has all the "swing" and "punch" and "pep" and "spirit" that is so characteristic of the bands whose names are a by-word at New Orleans dances. It is more proof that New Orleans sets the pace for "wonderful" dance music—a fact that is recognized and commented upon the country over.*
>
> *Come early for yours. Our supply is ample but not inexhaustive.*

Other advertisements in the paper placed by the local music stores read simply, "Some Record!"

For La Rocca and the rest of the band, however, the success of their first recording presented other and more complicated problems. In an early example of the difficulties inherent in the copyright practices of the new recording industry, they found themselves in legal jeopardy with both of the compositions on their single, and it took months for the legal issues to be settled. They had been completely new to the mechanics of the music business only a few months before, but as La Rocca told Brunn, "We sure learned fast."

The most serious problem was with the hit side of the record, "Livery Stable Blues." As the confused story of its origins makes clear, the original title had been "Barnyard Blues," which would explain the rooster, horse, and cow imitations of the three horns. This, apparently, was considered too coarse for the Victor audiences, so the title was changed just as the single was about to be released. In their haste, no one noticed that the composition had been copyrighted under its

NEW ORLEANS MUSIC STORES ADVERTISE THE FIRST RELEASE OF A RECORDING BY THE ORIGINAL DIXIELAND JASS BAND. "SOME RECORD!" MARCH 1917. COLLAGE BY THE AUTHOR.

original title, and the new title "Livery Stable Blues" was unprotected. Yellow Nunez, who had been with the band when the arrangement was created and certainly contributed to the final version, was working with Bert Kelly's band in Chicago and tried to buy a published arrangement of the piece to play with the new band. He was told that the piece hadn't been published, and when he inquired further he learned that it hadn't yet been copyrighted.

Still carrying on his feud with La Rocca, Nunez immediately copyrighted the hit song as a co-composer with Ray Lopez, who had played it with Tom Brown's band. When the Nunez/Lopez version was published, La Rocca and the others in the ODJB, through their publisher, brought suit against Nunez's publisher, asserting their prior claim. The legal battle, with attendant press coverage and virtually illiterate testimony by Nunez, wasn't resolved until the fall, when Chicago judge George A. Carpenter decided that the whole situation was so tangled it would never be possible to tell who had written the song. His convoluted decision is an unstudied reflection of the popular attitude toward jazz by most conservative Americans. He concluded the decision:

> *There is a dispute between the plaintiff and the defendant, two publishers, each claiming a right to the monopoly of this song, this musical production.*
>
> *No claim is made by either side for the barnyard calls that are interpolated in the music, no claim is made for the harmony. The only claim appears to be for the melody.*
>
> *Now, as a matter of fact, the only value of this so-called musical production apparently lies in the interpolated animal and bird calls—that is perfectly apparent from the evidence given by all the witnesses, and in a great many unimportant features the Court has great difficulty in believing what some witnesses on both sides of this case have told the Court under oath, but that does not go to the real merit of this controversy.*
>
> *. . . I venture to say that no living human being could listen to that result on the phonograph and discover anything musical on it, although there is a wonderful rhythm, something which will carry you along especially if you are young and a dancer. They are very interesting imitations, but from a musical stand-point it is even outclassed by our modern French dissonance.*
>
> *And the finding of the Court will be that neither the plaintiff nor the defendant is entitled to a copyright, and the bill and the answer will both be dismissed for want of equity.*[4]

Unlike "Livery Stable Blues, the problem with "Dixie Jass Band One-Step" was reasonably uncomplicated. The final settlement lacked the flair of Judge Carpenter's peroration. The third strain of the arrangement, the trio of the piece, used a melody similar enough to a 1909 composition by Joe Jordan titled "That Teasin' Rag" to bring on a quick claim of copyright infringement. No one had bothered to arrange any kind of rights for the use of the melody they'd quoted in their one-step, and it was unmistakably close to Joe Jordan's hit. In their inexperience, the ODJB's musicians might have felt that since they didn't put the name of the piece on the record, there wouldn't be a problem. It was necessary, however, to negotiate a contract with Jordan, and Victor Records immediately accepted a settlement. They could continue to sell the record, but the title on the newly printed labels would read "Introducing That Teasin' Rag," and La Rocca and the others would give up two-thirds of the copyright royalties.

While Victor was dealing with the problems of the first record, Columbia Records offered the band a contract in May, and they recorded a second single on May 31. This time they recorded a piece that was in their repertoire but not from New Orleans: the Shelton Brooks staple "Darktown Strutters Ball."

Probably because the record company had a tie-in with the publisher, for the other side they recorded a newly published song, "(Way Back Home In) Indiana." They remembered listening to it in the company office, played over and over for them by the company's demonstration pianist, then humming it to themselves on the way to the studio so they wouldn't forget it. It is also likely that, because Edwards was a skilled reader, they took a copy of the score with the lead and the harmonies. The sound quality was even less satisfactory than the Victor engineers were able to achieve, and it was the weakest of their early recordings.

Two and a half months later, while the lawsuit still was pending on "Livery Stable Blues," on August 17 they made their first recordings for even less experienced recording engineers—the employees of the Aeolian/Vocalion company, which had been active in the piano roll market. Aeolian's experience was largely with classical music, and their solution to the problem of the band's unique sound was to record them the way they would a classical group: with their natural balance, and with the musicians placed a little further away from the recording horns so there was some ambient sound in the empty concert hall where they did their sessions. In these recordings the sound of the band came closer to their bandstand balance. With Shields balanced as part of the ensemble, instead of featured as in the Victor recordings, it's possible to hear them as they might have sounded from the back of a large restaurant with the dance floor filled with noisy couples. La Rocca's cornet was clearly the center of the ensemble, with Shields as a strong counterfoil, while Edwards extended the harmonies with trombone lines that move effortlessly from staccato harmony accenting the rhythm to looser "smeared" phrases that add color to the arrangements. The sound of the cornet in the new version of "Barnyard Blues" is a revelation—supple and relaxed, with the kind of assured, centered tone that had always been characteristic of the Italian brass style. La Rocca's playing usually has been judged solely on the basis of the Victor recordings, on which he was so far from the recording horn that the subtleties of his phrasing were indistinguishable. Although the piano and drums are almost inaudible in the Aeolian version of "Barnyard Blues," La Rocca's cornet lead clearly represented the essence of the new band style. Anyone interested in what La Rocca might have sounded like in 1917 should listen to his rhythmic syncopation and the vocalization of the melodic line, with their subtle glissandi and variety of attack. The band also rerecorded the other piece that had caused a legal problem; "Dixie Jass Band" was redone as "Reisenweber Rag," with Jordan's melody dropped and a different melody that La Rocca improvised in its place.

For a session on September 3, 1917, the band recorded another uptempo specialty for Aeolian, "At The Jazz Band Ball," in which some choruses were deliberately played at half volume, as bands had done in New Orleans dances to give a little variety to their arrangements. It was a trick they'd picked up from the brass band compositions they all played. On one of the medium-tempo dance pieces recorded for Aeolian, "Look At 'Em Doing It," Edwards suddenly broke away from his rehearsed part for the final measures and improvised a swinging counter-melody. It was one of the moments the New York reviewer must have been describing when he wrote, ". . . every once in a while the trombonist gets excited about something and takes it out on his instrument."

The Aeolian Company, however, was completely inexperienced in the areas of sales and distribution, and made no announcement that they had records to sell for several months. La Rocca and the others had only a six-month contract with the company, and since Aeolian didn't renew it and the records hadn't reached any substantial market, the band felt free to return to Victor in March 1918. In the next months they redid the pieces that they had done the summer before for Aeolian and added new compositions. In sessions stretching over March, June, and July they recorded the classic repertory that was to define what came to be known as the early "Dixieland" style, which took its name from them. On March 18 they redid "At the Jazz Band Ball" and a new arrangement, "Ostrich Walk." On March 25 they recorded "Skeleton Jangle" and "Tiger Rag." On June 25 they continued with "Bluin' The Blues," "Fidgety Feet," and "Sensation Rag," and on July 17 they finished their New Orleans repertoire, adding "Mournin' Blues," "Clarinet Marmalade," and "Lazy Daddy." With Victor's better distribution and the earlier success of their first release, these pieces were to become basic source material for the New Orleans small-group style inspired by the ODJB.

These recordings have a wide variety of tempos and moods. "Bluin' The Blues," credited to the pianist Henry Ragas, was a brilliant small-band blues arrange-ment that featured Ragas in a series of breaks as well as solo passages played against repeated figures in the horns. La Rocca's playing was in its loosest blues mode, and during one of the instrumental passages Ragas suddenly shifted into repeated triplets against the basic pulse, one of the early tricks of the piano blues style as it cropped up in sheet music and piano rolls. The arrangement was picked up by several groups for cover versions; Wilbur Sweatman's newest band, includ-ing Harlem veterans of Jim Europe's Castle House orchestra, had their version on the market in December 1918, only a few months after the original recording.

In several of the arrangements Shields continued to be featured; he also played what could be considered the first recorded solo chorus in "Tiger Rag." As the band conceived their arrangement, the melody of the strain was a repeated riff figure played by La Rocca and Edwards, while Shields played a skillfully phrased obbligato over their rhythm. This little rhythmic riff was to become a standard effect in bands following their style. Clarinetists certainly heard Shields's chorus as a solo, however, and even today it usually is imitated as a part of the arrangement.

Other arrangements featured different members of the band, and for each of their selections their instrument was moved closer to the recording horn. La Rocca had the fiery breaks on "Fidgety Feet," and his cornet dominated the ensem-ble. Edwards was featured on "Skeleton Jangle," and his melody—along with Sbarbaro's percussion effects—invariably is included in later versions. Shields and

Edwards were both featured on "Lazy Daddy," which was named for Edwards, who had married a girl he'd met who was part of the show at Reisenweber's, and had become the band's first father. He never managed to make their afternoon rehearsals on time and he'd passed the work of keeping track of the band's financial affairs to La Rocca, so he became "Lazy Daddy."

Another complicated aspect of the band's success—one that cast a shadow over later discussions of La Rocca and the band—was the situation with the copyrights of their New Orleans material. At least two of their early successes, "Livery Stable Blues" and "Tiger Rag," were already known in New Orleans under a variety of names. The band led by Jack Carey may have been one of the first to adapt the European quadrille melody as the first strain of "Tiger Rag." Other musicians who were also playing at that time must have heard material that became part of some of the other pieces. In his 1924 half-tempo recording of what the ODJB had titled "Tiger Rag," New Orleans bandleader Johnny DeDroit gave his arrangement one of its original titles, "Number Two," adding the word "Blues." With these changes he felt free to copyright the arrangement as his own composition.

It seems certain that all of the arrangements of the eight compositions the band copyrighted in this series of recordings for Victor were the result of long afternoon rehearsals in the empty ballroom at Reisenweber's, but there was an agreement among them that certain compositions were more closely related to one band member than the others. It was to be expected that the composer credit for the brilliant piano specialty "Bluin' the Blues" was assigned to the pianist, Ragas; and Shields's name, with Ragas, is on "Clarinet Marmalade." For at least some of the pieces they resorted to drawing names from a hat at one of their rehearsals to share out the copyright credits. In a letter to Shields in 1952 Edwards wrote, "If memory serves, you will recall that the names of the numbers were decided at a rehearsal in the 400 Club Room, Reisenweber's, by drawing out of a hat."[5] When neither Edwards's or Sbarbaro's names were drawn, Edwards's name was put on "Sensation Rag" and Sbarbaro was assigned "Mournin' Blues."

There was resentment among the other band members when they found that, although the royalties for the piece were shared, La Rocca's name appeared alone on "Tiger Rag." In the band's archive is correspondence between people representing them and the lawyers concerned, making it clear that all of the band members were to be included, but through a series of mistakes only La Rocca's name was on the final copyright. Also, when their agent Max Hart filed the copyright papers for "Dixie Jass Band One-Step" he assigned the royalties to himself. Despite continual, increasingly rancorous protests from La Rocca, the rights to the royalties weren't relinquished until Hart's death in the late 1920s.

Some writers have insisted that the band "stole" this first group of compositions, which were considered to be the common property of all of the New Orleans's ragtime musicians. Many of the men who worked with Jack Laine's Reliance orchestras surely would agree. The usual implication is that the band "stole" from the city's black musicians; but the two groups of musicians, white and black, very seldom had more than superficial encounters, and their repertoires and ways of playing came out of separate cultural backgrounds. What Laine's musicians complained about angrily was that La Rocca had stolen from *them*. All the bands had been playing some version of "Tiger Rag" under its various names, and there was consternation when it turned up copyrighted by a cornet player who hadn't even been part of their regular circle.

Certainly La Rocca and the rest of the band showed a quick opportunism over some of the arrangements in their repertoire. In every instance when a new reservoir of American vernacular music material has been tapped—from classic ragtime, to the country blues, to the Anglo-American folk song heritage—there has been considerable opportunism on the part of musicians, agents, and music publishers. In his recordings of Appalachian folk song that the talent scout for Victor Records, Ralph Peer, initiated in his sessions with the Carter Family in 1927, there was no hesitation about copyrighting everything that was recorded as an original composition, which was then published by Peer's new music company. Even large segments of the Library of Congress field recordings were registered by one of the collectors, Alan Lomax, as a "co-composer" of the material that was gathered.

With the Original Dixieland Jass Band and their first recordings, however, the situation is considerably more complicated. The arrangements of the material have a distinctive character that wouldn't have been the case if they'd simply taken other musicians' material. It was more than a question of the melodies themselves. The band members were obviously a catalyst in the creative process. The consistency of the formal structuring of the pieces as they performed them, the uniformity of their balances between ensemble, breaks, and proto-solos make it clear that if some commonly used strains or melodies had been incorporated into the new compositions, they had been assimilated and adapted in the group's long rehearsals. Even if there was a familiar source for something in one of their arrangements, they had changed the original source so significantly that the compositions could have been copyrighted as "traditional/arranged," a valid copyright category. Of their music, however, only "Livery Stable Blues"—or "Barnyard Blues," as they had originally titled it—and "Tiger Rag" have been consistently claimed as material shared by the city's ragtime musicians, white and black; and there was general agreement that, because the source for the first melody of "Tiger Rag" was an "old European quadrille," no one could claim the piece as an original composition. I never heard anyone claim some prior source for less commercially valuable compositions like "Ostrich Walk," "Bluin' the Blues," or "Clarinet Marmalade," and La Rocca named a local dance tune he'd heard played by Ray Lopez as the source for the first strain of "Livery Stable Blues."

Whatever he thought of the court decision that denied his claims on "Barnyard Blues," Yellow Nunez soon was busy enough himself as a recording artist to salve whatever bruises he'd suffered in the legal battle. No band with an entirely New Orleans personnel was to record again for several years, but two bands that included musicians who had worked as members of Jack Laine's Reliance Orchestra recorded within months of each other after the first success of the ODJB's Victor Records releases. Frank Christian, the highly regarded trumpet player who had been one of the original choices to travel to Chicago with the earliest bands, was a member of the second band to record, the Original New Orleans Jazz Band. Nunez was the musical showpiece of the third band, The Louisiana Five, though the drummer Anton Lada was the manager and leader. Christian's band is particularly interesting, since it features a trumpet player who was generally considered one of the best in the city, with much more of a reputation than La Rocca. The group only recorded seven sides, and unfortunately for modern listeners, one of them was a minor hit—their version of "Jada"—so four of the seven sides, for different companies, repeat the "Jada" arrangement.

With the kind of casual shuffling of members that was part of the New Orleans band scene, Christian had left New Orleans with a band led by Lada that was called The Five Southern Jazzers and featured Lada's virtuosity on the marimba. A few months after they came north, a neophyte New York ragtime pianist and entertainer named Jimmy Durante was asked to bring a jazz group into the Alamo Café, a restaurant in Manhattan. He soon was in touch with drummer Johnny Stein, who had brought La Rocca, Ragas, Edwards, and Nunez to Chicago the year before. The band that Stein assembled for Durante included Christian, Frank L'Hotak on trombone, Durante as pianist, and Stein as drummer. The clarinetist was the regular member of Jack Laine's Reliance Orchestra, the Creole Achille Baquet. His playing on their recordings is of considerable documentary value for the understanding of the development of early jazz, since he plays in a style similar to that of Shields, though he clearly comes from a slightly earlier generation and his style is less fully developed.

The band took a series of publicity photos when they arrived in New York, and in one of them the photographer posed the three horns pretending to play in strained athletic poses as they turn to look at drummer Stein. Even a smiling Durante has swiveled on the piano bench to look over at him. Stein is sitting at his drums with a smugly satisfied expression and a very large cigar in his mouth, wearing a derby hat pushed down on his forehead. He was doing his impersonation of their friend and booster, Joe Frisco! Stein, however, was with the band only long enough for their publicity photos. By the time they recorded in November 1918 he'd been replaced by Arnold Loyocano, who had come north with the band Tom Brown brought to Chicago in 1915. For the new band he was playing the drums instead of the bass. Christian's band, under the name The Original New Orleans Jazz Band, did their first recording for the fledgling Okeh label, which used inadequate equipment and even poorer materials for their pressings. Despite the disappointing sound quality, the first single was a success: their version of "Jada," with a second strain of "You'll Find Old Dixieland in France," and W. C. Handy's popular rag "Ole Miss" on the reverse.

ORIGINAL NEW ORLEANS JAZZ BAND

THE ORIGINAL NEW ORLEANS JAZZ BAND, 1918. FROM LEFT: JOHNNY STEIN (IMPERSONATING JOE FRISCO), ACHILLE BAQUET, FRANK CHRISTIAN, FRANK L'HOTAK, JIMMY DURANTE. SAMUEL CHARTERS COLLECTION.

Unfortunately, to capitalize on their initial success, the next companies to record them repeated their "Ja Da" arrangement.

There has been some question as to whether the lead on the recordings was played by Christian or Jack Laine's son Alfred "Pansy" Laine, who also came north and jobbed around with the other New Orleans musicians. However, in a letter sent by the members of the band to the *New York Dramatic Mirror* in December 1918 as their contribution to the first debate about the origins of New Orleans jazz at this time, Christian was one of the band members who signed it, which means he was with the band at the time of the first recording. Also, before the 1920s Laine, who looks considerably like Christian in early photos, was always shown with a cornet, and it is unmistakably a trumpet on the recording.

The records are mostly known to collectors for the first appearance by Durante, who later became famous as a comedian. Despite his jokes about his band days, he played a solid, full band accompaniment. As with the Dixieland Band, the lead was centered in Christian's horn, with an obbligato-styled clarinet part and a trombone line that clearly came from a background of Tom Brown's and Eddie Edwards's playing. There was a difference in the band's attack, however, because Christian was one of the few musicians to play the brighter-toned trumpet instead of the cornet. His lead was cleanly stated, rhythmically varied, and alive; it had the swaggering confidence of years of playing in the city's dance halls and for Sunday dances at Quirella's Restaurant at Milneburg, where his band had been photographed a few years before. He took a ringing break on "You'll Find Old Dixieland in France" that makes it clear why veteran New Orleans musicians wondered why he wasn't the first lead player to go north. Christian's playing was more assertive than La Rocca's, and he had a touch of flamboyance that La Rocca kept under wraps. Christian's lead on "Ole Miss"—what can be heard of it through the poor quality of the surviving copies of the 78 single—was in the classic New Orleans lyric ensemble style.

Achille Baquet's clarinet playing on the recordings hints at why several musicians felt that he had been one of the best ragtimers in New Orleans until he decided to take lessons from Professor Santo Guiffre. His playing still had the warmer New Orleans tone, and he was working in the new obbligato style, but he occasionally he fell back on the squalls that had become a dissonant element in many of the early jazz recordings. What Baquet's difficulties suggest, perhaps, is that at the time when he was considered one of the city's best clarinetists and was working regularly with Jack Laine's Reliance Orchestra, he was still playing in the old unison band style, with everyone staying close to the melody. When he took lessons and began experimenting with the new style that was prominent on Shields's recordings, he may have felt that he was beginning again. Johnny Stein usually managed to be in the wrong place at many points in his career as a bandleader, but he finally recorded in 1920 with other members of the Original New Orleans Jazz band, now under Jimmy Durante's name. One side of a single, "Why Cry Blues," was recorded for Gennett Records in May.

Of the three bands to record that were made up of Reliance musicians, only the singles by the ODJB are still well known, but Nunez's group actually did the most recording. In less than two years, between December 1918 and September 1920, they produced more than fifty titles and additional unissued tests in more than a dozen sessions for Emerson, Edison, Columbia, OKeh, and Little Wonder, with test sessions for Victor that failed to produce a usable master. Most of the recording was for Emerson Records, who licensed many of the masters to other labels for sale in special locations. Often the band recorded two or three takes of a piece, and these generally made their way to the market on one or another of the related labels, sometimes under other band names. After La Rocca had fired him in Chicago, Nunez joined Bert Kelly's band in New York for some months; by the time the lawsuit over the rights to "Livery Stable Blues" was settled he was also on the road, touring the vaudeville circuits with a quintet that was led by drummer Anton Lada but featured Nunez's clarinet.

For two of these recording sessions the band included a cornetist, another New Orleanian, Bernard "Doc" Berendson, who had come north to replace La Rocca after the breakup of Stein's band at Lamb's Café. His playing on the two sides where he appeared make it clear that the unique, laid-back New Orleans swing was something all of the city's musicians shared. On "Slow and Easy," recorded on December 16, 1919, for Columbia Records, Berendson's full tone and rhythmic swing were clearly evident, and he added a confident cornet break to the arrangement. Like many of the New Orleanians he was a multi-instrumentalist.

He was an excellent clarinetist and recorded on that instrument with early New York jazz groups, influencing younger New York clarinetists like Jimmy Lytell, who was associated for many years with the Original Memphis Five. One of Berendson's recordings with a New York group, a version of "Shake It and Break It" from an August 1921 session with a studio band named Lanin's Southern Serenaders, was an excellent display of a fluid, classic New Orleans ensemble clarinet style. The group, including cornetist Phil Napoleon, trombonist Moe Gappell, and pianist Jimmy Durante, had already absorbed the ensemble style of the Original Dixieland Jazz Band, and the arrangement had a relaxed swing that is still fresh almost ninety years later. Berendson's clarinet playing had none of the shrill glissandi of Ted Lewis, and it demonstrated the supple New Orleans phrasing that also marked Gussie Mueller's playing with the Paul Whiteman orchestra the year before.

Yellow Nunez's band, The Louisiana Five, had a hit of their own, "Yelping Hound Blues," which they recorded for three companies—including a 12-inch version for Emerson Records—and which they featured in their vaudeville act. Nunez's high, wailing tone did for a "yelping" hound what the ODJB had done for a rooster, a horse, and a cow. Emerson Records obviously considered the Louisiana Five one of their premier groups. The 12-inch of "Yelping Hound Blues" recorded in September 1919 was a special version, for dancers, of the hit they'd recorded for Columbia the April before. It was marketed at $1.50, a very high price for a dance record when a dollar was still regarded as a fair day's wages. The label of this record also featured a simulated signature by the band, "OK, 'Louisiana Five'". The original hit was marketed with a specially printed record jacket that read, "By a clever manipulation of the clarinet the effect of yelping hound is realistically brought out and at the same time a perfect Fox Trot rhythm and also a humorous melody are maintained."

The promotional material on the sleeve also mentioned the other side of the single in more ambiguous terms: "Clarinet Squawk" was described as ". . . a concentrated essence of contortive jungle music." On all of the recordings Nunez's playing was strong and lyric, and the accompanying group—Charlie Panelli on trombone; Joe Cawley, piano; Karl Beyer, banjo; and leader Lada on drums—had the Milneburg Sunday afternoon boisterousness. Nunez was playing a C clarinet, which is a tone higher than the standard B♭ instrument, and he almost invariably played the lead melody. If he insisted on playing with the same noisy assertiveness when he was in the band with La Rocca in Chicago, it is obvious why they couldn't spend a lot of time on the same bandstand.

All these recorded performances are invaluable documentation of many elements of the early New Orleans band styles. By imaginatively balancing the performances against each other it is possible to create a musical collage of how the ragtime or early jazz that Jack Laine's bands were playing in the New Orleans dance halls and cabarets might have sounded. Missing from the picture is the music of the African American musicians—the Downtown Creole orchestras and the Uptown ragtime bands. Within a few years, however, as Chicago and New York changed with the influx of hundreds of thousands of African Americans from the South, the musicians themselves would emigrate north to follow their audience. In their new setting they would ultimately create a flood of essential recordings that would deepen and strengthen the perception of New Orleans as the root source of the new dance craze.

10

Southern Stomps

When the train pulled in all the Pullman porters and waiters recognized me because they had seen me playing on the tail gate wagons to advertise dances, or "balls" as we used to call them. They all hollered at me saying, "Where you goin', Dipper?"

"You're a lucky black sommitch," one guy said, "to be going up North to play with ol' Cocky." (King Oliver) . . .

When the conductor hollered all aboard I told those waiters: "Yeah man, I'm going up to Chicago to play with my idol, Papa Joe!"

LOUIS ARMSTRONG REMEMBERING THE DAY HE LEFT NEW ORLEANS TO
JOIN KING OLIVER'S CREOLE BAND IN CHICAGO, AUGUST 8, 1922[1]

When the New Orleans musicians began to scatter out of the city, they sometimes found that their casual habits of making music didn't make much of an impression on the new audiences they encountered. Sitting uncomfortably in their new tuxedos on a bandstand in St. Louis, or trying to keep up with a busy arrangement to accompany a cabaret floor show in Memphis, they were in somebody else's neighborhood, and they had to fit themselves into the new situation. Many of them soon realized that they needed some kind of half-way house that would let them work with the lyric and rhythmic skills they had nurtured at home, but would also let them acclimatize themselves to the new musical challenges. For many of the musicians who came out of New Orleans hoping for a job that paid more than $1.50 a night, and for an audience that was larger than the neighborhood dance hall, this half-step into the larger musical world was Chicago.

The musicians came in two distinct waves: first, the early white jazz groups who played in the cabarets, beginning with Tom Brown's band in 1915; followed by the Uptown black musicians, who began making the train trip north a few years later. A handful of legitimate Creole musicians also began appearing for occasional jobs at the same time, often brought north by the ambitious young Downtown violinist, Charlie Elgar. Their polite music, however, represented an effort at social assimilation, and the Chicago dancers wanted what was new. In the period from 1915 to 1925, what was new were the boisterous dance styles coming out of New Orleans.

There was a change in New Orleans that affected its music scene between the departure of the first white bands to work the Chicago cabarets, and the generation of African American musicians who followed as the war ended. The Restricted District in New Orleans was forced to close when its brothels were placed off limits to army and navy personnel. New Orleans wasn't singled out; the directive from the Secretary of War in August 1917 forbade prostitution within five miles of any military encampment, and this was supplemented with a similar directive from the Secretary of the Navy. The reason was more than simply moral discomfort; prostitution was a major source of venereal infection, and the medical resources of the Army and Navy Medical Corps weren't adequate to cope with an influx of cases. Despite a lobbying effort by New Orleans's mayor to keep the District open, the city was forced to give in, and the City Council adopted an ordinance on October 2, 1917, that abolished Storyville on orders of the Department of the Navy.

Many musicians insisted in later interviews that they hadn't played in the brothels themselves, which usually used only a pianist or a string duo or trio, if there was any live music at all. Many of the establishments had only mechanical pianolas, which the customers were expected to feed with their spare change. At its height, however, Storyville—by the police chief's estimate—employed 2,000 prostitutes working in 230 brothels, and there were 30 "houses of assignation," where prostitutes working on the street could rent a room with a customer for an hour.[2] If the suppliers of the food and the liquor for the brothels are included in the calculations, as well as the hundreds of casual workers employed as maids or delivery boys, it is obvious that prostitution in Storyville was a large and prosperous business, and its closing meant a major economic loss to the city. The bands may not have been employed in the houses themselves, but the District attracted steady crowds, and many musicians found regular work in the District's cabarets and in its two dance halls, the Tuxedo and the 101 Ranch.

So many myths have sprung up around Storyville that it isn't surprising that there are persistent stories about the bands and the prostitutes staging a procession through the dark streets when it came time to close, since it seemed like a reasonable way to end the nearly twenty-year experiment in regulating social morality. Stephen Longstreet, in his extravagantly romantic account of early New Orleans jazz and the Storyville brothels, *Sportin' House*, quoted extensively from what he described as an unpublished memoir he was given in 1933 by a retired madam named Nell Kimball, who had run one of the more elegant houses.

A SOUVENIR POSTCARD OF STORYVILLE, WITH TOM ANDERSON'S SALOON ON THE CORNER, ABOUT 1900.

As Longstreet presented her story, she remembered that the closing hours were "sentimental," but midnight itself—the closing deadline—arrived with considerably less flamboyance.

While there has been some question about the source of the manuscript Longstreet quoted, the essence of the story is similar to the accounts of others who visited the District, even if it contradicted the extravagant invention of trombonist Preston Jackson, who told interviewers about a sorrowful march of the prostitutes and their employers through the streets with the bands playing alongside them (though he wasn't living in New Orleans at the time). Many of the houses simply moved out to other parts of the city, and reopened in less lavish circumstances. The line of cabarets and saloons just outside of the District, the so-called "tango belt," wasn't effected by closure except to have increased business, and Tom Anderson's café, the old headquarters of the District, continued its music by hiring some of the finest young jazz musicians.

The story in Nell Kimball's memoir was that for two weeks there had been steady traffic in the district as wagons came to take away the furnishings in the houses. She had sold her own lavish furnishings to a Greek businessman who was opening a less pretentious brothel close to the army base, and he was going to cart everything away the next morning. Kimball wrote with a touch of sarcasm that they would have to "put out the old red lantern on the stroke of twelve like some wall-eyed Cinderella."[3] When it was time to unlock the doors, the girls in the house had put on their makeup and done their hair and were talking so loudly that it "sounded like a fire." Half of the girls were also drunk, since they'd bribed the maids to bring them bottles from the cellar. The liquor in the private cellar had already been sold—for $10,000—to a neighboring restaurant, but for the night, Nell opened the house for her own party.

> *I had a keg of lager open in the big parlor and Harry (bartender and handy man) tending bar in the private one. Harry was a bit soaked himself, and he had the big house watchdog, Prince, with him behind the bar nibbling at the buffet where I had the last of the turkey and the fish tidbits and stuff, a whole spread of shrimp, gumbos, lobsters, and soft shell crabs. It wasn't costing anybody a cent but me—girls, food and drink were on the house. If any of the whores asked for a going away present, well that was up to the John. It didn't matter no how to me anymore. . . . After awhile I got tired of everything and sat in my bedroom with just a few old clients, and they looked old and I felt I was old too. I didn't get drunk as I had expected. The stuff had no bite that night. We just sipped and jawed about girls that were dead, and crazy New Years and Fourth of Julys, the time we all went to a mass to see a Richmond whore marry a street paving contractor's son, and we talked of the kind of people who were becoming whores these days. . . .*
>
> *Midnight I stood under the big hall chandelier, some of its crystals gone, and we all had the last drink of flat champagne, the whores crying, the naked and dressed ones and half-dressed Johns coming down from upstairs. It was real sentimental, and I just looked at the ruin of the bar and buffet and the town cushions and all I could think to do was to figure out what the night would have brought in if it hadn't been on the house.[4]*

For two of the most important Uptown cornetists, Freddie Keppard and Joe Oliver, the cabarets in the District had occasionally given them steady work. Until he left for Los Angeles to join Bill Johnson, Keppard often led a small group at Hanan's Saloon at the corner of Liberty and Customhouse, across Canal Street. Oliver generally played with the Olympia Orchestra for society functions, but when Edmond Souchon, a very young white jazz enthusiast snuck into the District with his friends sometime around 1910 or 1911 to hear Oliver play, the Big 25 was where they found him. To get into the District, which was strictly patrolled by the local police, he and his friends had to dress as newsboys, and carry late editions under their arms.

> *Except for faint red lights that shone through half-drawn shutters and the sputtering carbon lights on the corners, there was not much illumination. We could see strange figures peering out through half-open doorways. A new cop on the beat immediately tried to chase us, but the peeping female figures behind the blinds came to our rescue. They hurled invective of such vehemence—"Let the poor newsboys make a livin' you——"—that he let us go. We told him we were only going as far as Joe Oliver's saloon to bring him his paper. It seemed to satisfy him.*

We could now hear that music from half a block away; it would probably have taken more than one policeman to stop us. The place was twice as long as it was wide. It was [a] one-story wooden frame building at sidewalk level, lengthwise parallel to the street. There was a bar at the Iberville end, and a sort of dance hall to the rear, nearer Canal Street. Quick glances through the swinging doors showed us that the inside was fairly well lighted. But outside the building there were many deep shadows, and the sputtering carbon arc-light on the corner was out more than on.

Some nights the boys had a chance to exchange a few words with Oliver when he came outside for a quick break. "I'll never forget how big and tough he looked! His brown derby was tilted low over one eye, his shirt collar was open at the neck, and a bright red undershirt peeked out at the V. Wide suspenders held up an expanse of trousers of unbelievable width."[5]

Although Oliver is often considered one of the most representative of the New Orleans Uptown musicians, he wasn't born in the city. There has been some question about his birthplace, but among my notes there is an interview with his widow, Stella, from 1957, in which she said without hesitation that he'd been born in the country, on the Saulsburg Plantation about fifteen miles from Donaldsonville. His birthdate was May 11, 1885. His mother was a cook on the plantation. Stella was certain in her memory, because she'd grown up on another plantation only three miles away, and when she met Oliver later in New Orleans she remembered him from her childhood. She also recalled that something had been thrown in his eye when he was a boy—she thought it might have been pepper—and he had been partially blinded. He came to New Orleans when he was still a boy and took care of the yard for a family named Levy, who lived close to the Irish Channel at Second Street and Magazine. He lived with the Levy family during the week, then spent the weekends across Lake Ponchartrain in Mandeville with his aunt.

Oliver's first instrument was the trombone, but he played it so loudly he was encouraged to turn to the cornet instead. Some of the musicians I spoke to from this early period remembered that he had to struggle with the instrument before he seemed comfortable with it, and unlike most of the New Orleans instrumentalists, he was in his late teens before he began playing with neighborhood bands. About 1907, when he was twenty-two, a friend who played the trombone got him into the Melrose Brass Band, which included the Creole veteran Paul Beaullieu and a young trombonist, Honore Dutrey. Oliver began reading music with the Melrose band, and when Freddie Keppard left the Olympia Orchestra to travel to California, bandleader Armand J. Piron brought Oliver in as the replacement. Two or three years later Edmond Souchon, now a university student, had new opportunities to hear Oliver play with Piron's orchestra at the Tulane University gymnasium for the student "script" dances, as they were called, since students paid their way in with student "script." Souchon and his friends would gather behind the bandstand, hidden by a curtain, and the drummer would sing off-color verses to the songs under his breath for them. Oliver posed for a formal photograph about this time. He was broad shouldered, still slim, and he looked into the camera with a direct, confident expression. In his neat suit and tie he looked like someone who might be taking a job with a local business. There was no suggestion that he would go on to a major musical career.

By 1915, Oliver was leading the orchestra at the Big 25, with clarinetist Sidney Bechet; violinist Peter Bocage, who had helped the young Bunk Johnson learn to read music in the Superior Orchestra; pianist Arthur Campbell, and drummer Jean Vigne. Like all of the New Orleans groups, there were often changes in personnel, and Henry Zeno took over as the drummer, Buddy Christian became the pianist, and Lewis Mathews played the bass. Bechet left to tour through Texas with a band led by pianist Clarence Williams, and a young clarinetist named Joe Nicholas replaced him. The crowd at the "25" was rough and noisy, but the bands made more from tips than they did from their salary. The doors were left open to the street, and there were crowds until late at night. People remembered Oliver playing with his chair tipped back against the wall, a derby hat tilted over his eyes to hide his forehead. The childhood injury to his eye had left him "cockeyed," as people called it, or "Cocky," the nickname that Armstrong remembered. Then he'd come back from a job across the lake in Mandeville with a bad cut on his forehead, which he refused to talk about. Other musicians in the District heard that there had been a fight between several band members and people in the crowd, and he'd been hit with a broomstick handle, and leaving a scar that partly closed his other eye.

During this time Oliver and his wife became a kind of surrogate family to the much younger Louis Armstrong, whose own father had left his mother. Armstrong had been placed in the Waif's Home, where he began playing the cornet, and when he was released he spent time with Oliver and his wife, taking informal cornet lessons and running errands. Armstrong was in his teens at this time, and in need of the kind of emotional support he found in the Oliver house. These early ties of family and neighborhoods, as well as their familiarity with each other's playing style, kept the New Orleans musicians close to each other when they began to leave the city to pick up their careers in other places. There was already talk of jobs that were waiting in Chicago, but for someone with Oliver's local popularity there didn't seem to be any reason to take a chance on the uncertain situation in the north. He was now the most solidly established of the Uptown cornetists, and also often was hired to play with one of the most respected of the Downtown street bands, the Onward Brass Band. On one parade, when the band's third cornetist failed to appear, Oliver and the legendary Manuel Perez played the entire parade as a two-cornet duet.

When musicians later talked about Oliver's playing before he left New Orleans they remembered his warm tone, his innate lyricism, and his natural instrumental technique. He was considered a thorough musician who could play anything.

In addition to his more legitimate playing with the Olympia Orchestra, he developed a repertoire of effects with mutes: growling or calling, imitating crying babies or people's laughter. He still specialized in comedy routines with the mutes when he worked with his own bands later on Chicago's South Side.

When Kid Ory's cornetist Mutt Carey left for a job in Chicago to replace Sugar Johnny Smith in the orchestra led by clarinetist Lawrence Duhe, Oliver moved over to Ory's band, which at that point was probably the busiest of the Uptown bands—still playing what was called ragtime, with a heavier emphasis on the "slow drag" numbers. Bill Johnson, the bass player who had organized the Creole Band and led them for their long three years on the vaudeville circuit, returned to Chicago and got in touch with Oliver, offering him a job. Oliver still hesitated, but he had begun having trouble with the police on some of his jobs; on June 19, 1918, he was one of a crowd of people picked up in a police raid on the cabaret where he was playing, and he spent the night in the city prison. It was the second time he'd been picked up, and when he was released he decided it was time to leave New Orleans. One of the jobs he could have taken was cornetist with Lawrence Duhe's band at the Dreamland Café, as a replacement for Sugar Johnny Smith, who was suffering from tuberculosis. but it was Mutt Carey who took the train north. Carey, however, made the trip in the winter and found he couldn't stand the cold weather. After a few weeks he told Duhe that he had to go home for his sister's wedding, and once back in New Orleans he announced emphatically that nothing would get him back to Chicago again. When he heard that Oliver was about to go north to join Bill Johnson's band, Carey told him to go ahead and take the job with Duhe at the same time. Oliver found himself finally in Chicago, working with two bands at the same time, Bill Johnson's at the Pekin Café, and Duhe's, which had moved to the Dreamland Café.

With the New Orleans habit of dealing with whatever happened to come along, Duhe accepted the arrangement, and Oliver split his nights between the two bands: from 9:30 to 1:00 a.m. at the Dreamland, and from 2:00 to 6:00 a.m. at the Pekin.[6] Oliver was still with Duhe in the fall of 1919, when some of the band members were photographed playing in the bleacher seats at the World Series that was "thrown" by the Chicago Black Sox. There were problems, however, since the band's trombonist, the exciting but unreliable Roy Palmer, sometimes fell asleep on the bandstand. Oliver demanded that Duhe fire him, and when Duhe couldn't bring himself to let Palmer go, Oliver took over the band and got rid of both of them. Oliver had no difficulty replacing the Creole clarinetist with another friend from the Uptown neighborhood, Johnny Dodds. They had played together in Kid Ory's band; after Ory's move to California, Dodds had left on a vaudeville tour with the Billy and Mary Mack Minstrel Company.

Most of his musicians remembered Oliver as generally relaxed and easy to get along with as a bandleader, but he could also be difficult and unpredictable. He insisted on a tight level of discipline in his groups, and he carried a pistol in his briefcase with his music. Jobs in Chicago, however, often ran down, with so much competition between the ballrooms and the cabarets, and the music they offered changing its rhythms and styles almost monthly. When business slumped at the Dreamland the owner first blamed Oliver and let him go, but then hired him again in April 1920.[7] The Pekin, a much rougher establishment, closed in the fall, following a shooting that caused the death of two detectives. Oliver continued to lead the band at the Dreamland, but a few months later, when he was offered work in California, he took the band there. Kid Ory, who had employed Oliver when Carey left for Chicago, was now leading a band in California, and he was offered a contract at the Pergola Dancing Pavilion on Market Street in San Francisco. He couldn't leave the job he already had, so he suggested instead that the Pergola hire Oliver's band, which had been getting positive reviews in Chicago.

Oliver and his musicians left for San Francisco on May 21, 1921, and stayed in California for almost a year. The group was essentially a New Orleans–style rag-time orchestra, with a violinist, Jimmy Palao from the Creole Band, as one of the lead instruments; clarinetist Johnny Dodds; pianist Lil Hardin, who had taken her first band job when it was still led by Lawrence Duhe; trombonist Honore Dutrey; bassist Ed Garland; and drummer Minor Hall. The ballroom didn't draw the crowds that had been anticipated, and soon they were finding themselves scuffling for employment. At some point in these early months the band toured on a local vaudeville circuit. They dressed in a variety of southern costumes: Lil wore a gingham dress, Dodds was dressed as a mechanic, and Palao was in over-alls and a straw hat. As work got scarce, Oliver decided to cut his expenses by letting violinist Palao go. Minor Hall threatened to quit, because he had been close to Palao's family in New Orleans, and Oliver angrily replied by firing Hall and sending for Johnny Dodds's brother Warren "Baby" Dodds to take his place. Hall went to the union to protest the unauthorized hiring of the new drummer; Oliver was fined and then forced to pay for Hall's return trip to Chicago when he didn't pay the fine.

In their months in California, however, the band was never far from New Orleans. Kid Ory had been playing in San Francisco, with Mutt Carey as his new cornetist, and Carey had already gotten audiences used to the muted effects that he and Oliver had been using on their jobs in New Orleans. For some weeks Oliver found himself dismissed as a Mutt Carey imitator. As the months passed they worked wherever it was offered. They began taking jobs in southern California and were booked for a long weekend into a bare, wood frame dance hall at an artificially constructed pond outside of Los Angeles called Leake's Lake. The hall had been built and operated by two Los Angeles music entrepreneurs, Reb and John Spikes, but when Oliver brought his band down, they found that the manager of the resort was another New Orleans wanderer, Jelly Roll Morton.

There was also union trouble—the kind of lack of attention to business details that continually got the New Orleans bands into trouble. By the spring of 1922 Oliver was combining the members that were left of his band with Ory's as the "Celebrated Creole Orchestra."

On June 21, 1922, Oliver, back in Chicago, opened at the Lincoln Gardens, at 459 E. 31st Street. It was the same place he'd played when he first came to Chicago in 1919, but there had been a name change while he was on the coast. It was the largest dance hall on the South Side. Drummer George Wettling, who heard the band there when he first was discovering jazz, described it as it looked then. "The thing that hit your eye once you got into the hall was [a] big crystal ball that was made of small pieces of reflecting glass and hung over the center of the dance floor. A couple of spotlights shone on the big ball as it turned and threw reflected spots of light all over the room and the dancers. The ceiling of the place was made lower than it actually was by chicken wire that was stretched out, and over the wire were spread great bunches of artificial maple leaves."[8]

Wettling also wrote that a large canvas sign was hung on the outside of the dance hall announcing that the orchestra was King Oliver and his Creole Jazz Band. As an advertising device Oliver had been given the title of "King" for his first Chicago job. No musician was ever advertised as "King" in New Orleans, and when Louis Armstrong came to join the band he was startled to hear people referring to him as King Oliver. By 1926, after the excitement of his first recordings wore off, Oliver was sometimes advertised in the Chicago press as simply "Joe Oliver."

The popularity that met Oliver in his Chicago career partly reflected the changes that had occurred in the city's population since the first New Orleans bands had opened in the cabarets only few years earlier. The entry of the United States into World War I in the spring of 1917, had led to a rush to supply war materials to the hurriedly assembling army, as well as to the forces of what were now the "Allies," France and Great Britain. In the scramble to arm, factories in the northern cities quickly expanded, and the need for manpower meant that African Americans from the southern states suddenly found themselves with employment opportunities that had never existed before. Within months the migration became a flood that drew hundreds of thousands out of the South to work in cities like Chicago, Detroit, and New York. For the New Orleanians, Chicago, on the L&N Railroad lines, offered the most opportunity, and there had already been a small but steady move north for some years. With this new audience that still had New Orleans music in their ears, it was only a matter of months before the cabaret operators began hiring the musicians who knew how to play it. For both the workers, who were earning more than they ever had in their lives, and the musicians who followed them, the emotions also were tied to their dreams of leaving the oppressive racism of the South behind them.

All of the newcomers quickly found that Chicago had its own racial antipathies, but the economic opportunities helped sweeten the air, and the racism they met now was a less pervasive presence in their lives. In the summer of 1919, the tensions in Chicago that had risen with the arrival of thousands of African Americans from the South—and aggravated by the problem that jobs had been taken over by the new arrivals—burst into the open in a murderous race riot that left dozens dead and injured. Despite police intervention the violence in Chicago raged for days. But the tide of immigration continued without a pause: in 1910 Chicago's black population was 45,000; by 1930 it had risen to 235,000.

Chicago had already become home to the Creole violinist Charlie Elgar, who began bringing up Creole musicians at the same time that Tom Brown's band was working at Lamb's Café. Two of the more ambitious music entrepreneurs from New Orleans, pianist Clarence Williams and violinist Armand J. Piron, had already had some success with their music publishing company in New Orleans, and they opened a combination publishing office and music store, advertised as "The House of Jazz," at 3129 South State Street. The store stayed open for several years, although Piron returned to the south to organize a successful dance orchestra, and after the riots Williams left for New York, where he became a very successful recording director for OKeh and Columbia Records, returning only for occasional visits. Many of the New Orleans musicians who had remained in the South tried out Chicago at least for a few weeks, often making the House of Jazz their first stop. For the ones who stayed, however, their music inevitably changed during their Chicago years, just as their way of playing changed the jazz scene that they found on their arrival.

Two of the innovations that changed the way their music sounded in the new circumstances were more or less forced on the New Orleans instrumentalists. They found they had to expand their usual New Orleans instrumentation, which was still built around the small quintets and sextets that were customary in the southern city's casual cabarets and small neighborhood dance halls. The style in Chicago was for a two cornet or trumpet lead, with the horns playing the melody in harmony. The dance halls were large and the bands had to make a big sound. All of the dance orchestras playing in the major ballrooms, white and black, used a double lead, with the musician playing the second lead often also used for the busier solo sections. Responding to the change that was coming to the small jazz ensembles everywhere in the country, they were expected to add saxophones. The leaders of the black dance orchestras that controlled most of the Chicago jobs—Erskine Tate, Dave Peyton, Ollie Powers, Sammy Stewart, Carroll Dickerson, and Doc Cooke—all played arranged scores with two horn leads and added two or three reed players who doubled on saxophone and clarinet. Their sound was identical in musical texture to the instrumentation of the Chicago orchestra with the largest national audience: the white band led by Isham Jones, with his strong lead cornetist, Louis Panico. The Isham Jones Orchestra set the style for Chicago dance music for most of the decade.

Even more important was the change in tempo. Every band performing in the North had a few uptempo one-steps as part of their dance offerings, and these were played at blistering tempos—like the Original Dixieland Jazz Band's "Dixie Jazz Band One Step" or "At A Jazz Band Ball"—but in New Orleans the tempos were generally slower and more subtle, closer to the easy slide of the ODJB's 1917 recording of "Barnyard Blues" for Aeolian Records. In Chicago, however, the operators of the largest dance halls began having serious problems with a self-appointed group called the Juvenile Protective Association, who sent representatives to monitor the dancing. What the Association found was that the couples—now that the women were out of their corsets and wearing lighter clothing—were often dancing pressed against their partners. In his important study *Chicago Jazz*, William Kenney emphasized the role of the Association in the development of Chicago's dance style.

> *The biggest of the twenties "ballrooms," most of them built in the nineteen teens, offered the public carefully engineered and sanitized musical and dance experiences. While it was waging its fourteen year war against "vice," the Juvenile Protective Association came to a culturally influential understanding with the owners and managers of nearly all of Chicago's largest dance halls, where some important jazz musicians earned a living. In 1921, the owners of the Midway Gardens, Merry Gardens, White City Ballrooms, Trianon Ballrooms, Marigold Gardens, Dreamland Ballroom, and the Columbia Ballroom formed the National Association of Ball Room Proprietors and Managers. Together, they pledged to work out their differences with the Juvenile Protective Association.[9]*

Some of the ballrooms drew as many as four thousand customers a night, so the economics of their situation demanded some accommodation of the JPA. At a meeting in 1921 the managers asked the Protective Association, "'What can we do to make our dance halls more respectable?' The JPA's answer: 'Speed up your music.' . . . Within twenty-four hours, every orchestra in the ballroom group had doubled the tempo of its melodies. The toddle, the shimmy and kindred slow syncopated motions were impossible at the brisk pace the music set, and the managers found most of the bad dancing eliminated."[10]

Other New Orleans musicians who were trying to adapt to the new situation were playing in new nightclubs like the popular Kelly's Stables, or the Friar's Inn, where the white musicians of the New Orleans Rhythm Kings were drawing steady crowds. The cabarets didn't have to face the restrictions of the JPA, but they had problems of their own. The Prohibition laws, which had been in effect since 1919, meant that they couldn't rely on income from liquor sales. The Friar's Inn was small enough that the band could satisfy their customers with a mixture of dance music, jazz specialties, and occasional entertainers, but at larger places like Kelly's Stables, the owners had to find ways to fill their tables without liquor. If the clubs did choose to skirt the edges of the laws prohibiting the sale of liquor, they went only as far as providing "set-ups." The waiter brought a glass, some ice, water, and a mixer like ginger ale, and the customers could add whatever they'd smuggled in with them. The set-ups were included in the tab the customers were charged for the opportunity to dance and to watch a show. To give the evening some excitement the owners added entertainment, which quickly turned into floor shows, with solo dancers, singers, and chorus lines.

The cabarets, by this time, were controlled almost entirely by the bootleggers, who competed with each other in the level of entertainment in their places. To play a floor show musicians first had to join the musicians' union, which meant passing a test for reading music and waiting out a "residence" period. Even if they managed to slip past the union's test, they soon learned they had to read music to accompany the floor shows. There was no possible way to accompany a shifting roster of vocal soloists, dance numbers, and elaborate transitions from one song to another, often in a different keys and tempos, without learning to read music. Most of the New Orleans men spent some time in their early months in Chicago studying music with local teachers. Listening to the changes in the playing of clarinetist Jimmy Noone from his first Chicago recordings with Doc Cooke's Dreamland Orchestra in January 1924 to his 1926 recordings leading his own Apex Club Orchestra, it is obvious that something has changed him from a generally tame and often tentative soloist to an assured and technically brilliant bandleader. What happened were his studies with the well-known white concert clarinetist Franz Schoepp. Writers have noted the similarities in the playing of Noone and Benny Goodman, but the influence may have come from Schoepp, who was also Goodman's teacher.

The policy of allowing the customers to bring in liquor—which violated the law, but put the responsibility on the customer—was ended by a court decision in December 1926. Within a few months the cabaret scene had all but closed down, leaving many musicians without work at the same time that new sound systems were also allowing some movie theaters to let their musicians go.

When Oliver returned from California a few years before the closedown, there were still jobs and opportunities to record, and he made the most of the situation. What was left of his band returned to Chicago in the spring of 1922, and Oliver finally agreed that, to move along with the times, and to meet the competition from the other ballrooms, he would have to add a second cornet. He was also beginning to experience the gum trouble that would effect his playing for the rest of his career, but the now widespread practice of adding a flashier soloist as the second lead made it possible for him to continue leading his bands through the rest of the decade. Oliver himself was a strong cornet-ist with an individual style, and he led some of the most popular New Orleans–influenced orchestras in Chicago, but he will always have an important place in the history of jazz because of the telegram he sent to New Orleans in the summer of 1922, asking his young protégé, Louis Armstrong, to join his band at the Lincoln Gardens. Armstrong, as everyone had known almost from the beginning, was something new.

For most of his long and richly successful career, it was accepted that Louis Armstrong was born in New Orleans on July 4, 1900, but baptismal records make it clear that he was off by a year in his own counting. He was born on August 4, 1901, which means that he was only twenty-one when he received the telegram

LOUIS ARMSTRONG, WITH HIS
MOTHER AND SISTER, 1920.

from Joe Oliver. When he was a boy, and his mother (whom Armstrong surmised probably worked some of the time as a prostitute) was struggling to bring him up, there was nothing in his life to give a hint of what was to come later. He was born in a room in a back alley in what was called "the battleground," a raucous Uptown neighborhood around Perdido Street and Liberty. Virtually every trace of the streets he knew was obliterated with the rebuilding of the city's center in the 1950s and 1960s. Men came and went in his mother's life, but he always remembered her struggles to raise him to be obedient and helpful with deep love and loyalty. Although he knew his father and for short periods lived with him and his new family, it was his mother and grandmother who raised him. Armstrong wrote about his childhood in three poignant autobiographies, published over a twenty-year period, as well as giving countless interviews and responding to letters and questions.

Many of the things that happened to Armstrong in his long career seemed serendipitous, but what set all of them in a framework was that, as he matured, it was obvious that he was blindingly talented—and that it was a unique talent shaped by a warm, generous, and seemingly limitless affection for his audiences and his fellow musicians. When he joined in the noisy New Year's Eve celebrations at the end of 1912 by firing a pistol that had been left by one of his mother's men friends, he found himself in city prison; and because he was eleven years old at the time of his offense, he was ordered to the Colored Waif's Home on January 1, 1913. At first he was miserably unhappy at the home, but he was given the chance to learn a musical instrument, and as he wrote later, "That shot, I do believe, started my career. My whole success goes back to the time I was arrested as a wayward boy of thirteen [sic]. Because then I *had* to quit running around and began to learn something. Most of all, I began to learn music."[11]

For the first few months the music director at the home, Professor Peter Davis, kept him at a distance, because he felt Armstrong was too undisciplined to be admitted to the band. Finally Davis asked if he'd like to learn to play the bugle, and within a few months Armstrong had moved from the bugle to the cornet and then to leading the band on their modest jobs for parades and picnics outside the home. When he was released, on June 16, 1914, at the request of both his father and mother, who still weren't living together but spoke up together in the appeals to the judges, he was so accustomed to the life that he remembered his unhappiness at leaving for the rest of his life. His first months out of the home were spent unhappily with his father's new family, but finally he was permitted to return to his mother and sister in their shabby room in one of the poorest, roughest neighborhoods in New Orleans.

Armstrong later said that he didn't play the cornet again for three years, and he found work hauling a coal cart. The cornet wasn't completely forgotten; he would slip out at night to find a "tonk"—a rowdy bar—that would let him play a few numbers. He never had a chance to play with one of the established orchestras, so the rough bars and their late-night crowds served as his musical apprenticeship. He was interested in music of every style, and like many apprentice musicians of the period he was drawn to the new Victor red label, 12-inch 78 r.p.m. recordings of the Italian opera stars, led by tenor Enrico Caruso, that at the time were among the fastest-selling discs in the United States. With so many Italians in the city, and so many of the concert bands at resorts like Spanish Fort led by Italian bandmasters, there was a responsive local audience for the stentorian vocal recordings. Armstrong recalled that sometimes he would take some of the money from his days of hauling coal and buy opera discs for himself. His later recordings often displayed reminiscences of the unstoppable bravura and soaring melodies of the soprano and tenor arias he played for himself on a wind-up phonograph when he was still a teenager. Occasionally the fiery cadenzas he interpolated in his music had their origins in the concert cornet solos of the period. The family of Sidney Bechet, a friend who was learning to play the clarinet and who shared Armstrong's excitement over Italian opera, had more money than Armstrong's household, so Bechet often was taken to the French Opera House where he heard live performances. He insisted that his trademark throbbing vibrato was something he'd learned from Enrico Caruso recordings.

For Armstrong, everything that he heard simply became another facet of his evolving style. Kid Ory, the trombonist from LaPlace, Louisiana, who came into the city in 1910 and in two or three years, with a combination of showmanship and a flair for the business side of bandleading, turned his orchestra into the bus-iest of the Uptown bands, also began to hear about Armstrong and his playing in the tonks. One afternoon his band had an advertising job on a wagon and their regular cornet player, Mutt Carey, couldn't make the job. As they were moving down the street, the bass player, George Foster, saw Armstrong standing along the curb and he told Ory to let him come up with them for the afternoon. Foster was certain this was the adolescent cornet player's first experience with a real band. He also laughed that the only thing Armstrong could play was the blues, so that was what they played for the whole day.

In the summer of 1918 Armstrong again had one of those moments of good fortune that he turned into an opportunity to expand his musical range. The fine Creole cornetist and violinist Peter Bocage had been working with Fate Marable and his orchestra on the river steamer the SS *Sidney*. When the boat headed north for the summer season Bocage decided to stay in New Orleans, and he recommended Armstrong for the job. Armstrong was not an obvious choice, since his reading skills were rudimentary, but Marable's bands were considered a "conservatory" for musicians who were short on skills. Armstrong stayed on the boat for two seasons, getting help with his reading from the first cornetist Joe Howard, and by the end of his time on the *Capitol* he said of himself that he'd become a mature musician. "I could read music very well by now and was get-ting hotter and hotter on my trumpet [*sic*]. My chest had filled out deeper and my lips and jaws had gotten stronger, so I could blow much harder and longer than before without getting tired. I had made a special point of the high register, and was beginning to make my high-C notes more and more often. That was the greatest strain on the lips."[12]

Also, when the boat tied up at cities like St. Louis he found that audiences outside of New Orleans had the same jubilant response to his music.

Armstrong's first marriage, to a teenage prostitute who was wildly emotional, dangerously jealous, and attacked him in her fits of rage, ended sometime before he left New Orleans, although to his dismay she turned up again when he was in Chicago. His second marriage, however, to the pianist with Oliver's band, Lil Hardin, was another moment of serendipity. Hardin was born on February 3, 1898, three years earlier than Armstrong, and was as much of an individual as he was. Her background, though very different, was almost as colorful. She grew up in Memphis, the daughter of a deeply religious mother. Although encouraged to play the piano, she was permitted to play only religious hymns and light classical pieces. Hardin's later accounts that she was training to be a classical pianist were a little far from the truth, along with her memory of being class valedictorian at Fisk University. The school records show that she was a student at Fisk for less than a semester.

Her musical career began in Chicago in 1917 when she came for a visit and found a job demonstrating sheet music at a neighborhood store. She later told a story of Jelly Roll Morton listening to her play on her third week on the job and showing her how to play jazz variations on the melodies. Whatever happened in those early weeks, she soon was popular enough at the music store to be asked to come and audition for Lawrence Duhe's New Orleans orchestra. Her memory of her first experience playing with a band has a distinctly New Orleans flavor.

> *When I sat down to play I asked for music and were they surprised! They politely told me they didn't have any music and furthermore never used any. I then asked them what key would the first number be in. I must have been speaking a different language because the leader said, "When you hear two knocks, just start playing."*
>
> *It all seemed very strange to me, but I got all set, and when I heard those two knocks I hit the piano so loud and hard they all turned around to look at me. It took only a second for me to feel what they were playing and I was off. The New Orleans Creole Jazz Band hired me, and I never got back to the music store—never got back to Fisk University.*[13]

She stayed with the orchestra when Joe Oliver took over the leadership, and traveled with them to San Francisco. A few weeks of their vaudeville tour tired her of life on the road; she returned to Chicago, where she took a job with a band led by a violinist named Mae Brady. When Oliver returned to Chicago in the spring of 1922 and began working again he used another pianist, Berthat Gonsoulin. After a few months, however, Hardin rejoined the band. She was slim and fashionably dressed, a beautiful woman who had come through a brief marriage and divorce a few months before, and she was courted by most of the younger members of the band. She kept them at a distance, but Oliver kept telling her about the new cornetist he was bringing up from New Orleans. Armstrong arrived in Chicago on July 8, 1922.

At the beginning, Hardin didn't think much of him. "I was a little disappointed," she reminisced later. "All the musicians called him 'Little Louis,' and he weighed 226 pounds! And I said, 'Little Louis?' Wonder why they call him 'Little Louis,' as fat as he is."[14] She didn't like his clothes and when she first saw him he was wearing his hair in bangs. "And they were sticking right straight out!" In a photo taken around this time of Armstrong and Oliver together, Armstrong, standing behind a grandly seated Oliver, was so overweight that his face was the shape of a balloon. He was wearing new clothes, crowned with a sharp hat, but he didn't look comfortable in them. He seemed to be a green country boy, just as Lil Hardin suspected. She also didn't think much of his playing, but as time passed she began paying more attention, and they soon began hanging out together—the slim, brown-skinned woman from Memphis and the dark-skinned, pudgy cornetist from New Orleans.

When they decided to be married she quickly began to remake him for the next stage of his career. She made him lose weight, she picked out new clothes for him, and with her broader musical background she began introducing him to more ambitious music. Armstrong already had the love of Italian opera that had been with him since his coal-cart days, and with Lil he began to explore musical equivalents on the cornet. The young musician and composer Hoagy Carmichael knew them at this time, and he remembered that Lil "got a book of the standard cornet solos and drilled him. He really worked, even taking lessons from a German down at Kimball Hall, who showed Louis all the European cornet clutches."[15] Lil also continued to study herself, and finished the requirements for a teaching certificate from the Chicago College of Music.

On April 5 and 6, 1923, Armstrong made his first recordings with "King Oliver's Creole Jazz Band" for a small company named Gennett Records, with its office just over the state line in Richmond, Indiana. The sessions were, in reality, the first recordings by any of the members of the band. The singles released from these sessions are sometimes regarded as the first by an African American jazz orchestra from New Orleans, but Kid Ory, in California, had beaten them into a recording studio almost a year before. One of the compositions that Oliver recorded, "Krooked Blues," had been recorded first by Ory's band, and Oliver paid them the tribute of repeating their arrangement and using some of Mutt Carey's muted cornet fills.

For many jazz writers, the Oliver sessions dominate the story of South Side jazz, but it is difficult to imagine that the sessions would have come to occupy such an important place in the history of New Orleans jazz had it not been for Armstrong's presence. The rhythm section had little of the loose elasticity of the classic New Orleans bands of this period of the 1920s. Lil Armstrong had played in her family's parlor in Memphis, and although she was familiar with the band's style, her playing was derivative and rhythmically stiff. She had none of the technical assurance of other pianists like Jimmy Blythe, Tiny Parham, or Teddy Weatherford who were also working with the South Side bands. The banjo player was Bill Johnson, who had been the organizer behind the Creole Band and toured for three years on vaudeville with the band, and in his later recordings he was much more effective on his original instrument, the bass. The drummer, Baby Dodds, was certainly the most skilled of the rhythm section—like Armstrong, he'd come up through Fate Marable's "conservatory"—but in the poor acoustics of the sessions he's virtually inaudible except for his busy woodblock.

The band's greatness was in its horns, but there were also problems there. All of the New Orleanians were close friends with the trombonist Honore Dutrey, and they'd often played together in marching bands before the war. Dutrey, however, had spent the war years in the Navy and his lungs were badly damaged in a training accident. Often he had to leave the bandstand between numbers to use an inhaler to catch his breath. Of all the New Orleans trombone players who recorded during these years, Dutrey was probably the most limited, and he had none of the feeling for the varied staccato rhythmic passages that had been such a basic element in the style of most of the other New Orleans trombonists. Dutrey sometimes repeated the same simple combinations of notes with a sliding legato over and over again, adding an effect to the ensembles that at times became unintentionally comical. Between the clumsy rhythmic sense of the piano and the trombone, the band sometimes seemed to be laboring through wet sand. Clarinetist Johnny Dodds was to become one of the great New Orleans instrumentalists, and although his playing was restrained on some of the arrangements, there were already hints of the brilliant, flashing energy that was to make him one of the most recorded sidemen on the South Side. Balanced against him, however, was an obligatory saxophonist, "Stump" Evans, whose playing was heavy and lacked an essential swing. The band recorded for three companies within a brief period, and they duplicated material; in comparing the performances, it is clear that, like the white New Orleans bands, the arrangements were more or less set and there was very little improvisation.

It was in the intimations of the half-acknowledged tensions between the two cornetists, Oliver and Armstrong, that the recordings struck fire. The others remembered that in the first test in the studio, Oliver was virtually inaudible. This had been the same experience of many musicians in Chicago in this period when the studios still were recording with acoustical horns. The technical aspects of the equipment favored mid-range frequencies, and this was Armstrong's great strength. In session after session musicians standing beside him would play as loudly, but on the playback it seemed that Armstrong had virtually been playing a solo. Since Oliver was playing the melody and Armstrong the harmony, to deal with the problem Armstrong was moved further away from the recording horn. Then Oliver was also moved back because his strong tone was effecting the cutting needle, just as La Rocca's cornet had overbalanced the ODJB's first session seven years before. The final placement, as had also happened with the ODJB, overbalanced the clarinet, and Dodd's obbligato was the most clearly audible element of the ensemble.

The ensemble texture on these first singles is one of the most impenetrable of any New Orleans band recording, which was only partially the result of the inadequate recording techniques of the Gennett engineers who did the first sessions. A few months before, the same engineers, working in the same studio with another New Orleans band, the New Orleans Rhythm Kings, had achieved balanced, musically sensitive sides with a tonal warmth and clarity for the three lead horns. It was the volume of the Oliver band that defeated them. Oliver and the band went on to record essentially the same arrangements with other companies over the next few months, and there was the same difficulty with all of the recordings: the acoustic recording horns were unable to deal with the band's raw power.

On all of their recordings the emotional thrust of the music was breathtaking, but the confused mass of sound was almost impossible to separate into its musical components. It was the two cornets who suffered the most, but Armstrong was at least audible on his first recorded solo in "Chimes Blues," one of the pieces recorded the first day. The solo's angular, arpeggiated melody—which he played twice—had so little of the unique style that the musicians around him described that some of his Chicago friends were surprised. In New Orleans, however, several musicians recognized the solo as one of the familiar choruses that Buddy Petit featured. The same solo turned up a few months later played by the trombonist on a recording by Charlie Creath's orchestra in St. Louis. Creath (pronounced like "breath") was a gifted cornetist and a close friend of Armstrong's from the summers on the riverboats.

Several times on the recordings Oliver and Armstrong performed the celebrated two-cornet breaks that they used on the bandstand, as well as the carefully rehearsed descending chromatic lines played in harmony on "Snake Rag." The short interludes were as carefully rehearsed, and on the bandstand they would hum to each other the break they wanted to use next. The breaks were also repeated in their subsequent recordings of the same arrangements. "Dippermouth Blues," also recorded on the first day, drew the most intense performance from the band. There was some adjustment of the balance, which helped give the recording some of its brilliance. Since Oliver was featured in a muted solo, he was moved closer to the recording horn, and the rhythm section launched into the arrangement with a relentless energy. The composition—under a new title, "Sugar Foot Stomp"—was the only one of the pieces recorded that became part of the new jazz repertoire of the 1920s. The first solo by Dodds, accompanied by stop-time chords, was imitated again and again, and Oliver's three choruses, building to a stinging climax—broken with a pause and Bill Johnson's unexpected shout of "Oh, play that thing!" to give Oliver time to take out his mute and step back from the recording horn—became embedded in the piece. They were repeated in countless arrangements in the swing era.

The drama being played out between the two men came out in the open most clearly in an arrangement of the piece "Southern Stomps" recorded in December 1923 for their final session with Gennett. A bass saxophone had been added to the rhythm, giving it an even clumsier tread, but the arrangement was the first where Armstrong's melodic and rhythmic innovations could be heard clearly. The tune was a commercial composition with a standard form of verse, then a bridge that transposed to a different key for the chorus. After the first bridge, which featured Dodds, Armstrong was given what was virtually a solo; following the repeat of the bridge, again with Dodds playing the melody, the ensemble returned, this time led by Armstrong. It was not until the final chorus that Oliver's cornet abruptly reasserted his authority with a fierce, muted entrance, while Armstrong could be heard moving a few steps back and resuming his backup role. The sheer force of Oliver's entrance emphasized that he still was the band's leader, but he clearly was pushing himself to bring off the effect. As the months passed and his problems with his embrouchure worsened, it became more and more obvious that the musical direction of the band was passing to the younger man.

"Southern Stomps" also provides invaluable insight into Armstrong's growing confidence, because it was one of the few pieces where there was a second take. The solo on the first take already stretched the boundaries of what any other

PARAMOUNT RECORDS AND COLUMBIA RECORDS ADVERTISE KING OLIVER'S JAZZ BAND, 1925. COLLAGE BY THE AUTHOR.

cornetist was doing at the time, but the second solo chorus effortlessly reached beyond what he had already achieved on the first take. For any musician who was listening, it was a sign that something they couldn't have expected had already happened, and with Louis Armstrong their music was moving into new dimensions.

Although Lil Armstrong had been a member of Oliver's band for some years and was featured even more prominently on their first recordings than her husband, she was conscious that as long as Armstrong stayed with Joe Oliver, he would always be second cornet. As Oliver told her in an unguarded moment, he didn't need to be afraid of her husband as long as Armstrong was in his band. When she found inadvertently that Oliver was "skimming" his second cornet player's salary—the management was paying $95 a week, and Oliver was passing on $75—she demanded that Armstrong leave the band, though she stayed on herself. In his first weeks of unemployment Armstrong was confused and uncertain over what he'd done, and the first legitimate orchestra leader he approached, Sammy Stewart, turned him down despite his growing reputation. Stewart's orchestra was made up of light-skinned musicians, and Armstrong was black. However, the second leader he approached, Ollie Powers, who was leading the orchestra at the Dreamland, hired him. He was already established with Powers when the other members of Oliver's band found that he was also skimming their salaries and the historic group broke up.

Once again, for Armstrong it was a serendipitous moment. Fletcher Henderson, at that moment the most successful African American orchestra leader in the country, offered him a job with his orchestra in New York City. After much prodding from his wife Armstrong took the job, and his new career began. The music he would play in future years would only occasionally return to the styles and musical idioms of where he began, but there would always be some echo of his long New Orleans apprenticeship.

In the volatile world of the South Side cabarets, Oliver always faced considerable competition from other groups. Despite his own personality, and the sales of his band's recordings, for some months after the breakup of the Creole Band he found himself scuffling. He was to regroup, and with his later Dixie Syncopators have more success than he'd experienced with the Creole Band, but by this time he'd been away from New Orleans for several years. Even with the addition of younger New Orleanians like reedmen Barney Bigard and Albert Nicholas and trumpeter Lee Collins, the new orchestra's arrangements were now more of a piece with the South Side sound than with New Orleans. Sometime toward the end of 1924, Edmond Souchon heard Oliver play again, and described his music in his vivid memoir. New Orleans jazz enthusiast Souchon had first heard Oliver in the District, and with his friends had clustered around Oliver and the Olympia Orchestra when they played for student dances at Tulane University. Souchon had been in Chicago for two years finishing his medical internship, and decided to celebrate with some friends before returning to New Orleans and a medical practice. He went with them to the South Side, not knowing what cabaret they were going to visit, only that someone said the "greatest jazz band of all times" was playing there.

Prohibition was at its maudlin height. The place was far from inviting from the outside, dingy and needing several coats of paint. Ancient paper decorations and faded flowers hung dejectedly from unpainted walls and peeling columns. A long, winding ill-lit hallway seemed to take us back of some large hotel or building. The place smelled of last week's beer. But the closer we got to the dance hall, the more excited we became. No one had mentioned the name of the band playing there, but it was only necessary for a few musical strains to meet us for us to realize that something familiar was greeting us.

A rather pretentious floor show was in progress as we made our way to our table. A brilliant spotlight followed the performers on the dance floor, but gloom made the faces of the musicians indistinguishable. The bandstand supported about ten chairs, and the musicians were decked out in tuxedos or dress suits (I am not sure which) with much tinsel and fancy braid. A heavy man was their leader, and he was following the cues of the dancers and singers. The floor-show star that night was Frankie "Halfpint" Jackson [sic].

When they got to the table, Souchon realized that the figure they could make out behind the spotlight looked like Joe Oliver, and he sat impatiently waiting for the lights to come on for the dancing. "It was Oliver all right, but his was a much more impressive figure now. The transition from the red undershirt and suspenders of Storyville's 'Big 25' to the clean white shirt at the Tulane gymnasium to the formidable figure he now presented, was almost too much to believe. He was now 'King,' the most important personage in the jazz world, surrounded by his own hand-picked galaxy of sidemen. His cordial welcome to two old New Orleans friends almost made us ashamed of the lumps in our throats . . ."[16]

11

Rhythm Kings

I saw Mike Fritzel last night and he sure seemed impressed when I told him about you boys wanting to come to Chi and that you would consider the Friar's Inn if everything—"Do" and hours were satisfactory—I sure poured it on thick, well Nick Mike wanted to know the dope in regard to the money you boys wanted etc. and I said that you would write him the full particulars that I just didn't know. All I knew was that you were the best band in the country. Well he expects a letter from you Nick. I'm sending your address to him so he can write you—I was supposed to meet him today at 3 but I left early so I left your address addressed to him at Friars.

BIX BEIDERBECKE WRITING TO NICK LA ROCCA, NOV 20, 1922[1]

Back in New York, at the height of the excitement over their music in the spring of 1919, the Original Dixieland Jazz Band did the one thing that a band that has scrambled to the top of the commercial heap is not supposed to do. They left. When they returned a year later, so much had changed in their world that there was no way they could find their footing again, though for the first months they continued to ride their crest of popularity. In part what had happened was almost inevitable. Their first single had been released in March 1917, only a month before the United States entered the war against Germany. The war meant that they immediately faced the draft. When they were called up for their physical examination in the spring of 1918, four of them, for various reasons, failed to pass. Shields, who had always been high-strung and temperamental on the bandstand, was considered too nervous to be a successful soldier, and La Rocca had a muscular tic in his left shoulder. Only Edwards was taken into the service, but with his departure the rest of them abruptly realized that their distinctive repertoire of compositions and arrangements presented them with a serious problem. As H. O. Brunn pointed out in his story of the band, the old days in New Orleans, when anybody could show up for a job and expect to fit into the casual ensemble, were part of the past. The band now had a repertoire of hundreds of pieces, many of them original compositions that they performed in their own arrangements, and all of it was in their heads. Nothing that they played was written down. To bring in another trombone player, it would be necessary to teach him the entire repertoire, as well as Edwards's own style as a trombonist, since the arrangements had been tailored to their individual musicianship.

New Orleans and its reserve of musicians saved the situation. Emile Christian, who had been one of the original choices as a cornetist when they'd first organized three years before, agreed to try filling in, though with some reluctance, because he usually played the cornet and had thought of giving up the trombone. The band took a break in the middle of the summer in 1918, and rode the train back to rehearse with Christian in New Orleans. For five weeks he listened to the recordings at Shields's house, playing along as they coached him in the elements of Edwards's style, with its complex shifts from legato melodic phrases to the more staccato rhythmic emphasis. The "feel" of what Edwards had been doing was certainly familiar to Christian. He'd grown up playing together in bands with all of them.

They continued to be one of the popular stars of the season in New York City, even with the change of personnel. They played for private parties hosted by theater stars like Al Jolson, appeared at concerts and War Bond rallies, and for an occasional private Long Island dance were paid as much as $1,000 for an evening's work. At the same time they continued at Reisenweber's, occasionally doubling in vaudeville as a specialty act. The continual stress had its effect on their personal lives, but so much was happening that they couldn't take time to deal with any of the problems. Ragas was the only one who was married when they left New Orleans, and there were increasing difficulties, since he was living in New York and his wife remained back home. His mood grew steadily more depressed and he was drinking more heavily. In November he traveled to New Orleans for a short trip to try to patch up the situation, but after his return to New York the next month he spent most of his time in his hotel room, avoiding the others when he didn't have to be on the bandstand. He soon was too debilitated to perform, and influenza developed into pneumonia. He died in Bellevue Hospital on February 18, 1919. Fearful of the influenza, the band had avoided his room, and the expenses of his illness had taken what he'd saved from their run of success. His widow arranged a memorial service for him in New Orleans, and the body was sent back by train.

In the weeks of his illness the band had already been struggling with the same problem they had just weathered when Edwards was taken in the draft: a large repertoire of unique arrangements, with nothing scored and all of it in each band member's memory. This time New Orleans wasn't able to fill in with a replacement. Larry Shields's younger brother Eddie was just beginning to work as a band pianist and he immediately took the train north in the hope that he could solve the problem, but he found that the music was too difficult and after a two-week trial he returned to New Orleans. Since the newspapers had been treating the band like celebrities, La Rocca had gotten used to making grandiose statements to the reporters, and he complained that they were having difficulty finding a new pianist because they couldn't find one who couldn't read music. The situation now was even more pressing—they had been scheduled to sail for an engagement in London, two days after Ragas's death.

There had been continual offers for the band to appear outside of New York, but a proposal from a London theater finally convinced La Rocca it was time to present their music to new audiences. They had been offered a job appearing in a London musical *Joy Bells*, starring the comedian George Robey; La Rocca immediately wired the producers and asked for a month's time to find a new pianist, which the producers accepted. The other three band members were as ready to get away from New York, if only for a short break. Shields had met a woman named Clara Ferguson in Chicago, when they first played at Schiller's in 1916, and she'd been one of the band's early fans. La Rocca recalled to H. O. Brunn that one night just before they were finally about to sail, he was walking to his hotel room when Shields came running up the stairs, waltzed him around the corridor, and announced that he and Clara had just gotten married, and she'd be joining them for the trip.

The problem with the pianist to replace Ragas was solved when a pianist already working in New York found their hotel, and knocked on La Rocca's door. J. Russell Robinson was a successful ragtime composer, with a busy career cutting piano rolls. More important was that he and his brother, a drummer, had worked in New Orleans in the nickelodeons on Canal Street, and part of their act had featured playing along with the band's recordings, so he was familiar with the basic repertoire. When the band sailed on March 22, 1919, Robinson and his wife joined them.

The London trip grew into an extended stay and introduced the New Orleans jazz style to England, but it almost ended as soon as it began. They were to play in a cabaret sequence in the musical, and at the moment, with the war over, London, and the theater, was swamped with American soldiers who were on their way back from France. The Original Dixieland Jazz Band was a memory of what they'd left behind in America, and they gave the band's appearance a tumultuous reception. It was never clear if the musical's star, Robey, was upset with their music or with the audience's applause, but at the end of the first night he summoned the show's producers and demanded that the group be fired. If they didn't leave, he would, and the management had to tell the band their engagement was over. The magazine *Town Topics* noted,

The Dixieland Jazz Band appeared in "Joy Bells" at the Hippodrome last Monday, but since has been withdrawn, probably on account of that ubiquitous complaint, influenza. On the occasion of their performance, they gave us

a demonstration of undiluted jazz, and it must be admitted, despite all that has been thought and said to the contrary, there was a certain charm in the mournful refrains, dramatically broken by cheery jingles and a miscellany of noises. . . . At one moment, the whole orchestra would down tools while one member tootled merrily or eerily on his own account, and the whole would resume again, always ready to give a fair hearing to any other individual player who suddenly developed a "stunt." The conductor was most urbane about it all, but everybody was perfectly happy, not excluding the audience who appreciated a novelty not unartistic. [2]

The confusion of their first night's appearance, widely reported in the press, brought them immediate attention, and they began a series of engagements that took them up and down Britain, including lengthy stays in London's busiest dance halls, among them the fashionable Rectors on Tottenham Court Road, and the mammoth Palais de Danse in Hammersmith. It was reported that nearly 6,000 patrons paid to dance to their music on their opening night in Hammersmith. Although their London stay was continually extended with new job offers, Robinson left in the winter. La Rocca felt he'd gotten tired of the audiences, but Robinson's wife was also having health problems with London's damp weather and the winter fogs. For some time, the band had been alternating with an English tango orchestra that included a young English ragtime pianist named Billy Jones, who became familiar with their repertoire and was the obvious replacement. The new pianist, who was gangling and red haired, was comfortable with the band's brand of showmanship, and he became the first European to perform American style jazz with a New Orleans orchestra.

The months in London were hugely successful, with large street billboards advertising their appearances and continuing crowds at the dance palaces. The musicians were more lavishly paid than they would have been even in New York. As important to the band's story is that Columbia Records decided to take them into the studios to produce singles for their 12-inch dance series. The band had been booked into the popular Palladium immediately after the fiasco with *Joy Bells*, and on April 16, less than a month after they'd left New York, they began their series of English recordings. Between April 1919 and May 1920 they recorded seventeen titles, with sound that was clearer and presented the ensemble sound more fully than their earlier studio experiences. For the first time Sbarbaro's snare drum was audible, and it was possible to follow the piano in the loudest passages. The most immediate advantage of the new recordings was that with the longer playing time, and the more relaxed London atmosphere, they could rerecord some of their standard repertoire at more relaxed tempos. For the first eight singles, recorded over the rest of the spring and the summer, they repeated familiar material. Since this is what London audiences were responding to, it was obviously to the company's advantage to be able to offer them the compositions that were causing all the excitement.

The recordings still reflected the limitations of the acoustical recording horns, and as in New York the sound technicians reacted to the repeated breaks of Shields's clarinet in the ensemble arrangements by altering the band's balance to bring him forward. For two of their less showy dance pieces, however, "Look At 'em Doing It" and "Satanic Blues," the cornet was brought closer to the center of the ensemble, and it was possible to hear some of the nuances in his playing that had been so evident in the Aeolian sessions. In "Satanic Blues" they repeated the old New Orleans habit of playing alternate choruses at half volume, as they had done on their recording of "At The Jazz Band Ball" for Aeolian.

There was a gap of five months between the last session using their familiar material and their next date in the studio in January 1920. Robinson and his wife had returned to New York and Jones was now the band's pianist. They recorded nine singles over the next five months, and it was immediately evident that they had exhausted the store of compositions either composed by La Rocca and the original members of the band or adapted from the store of shared band material in New Orleans. All of the new singles were popular songs, and although the playing had lost some of its intensity, what also emerged was their easy, skilled casualness in the ensembles. From a historical standpoint, the two waltzes that were recorded, "I'm Forever Blowing Bubbles" and "Alice Blue Gown," documented a less well-known side of the band's repertoire, because they were the only jazz recordings from that period of the endlessly popular dances that were part of every band's dance repertoire, whether or not they considered themselves a jazz orchestra. On the first of the waltzes Shields played the melody in the lower register, while La Rocca softly harmonized behind him; for the second waltz La Rocca played the melody, and it was Shields's turn to improvise a harmony.

Even though much of the material they recorded was less than compelling, for modern listeners the band's recording of a popular song by Irving Berlin, "I've Lost My Heart in Dixieland," has taken on a new significance, with its two choruses taken at half volume—La Rocca playing softly, using a mute, and Shields responding to his melody in the clarinet's lower register. The gentle charm of the performance could be considered a response to the critics who have found the band's brash manner and aggressive strut without charm of any kind.

The return to the United States came unexpectedly. The band had taken a break after a year of steady dance work, and Shields and his wife were finally enjoying a honeymoon trip to Paris. La Rocca had always relished the side benefits of his popularity, and he had been continually involved with their women dance fans. In London, however, the current young woman was the daughter of a highly placed member of English society, Lord Harrington, and after angry threats from her father, La Rocca hurriedly wired Shields and his wife to return from Paris while he arranged for their passage to New York. When they sailed on July 8, 1920, there were only three band members on the ship. Robinson and Edwards were waiting in New York, still members of the band, and their two replacements, Billy Jones and Emile Christian, stayed behind. Billy Jones returned to his tango orchestra in London, but Christian decided to try to put together a band to take a job in Paris. Despite help from La Rocca he was unsuccessful, but he decided to look for work with orchestras in Europe. In one of his letters, using La Rocca's nickname "Joe Blade," he referred with some amusement to the difficulties that had led to the rushed departure. "Joe, take a tip from me, from what I understand Old Man Harrington is going to fill you full of bullets if you ever put your foot in England again. So be careful and watch yourself if you ever intend to come back to England."[3]

A few months after I found the copy of the ODJB's first record in a pile of singles at the Salvation Army store in Sacramento, I found a second record by the Original Dixieland Jazz Band in another gritty pile of used 78s on the shelves of the Salvation Army thrift shop. I took it home and washed it, then put it on the phonograph. Instead of the raucous jazz sound I expected, what I heard was a novelty dance piece led by a hurrying saxophone with a clutter of instruments behind its insistent melody. It was the first recording the band made on their return from Europe, an arrangement of a new composition by Robinson titled "Margie." Despite my adolescent enthusiasm for whatever turned up in the Salvation Army bins that sounded even close to jazz, I never got over my first dismayed reaction, and for everyone who had taken the music of their earlier releases with any seriousness, "Margie" was a cold splash. In many anthologies of their recordings the song isn't even included, even though they were identified with it for the next four years. It was predictably their best-selling release, and if they had had the stamina they could have gone on touring and featuring "Margie"— adding the "Livery Stable Blues" if there were older fans in the audience—for the next two decades.

On their return to New York, La Rocca and the others found that there had been a major change in the public who had been their supporters when they left. They were abruptly thrust into a jazz world that had been changed by a new artist who had done his recordings while they were pleasing the dancers at the Palais de Danse. They had come back to the world of Rudy Weidoeft and his saxophone.

In the spring of 1917, in the weeks that followed their sensational breakthrough at Reisenweber's and other New York dance restaurants looked for a "Jass" band of their own, the first new band that turned up in the advertising columns of the *New York Times* opened at the Montmartre at 50th and Broadway, only a few blocks away, on March 21, two months after the New Orleans band had opened. The advertisement announced:

The ORIGINAL CALIFORNIA "JAZZ" BAND
From Frisco in "JAZZ" MUSIC

As far as Reisenweber's and its band were concerned, the Montmartre was simply trying to catch up with a good thing, but to the new arrivals, their music had been stolen by the Italians from New Orleans. The word "jazz" had been circulating for years in Los Angeles and San Francisco before it made its way east to Chicago, and the first band to be described in print as a "jazz" band was Art Hickman's San Francisco dance band when they entertained the crowd at a boxing training camp. With "jazz" suddenly the hot novelty, the California band that had opened at the Monmartre was offered a contract almost immediately by Edison Records, who recorded them on May 10, and during the next few months released ten singles by the group on both discs and cylinders. It's obvious from the recordings that their music still hadn't crossed over from "peppy" ragtime to what would be considered jazz, but it was their saxophonist who attracted attention.

The arrangements of the new band, titled on the Edison labels The Frisco Jazz Band, featured the lead melody played by a violin and a C-melody saxophone, a particularly assertive variant of the saxophone that in pitch comes between the alto and the tenor horns. The band also worked without a cornet on some of the recordings, relying on the saxophonist for the leads. The band's success didn't last beyond the spring season, but the saxophone player, Rudy Weidoeft, a twenty-four-year-old musician originally from Detroit, went on to be featured the next spring in a novelty number he played from his seat in the pit orchestra of a Broadway musical comedy titled *Canary Cottage*. Edison quickly realized his playing was attracting attention and recorded him in a series of uptempo, virtuoso saxophone solos in the new style that would come to be called "novelty ragtime." One of his recordings, "Sax-o-phobia," which he'd written in 1918, became one of the biggest-selling records of the year, and it is probably the biggest-selling saxophone solo record ever released. His stylishly tricky composition still turns up in recitals by ambitious student performers.

On their return to New York, the ODJB found themselves in the middle of a saxophone craze, and Victor Records insisted that they add a saxophone to their ensemble. The New Orleans bands had a problem that still has never been satisfactorily solved: after a long period of experimentation they had created a collective ensemble style that balanced three melodic instruments—clarinet, cornet or trumpet, and trombone—in a contrapuntal structure that was a logical musical response to the tone and distinctive attack of each instrument. Suddenly the bands were asked to absorb a fourth horn that had no obvious place in the tonal balance. The alto saxophone was in the same range as the cornet; did it play the melody with the cornet, replace it, harmonize with it? A tenor saxophone was in the same range as the trombone and presented the same problem. For their recording director at Victor Records there was no problem. Their new saxophonist, Benny Kreuger, who played an alto, was given the lead, and in the new balance Shields was virtually inaudible, with La Rocca reduced to a dim echo behind the busy runs of the saxophone.

The overwhelming success of "Margie" meant that the band would continue to do sessions with Kreuger, and the recording director the next year added a Broadway comic vocalist named Al Bernard whose contributions to the recordings pushed them even more firmly into the "dance novelty" category. The same producer a few years later was to object to the arrangements by the Gene Goldkette Orchestra that featured their cornetist Bix Beiderbecke, which would make him one of the handful of studio producers whose effect on the music they supervised was a creative disaster.

Out of the shambles of their old style, however, the band managed to create a moment that found its way into jazz history. W. C. Handy was anxious for them to record his "St. Louis Blues," and La Rocca finally agreed to do it in return for a share in the royalties. The recording featured a vocal by Bernard that was even dismaying by his standards, but it was followed by what is generally considered the first recorded jazz solo. Unlike the obbligato chorus Shields played on "Tiger Rag," with the cornet and trombone playing a loud rhythmic figure, on the new recording he played two choruses with only the rhythm section accompanying him. His beautifully shaped improvisation became the model for hundreds of versions of it that appeared on record over the next decades. His younger brother Harry continued, for the rest of his career, to play it just as his brother had.

The band, with the new successes, continued to draw crowds and to command large fees. They were traveling steadily now, however, and Shields's wife became tired of the continual nights in hotel rooms. She moved to Los Angeles and opened a beauty salon. Within a few months her husband, discouraged by the band's direction, and as usual quarreling with La Rocca, gave his notice and, following a weeklong theater engagement in Philadelphia, left the band to join his wife in California on December 20, 1921. Robinson had already left after a quarrel with La Rocca, who insisted that there was an agreement for the band to be paid an extra bonus from the royalties of "Margie" if the record had done well. Even with replacements who struggled to recreate the original arrangements, they were still so popular that La Rocca managed to keep touring. By 1924 it all became too chaotic and La Rocca suffered a nervous collapse. He returned to New Orleans, took up his old trade of building houses and doing electrical wiring. He put his horn away, and it seemed that the long musical road for the band, and for La Rocca himself, had finally ended.

Although at the time of their breakup the music of the Original Dixieland Jazz Band was still considered a novelty that would experience the same changes and adaptations of any popular musical style, jazz had already gone through a metamorphosis and emerged with an ensemble sound that absorbed the elements of their arrangements but made them recognizably new. It had become obvious, by the time of Shields's solo on "St. Louis Blues," that a recording didn't need to be only something danceable. It could offer arranged passages and solos that weren't fashioned for the dance floor. If La Rocca had even felt the need to change, however, the continued popularity of their familiar repertoire made it difficult for his band to think of moving into new musical territory. A younger New Orleans band did the job for them.

In the summer of 1920, with New Orleans ensembles still popular in the Chicago cabarets, Mike Fritzel, who was now running a cabaret called The Friar's Inn,

PAUL MARES, PROBABLY MID-1920S.

downstairs at 343 South Wabash Street, got in touch with a twenty-year-old cornetist from New Orleans named Paul Mares who was in Chicago staying with a friend, a member of the Chicago police force. (The pronunciation of his name has given generations of jazz enthusiasts difficulty. It is pronounced Ma-REHS, with the accent on the second syllable.) The policeman that Mares was staying with worked in the downtown Loop district, with Fritzel's cabaret in his neighborhood. Through him, Fritzel heard that another New Orleans musician was in town and contacted Mares to offer him a job. He was looking for a New Orleans band, and would pay a decent salary—$ 90 a week for each musician—if Mares could put one together for the Inn. Mares immediately began contacting other young New Orleanians who, like him, were drifting through a series of local orchestras in the Midwest, playing as much for the pleasure of it as for the opportunity to advance a "career."

Mares was only one of a number of talented young New Orleans musicians who had grown up playing jazz, and it was as much a matter of circumstances that he happened to be the one that Mike Fritzel got in touch with. The period when the band that he led worked together was relatively brief—less than a year and a half—but his own musicality and his consciousness of the new directions jazz was taking helped set their stamp on the younger musicians who clustered around them. Teenagers from Chicago's Austin High School hung out with the band members, devouring their recordings, and the teenage Bix Beiderbecke spent so much time listening to their music that he flunked out of the boarding school where his distraught parents had sent him to help cure his addiction to jazz. Beiderbecke's initial inspiration had been Nick La Rocca and the energy of the Original Dixieland Jazz Band, but the lyricism and the melodic inventiveness of his playing drew even more directly on the sound of Mares's playing in the cellar of the Friar's Inn.

Throughout his life Paul Mares was regarded as one of the most pleasant and least self-conscious of all the city's cornetists, and he never lost touch with his New Orleans roots, though for much of the Depression he and his wife ran the successful Bar-B-Cue restaurant in the Chicago Loop that became a popular musician's hangout. He was dark haired, modestly good looking, even in his formally posed portrait photos managing to seem unassuming. His father, Joseph E. Mares, whose family was of French ancestry, was, like Nick La Rocca's Sicilian father, a part-time musician, a cornetist with Tosso's Military Band who performed at West End. Unlike La Rocca's father, however, he encouraged his son to play, with the understanding that music would always be a sideline. Paul Mares learned on his father's cornet. The elder Mares established a successful business dealing in leather and hides, which in Louisiana meant muskrat pelts that Cajun trappers brought in from the bayous.

Mares was born on June 15, 1900, and was still a teenager when he left New Orleans. In the last year of the war he spent some months in the Marines, and at the same time was learning his father's business. He also was excited at the chance to play professionally, and there was an edge of adolescent restlessness in his moves from job to job. He had already played for occasional dances with most of the New Orleans musicians who were the same age, but even then it was another cornetist named Emmett Hardy, three years younger, who was attracting the most attention.

Trying to trace the movements of Mares and the other New Orleanians who would become the heart of the new band as they drifted through the Midwest in the months before Mares managed to get them together in Chicago is almost like trying to follow a skittering of birds in the first weeks of spring. Some of them spent time in an orchestra in Davenport, Iowa, the hometown of teenage cornetist Bix Beiderbecke, who was still in high school when they played in Davenport, teaching himself to play the cornet by fingering along with records by the Original Dixieland Jazz Band.

Another Italian American musician whose parents had been part of the wave of immigration from Sicily to the United States, clarinetist Leon Roppolo, had left New Orleans with Hardy in an orchestra led by trombonist Santo Pecora that had been hired to accompany an entertainer named Bea Palmer, whose act featured the "shimmy dance"—a dance routine where she just held her arms wide, put her feet together, and shook her body. The shimmy was already an established cabaret novelty featured by the dancer Gilda Gray, who had employed Frank Christian for her orchestra for a few years, but it was still a little advanced for audiences in small Midwestern cities. For the tour, Palmer had given her band the name The New Orleans Rhythm Kings.

The act played at the local Davenport theater, the Columbia, in the late winter of 1920, but there were already complaints that Palmer's dance exceeded the level of decency permitted for family audiences. She persisted with the tour to Peoria, Illinois, but there was so much criticism that finally she abandoned the act, and the musicians were left stranded. Roppolo and Hardy returned to Davenport, and joined the orchestra led by a pianist named Carlisle Evans at the Coliseum, a seedy dance hall that that was popular with Davenport's young dancers. Bix Beiderbecke had been playing only for a short time and he spent as many hours as he could for the rest of the spring getting away from his high school studies to hear the orchestra. The banjoist was named Louis Black, and as Lou or Lew Black he was to follow the New Orleans musicians as they restlessly tried different towns.

The casualness of the lives of dance band musicians in these years was part of a musical culture that has almost nothing to do with the emphasis on the distinctive personalities of the popular rock and punk bands touring today, with their stagey personae and each band's individual repertoire. In 1920 a dance band musician could spend a few nights in one group, go to the next town and spend a few nights with another group, without the dancers noticing much difference. The newcomers didn't have a real need for rehearsal, since most of the bands used stock arrangements, and even if younger players like Beiderbecke were poor readers, all the bands played the same dance pieces, with an occasional jazz novelty. All the new members of the orchestra had to do was follow what the rest of the band was doing. Roppolo and Hardy stayed with Evans's orchestra until the end of May when the Coliseum closed for the summer. In those years before theaters and dance halls could be adequately cooled, the owners had learned through unhappy experience that the only thing they could do about the summer heat was close down until the fall. For the hot months the dancers moved outdoors to fairgrounds or resorts, and the Carlisle Evans band had a job at Electric Park in Waterloo, Iowa.

Hardy and Roppolo decided to move on, and first Hardy and then Roppolo joined the band on the SS *Capitol*, the same river excursion boat on which Louis Armstrong had spent two years with Fate Marable's Orchestra. One of the musicians they'd grown up with, the nineteen-year-old trombonist George Brunies, was already with the band, and he'd told the leader about them. The job lasted less than a month. The New Orleanians couldn't get along with the orchestra leader, a drummer named Doc Wrixon, and they quit in July. For a brief time Beiderbecke was hired as Hardy's replacement, but he wasn't a union member, and he had to give up the job. He filled in with local bands until he went back to high school to finish his senior year.

By the time Mike Fritzel talked to Mares about a job at the Friar's Inn, Mares had been working in Chicago for some months. A drummer who had been with Jack Laine's Reliance Orchestra, Ragbaby Stevens, had contacted him some months before. Stevens had been among the first group of musicians to follow Tom Brown and later the ODJB to Chicago, and he had a chance to bring a band into a dance hall called Campbell Gardens. He first sent a telegram to trombonist George Brunies's older brother Albert (called "Abbie"), another cornetist. Abbie had just taken over as leader of the band at the Halfway House, a dance hall on the way out to Lake Ponchartrain, and had a part-time job driving a taxicab. He felt he was secure enough where he was. Stevens, in his telegram, added that Abbie could bring his seventeen-year-old younger brother George with him. Brunies later remembered his excitement at the chance to go, and his disappointment when his brother turned down the job. His friend Mares, however, could look ahead to a secure future in his father's business and he was interested. Brunies's memory was that he was the one who told Mares about the offer that Abbie turned down. "So I says Paul, I says, Abbie don't want to go to Chicago and I'm kind of leery, I'm afraid. Paul says, 'Man, give me that wire. I'll go.' So Paul went up and introduced himself to Ragbaby Stevens and Ragbaby liked him."[4]

Stevens offered Mares the job and told him to bring Brunies. Mares had less of a problem with money than the others because his father was helping him, so he loaned Brunies the $60 for the train fare and promised to lend him one of his younger brother Joe's overcoats, as it was still winter in Chicago. The job with Ragbaby Stevens lasted into the spring, and Mares and Brunies met the members of a young Chicago band who were playing at a ballroom called the Blatz Palm Garden. Three of the new contacts, pianist Elmer Schoebel, banjoist Lou Black, and drummer Frank Snyder, were to become members of the band that Mares would assemble a few months later.

The job at Campbell Gardens ended early in the summer, and during the next few weeks Mares and Brunies drifted from job to job. These were the same weeks that the musicians from Bea Palmer's band were wandering through the same territory. Mares, Brunies, Roppolo, and Hardy seem to have finally run into each other, and perhaps even worked together on the SS *Capitol*. All of them were still young, without any responsibilities, and along with the dance music that was the standard fare of the orchestras that picked them up, they were having a chance to play some jazz. Mares went into Chicago whenever he had a chance, staying with his friend and looking for a steadier job. In August Roppolo and Hardy managed to find a few weeks' work in Chicago with Bea Palmer, who was doing her shimmy in a basement cabaret, with Paul Mares finally joining them when he left the orchestra on the boat. When Mares got the offer from Fritzel, he got in touch with Roppolo, and sent a telegram to Brunies, who had temporarily returned to New Orleans.

Of the many clubs that Mike Fritzel owned or managed in his long career operating dance places in Chicago, the Friar's Inn was remembered as one of the least impressive. It was in a basement at 343 South Wabash, with a ceiling so low the bass player remembered that when he was on the bandstand he could reach up and touch it. All of the band had to adjust to playing at a softer volume, and Mares started using a felt hat hung over the bell of his cornet, a habit that became an affectation with a generation of younger Chicago cornetists. In the beginning, the band was filled out with the musicians they'd met in Chicago. The three New Orleanians picked up bassist Deacon Loyocano, who had come north with Tom Brown in 1915, but Loyocano took a break from the job and they replaced him with Tom Brown's brother Steve. Mares was the nominal leader of the band, but the pianist he'd met at the Blatz Palm Garden, Elmer Schoebel, did most of the band's arranging, and Schoebel brought the drummer, Snyder, and the saxophonist Jack Pettis with him. Schoebel was the only one of the band who was a skillful reader, and he played over new material for them on their occasional rehearsals. The banjoist was Lou Black, whom they'd met in the Davenport orchestra and who was now one of the crowd.

Of all of them in the band it was Schoebel who did the most work. He had to teach new material to the others, and he sketched out harmony parts for them and then rehearsed them until they could perform the new numbers. The Friar's Inn, like the other Chicago cabarets, also brought in occasional variety acts and the band was expected to play their accompaniment, which meant even more work for Schoebel. Schoebel was older than the others, though only in his mid-twenties. He was born in East St. Louis in 1896, and already had years of experience accompanying silent films and theatrical acts. He was also a talented composer. Several of his instrumentals had already been picked up and recorded by other orchestras, and some would become jazz standards.

In the beginning, Mike Fritzel demanded long hours from his musicians, in addition to the hours they spent after they woke up, learning new material in the afternoon rehearsals. When Loyocano decided to take a break, and the band brought Tom Brown's younger brother Steve to replace him on bass, Loyocano moved on. In the first months, Schoebel and the rhythm section played for the dinner hours, then the rest of the band joined them about ten and played as long as there was somebody in the club who was spending money. It quickly became a mecca for Chicago's white musicians, and Mike Fritzel let them sit in a section beside the bandstand. Beiderbecke had been sent away from Davenport by his parents, who were upset with his passionate interest in music, and he was now failing his studies at a private academy outside of Chicago by coming to the Friar's Inn every time he could get away from school. It was also at this point that the group of Chicago high school students, who would later get the name "The Austin High Gang," discovered the band, and they joined Beiderbecke in the side section.

When he was asked many years later, Mares still had pleasant memories of the band's months at Friar's Inn. He didn't feel that he should get a lot of credit for putting the group together: ". . . it was just because I knew the boys who could really fill that bill." He was certain that if his brother Abbie, who turned the job down, had decided to go to Chicago instead of staying at the Halfway House, he would have had as much success. What Mares remembered most vividly was that they were very young.

Friar's Inn was . . . cabaret style, with tables and a dance floor. There was a post on one side of the bandstand, and Rapp used to play with his clarinet against it for tone. He used to like to play in a corner, too.

Something happened every night at Friar's. There was always lots of fun and lots of clowning in the band. I remember we used to put oil of mustard on each other's chairs on the stand. Fritzl [sic] could never figure out what all the confusion was about at the beginning of a set. Jack Pettis would always go to sleep on the stand during the floor show, and we'd wake him up by holding the oil of mustard to his nose. . . . Nobody drank much at Friar's. We were all too young.

The band had lots of other offers for better money, but no one wanted to leave Friar's. Sam Levin wanted us for the New York Roseland, and they tried to get us for Ford's Arcadia in St. Louis, but nobody would leave. We used to try to hold rehearsals, but no one would show up. So we did our rehearsing on the job. The crowd never knew the difference. . . . We used to play Farewell Blues *a lot; Rapp wrote that one, you know. Also we played* Bugle Call Rag *and* Tin Room. *Bix—he was in school at Lake Forest Academy then—used to sneak down and pester us to play* Angry *so he could sit in. At that time, it was the only tune he knew.*[5]

Through Schoebel's connection with a very new and very ambitious music publishing company, the Melrose Brothers, in only a few months a session was arranged with Gennett Records, a subsidiary of the Starr Piano Company. The company had a crude studio set up alongside a railroad siding at their factory in Richmond, Indiana, just over the state line south of Chicago. The Melrose Brothers publishing company was owned by two young, neophyte Chicago businessmen, Walter Melrose and his brother Lester, who were operating a struggling music store on Cottage Grove Avenue on the South Side. Phonograph records were beginning to sell in larger numbers during these years, but for publishing companies like the Melroses sales of sheet music were still the largest source of profit. Many of the music publishing houses were steady advertisers in the pages of the country's most important African American newspaper, the Chicago *Defender*, and they advertised the month's new publications with the same promotional hype the record companies used for their singles.

Within a few years the Melrose brothers had signed publishing contracts with most of the city's important white and African American jazz composers, and they also engaged several of them to create the piano solo versions and the orchestra arrangements of the pieces they were publishing. The youngest Melrose brother, Frank, who recorded as "Kansas City Frank," was also a fine South Side–style pianist and had an insider's knowledge of the musical scene. In their tireless struggles to establish their business, Walter or Lester often provided financial backing for recordings using their compositions, and generally brought the arrangements they published to the studios or to rehearsals to make sure what was going to be recorded was the music they were selling.

Although an area of the music industry that generally functioned below the level of interest of dancers and new record buyers, there was a large market for

published orchestrations—usually called "stocks," short for "stock arrangements"—
that sold to thousands of orchestras performing everywhere, from Iowa roadhouses to bustling New York theaters, even to Europe and South America. The
Melrose orchestrations were generally done on a fee basis by local musicians
who worked as "house arrangers." The Melroses published these "stocks" as their
popular "Syncopation Series," and in their business calculations the recordings
functioned as promotion for the sales both of the orchestrations and of the sim-
plified solo piano versions. Schoebel was one of the musicians they employed for
their arrangements, and he also composed some of the company's early successes.
Other arrangements were credited to a pianist named Mel Stitzel, who, like
Schoebel, was to play an important role in the brief recording career of Mares
and his band.

The band's first trip to the Gennett studio was in April 1922. They tried to
do a take of the ODJB's "Livery Stable Blues," but failed to produce anything
that was usable. When they returned on August 29, 1922, they recorded four
titles, the first of them a composition titled "Eccentric" by J. Russell Robinson,
the ODJB's pianist. La Rocca and his band had been performing the piece on
their tours but hadn't had an opportunity to record it. The band that Mares took
into the studio played with a warm ensemble tone and a comfortable rhythm,
but Pettis's large-toned saxophone, playing the melody, dominated the recording
balance, and except for Roppolo's breaks the other instruments were crowded to
the edges of the ensemble. Despite these problems, the recording was immediately popular with other young jazz groups. Their arrangement quickly became a
small-band standard, and there has been a continuing series of recordings based
on their version.

Through most of the first session Mares played with a mute, which has led to
the assumption that he had been influenced by Joe Oliver. Mares encouraged the
comparisons by describing nights that he spent listening to Oliver's band, which
was playing at the same time at the Lincoln Gardens, but Oliver had already left
New Orleans in 1919, and although Mares also had some of Oliver's mannerisms,
temperamentally he was a different style of musician. His playing was more typical of other white New Orleans cornetists of the early 1920s. He played with the
same clean, uncluttered line and the assured Italianate tone characteristic of the
musicians who worked with Jack Laine's bands. It was a style that was essentially
modest, scaled to the small clubs where they were performing.

For many jazz writers the playing of the band's clarinetist, Leon Roppolo,
was considered to be their enduring contribution to the developing jazz idiom.
He has long been considered the first instrumentalist of the early jazz period to
emerge as a true soloist. Fortunately, there are second and sometimes third takes
of several of the pieces they recorded, and they show Roppolo working within
a melodic outline obviously already rehearsed, but improvising a variation on
each take. The major influence on his style was clearly Larry Shields, and often
the phrasing of Roppolo's breaks and the outline of his solos brought the listener

back to Shields, but his playing was softer, more introspective. All of them were occasionally using marijuana, which was just beginning to come into the jazz world, but Roppolo was one of the few among that generation of jazz artists whose careers were shortened by some other stimulant besides the ever-present alcohol. The others in the band felt that some of his most unique choruses came out when he was high.

Roppolo was thin and dark haired, with the intent stare of an Italian character actor in a silent film. His family were Sicilian immigrants and he was born outside of New Orleans in the small community of Lutheran on March 16, 1902. He began playing the violin as a boy; there is a family photograph of him in a band uniform at about age ten, posed with the violin. The family moved into New Orleans, however, and he dropped the violin when he found out he couldn't play it in street parades. He was in his mid-teens when he left New Orleans with Bea Palmer's band. Some of his solos were so unique that the band turned them into arrangements as compositions on their own. Brunies described the solo that they turned into their "Farewell Blues": ". . . we were playing the "Weary Blues" one night, so all of a sudden Rapp takes a chorus, just playing by himself. He didn't care nothing about the people, he's high . . ."[6] When they arranged Roppolo's solo melody as "Farewell Blues" they tried to work the feeling of a train whistle into the harmonization of the first chorus, and the distinctive voicing they created turned up in the later composition "Mood Indigo" by Duke Ellington, who adopted the voicing and a suggestion of the melody, altering it to a slower tempo.

The phonograph industry was considerably less formal than it was to become later, and the singles the band had done were released under the name of the cabaret, as the Friar's Society Orchestra. The name of a local promoter, Husk O'Hare, who had nothing to do with the band, was also added, and on the record labels the singles were credited to "Friar Society's Orchestra, direction Husk O'Hare."

In the crowded months between August 1922 and March 1923, the band—now known under the name Bea Palmer had given them, the New Orleans Rhythm Kings—dominated the white Chicago jazz scene. Joe Oliver returned from California and opened with his Creole Jazz Band at the Lincoln Gardens in June, bringing the other New Orleans jazz style to Chicago dancers. When his protégé Louis Armstrong joined the band in August, there were nightly crowds in the Gardens to hear the new cornetist, but for the musicians who were to become the "Chicago School" of jazz it was the sound of the band downstairs in Friar's Inn, with Roppolo leaning against the wooden pillar and Mares slouched with a felt hat over the bell of his horn that left the deepest imprint on their own playing. Cornetist Jimmy McPartland remembered that they would play the NORK recordings at the slowest possible speed on their hand-wound phonographs, and pick out the notes of each part in the arrangement. When these young players themselves began to record within a few years, it was the repertoire and the band style of the NORK that they imitated.

THE NEW ORLEANS RHYTHM KINGS, UNDER THEIR EARLIER NAME, THE FRIAR'S SOCIETY ORCHESTRA, 1922. FROM LEFT: GEORGE BRUNIES, PAUL MARES, LEON ROPPOLO, ELMER SCHOEBEL, JACK PETTIS, LEW BLACK, STEVE BROWN. THE DRUMMER, BEN POLLACK, IS IN THE LEFT REAR.

What the success of the 1922 and 1923 NORK recordings made clear was that there were already two clearly defined New Orleans jazz styles; one white, one black, both of them popular and both growing in poise and musical assurance. The Rhythm Kings' next sessions at the Gennett studio in Richmond, Indiana, in the spring of 1923 were to define many of the directions white jazz would follow for the next decades, though only through a series of coincidences that the recordings were made at all.

Once again the Melrose brothers were behind the trip to Indiana, probably even paying the musicians and the studio costs for at least one of the two days they were scheduled to be in the studio. The material to be recorded included some of the strongest new compositions that the Melrose brothers were publishing, from "Sweet Lovin' Man," a popular piece played by King Oliver's band that was co-composed by Lil Hardin and Walter Melrose, to "Wolverine Blues," a composition by one of the company's newest discoveries, pianist Jelly Roll Morton. Each of the eight titles they recorded became part of the bedrock of the style they had refined and reshaped. The Rhythm Kings were booked into the studio on March 12 and 13; the first session by Oliver's band was scheduled for the studio three weeks later, on April 6. In those three weeks, between the recordings by the two bands, much of the outline of the two diverging jazz traditions was documented and clarified.

The near-cancellation of the sessions with the New Orleans Rhythm Kings almost inadvertently shaped the music that emerged. Shortly before the sessions were scheduled, Mares found himself without a band. Elmer Schoebel and the others in the rhythm section had gotten tired of the long hours, and Schoebel

Recording Information of Wax No. 11352
11352A
11352B

Date Recorded 3-12-23   By E C A Wickemeyer   Richmond, Ind.

Subject "SWEET LOVIN' MAN"

By New Orleans Rhythm Kings, Formerly Accompanied by
    Friar's Society Orchestra

Composed by   Music by   Hardin-Melrose

Words by   Hardin-Melrose   Published by   Melrose Brothers, Chicago

Copyright   19   Royalties

Recording Expense

Wax Shipped   Trunk No.   Via

Suggest Using in   Supplement

Remarks

RECORDING LEDGER SHEET FOR THE NEW ORLEANS RHYTHM KINGS SESSION, MARCH 12,
1923. THE LEDGER LISTS THREE TAKES OF "SWEET LOVIN' MAN," 11352, 11352A, AND
11352B, EACH ON A SEPARATE WAX MASTER. THE SESSION WAS SUPERVISED BY E. C. A.
WICKEMEYER, AND THE COMPOSITION WAS CREDITED TO LIL HARDIN, WHO WOULD LATER
MARRY LOUIS ARMSTRONG, AND WALTER MELROSE.

was also exasperated with the casualness of the New Orleanians, who were still
in their early twenties and often acted like schoolboys. They were careless about
rehearsals; they didn't bother to learn to read music, so he had to play new material over and over for them and teach them the arrangements—which they then
wouldn't bother to follow. They also continually upset Fritzel by insisting on playing their own music when the customers would have been happier with more
dance numbers, and by their habit of playing noisy practical jokes on each other
on the bandstand. Some nights they spent more time talking to the even younger
Chicago musicians who clustered beside the bandstand than they did entertaining
the crowds. When the Midway Gardens offered Schoebel a job as leader of the
orchestra there, he immediately accepted, and took the rhythm section with him.

What could have been a disaster turned out to be the moment when the classic New Orleans ensemble style was most clearly defined. Mares went to the studio in Indiana without their saxophonist Jack Pettis, who had also left after the
others moved to Midway Gardens, and there was no effort to bring in another
banjoist. For two days they recorded with the classic ensemble of the Original
Dixieland Jazz Band: cornet, clarinet, trombone, piano, and drums. Mares called
Mel Stitzel, who was working as a relief pianist at the Midway Gardens, to replace
Schoebel. Stitzel was another of the Melrose staff arrangers and had played occasional nights with the band at Friar's Inn. The drummer Mares decided on was
a young fan named Ben Pollack, who was to become an important figure in the
Chicago scene that emerged over the next years.

With only the three horns, Mares and the others were able to document the
now fully developed ensemble that had begun to take shape with Jack Laine's

musicians only a decade before. They didn't have to find a way around the turgid phrasing of Pettis's saxophone, which still clung to dated "jingly" mannerisms. Without the banjo doubling the beat, Stitzel could shape the accompaniment of the horns with a quick responsiveness. A bass player—particularly one of their friends from New Orleans, Steve Brown or Chink Martin—would have been the ideal ballast, but listening again to the singles they made it is startling how full they managed to sound with only five musicians, even with recording horns that were set up much closer to the instruments than the boomy recording horns that the first bands like the ODJB had to contend with. Stitzel was in the difficult situation of filling out the arrangements, but his playing was fresh and continually musical.

The essence of the eight titles they recorded was the interplay between the three horns, for once balanced both in tonal quality and in musical conception. The three of them had known each other since they were boys and had grown up in the same neighborhoods, which gave them an intuitive feel for each other's phrasing. Mares was particularly effective on the arrangements, emphasizing his spare melodic drive. He was only twenty-three, but there are elements of the New Orleans style on an arrangement like "That's A Plenty," a new composition by drummer Pollack, that seem almost to sum up and refer to a decade of musical change and expansion. Pollack himself was the ideal drummer for the group, with a steady pulse that anchored the New Orleans light-footedness. Just as jazz ensembles everywhere had picked up their "Eccentric" the year before, their version of "Maple Leaf Rag" became a kind of test piece for other bands, and their brilliant first recording of "Wolverine Blues" brought the tune the attention that the Melroses had been hoping for.

Of the three instruments of the basic New Orleans front line, the clarinet's obbligato style had taken the longest to work out its unsteadiness, but with Roppolo's playing all of the raw edges were rubbed smooth. His melodic figures worked at any tempo and he moved without loss of intensity from the lowest register of the instrument to notes at the limit of the ability of the recording stylus to capture them.

Their recording of "Tin Roof Blues," one of the band's compositions, could be considered the stylistic source of almost all the small-band white jazz that followed in their wake, with its semi-arranged passages and warm-toned solos by all three instrumentalists. There were three takes, which makes it possible to hear Roppolo considering and reconsidering his haunting solo. In his book *Lost Chords* Richard Sudhalter[7] included transcriptions of all three solos, and a comparison of the three melodic lines shows that although Roppolo entered on the same high note and ended each solo with the same sequence of notes to bring back the cornet melody, each of the versions was subtly altered in the middle measures, giving new depth to his interpretation. Both his solo and Brunies's gruff trombone solo have been repeated by thousands of musicians who have continued their traditions.

The three versions of "Tin Roof Blues" have been analyzed many times, but also a controversy over the composition itself is continually revived. Two months after the NORK's single was released, on June 23, Oliver's band recorded a new composition by New Orleans pianist Richard M. Jones titled "Jazzin' Babies Blues," which included a melody strain similar to the chorus of "Tin Roof Blues." Mares and the band, however, were surrounded by enthusiastic listeners who insisted that the group was already playing the piece in their first sets at Friar's Inn months before they recorded it. Brunies remembered that it was an arrangement they had worked out on the bandstand, and that their name for it was "The Rusty Rail Blues." Walter Melrose heard them play it and liked it enough to offer them a $500 advance for the rights. Because the piece had been popular at the Inn, they put all of their names on it as composers.

Melrose felt the piece needed a new title, so they decided to name it after a place they'd played in New Orleans they called the Tin Roof Café. Despite the similarity in the melody of the chorus, the Rhythm Kings' version is different in feel and presentation from Oliver's later recording of "Jazzin' Babies Blues"; and the semi-arranged sections in the Rhythm Kings' arrangement point toward the new direction the New Orleans ensemble would take over the next years. It was also the performance that most clearly caught the personal tone and thoughtful phrasing of Mares's lead, which was to leave its own traces in the style of many later trumpeters.

To distinguish the new sessions from the singles credited to Husk O'Hare and his Friar's Society Orchestra, the band got back the name they'd been using on the job, "The New Orleans Rhythm Kings," with a parentheses on the record label ("Formerly Friar's Society Orchestra").

The difficulties of keeping a band together were wearing down Mares, who was one of the most good-natured of the New Orleans musicians, and he found it almost impossible to keep the band organized without Schoebel. The previous fall, with another of the young Chicagoans who hung around them, Volly DeFaut, filling in on clarinet, Mares sent Roppolo back to New Orleans to bring up more musicians. Bassist Chink Martin joined them, along with violinist Oscar Marcour, clarinetist Nunzio Scaglione (to make it possible for Roppolo to move over to the alto saxophone), and cornetist Emmett Hardy. This time there were more than the usual difficulties. The new arrivals were required to wait for a period before the musicians' union would let them work, but only Scaglione passed the reading test, and Hardy was so ill with tuberculosis that he had to return to New Orleans.

After the sessions with Stitzel Mares finally came to the end of his patience, and disbanded what was left of the group. He and Roppolo went to New York and found work with a band led by Bea Palmer's husband Al Siegel in Greenwich Village, while the other two, the drummer Ben Pollack and Brunies, scuffled with different groups in Chicago. The band still wasn't finished, however. Walter Melrose had another two-day studio session planned in Indiana, and of their three periods of recording in the Gennett studio this was to be the most discussed. To get their published material out on record the Melrose brothers reasoned that, once in the studio, they could bring together musicians who would play what the brothers wanted, and the way they wanted it played. In Richmond, Indiana, on July 17 and 18, 1923, they brought together the already successful New Orleans Rhythm Kings and the publishing company's new composer and piano soloist, Jelly Roll Morton, for two days of recording. The music that was recorded has been so often discussed in relationship to Morton's career that the story of the circumstances of the sessions and the singles that came out of the two days belongs in the story of Morton's itinerant life and career in the chapter that follows.

There is also a poignancy in the last sessions of the Rhythm Kings, since for Roppolo and Mares, the two days in July essentially marked the end of their musical careers. Mares was only twenty-three but decided it was time to walk away from the trials and uncertainties of leading a jazz band. He returned to New Orleans and his family's business in furs, hides, and muskrat pelts. He joined Santa Pecora in New Orleans in 1925 for a recording session that used the Rhythm Kings name; in the 1930s he played again occasionally with friends. But the family business—and later operating successful restaurants in New Orleans and Chicago—took all of his time. In those short months that he'd led his group, however, he had given a new shape and focus to the style of jazz that would always be associated with them.

Roppolo spent the next months after their last sessions filling in with different bands, but his moods were becoming increasingly unpredictable, and he returned to New Orleans, where he worked for some months with Abbie Brunies's Halfway House Orchestra. His last recordings were done at a session that produced two sides with that band on January 22, 1925. He played an extended duet on alto saxophone with tenor player Charlie Cordilla on one arrangement, and a characteristic low-register clarinet solo on the other was probably by Roppolo. When Pecora and Mares came into the studio three days later to record as The New Orleans Rhythm Kings, they intended to use Roppolo, but Cordilla had to fill in when Roppolo couldn't play. Roppolo was committed to an asylum a few months later, and except for occasional periods in the 1940s when he spent a few weeks outside, his life ended there. He was only twenty-three when he was institutionalized and forty-one when he died in 1943.

12

Mister Jelly

By that time I was thinking of leaving Chicago—a different class of people were invading the city at the time. So when a very prominent figure around town by the name of Lovey Joe Woodson came to me and told me they had a job for me in Los Angeles, I didn't even wait to ask him the salary, I was so anxious to get away.

I had a lotta clothes those days, which I packed and shipped. It happened to be summertime and the dust was terrible in that tourist car. I was almost as dusty as a boll weevil when I arrived in Los Angeles. It was a funny situation. They had a brass band to meet me at the station, but when I got off covered in all that dust, the newcomers who didn't know me asked was that the hot Jelly Roll people had talked so much about? "The first thing this guy needs is to go to the cleaners. He's got a dirty suit of clothes on."

JELLY ROLL MORTON DESCRIBING HIS ARRIVAL IN LOS ANGELES IN 1917[1]

Once the New Orleans musicians began traveling, the easiest place to find many of the city's best artists was almost anywhere else, since that's where they found jobs. These were the traveling days of New Orleans jazz, and the story of the music has to be told in part through the stories of the musicians who were on the road. The sound of much of their music also has to be traced out on the road, where many of them recorded. Only a handful had an opportunity to record in their hometown. Like most smaller American cities, New Orleans didn't have any recording facilities. It wasn't until the mid-1920s that the companies developed the practice of sending their engineers out on the road with a recording director to see what they could find. As the interest of music buyers shifted from sheet music to recordings, the companies were learning that popular local artists could also bring in local sales.

THE SEVENTEEN-YEAR-OLD JELLY ROLL
MORTON IN NEW ORLEANS.

Of all the early traveling musicians who managed to get into a recording studio, Jelly Roll Morton is the most flamboyant and the most difficult to bring into
focus, because it's so often uncertain where he was or what he was doing. To
compound the difficulties, his own accounts of his life and adventures often had
only a tenuous connection to what really happened. His early New Orleans years,
ironically, come down to us with the most clarity, though this is only the result
of persistent digging by modern researchers who finally succeeded in confirming some of the most basic facts, among them his birthdate and proper name.
He claimed that his family were all descended from the original French settlers,
but his younger sister Frances Oliver mentioned in an interview in 1969 that
their maternal great-grandmother was a German Jewish immigrant. "My brother
and I both got our large Jewish noses from our great grandmother Mimi, who
was a German Jew—Felice Schmidt, so, of course, we're Jewish."[2] What is certain is that her brother was born on October 20, 1890, his name at his baptism
was Ferdinand Joseph Lamotte, and his parents were named Edward Lamotte
and Louise Monette. His mother was light-skinned enough to pass for white,
and since Morton himself had very fair skin his father probably was also light.
In 1894 his mother married a man named William Mouton and they moved to
her mother's house at the corner of Frenchmen and North Robertson Streets.
The two-story frame house survived the flooding of Hurricane Katrina, and it is
marked with a hand-painted plaque beside the door.

Morton is an anomaly in many ways, not only because of the confusion that clouds much of his story but because he continues to fascinate so many writers drawn to this period of jazz history. He has probably been the subject of more research than any other New Orleans musician. In 1938 Morton himself spent hours telling his story to Alan Lomax at the Library of Congress, and he also began an autobiography. William Russell, who was the owner of the small, important revival record company of the 1940s, AM Records, and one of the men behind the rediscovery of Bunk Johnson, devoted much of his life to locating and interviewing everyone who might have had some contact with Morton. The resulting book, *Oh, Mr. Jelly!*,[3] completed only months before Russell's death in 1992, is one of the most comprehensive compilations of material on anyone's life that has been ever been presented in a single volume. The book is in a large format, more than 700 pages in length, and is filled with photographs, interviews, background documentation, letters, and reproductions of Morton's music scores. What makes Morton's story even more complicated, however, is that even with this wealth of material, he *still* remains an elusive, complex figure. At least at one point he explained the name "Morton"—he didn't want people he encountered on his travels to think he was French, so when he left New Orleans he anglicized his family name.

Morton spent much of his life as a persistent advocate of New Orleans jazz, its place in musical history, and his own role in its development; but except for occasional short visits later, he worked only for a short period of time in the city as a musician, and the playing he did was in the Restricted District, where he began his musical career as a very young and very inexperienced brothel pianist. The pianists usually worked in the more expensive houses, where they played and sang popular requests and played for a little dancing. They did their heavier playing after hours, when they met at one of the Storyville cabarets and tried to outperform each other in "cutting" contests.

As a dutiful Creole son, Morton began working a menial job in a barrel factory in his early teens, earning $15 dollars a week, but he was also singing in little street serenading groups, and had learned to play the piano well enough to impress his friends. He spent considerable time in Biloxi on the Mississippi coast, where he stayed with his godmother, Eulalie Hecaud (or Hecault, the spelling is uncertain). After the death of his mother when he was fourteen his grandmother became responsible for him, but at the same time he began to drift along the sidewalks in Storyville with his friends to stare at the girls and watch the crowds. In his autobiographical sketch he described his first experience playing in one of the houses.

One Saturday night, whilst on one of the wild jaunts, we heard that one of the houses was stuck for a professor (pianist). My friends encouraged me to go for the job, but my fear was so great the only way I would go was if my friends would go with me. They only wanted me, however, so that was impossible. They finally *agreed to take the other upstarts along and put them in a rear room, so their guests could not see them. (I felt sure that it was a plot to kidnap me, since I had a narrow escape when I was younger on Melpomene and Willow Streets.) So they agreed to let them stay where I could see them. I was so frightened that when I first touched the piano the girls decided to let me go immediately. One of my friends spoke up, "Go ahead and show these people you can play." That encouraged me greatly, and I pulled myself together, and started playing with the confidence of being in my own circle. (Remarks of the inmates and guests) "That boy is marvelous." The money was plentiful, and they tipped me about $20, but I did not want to accept (it) because I was not taught that way.*[4]

Morton was finally persuaded to take the job, but he was afraid that his family would find out what he was doing, and for some months he managed to conceal his activities by telling his grandmother that he'd been changed to night work at the barrel factory. He brought home the same weekly salary. He picked up his nickname in these first months in the District—"jelly roll" was a sexual term that could mean either the vagina or the penis. He also was known as a "winding boy," which meant that he moved his hips when he walked and danced, and also inferred that he employed the same movements when he spent a little time with one of the girls in the houses. A photograph of him taken when he was about seventeen shows one of the skinniest, youngest, most uncomfortable-looking professors who ever worked in a brothel, but in his later memories he always thought of himself as the "sport" he later became, with closets filled with suits and a diamond set in his front tooth.

The District was like a small town, however, and his uncle, one of his mother's brothers who also lived in the house and spent occasional nights in Storyville himself, was aware of what he was doing and sometimes borrowed one of Morton's new suits when he went out. One night Morton caught him and beat him, and in the confusion of their fight his grandmother finally realized what her grandson was doing. His sister remembered that she was about eight years old when Morton and his grandmother quarreled. "She just didn't approve of him playing in those shady places and coming back home where children were. She wanted him to respect a girl, and not come in and tell his experiences of the night before to my uncles. I mean, some of those things were shady, I guess. Also, my grandmother was afraid of venereal diseases and thought he might bring them home to the family."[5]

Her teenage brother was forced to leave the house and went to live with his godmother in Biloxi. In his new situation Morton was left in an emotional vacuum, and soon there were scrapes with the law. At one point, after some confusion over his identity following a local crime, he found himself working on the city chain gang. An actor named William Benbow rescued him from that situation. Morton became part of a blackface vaudeville act with Benbow and his wife on a tour of small theaters that led them through Mississippi and up to Memphis.

He eventually became part of a comedy duo with a woman he introduced as his wife. She sang while he accompanied her on the piano, and he did a comedy routine and performed a piano solo. He appeared in blackface, wearing a ragged tramp's outfit, and there were occasional mentions of their act in the trade journals, generally praising his work and singling out his piano playing.

At this point following Morton's travels becomes more problematic. His wandering took him from one city to another, sometimes with one of the shows, sometimes on the trail of an optimistic financial scheme, sometimes just with a hunch he might find a job as a pianist. He was in New York about 1911 or 1912 and in Chicago sometime later, but couldn't find enough opportunities in either city to keep him long. In New York at least, he had a chance to show off his piano skills, and the stride-style veteran James P. Johnson remembered that Morton was "hot" when he hit town. Morton's penchant later in life for insisting that he had invented jazz (he set the year as 1902, when he was twelve), as well as virtually every musical phrase he heard on contemporary jazz and swing recordings, irritated many musicians, though some found it entertaining. Younger musicians often were impressed, while musicians closer to Morton's age had considerably more difficulty with his obsessive boasting. One of the New Orleanians who glimpsed Morton on one of his occasional trips back home to New Orleans before World War I was a young drummer named Zutty Singleton, who was eighteen at the time and just beginning his own long and successful career, which many years later included sessions with Morton. He first saw Morton in one of the Storyville cabarets where pianist Steve Lewis (who was leading the group Singleton was playing with) had taken him, probably in 1913 or 1914.

I didn't get a chance to speak to Jelly that night, I just saw him. Several times, later, I'd go around this bar, 25, and I'd see him with Louis Wade, a pianist and Manuel Manetta, and Fred Washington and all those guys. They played at the big sporting houses. They all had different times to play their sessions at those houses and there were about five or six piano players that made those rounds. Jelly was among those piano players that used to do that kind of work you know. Tony Jackson had gone by that time. He was Jelly Roll's favorite piano player. He loved him—he was crazy about Tony . . . The first time I heard Jelly play was at Big 25. That was the headquarters where a lot of piano players used to hang out in New Orleans. One evening, I happened to go in there. I had to have on my long pants, and Steve Lewis, he taken me in there. Different guys were sitting in on the piano, in the wine room they called it, you know, and I heard Jelly play then. I thought he was great. I liked his time. I liked his tempo. I liked the way he played the piano. I felt I could keep time with him, you know.[6]

In February 1969, at the same time that Singleton was talking with Bob Green about Morton in New York, William Russell had an opportunity to interview Singleton's wife Marge Creath Singleton, who was considerably less enthusiastic about Morton than her husband was. She had much more contact with Morton during this same period, after he'd made his way north to St. Louis, and—as is characteristic with so many of the glimpses we have of him from these years—her description of him gives a less sanguine picture of his life. She was the younger sister of cornetist and bandleader Charlie Creath, whose early recordings featured his stunning muted work and also presented an ambitious arrangement of one of Morton's compositions, "Grandpa's Spells." Marge Creath became a pianist herself, and played with her brother's band for their OKeh sessions. Morton was twenty-six when he showed up at the house with her brother.

> *Jelly was a friend of my brother, Charlie Creath. They were both alike—a whole lot alike, bragged a lot. My home was in East St. Louis and we used to go to the nickelodeon on Sunday to see the movies. They weren't even talking movies and Jelly Roll was playing an upright piano down there. . . . I know it was in 1916, because I was just finishing high school. I used to go to the movies every Sunday. It was only a nickel to get in on Sunday afternoons, and Jelly played piano. The piano was right to the side of the screen, a big upright piano. And Jelly was accompanying the movie, sometimes sad music, you know, sometimes fast, and ragtime. It was just nickelodeon piano, that's all.*

She remembered that Morton spent much of his time gambling, and he'd been given the job playing for the movies by two friends of her brother named Lobe and Don, whom she referred to as uncles although they were the uncles of one of her best friends. She was uncomfortably aware that Morton was also earning money by pimping for local prostitutes.

> *The Hawkins brothers gave Jelly this job playing in the nickelodeon, just to keep him with gambling and eating money, that's all. He wasn't dressed sharp then. . . . He played just to have some money to gamble with. He gambled a lot, my brother gambled a lot, and the Hawkins brothers gambled a lot. Jelly Roll and my brothers were enough alike in ways and talk to be brothers, because they were very much braggadocios. . . . In that period, Jelly Roll couldn't have been thirty years old. He must have been in his twenties. They were all young men and they all dressed very sharp, but Jelly Roll wasn't as sharp as they were, but Uncle Lobe and Uncle Don were crazy about him because he played good piano on Broadway. At that time, Jelly took himself more seriously as a gambler than a musician—as a gambler and a hustler. The music was just a side issue with him, that's all. Nobody in East St. Louis didn't notice him, or care anything about Jelly Roll. He didn't mean a thing. There were too many piano players around.[7]*

A year later, in 1917 or 1918, a photograph was taken of the entertainers at a very successful Los Angeles cabaret called the Cadillac, and in the center of the line of six well-dressed, smiling performers is a trim, satisfied-looking Morton.

JELLY ROLL MORTON WITH THE CAST OF ENTERTAINERS AT THE CADILLAC, LOS ANGELES, ABOUT 1917. FROM LEFT: "COMMON SENSE" ROSS, ALBERTINE PICKENS, JELLY ROLL MORTON, ADA "BRICKTOP" SMITH, EDDIE RUCKER, MABLE WATTS.

He is in shirtsleeves, but his shirt is buttoned and he's wearing a bowtie. The group are posed half turned from the lens with their hands on each other's shoulders, and Morton's hand is on the shoulder of Ada "Bricktop" Smith, who was to become one of the legendary cabaret entertainers and night club owners in Paris in the 1920s and 1930s. Again, it's difficult to sort out what he was doing and how long he lasted with the job, but he seems to have been working as the accompanist for the acts with a solo number of his own. His own account of the engagement, however, is considerably more extravagant: "On my opening night they had to have the police department to stop the crowd, because I was pretty well advertised. Then the movie-star trade began, and we didn't have anything but movie stars as long as I stayed there . . ."[8]

Whatever Morton's part was in the show, he lasted only a few weeks. He went to the manager and claimed to have seen Bricktop stealing some of the money that was supposed to go in the common "kitty"—the tips for the night for all of the employees in the cabaret—but after an argument, he was the one who was fired. In his own version of the events, his response was to close down the Cadillac, the cabaret where they'd been working. "There was a road house out in a little place called Watts, about nine or ten miles from Los Angeles. The colored owner, George Brown, wasn't doing any good, so, when I offered to come out there, he immediately accepted. I told him I didn't want to open until he notified Hollywood that I'd be working there. We had invitations printed and, my opening night, all Hollywood was there. That ended the Cadillac. They kept on going down and down until they had to close."[9]

Los Angeles continued to be Morton's nominal base for the next six years, as he continued his itinerant career up and down the West Coast, sometimes leading bands and sometimes operating cabarets and restaurants, none of them very large or very successful. What drew him to Los Angeles was the woman who was as close to being a companion as he had in his life. Sometime in his wanderings—perhaps on an earlier trip to California—he got to know Bill Johnson, the New Orleans bass player and small business owner who had put the Creole Band together in 1914, and who toured with the band on the vaudeville circuit for four years. About this time Johnson had broken up the band after problems with the cornetist, Freddie Keppard, and was spending time in both Chicago and Los Angeles. Morton also became close with Bill's younger sister, who was now calling herself Anita Gonzales. As soon as Morton reached Los Angeles he tried to find her again, even though for some reason he never explained, Johnson was evasive. But Morton persisted.

> *Finally I runned up on her old lady, her mother, and she says, "Oh my, how Anita would like to see you!"—and she got me in touch with Anita. Anita had bought a saloon business in a little town called Las Vegas, Nevada, and she had made a lotta money. When her mother notified her I was in L.A., she came up to see me and we got back together. She said she should let the saloon go unless I decided I liked Las Vegas. So I tried Las Vegas a while, but it was too dog-gone cold in the winter and too hot in the summer. We turned the place over to Bill Johnson and, when we saw him next, he was riding in a MacFarland automobile, which they was plenty high those days.[10]*

Like everything else in Morton's life, it is difficult to sort out what his relationship was with Anita Gonzales, except that they didn't get married and they fought continually. Despite his later marriage in New York, it was Anita who was with him at his death in Los Angeles in 1941, and who inherited his estate. It is even more confusing attempting to follow his musical journeys as he and Anita moved from city to city, once as far north as Vancouver, with an excursion boat trip to Alaska. He also drifted as far east as Casper, Wyoming, performing as a solo act while he and Anita tried living separately for a period. She was considered by her brothers to be a successful, enterprising businesswoman, and for a period her younger brother Dink, who had been the drummer with the Creole Orchestra and was now playing the clarinet, managed the saloon in Las Vegas. Anita was dark haired, with large, soulful eyes, and a buxom figure. In her photos she has an exotic, alluring image. She was the "Nita" of his composition "Mamanita."

Whatever their relationship was at any moment, Morton was intensely jealous of her, and to keep other men from showing an interest in her when he was performing, he made her sit on the bandstand beside him for the entire night. He displayed the same jealousies with the woman he eventually married in the 1920s, a cabaret singer named Mabel Bertrand. Neither of the women was permitted to be part of the entertainment, though they both were used to working in the cafés themselves. When the jazz promoter and local supporter of Morton's music Floyd Levin interviewed Anita Gonzales in 1950 she still remembered her difficulties with his Creole attitudes. "I used to sing, you know. Not really as a professional—but I had a good voice and knew all the old songs. I pleaded with Jelly to let me sing with his band, but he never let me. He was very old-fashioned. He didn't want me to work. When I ran a hotel, years ago—1918, I think—he made me hire people, to clean and rent the rooms. He refused to let me do any of the work."[11]

One night when Anita was sitting on the bandstand beside him, the singer who was appearing with the band didn't show up, and without saying anything, Anita went out onto the dance floor, and began singing and dancing. Morton instantly stopped playing, and since he was the pianist and leader, the band stopped playing as well. She continued singing, and when she finished the customers threw a shower of coins. Morton made her sit down again and, chastened, she spent the rest of the evening on her chair.

With Anita there was sometimes a little money, and although it wasn't openly acknowledged, Morton still had his sideline pimping for a few of the women working in the cabarets. Anita sometimes would put together some small operation that made a profit, then lose the money in a stock swindle. Much of Morton's money went into his collection of suits and silk shirts, and it was at this time that he had a diamond set in one of his front teeth to add to the sartorial effect. He was gambling even more heavily than he had been when Marge Creath knew him in St. Louis. The one area of his life where he didn't make much money was as a musician, since none of his jobs lasted very long, and what jobs he did get usually involved long train rides and nights in hotels. With all the enterprises he and Anita involved themselves in—his outside activities, Anita's ventures, and his sporadic luck as a pool shark—there were occasional periods when he was flush. He later reminisced about Anita's fur coats and diamonds, and he had diamonds sewn into his underwear himself to keep from being robbed. When he did have a bankroll, though, it usually went on a gambling spree, and when Anita looked back at their years together she sighed that he often would go broke in a weekend.

Sometime during his West Coast adventures Morton found that he could send notices of his activities to the Chicago *Defender*, the pioneering African American newspaper that had become the voice for the beleaguered black community in the United States. The brief appearances of his name make it possible occasionally to follow his wanderings, but they also make it clear that he never managed to stay anywhere long enough to build up an audience or pick up local contacts that would have helped his career. On February 22, 1919, he wrote that he had organized a jazz band in San Francisco, and was driving a "12 cylinder touring car that makes the natives sit up and take notice." In July 1920: "Kid Jelly Roll and Ralph Love, the Whirlwind Entertainers, are doing their stuff in Portland enroute to the Entertainers Café in Seattle." In June 1921, once again in Los Angeles: "Kid Jelly Roll the pianist just blew into town, has taken a band into Paradise Garden, L. A." October 15, 1921, he was at the Kansas City Bar in

Ti Juana, Mexico. On November 5, 1921, he wrote from San Diego, wanting to get in touch with the champion pool player, the Pensacola Kid, and he said there was a "Nice set-up for band" at a hotel in South Dakota. In November 1921 he was still in San Diego, but on April 22, 1922, he announced that he was in Los Angeles managing Wayside Park, as Leak's Lake was sometimes called, and the next weekend he announced Joe Oliver's two-day guest appearance there. The last *Defender* notice appeared on September 23, 1922, when it was announced that "Jelly Roll Morton's Incomparables left Wayside Park (Los Angeles area) when it closed for the summer to play a Southern California tour presenting Mantan Moreland, comedian-entertainer."

One of the most successful black orchestras working the cabarets in Los Angeles and San Francisco at about the same time was the So Different Orchestra, led by pianist Sid LeProtti. LeProtti had great respect for Morton's abilities as a pianist, but he had the usual difficulties with Morton's business style. One afternoon after Morton had opened at a club on Columbus Avenue in San Francisco, close to where LeProtti was leading his group at the corner of Jackson Street, LeProtti ran into him on the street.

The place he had was right on Columbus Avenue, downstairs in a cellar; you went downstairs to get into it. Well, he had a bad spot because everything was on Pacific Street. . . . So Jelly went on over there and got him a little band there, and he started out pretty good. My boys used to slip over there at night to hear them. Jelly started with three pieces; he had a clarinet and a cornet.

I met him on the street one day and said, "How're you doin', Jelly?"

He said, "All right! I'm doing all right!" And then he asked, "How much do they pay your men over there?"

I said, "Why do you want'a know?"

He said, "Because I'm gonna give them fifty dollars a week. I'm gonna take all your men."

That's the kind of fellow he was, kind'a boastful, and then, on the other hand, you'd catch him in the right mood, and he was a swell guy. Looked like sometimes he had something that was itching him all the time; he'd have to scratch it. He had no right to tell me he was gonn'a take my band, but sure enough the boys came back to me and said Jelly had offered them fifty dollars a week to go over there and play.[12]

The musicians turned down the offer, because Morton was notorious for criticizing the playing of his men on the bandstand. He usually also managed to argue with the management and customers, which meant that a club with Morton in it had more than its share of fights.

In his first weeks in Los Angeles Morton renewed an old acquaintance with the Spikes brothers, Reb and John, enterprising African American businessmen whose music store on Central Avenue, close to the railroad depot, functioned as the informal headquarters for black musicians in Los Angeles. It was through the Spikes that he spent a season managing the dance hall they'd opened at Leak's Lake, and it was to be through the Spikes that he made his way back to Chicago in the spring of 1923. Reb Spikes, the younger of the brothers, first met Morton about 1911 in Oklahoma, when Morton was doing his blackface comedy act. Spikes agreed he was a good pianist, but as a comedian he once commented that Morton was as funny as a sick baby. The next year, 1912, Reb and his older brother John were working with a show called McCabe's Troubadours, and the show was looking for a comedian. Reb remembered Morton and, despite his misgivings about Morton's ability to make audiences laugh, located him by telegram, and Morton joined the show in Kansas City. There was an accompanist for the show itself, but Morton performed the "overture." "We had a little girl playing the piano. She could read the music so she could play all the songs and things for the show. But after they heard Jelly play, they wanted him to play the overture. So we persuaded Jelly—at least he wanted to—he'd go out and play the overture. Oh, he'd wear them out. He was great, you know; he'd play, he'd run the people crazy. He wasn't paid to play the overture. Then he'd come up to do his comedy blackface comedy act on the stage, and the girl would take over the piano for the show."[13]

Spikes also remembered that Morton read music, but he never commented about Morton's work as an arranger. Of all the confusion about Morton's early years, one of the most intriguing questions is where he picked up enough musical training to become proficient as a reader, as well as how he learned to write arrangements, which involve a specialized knowledge of scoring and instrumental voicing. Throughout his career musicians disagreed over his skills, sometimes claiming that he'd played his material over for them first, asking them to do the basic score for him. What is evident is that during this long period Morton slowly developed the group of solo piano compositions that were to be at the center of his creative achievement, and that he would continue to perform, sometimes under different titles, for the rest of his life. The pieces were based on the popular styles of the period when his playing matured, but as integral to their effect were the personal innovations that he brought to the pieces as a performer.

Morton's classic solo compositions are multi-sectioned, extended pieces using the harmonic forms of classic ragtime: sixteen-bar strains, repeats, short bridging interludes, and a melodic central strain. With these structural elements he blended the emotional phrasing of the period's popular songs—the nostalgia and the sentimentality—and in a final transformation, he drew on harmonies and melodies from the vital traditions of African American vernacular music he found everywhere in his travels. Since the pieces were never entirely free of their ragtime roots, however, for a new generation of musicians they were perceived to be part of a generally unusable past. Also, from a business point of view, their rhythms weren't as comfortably suited to the newest dance styles. Morton's own performances were powerful and insistent, with an individual style that emphasized cascades of octaves in the right hand and a driving left hand that amplified the melodies of the treble with answering melodic figures in the bass. Because of the long gestation period of his finest compositions, when he finally was able to record them he amplified them with a vocabulary of variation and restatement, honed in hundreds of cutting contests with other pianists, that turned each new version into a continually exhilarating experience.

Wayside Park, where Morton finally ended his Los Angeles adventures, was one of the Spikes brothers' many business ventures. It was a crudely built dance hall they constructed in 1921 at a picnic ground and artificial pond in Watts, then an outlying Los Angeles suburb. The premises had originally been built as a spot for picnics and parties by a man named Leak, who named it Leak's Lake and who continued to operate a barbeque concession close to the new dance hall. His venture wasn't successful, and when the Spikes brothers took it over, their plan was to bring in more business with the wooden building they had put up at the side of the pond in 1921. It didn't do much business, perhaps because they couldn't find time from their other ventures to manage it, so they sold it to the members of the band who were working there on weekends. Morton was leading the band, but it was the trombonist, Willie Woodman, who put up most of the money. Nearly fifty years later, Woodman's memories of his experience were still painful. "Spikes built Leak's Lake. When things got rough, he sold it to me. It was a 'white elephant.' I got stuck with it. I mortgaged my home and gave him a down payment on it, but I paid him off. It was just a big plain hall, about seventy-five by a hundred feet long, with no trimming, no porch, or nothing. It was on Imperial, close to Willowbrook Street. Imperial is now 117th Street, close to the Watts Towers. The bandstand was low, just about a foot from the floor."[14]

As the *Defender* had noted, Morton managed the dance hall the next summer, 1922, mostly opening it for dancing on the weekends. Woodman also remembered the engagement with Oliver in April, shortly before Oliver returned to Chicago. "I'll tell you when we had a good week. Jelly Roll knew King Oliver, and when Oliver came down through here from Frisco he played a week with us at Leak's Lake. We packed them in that week. Oliver was our guest and just sat in with Jelly Roll's band. We also featured Kid Ory's band, with Mutt Carey, out there. They did good there, good drawing power. So we made money when we could get them."[15]

The relationship between Morton and the Spikes brothers was never comfortable, though their only actual venture together was a publication of his piece "Froggie Moore." The brothers also wrote the lyrics to Morton's composition "Wolverine Blues," although he seems to have been unaware of their addition to his music until he learned it was to be published. He had no use for their verses, but what caused real trouble was that they copyrighted it with the lyrics as a composition by all three of them. Jelly's version of what happened was, as usual, at odds with Spikes's recollection, but in this instance it is probably

Morton who was closer to the truth, though he certainly exaggerated the amount of the advance he was offered.

> *I was in the music-publishing business with Reb and Johnny Spikes, whom I had met on the stage in the old days. Johnny played piano, and Reb, sax. They could read, but had no ideas. Occasionally I condescended to play with these cornfed musicians. Two of our early tunes became big hits and made the Spikes brothers famous. The first,* Someday Sweetheart, *was my idea and the second,* Wolverine Blues, *was my tune. . . .*
>
> *I'm not sore, but I did get hot about how they handled* Wolverine Blues, *which they misnamed because it is not a blues. I first wrote the* Wolverines *in Detroit in the early days. It was just one of those things that float around in my head and one day, when I sit down at the piano, it comes out of my fingers. . . . The tune got to be famous around Chicago and Melrose wrote and offered a $3,000 advance for it. Somehow the Spikes brothers got the letter and jumped up and wrote some words and published my song as written by Spikes-Morton-Spikes. Right there we had an argument, because they just wanted to drag me over the fence, to tell the plain truth.*[16]

It was Joe Oliver who introduced "Wolverine Blues" to Chicago. He heard the piece when he was working with Morton's group at Leak's Lake, and began playing it when he opened with his Creole Band at the Lincoln Gardens. Soon there were many requests for copies of the sheet music from customers who still played the piano or performed with orchestras of their own. Through Oliver, Walter Melrose found where Morton was living in Los Angeles and wired him an advance for the rights to publish his composition. Morton's relationship with Anita Gonzalez had soured and the tour with Mantan Morland that had been announced in the *Defender* hadn't stirred much interest, so Morton immediately took a train to Chicago to demand that the piece be published with himself as the sole composer. He burst into the Melrose shop wearing a western-style red bandanna, loudly announced himself with a description of what he could do, then sat down at the shop's piano to play and show them what he had to offer. The Melroses were immediately aware that he had a great deal to offer them.

Over the next few years the Melrose brothers published most of Morton's important compositions, both the piano solo versions and orchestrations. Although some later writers have intimated that they exploited many of the jazz and blues artists they worked with over the years, in their early days as publishers, promoters, and record producers they offered the most consistently helpful services to Chicago's jazz musicians. The Melroses immediately set up Morton's first recording sessions to promote the music they were publishing, and they also were instrumental in publishing the orchestra arrangements used by the pick-up groups that accompanied Morton on the recordings.

As Walter Melrose worked to create what was to become the keystone in the legacy of Morton's music, the most important step he took was to set up sessions with Gennett Records for solo piano versions of all of the major Morton compositions that he was publishing. In two days in the studio in Indiana shortly after he arrived from California, Morton recorded the classic versions of fourteen of his signature works, including "King Porter Stomp," "The Pearls," "Grandpa's Spells," "London Blues," "New Orleans Blues," and "Original Jelly Roll Blues." The first releases were included in the Gennett advertisements in the *Defender* on October 20, 1923, for "Grandpa Spells" and "Kansas City Stamp" [*sic*] ("Jelly Roll Morton Makes the Old Piano Talk") and on November 24 for "Wolverine Blues" ("Another Wonderful 'Jelly Roll' Morton Piano Solo").

Even before the solo records began to reach the market, Melrose also involved Morton in another recording project in July 1923, including him in a session with the New Orleans Rhythm Kings. Melrose had already helped the band with Gennett sessions to produce band versions of some of the pieces that he felt might sell as orchestrations. One of their recordings was an exuberant version of "Wolverine Blues" made in March 1923, about the time Morton arrived in Chicago, with pianist Mel Stitzel. When the band arrived in Indiana with Morton for the new session in July, they ran into some of the usual problems. He was booked into the one local hotel with the other band members, but the management at first refused to rent him a room. The trombonist George Brunies later said that he was the one who told the person behind the hotel desk that the tall, light-skinned man with them was ". . . not a Negro. I started to say he was from Puerto Rico, but some of them are black, so I said South American, and he's got these tunes and we've got to record them."[17]

The sessions on July 17 and 18 have been discussed many times before—not only because of Morton's presence but because they are generally considered to be the first interracial jazz recording. Although there were earlier sessions that could be considered as including musicians of both races, the Morton collaboration with Paul Mares's band was more or less openly known at the time, and Melrose's intention was to secure as much attention as possible for the special circumstances of the sessions. There is also considerable confusion and some controversy about what happened during their two afternoons playing into Gennett's recording horns. Some later writers have contrasted the effect of Morton's piano with what they regarded as the rhythmic weakness of the band's recordings done in the spring, but those sessions had been made with a quintet, with only Stitzel and drummer Ben Pollack as the rhythm section. For the new sessions, Melrose added Morton to the band, but he also brought back the band's banjo player from their first sessions, Lew Black, and included the solid New Orleans bassist, Chink Martin. For their two days in the studio Morton was working as part of a tight and very professional rhythm section. To add to the confusion about the recordings, there were three pianists who played during the sessions. Morton essentially was there to do his compositions; a Chicago pianist named Kyle Pierce was there to play the dance numbers that weren't in Morton's style; and Mel Stitzel, who had been on the sessions a few months before, was there for the standard jazz numbers they had scheduled to record.

Trying to sort out the pianists who played on the eight different arrangements has occupied jazz historians for years. Chink Martin remembered that Morton played only on his own compositions, and certainly it was Morton on "Mr. Jelly Lord" and "London Blues." He also played on a composition that he shared as co-composer with Mares and Roppolo, "Milneberg Joys." The pianist for the two commercial dance arrangements, "Marguerite" and "Mad (Cause You Treat Me This Way)," as well as for the uptempo instrumental "Angry" was Kyle Pierce. Of the two other arrangements, "Sobbin' Blues" and the ODJB's "Clarinet Marmalade," after many years of trying to decide which of them was playing, I would say that Morton plays on "Sobbin' Blues," which sounds as though it were a piece he was already familiar with. The flowing octave passages in the treble and the strong rhythmic figures in the left hand have the feel of Morton's distinctive solo style. Stitzel's playing was built around more busily arpeggiated figures in the right hand and a less assertive left hand, and on "Clarinet Marmalade" it does feel like his work. Even though it is a New Orleans jazz piece it is stylistically atypical for Morton.

There were problems in the studio over "Milneburg Joys." What seems to have happened before they came to the studio was that Melrose wasn't satisfied with the original composition by Mares and Roppolo, which had only two strains, so as a new Melrose composer, Morton added a four-bar introduction that was repeated as a bridge later in the arrangement. When there was a question about the composer credits, Brunies, who also had been playing the piece with the band and considered himself one of the composers, found he was being left out of the credits, and he stormed into the next room and began drinking. A few moments later Mares came in and began shouting at him, and it was several moments before the rest of the band could calm them down enough to begin recording again. The recording has some of the instrumental voicings and the overall structure of the arrangements associated with Morton, but it is difficult to know if Morton or one the Melrose arrangers did the final score.

The recording, however, also sounds as if Morton set the tempo, since it has the same feel as the tempos for the other two arrangements of his compositions. It is considerably slower than the usual Chicago dance tempo, and it's uncertain whom Morton intended as the buyers for the record. A year and a half later, Mares recorded the composition again without Morton's interpolations under the title of "Golden Leaf Strut," and in this version, with Mares using a mute to drive a fierce final chorus, the original piece turned into an exuberant, uptempo dance number that could much more justifiably be called "Milneburg Joys." Morton's admirers sometimes express their enthusiasm over his characteristic fills on the sessions with the Rhythm Kings, but as far as the band was concerned, his playing must have often felt intrusive. Roppolo's solo on "Mr. Jelly Lord" was almost lost in Morton's interpolations, and there was the same feeling of his crowding behind the solos of both Mares and Roppolo in "Milneburg Joys." On the second take of some of the numbers there was less of a problem; probably he was asked to hold back a little with his playing, but he continued to make himself heard.

Melrose continued to set up sessions for Morton, still pushing the compositions he was publishing. There were tentative early band sessions with obscure musicians, and in 1925 there were two duet sessions for the Autograph recording company, a miniscule operation with even more primitive recording facilities than Gennett. One of the duets was to become a legendary collector's item, Morton and King Joe Oliver playing two of Morton's pieces, "King Porter Stomp" and "Tom Cat Blues." Oliver, however, was clearly uncomfortable with the situation and the two performances have generally remained collector's curiosities. He performed "King Porter" in a flat, tentative tone, without his mute, simply reading the melody directly from the cornet part in the Melrose arrangement. With another musician, however, the young white Chicago clarinet player Volly DeFaut, who Morton always insisted was his favorite of the young Chicago clarinetists, there was a brilliant version of "Wolverine Blues," also for Autograph, and in the exuberant final choruses Morton demonstrated why he had often walked away as the winner in after-hours cutting contests.

During this period Morton became ill and sent for his sister Frances to come from New Orleans to nurse him. Although she only nursed him for three weeks, she stayed on for six months, staying with a family he knew. He generally kept her away from the musicians he was working with. He was driving an old car, and he insisted that she always had to remember that he was only twenty-eight years old. She protested that she knew he was thirty-five, but he insisted that she agree with him. She didn't see him with any of his associates, and except for a night when he took her to out to hear Albert Nicholas, Barney Bigard, and Paul Barbarin, friends she knew from New Orleans, he never let her hear any other music. They were playing with King Oliver at the Plantation Gardens, and she was only allowed to stay for an hour because it was her first time in a nightclub and her brother said her eyes were "big as saucers." The impression she had of Morton's life was that he didn't have close friends, and that probably his most important personal contact was his relationship with Walter Melrose.

The handful of recordings Morton recorded with generally inept bands under the name of Jelly Roll Morton's Levee Band and Jelly Roll Morton's Incomparables in 1924 and 1925 are a puzzling beginning to his work as a bandleader, since there was no clear musical direction in the ensemble playing or the arrangements. They would have remained among the many forgotten sessions from these tentative years—like the equally clumsy first recording by Duke Ellington's very inexperienced band from Washington, D.C., in 1926—but Morton was offered a recording contract by Victor Records, which came late to the South Side scene and had no major artists under contract. Again, the Melrose brothers played a role in setting up the sessions, and the level of the musicians who began rehearsals with Morton was much more promising than any of the groups he'd assembled before. The sessions by the group, under the studio name of the Red Hot Peppers, have come to be considered some of the most successful examples of the New Orleans small-group style that were recorded in the 1920s and, like the session Morton did with the New Orleans Rhythm Kings, they have been analyzed, discussed, praised, and admired for decades. Their first date in the studio was September 15, 1926, and one of the most exciting performances was "The Chant," a composition and arrangement by New Orleans Rhythm Kings session pianist Mel Stitzel.

Most of the musicians were drawn from the group of New Orleanians who were already working around Chicago. Kid Ory, who had come east to record with Louis Armstrong and his Hot Five, was playing for dancing with King Oliver's Dixie Syncopators. The banjo player Johnny St. Cyr was also part of the Hot Five and was in demand with many of the Chicago bands, including Oliver's. The gifted cornetist George Mitchell, from Louisville, was an unexpected choice; although he continually turned up in the recording studios, he essentially didn't improvise and always played from arranged scores. The clarinet player, Omer Simeon, was born in New Orleans and had studied with Lorenzo Tio Jr., but began playing in Chicago with Charlie Elgar's orchestra, and the sessions with the Red Hot Peppers were his initial recordings. The rhythm section was filled out with Johnny Lindsay, who had played the mandolin with his father's trio as a teenager in the Storyville cafes, and had been the trombonist with A. J. Piron's New Orleans orchestra for their sessions in New York two years before. With the Peppers he played the bass. The drummer, Andrew Hilaire, was also new to the recording studios, but he was experienced and musically sensitive and had no difficulty following Morton's very precise directions.

As is the situation with so much about Morton's career, there is still some confusion about how the sessions evolved. The arrangements have been singled out for much of the praise for the recordings, since the sound of the small group was different from almost anything else recorded in that period—but it isn't entirely clear who did them. The musicians themselves were asked again and again about the scores they worked from, and their answers were contradictory. Ory said that all he saw was a lead sheet, with only the bass line harmonies written out. "There wasn't enough in his parts, you know. After he wrote out what he wanted, the boys would add on to it. That's just what I did. He didn't have nothing but bass notes, and I wanted to put some harmony and some legato and you know, other stuff in it—mix it up. And so he told me, 'Don't worry about the music; I can't write your music.'"[18]

Simeon's memory was that they used the Melrose stock arrangements when they began rehearsing, but only for the first few run-throughs. He was also very specific about the role of Walter Melrose.

We had rehearsals for the recordings and Melrose always came down to the rehearsals to get an idea of what it sounded like. Walter Melrose published most of Jelly's tunes, and he would bring down some of the stock orchestrations from his publishing house. We used them merely as a guide until we got familiar with the tune and didn't need the music any more. We improvised the ensembles and we would always play the solos ad lib. . . . Jelly arranged special introductions that he had in mind, and then Ory, George Mitchell, and myself got together and harmonized it and tried it out. Jelly set a routine so the order of the solos was decided. We always played an ensemble, and the melody was going at all times until probably the last chorus, the take-out chorus, you know. Then everybody would give out, but the melody dominated most of the time.[19]

George Mitchell remembered two or three rehearsals at the Union Local on South State Street and one rehearsal at Melrose's office. He also remembered that Morton brought in the Melrose arrangements and would help him out with his own solos. "Jelly would always fix up something for me. He would show me and give me ideas about something to play. . . . But he always wanted you to play your own ideas, yeah. Then he'd tell us, 'Just throw the music away and play.' So, after I learned those tunes, then I just tried to play, tried to put in what little ideas came to me. I also remember that, for some of the tunes, Jelly brought a few of the printed copies of the orchestrations that Melrose published."[20]

It is clear from the alternate takes that the group had used the rehearsal time well. The sequences of the solos and the solos themselves were generally repeated without substantial changes. Not all of the pieces were Morton's; the brilliant uptempo piece by Mel Stitzel, "The Chant," was one of the most exciting of the first arrangements they recorded. But everything they played had a consistency in style and approach. The arrangements, it seems clear, were in part based on the Melrose stocks, in part suggested by Morton at the rehearsals, and in part worked out by the musicians themselves. When the arrangements were published only one of them was credited to Morton, the "Original Jelly Roll Blues" arrangement, which credits him with the orchestration while the "arrangement" was done by Mel Stitzel.

The sessions were sensitively recorded by the Victor engineers. New electrical recording techniques introduced since the Gennett session Morton had done with the New Orleans Rhythm Kings only three years before gave the instruments a warm, vibrant timbre that set a new standard for small-band recording. There was a richly harmonized clarinet trio for "Sidewalk Blues" with two other New Orleans reedmen, Albert Nicholas and Barney Bigard, filling out the harmonies with Simeon. The band was exciting at fast and slow tempos, and pieces like "Black Bottom Stomp" and "The Chant" were as technically challenging as they were exciting musical creations. To balance the mood, Morton also threw in some blackface hokum with spoken introductions and sound effects, and on "Dead Man Blues" he reenacted the ritual of a New Orleans funeral. Sensing the quality of theatrical entertainment in the performances, Victor released the first single, "Doctor Jazz," with a novelty number played by the Dixieland Jug Blowers on the reverse side.

Years later, the Red Hot Peppers recordings from these first sessions still have a strutting excitement, and the performances continue to have a freshness and a spontaneity. Morton had been away from New Orleans for so many years it's difficult to conceive how he could have had any real memory of what he might have heard twenty years before—although he certainly encountered other New Orleanians, like Buddy Petit during Petit's short-lived career in Morton's band in Los Angeles, and he went to hear groups like Oliver's Creole Band who were busy in Chicago. The ensemble style of these 1926 recordings hadn't yet evolved when his early playing career in Storyville essentially ended about 1907, but he'd certainly heard many recordings, and had spent two days in the Gennett studio with the New Orleans Rhythm Kings and their New Orleans manner. Even considering this background, however, nothing else left on record by any of the New Orleans musicians has the unique feeling of those sessions done on winter afternoons in Chicago by a diverse group of instrumentalists, some who had been away from New Orleans for several years themselves, some who had never lived there at all, and all who were performing pieces that had been written in other places for other times. How Morton managed to achieve this synthesis is another of the mysteries that we consider in our persistent efforts to follow the elusive trail of Jelly Roll Morton's life and wanderings.

13

Bouncing Around

Speaking of pep, poise, pleasing personalities, pretty faces, beautifully gowned ladies, we are reminded that the male of the species who attended the dance in the Garden of Joy on last Saturday night . . . Got eyes full of visions of loveliness . . . The consensus was that the Theophile Sisters are clever dancers and did their number quite pleasingly . . . Wasn't it nice to note that the affable Mr. Piron quietly asked that no money be thrown to the entertainers, as they were paid for their services.

E. BELFIELD SPRIGGINS, WRITING IN THE *LOUISIANA WEEKLY*, OCTOBER 11, 1927[1]

With the economic boom in the United States of the 1920s, many people seemed to have more of everything, or at least many people suddenly became potential customers for almost everything. With new audiences ready to dance to the current rhythms, within a few years the music of New Orleans's black musicians found its way into record stores everywhere and onto mail-order lists in newspapers like the Chicago *Defender*. The New Orleans artists whose music was recorded—and preserved—came from a broad spectrum of the city's black musicians. The recordings themselves were made from one end of the continent to the other. Even before the companies noticed what was happening around them in the Chicago ballrooms, the New Orleans émigrés had found their way into studios a continent apart—from Central Avenue in Los Angeles to Times Square in New York.

Whatever Jelly Roll Morton thought of Reb and Johnny Spikes, they had their hand in nearly everything that was happening in the African American musical scene in Los Angeles, and in the early summer of 1922, they decided to set up recording sessions to produce some singles to sell in their music store on Central Avenue. Their plan was to record vocal blues with two women singers who were performing locally, and for an accompaniment, back them with one of the popular local bands. Morton was still in Los Angeles, leading the band at Leak's Lake, and he hadn't yet quarreled with the Spikes brothers over the copyright to his tune "The Wolverines," but the band they chose was Kid Ory's. It would become an historic session, though no one seems to have thought at the time that this was the first recording of a black New Orleans group. It might have an even more fitting place in jazz history if the first session had been made by one of Morton's bands, but as his trombone player recalled when he was interviewed years later, their band didn't attract a lot of customers at Leak's Lake. Ory's band, on the other hand, ". . . did good there, good drawing power. So we made money when we could get them."[2]

The two women blues singers, Roberta Dudley and Ruth Lee, probably were of most interest to the Spikes, since this was the heyday of blues singles by statuesque women with stately voices. In the record company advertisements the women's blues were given the most space, with the instrumental jazz novelties usually included in the lists of other releases almost as an afterthought. Two of the three singles that the Spikes brothers recorded were by the two women, although only one of the pieces was titled a blues, and all four of the songs were standard cabaret style songs. The two sides by Ory's orchestra, however, are of particular interest not only as the first by one of the New Orleans Uptown bands. The musicians had been away for some time, and isolated from the continual changes that left New Orleans jazz with what seemed to be a different sound every few months.

Back home in Louisiana, Ory's band had most of their crowds in the Uptown dance halls—though, as he remembered with some pride, they often were hired for society engagements on St. Charles Avenue. The cornet players he hired— first Mutt Carey, then Joe Oliver, followed by Louis Armstrong—were among the best in town. Despite the band's success, there were personal difficulties in New Orleans for Ory in 1919, and he also was having health problems: the damp New Orleans climate was aggravating an asthma condition. He decided to try the drier air in southern California, and once he arrived immediately began to assemble his band again. Mutt Carey had left him to work with Lawrence Duhe's band in Chicago, but Carey couldn't stand the northern winter and hurried back to New Orleans, sending Oliver north as his replacement. When Ory sent Carey a telegram, asking him to join the new band in Los Angeles, Carey quickly agreed. During Joe Oliver's yearlong stay in California his bass player, Ed Garland, renewed an old friendship with Ory and elected to stay in California when the rest of the band returned to Chicago. Garland worked in various bands of Ory's for the rest of his career, despite occasionally furious arguments between them.

Slim and light skinned, with wavy hair and a genial manner, Ory was a skilled showman and tireless in finding jobs. His New Orleans ensemble was soon performing as far north as San Francisco and Oakland under the name Kid Ory's Original Creole Jazz Band, which probably was a conscious reminder for their audiences of the earlier appearances of the Original Creole Orchestra, led by

Keppard, that had played in Los Angeles in 1914. It was a job Ory had to turn down, at the Pergola Ball Room in San Francisco, that brought Oliver out from Chicago. In Los Angeles Ory and his musicians built up an enthusiastic following and as far as the Spikes brothers were concerned, their name was enough to help sell singles. The recordings were done in the small studio of a local music service and released on two labels, Sunshine and Nordskog, which was the name of the studio where they recorded. The brothers pressed 5,000 copies on the Nordskog and Sunshine labels to sell as an exclusive item in their store at 12th and Central Avenue. On the singles the band was either "Spikes' Seven Pods of Pepper" or "Ory's Sunshine Orchestra."

Roberta Dudley was large voiced, with a throbbing vibrato and the declamatory, plaintive style that had been introduced in New York the year before. With her they recorded a Spikes brothers co-composition, "Krooked Blues," in an arrangement that Oliver also used when he recorded it as an instrumental with his Creole Band the next year. Carey's cornet fills and muted breaks were an obvious source for Oliver's playing on his band's recording. The two instrumentals they did for the Spikes brothers were in very different styles. "Ory's Creole Trombone" was a trombone novelty in the style of the touring brass bands that had made popular favorites out of pieces like "Sliding Lassus Trombone" or "Slippery Hank." Ory's composition was in the classic march, rag format, but it also built to occasional noisier passages in the New Orleans ensemble style. The rhythm section was poorly recorded, but with pianist Fred Washington and bassist Ed Garland there was a strongly defined beat. Both of them, along with Carey, were to rejoin Ory when he assembled the band in the late 1930s. The band had the usual difficulty finding a clarinetist; they made do with Bill Johnson's brother "Dink" Johnson, who had left New Orleans as the drummer with the Olympia Orchestra in 1914, then worked for his sister Anita Gonzalez in some of her business ventures. In later years he entertained in his own tavern as a pianist and singer. His clarinet playing included many of the characteristic New Orleans melodic phrases, but he was obviously inexperienced. His rhythm was uneven and his intonation was rough.

On the single's reverse side, the band recorded an instrumental composition "Society Blues." In the recording balance Carey's muted cornet lead was sometimes overshadowed by the trombone. Ory wasn't using a mute and his repetitive ensemble part generally compensated in volume for what it lacked in subtlety. Although "Society Blues" used the term "blues" in the title, and its two strains were in the twelve-bar blues format, melodically it was closer to the vaudeville slow drag ragtime of the era. In Carey's playing the melody was sensitively shaped and there was a conscious ensemble feel to his playing, though he was hampered by the tricky arrangement. At one point he created an unexpected break that also turned up in Joe Oliver's Chicago recordings the next year.

Most distinctive about the ragtime blues side of the single was Carey's use of improvisation from chorus to chorus, instead of repeating the melody without change as earlier bands were doing. This same natural extension of the New Orleans style was also evident in the recordings of the New Orleans Rhythm Kings, who went into a studio in Chicago a few months later, and other New Orleans bands also began to stretch out their ensembles with looser instrumental leads. The mute makes it difficult to compare Carey's style with Paul Mares, who led the Rhythm Kings, but Carey didn't sound as technically assured, and he didn't have a decisive rhythmic push. His playing was consciously centered in its older stylistic elements, still employing many of the staccato and repetitive figures of the ragtime bands, as though he were looking back as much as he was looking forward.

Another black New Orleans cornetist named Ernest "Nenny" Coycault, who had begun playing even earlier than Carey, had also moved to Los Angeles from New Orleans, but the orchestra he was with, Sonny Clay's California Poppies, wasn't a New Orleans ensemble. Clay's eight-piece orchestra was as determined to be a part of its own time as Ory's band had chosen to look back to the older New Orleans sound. The two sides the orchestra recorded in 1923 were tight, bravura performances in the popular "hot" dance style. Clay didn't feature himself on the piano, which is a disappointment, because it's obvious from the solo recordings he made at the same time that he was an impressive jazz pianist. The group's most obvious weakness was a clarinetist even less suited to the New Orleans style than Dink Johnson, and for some reason the engineers decided to bring him forward in the recorded balance. Both of the pieces they recorded, "What A Wonderful Time" and "Lou," featured Coycault, though the solo passages in "Wonderful Time" were only a repeated riff figure. In "Lou" he played an extended two-chorus solo and a break close to the end of the arrangement. He was technically assured enough to be at ease with fast tempos, and his playing had the distinctive melodic sense of the classic early New Orleans style.

Ory and his band in California left behind them an irreplaceable document of the music and style of the Uptown bands at the beginning of the 1920s, and it will have to stand for the musicians who didn't make it into the studio—musicians like Buddy Petit and Chris Kelly, whose names will always be part of New Orleans's legendary past. A year and a half later another series of sessions made on the other edge of the continent by another New Orleans orchestra documented the music of the other New Orleans African American community, the Downtown Creole musicians. With their buoyant swing, warm musicality, and relaxed, proud professionalism, the singles made by Armand J. Piron's New Orleans Orchestra are as important a document as the single by Ory's orchestra. The orchestra was the only one of the Creole bands to record, and the style of these musicians in the gaudy rainbow of New Orleans music was as vital as that of any of the city's other social groups.

With the idea of having singles to sell by an orchestra that was well known to the society audiences along St. Charles Avenue, the Werlein music store on Canal Street arranged for Piron's orchestra to take the train to New York City in

December 1923 to record for Victor Records. The upstairs rooms in the Werlein building were later used for recording sessions, when the companies began sending portable equipment to New Orleans, but in 1923 that still wasn't considered a possibility. The only way to get the singles was to send the band to the studios. The Canal Street building stood up through Katrina, but although its large sign still stood on the roof in December 2005, Werlein's itself finally was forced to close its doors.

Armand J. Piron and Jelly Roll Morton were from the same Creole background and, because Piron was only two years older, they might even had some contact when they were growing up—but it would be almost impossible to find a Creole musician from the same New Orleans musical environment as Morton who was more his opposite in every way. For most of his career Morton seemed to be in a different city every other month; Piron left New Orleans only for a few months in Chicago in 1918 and 1919, then for a few months in New York in the winter of 1923 and 1924. While Morton tirelessly promoted himself and his music in endless monologues for anyone who had the patience to listen to him, Piron was personally so aloof and self-contained that, despite his success and his years of professional activity in New Orleans, he is almost never mentioned by other musicians. Even Peter Bocage, in conversation, didn't offer any colorful Piron anecdotes, though he'd played in the orchestra for most of the 1920s. In perhaps an even more indicative sign of their different temperaments, Morton expended much energy and emotion in his last years insisting that he'd invented jazz, while Piron's brilliantly successful Creole orchestra sometimes didn't seem to be concerned about playing jazz at all.

Piron in many ways epitomizes the musical tastes and social attitudes of the Downtown Creole world, though he was even more aloof than the other popular Creole orchestra leader, John Robichaux. In his own diffident way Robichaux competed with Piron for the society jobs both men spent their lives playing. Born in 1888, Piron was a short, light-complexioned man with a thin, handsome face and somber, watchful eyes. He walked with a limp as the result of a streetcar accident, and for some time after his accident there was a question whether he'd be able to walk at all. His father was one of the city's respected music teachers and led a group of his sons and students in the turn of the century Piron-Gaspard Orchestra. The "Gaspard" of the orchestra's name were two brothers, Tom, a bassist, and Vic, a trombonist, who were with the orchestra from about 1893 to 1902. Professor Piron's sons Milford, a cornetist; Albert, a violinist; and the youngest of them, Armand, also a violinist, and himself as pianist were the "Piron" of the name. Armand began playing with them about 1900, when he was twelve. Milford continued to play semiprofessionally after the orchestra was disbanded; Albert moved to St. Bernard Parish and for many years was the leader of a small orchestra playing symphonic music. In 1903, Armand participated in one of the most ambitious Creole music projects, the Bloom Philharmonic Orchestra, which included most of the Downtown musicians.

Piron also found, as many other Creole musicians were learning, that the new ragtime style of playing, whether they liked it or not, had a growing public, and he quietly accommodated himself to the changes, at the same time keeping his own sense of musicality and taste. He was a member of a number of Uptown bands during this period when the violin was still considered an essential instrument for an ensemble. He and Peter Bocage worked as violinists at the same time, Bocage with the Superior Orchestra and Piron with the Olympia Orchestra. When the Olympia's cornetist, Freddie Keppard, went to Los Angeles to join Bill Johnson, Piron took over the orchestra and replaced Keppard with Joe Oliver.

It was this Olympia Orchestra that Edmond Souchon heard playing for student dances at the Tulane University gymnasium. They occasionally played ragtime dance numbers, but their repertoire centered around popular songs and waltzes, with the expected repertoire of mazurkas and schottisches, as well as the obligatory quadrilles. They read from arrangements, though some of his musicians, including Oliver, had limited reading skills. The men working with Piron were among the best dance musicians in New Orleans: Oliver, clarinetist Sidney Bechet, trombonist Zue Robertson, either Henry Zeno or Happy Bolton, drummer. Louis Keppard, Freddie's brother who didn't make the California trip, played guitar. Clarence Williams, a pianist from Plaquemine, occasionally worked with them until Steve Lewis joined the group; Lewis was to stay with Piron until 1928. Like all of these orchestras—as musicians who were playing at the same time later recalled—the Olympia musicians played quietly. The halls were small, and with a violin playing the melodic lead the other instruments had to hold back to keep from covering him. As so many of the dance musicians maintained, they liked to hear the sound of the people's feet on the dance floor.

Piron had ambitions larger than merely leading a dance orchestra with his violin. In 1915 he and Clarence Williams opened an office as music publishers on Tulane Avenue. They quickly had a hit with a piece that Piron co-composed, "I Wish I Could Shimmy Like My Sister Kate"—still a standard with traditional bands. The title had to be modified to meet the strict dance codes in the Chicago dance halls; the word "shimmy" was dropped from the sheet music, and the published title became "Sister Kate." Williams also had a hit the next year, and the partners began rehearsing a large group for the Orpheum circuit. In a promotional photo they posed in the crude tramp costumes that were one of the acceptable personae for black artists on the stage, though they weren't wearing blackface. They probably intended to follow the Creole Band's success with their own ragtime comedy and song act. Besides themselves, the orchestra included cornetist Oscar Celestin, trombonist Bebe Ridgely, clarinetist Jimmy Noone, bassist Johnny Lindsay, drummer Ernest Trepagnier, and two banjoists, Johnny St. Cyr and Tom Benton, with Benton, who was regarded as the best singer around, also working as the group's vocalist. Before the tour began, however, there were problems with the contract, and the others said that Piron refused to sign it. The group broke up, and for a time the relationship between Piron and his business partner, Williams, was severely strained.

Peter Bocage was among the Creole musicians who moved easily between the two worlds—the ragtime music from Uptown, and the legitimate music of Downtown—and until his death in the 1970s he continued to be admired and respected by musicians from both sides of Canal Street. He was born on July 17, 1886, which meant he was two or three years older than Piron and Keppard, as well as many of the first generation of white jazz musicians, including the members of the Original Dixieland Jazz Band. It is probably attaching too much significance to the clannishness of the neighborhoods in New Orleans, but Bocage's family was from Algiers, across the river, and he might have grown up with fewer of the strongly divisive emotions that some of the Creole musicians carried with them. He was slight and soft spoken, still living quietly in Algiers when I talked with him in the 1950s. For many years he had worked as an insurance agent to give him a steadier income than he could expect as a musician. He spent much of his working life hurrying to the Mississippi River ferry at Canal Street to get back and forth from his jobs.

Bocage could speak with some authority of the early years of jazz: as violinist, he was among the members of the Superior Orchestra in a photo taken in 1910, along with a very youthful looking cornetist, Bunk Johnson, whom Bocage helped with his music reading skills. I have never lost my own admiration for him on the afternoons when he would help out the Eureka Brass Band or the Young Tuxedo Brass Band as a replacement for one of their trumpeters, and I followed him as he marched sedately for long hours in the sun, playing with experienced skill and technical assurance even though close to his seventies.

Although Piron always considered himself as the leader of everything he did, it was Bocage who helped him assemble the successful orchestra that Piron led for almost ten years. Bocage, who was equally proficient either as a cornetist or a violinist—but considered the trombone his favorite of all the instruments he played—worked for the spring of 1918 on the SS *Capitol* with Fate Marable's Orchestra. When the boat headed north at the beginning of the summer, he decided to remain in New Orleans and recommended the seventeen year old Louis Armstrong as his replacement. There was an opening for a group at Tranchina's Restaurant, one of the popular places at Spanish Fort, and Piron and Bocage organized an orchestra that, under Piron's name, was to be associated with the restaurant for the next ten years.

Bocage also functioned as the orchestra's musical director during Piron's absences on his other business ventures. The same year, Piron and Williams, their differences over the cancelled vaudeville tour smoothed over, opened a music store and publishing office in Chicago, the Williams and Piron Music Company, at 3129 South State Street, advertising themselves as the "House of Jazz." Williams left Chicago after the racial violence of the summer of 1919, but returned often and the store remained open, though Piron's involvement became more and more marginal.

The job at Spanish Fort was one of the most desirable that New Orleans had to offer, with its setting on the Ponchartrain lakefront and the background of the elaborate formal gardens of the resort's grounds. The musicians who worked with the orchestra were highly regarded. Lorenzo Tio Jr. was the clarinetist, also doubling on tenor saxophone; Louis Warneke, alto saxophone; Arthur Campbell, pianist (though he was replaced by Steve Lewis within a few months). The drummer was the veteran Louis Cottrell, the banjo was John Marrero, and the bassist was Bocage's brother, Henry. There were some temporary replacements at the end of the first summer. The Gaspard brothers, who had been part of the Piron-Gaspard Youth Orchestra, hired away Tio and Cottrell for their Maple Leaf Orchestra. Peter Bocage moved to trombone at Tranchina's, and Willie Edwards was brought in as cornetist. When their summer job ended with the Gaspards, Tio and Cottrell returned to Piron, and Johnny Lindsay began playing the trombone, which meant that Bocage went back to the cornet, and he also played occasional violin on some of the arrangements. For a few months Johnny St. Cyr replaced Marrero as banjoist, then was replaced by Charles Bocage, another of Peter's brothers.

It was this band that Piron was leading when Werlein's arranged for them to make their trip to New York three years later. For Piron, who had never made an effort to hide his ambitions to break away from New Orleans, the trip represented a long awaited opportunity. Soon after they arrived in New York he was able to secure a job at a successful cabaret called the Cotton Club. They were brought in for a night as an audition, but their New Orleans rhythms did so well with the dancers that they were immediately offered a contract. The New York musicians who heard them were surprised at their heavy rhythm section, which with four pieces—piano, banjo, bass, and drums—was fuller than the usual New York dance orchestra, and the local men were also surprised that the orchestra played the long job with only a single cornetist.

Piron and his stylish New Orleans ensemble made such an impression that the original Victor recording session on December 11, 1923, was followed by another for rival Columbia Records on December 21, and later in December two sessions for the enterprising jazz label OKeh Records. They produced a single for each of the labels, and for OKeh they also accompanied popular blues artist Esther Bigeou for her "West Indies Blues." Victor Records doesn't seem to have signed any kind of exclusive contract with the orchestra, and in January they resumed the sequence, beginning with a single for Victor on January 8, 1924, then after a break in New Orleans, recording a single with Columbia on February 15 and an additional single for OKeh in early March. The band returned to a desirable booking at the Roseland Ballroom, which would become the showcase for some of New York's best-known jazz orchestras, including Fletcher Henderson's, who remained as the house band for several years. Piron found to his intense disappointment, however, that his New Orleanians were voicing the familiar complaints about the North. They were unhappy with the food, they hated the cold, and they couldn't get used to New York's noise and crowds. He had no individual contracts with them, and he realized that he couldn't demand that they stay, even though the opportunity at the Roseland represented his life's musical dream. He assembled them in his hotel room and offered them the chance to vote about accepting the job. As he had unhappily anticipated, they voted to return to New Orleans.

Both OKeh and Victor Records still were interested in the orchestra, however, and recorded them again when they sent their mobile units to New Orleans. On March 24, after their return from New York, OKeh recorded a single for a local performer named Lela Bolden, with Piron and Steve Lewis playing the violin and piano accompaniment. The next day the entire band, without trombonist Johnny Lindsay, did a final single for Victor Records. Each of the companies continued to make recording trips to New Orleans over the next four years, but only Steve Lewis was recorded again. In 1926 Columbia brought him into the studio to accompany local entertainer and singer Willie Jackson. For Piron there was the disappointment of having come so close to major success on their New York adventure, but he returned to his job at Tranchina's Restaurant, and for some years he seemed satisfied with his Sunday afternoons accompanying the dancing at the New Orleans Country Club, and his comfortable life as the leader of a society jazz orchestra.

The Piron orchestra's seventeen sides are the most that were recorded by any of the New Orleans black orchestras, although Celestin's Tuxedo Jazz Orchestra follows closely with fifteen. Some writers have emphasized the obvious effects of the racial policies on the part of the record companies in their decisions about artists, but the number of sides by Piron compares favorably with the quantity of recording done with the local white orchestras. There were nineteen sides by various groups led by Tony Parenti, and eighteen by the most popular of the white orchestras, the New Orleans Owls. Columbia recorded twenty-two sides by the Halfway House Orchestra, but only seventeen of them were released at the time. As Piron's recordings were the only music of the Downtown Creole society to make its way onto record, they constitute unique and invaluable documentation of this often overlooked world of New Orleans music.

The music that Piron and his orchestra played was so different from any of the other New Orleans groups who recorded that it seems to have come from some earlier, less stressful era. In their understated rhythms, however, there was an irresistible dance beat, and in each of their complicated arrangement they demonstrated again and again just how well they were matched as an ensemble. Their instrumental blend and sense of phrasing and timing was perhaps the most sensitively constructed of any of the early jazz orchestras on record. In arrangement after arrangement they effortlessly moved from one instrumental voicing to another, interjected unexpected harmonic transpositions, shifted their phrasing to a sharply articulated attack, and as smoothly resolved it into a stylish solo or duet—all done with relaxed assurance and poise. Some of their arrangements included passages that had some of the feeling of the skillful "popular dance"

THE ARMAND J. PIRON ORCHESTRA, PLAYING AT TRANCHINA'S RESTAURANT AT LAKE PONCHARTRAIN, ABOUT 1926. FROM LEFT: PETER BOCAGE, JOHNNY LINDSAY, LOUIS COTTRELL, LOUIS WARNEKE, LORENZO TIO JR., STEVE LEWIS, UNIDENTIFIED BANJO, ARMOND J. PIRON.

groups that were recording at the same time, but Piron and his musicians performed everything with New Orleans warmth and grace.

For someone interested in the history of New Orleans jazz, the most important instrumentalist in the group was the clarinetist Lorenzo Tio Jr. Tio was the son of the famed Lorenzo Tio Sr., who with his older brother Louis taught their legato playing style to an entire generation of New Orleans clarinetists. Lorenzo Jr. was also a busy teacher and a continual inspiration to all the clarinetists who followed him, from Sidney Bechet to Johnny Dodds. He was tall, light skinned, pleasantly good looking with wavy hair, and had a genial interest in all of the music of the city. Often the clarinetist with one of the rough Uptown bands would look out over the crowd during one of their sets and see Tio leaning against a wall, listening to him. Two of the band's arrangements feature his limpid tone and impeccable rhythm—though in the most exciting of them, "Bouncing Around," recorded for OKeh in December, the studio engineer made a decision to bring the saxophone closer to the recording horn, mistakenly deciding that Louis Warneke was playing the melody. Behind the saxophone's lead, Tio had a series of flashing breaks and his final chorus was a loose improvisation in a classic New Orleans ensemble style that displayed his poise and flexibility.

Victor Records made the final single with the orchestra in March, three months later, and Tio was featured again on a slower dance piece, "Red Man Blues." This time the clarinet could be more clearly heard in the recording balance. His tone was liquid and his phrasing had a complete, easy assurance. It was obvious why he had so much influence on the younger musicians who heard him.

The arrangement even included a minor key "mysterioso" solo for the clarinet reminiscent of the "Egyptian" specialty that was featured for so many years by Sidney Bechet.

The ensemble had to work within the tonal frame permitted by a violin lead, which was the standard sound for virtually every New Orleans orchestra before the success of the bands that went north to Chicago in 1915. The answer to the question of how loudly these small orchestras played is clear from Piron's recordings: when the violin carried the lead, the other instruments had to accommodate their volume and tone down to it, which meant a busy use of mutes for both the cornet and trombone. Piron's violin can be heard in most of the arrangements, and on their instrumental version of "West End Blues" he played a bouncing duet with pianist Steve Lewis, who "ragged" with noisy enthusiasm under the "straight" melody played by the violin. For two of the arrangements, one of them the classic "Mama's Gone Goodbye," Bocage joined him with his own violin, in what were possibly unique examples of two-violin jazz in their time.

The record companies in the mid-1920s were still trying to find ways to market their singles through the musical changes that were occurring, and began to work with the concept of "popular dance" singles—usually by large white orchestras—and "hot dance" singles, which were understood to be "jazzy" whether played by white or black groups. Piron's group employed "hot dance" arrangements with the same easy swing, handling the often complex instrumental writing with a confident swagger that made the music seem as natural as a dance down a New Orleans sidewalk.

The impetus from the record companies that led to the recordings by Ory's Sunshine Orchestra in Los Angeles, King Oliver's Creole Jazz Band and Jelly Roll Morton in Chicago, and A. J. Piron's New Orleans Orchestra in New York also brought into the studio another of the strong personalities who had been part of the rough cabaret and dance hall world before World War I. Freddie Keppard, the irascible and uncontrollable cornetist who had left to join the Creole Band in Los Angeles in 1914, finally made his appearance in a Chicago recording studio at the same time that Oliver and Morton began their studio careers, and over a period of two or three years Keppard's New Orleans–style cornet could be heard on a number of recordings.

Like Oliver, Keppard had been away from New Orleans for some time before he had an opportunity to record. There has been a persistent story that Keppard was offered a chance to record when the Creole Band was touring as a vaudeville ragtime act in 1916, a year before the Original Dixieland Band, a story that researcher Lawrence Gushee concluded was apocryphal. Certainly it is similar to many of stories that musicians offer for their own failure to get into a recording studio. . By the time Keppard did record in Chicago, nine years had passed since the Creole Band had begun playing for dancers in Los Angeles, and he had settled into a new career with the Chicago bands.

The first session that included Keppard was done in Chicago in June 1923, with the large orchestra led by Erskine Tate at the Vendome Theatre. In the style of the Chicago orchestras at the time, there were two cornets and a three-man reed section, and it is difficult to pick out Keppard's cornet. The occasional breaks and transitions have a distinctive raggy flavor, but they also could have been played by James Tate, the other cornetist, who was also a strong lead player. Although the leader, Erskine Tate, directed a successful group in Chicago through the decade, he only took his Vendome Orchestra back into the studio for one other session of two titles that was done three years later. It is interesting that on this second occasion Louis Armstrong was playing the trumpet instead of Keppard, again with James Tate as the second horn. In the intervening years the band developed a fierce South Side rhythmic attack, including flashing solos by the brilliant pianist Teddy Weatherford. The two titles, "Static Strut" and "Stomp Off, Let's Go," were incandescent, and Armstrong played with a concentration and fire that were unique among his many early recordings.

By the next year Keppard had left Tate to join Doc Cook's Orchestra at the Dreamland Ballroom, and he made his first recordings with them in January 1924. It was a dance ensemble, this time with four reeds—one of them an old friend from New Orleans, Jimmy Noone, who played the clarinet. Again Keppard only briefly could be heard in the elaborate arrangements. None of the bands worked in isolation now, thanks to recordings and the radio, and the inspiration for Cook's style was clearly the very popular white Chicago orchestra of Isham Jones, which already had begun a very successful recording career. The Isham Jones arrangement of a piece like "Mamma Loves Pappa," from October 1923, set the ensemble style for Cook's own arrangements, and at this point what can be heard of Keppard's playing had strong echoes of the work of Isham Jones's cornetist, Louis Panico. The style of Cook's orchestra was 1920s roadhouse dance music, and they held the job at one of largest South Side dance halls for a long period. Occasionally on the recordings there were brightly played solo passages for a wah-wah style muted cornet, but another cornet, presumably Keppard, could be heard playing a more stentorian lead in the background, and the solos were probably by the second cornetist, Elwood Graham, much as Louis Armstrong, as second cornetist, was playing the busier solos for Fletcher Henderson's orchestra in New York.

As jazz become more of a commercial product that could be sold on its own terms, the companies began taking the stars of dance orchestras and theater bands and putting them together for studio sessions. Armstrong had set the pattern with his small-band recordings in New York with various groups put together by Clarence Williams, who had become a "race" recording director for OKeh and Columbia Records. Armstrong did the smaller sessions as a change from his nightly dance job at the Roseland Ballroom with Fletcher Henderson's orchestra. Keppard's first small-group session was in June 1926, with an ensemble from Cook's Orchestra that was given the comedy name of Cookie's Gingersnaps on the record labels. By this time Armstrong's recordings had begun to affect the entire jazz world, and in the opening choruses of the first title recorded by the Gingersnaps, "High Fever," the sound of the cornet and the clarinet was a close copy of the Armstrong recordings with the Red Onion Jazz Babies done two years earlier. Keppard played with a mute, as Armstrong had done, and the clarinet stayed close to him, in harmony with his lead. The little group's style, however, was still weighted down with Cook's stylish, and busy, arrangements, and though there were two other New Orleans musicians in the group, Noone and banjoist Johnny St. Cyr, the sound remained tied to contemporary Chicago.

In the tantalizing moments of Keppard's playing that could be heard filling in some of the space of the arrangements he labored through, it was evident that he still had a forceful tone and a commanding, though occasionally disruptive presence. The closest comparison to his way of phrasing the lead are the recordings by Oscar Celestin, who had been part of the pre–World War I New Orleans world, though Celestin was already a veteran performer by the time Keppard was leading his first band. Each of them was a self-conscious showman used to dominating a stagy presentation. Each also still included many ragtime phrasings in their playing, and neither of them ever entirely assimilated the changes that were occurring in jazz in the mid-1920s. With all of these hints, there was no way to predict that, in the summer of 1926, only a few weeks after the Gingersnaps session, Keppard would create a handful of recordings that would document the feeling of the older New Orleans idiom that at that earlier moment was still poised uneasily between ragtime and jazz.

Keppard was only in his late thirties, but he was grossly overweight, drinking heavily, and already in poor health, but for these weeks he was able to project something of the power that he must have shown ten years before. In the first of the sessions, a month after the Cookie's Gingersnaps date, he was still a sideman; the group, Jimmy Blythe and his Ragamuffins, was led by pianist Jimmy Blythe. On one of the titles they accompanied popular vocalist Trixie Smith. The rhythm was light, only piano and woodblocks, but this time Keppard had a strong foil to work against, clarinetist Johnny Dodds. In the first arrangement, "Messin' Around," Dodds played the lead on the alto saxophone, with Keppard filling in a muted second to the melody. There were two takes; on the first Keppard clearly was unfamiliar with the arrangement, and he fumbled through the short cornet bridge that led to the vocal. After Smith sang the verses, Keppard returned, this time without the mute, and in the final choruses for the first time he played with a rough, though uncertain sense of power. For the second take he was more familiar with the piece, and when he returned after the vocal there was some of the New Orleans strut in his ensemble choruses. The session closed with an extended instrumental, "Adam's Apple," that chugged through an undistinguished Blythe melody with some of the excitement of the final choruses of the first piece they'd recorded, but sounding at the end as though Keppard's lip was tiring.

In September of 1926 he finally was able to come into the studio as leader of a small group under his own name. It was the only time his name was featured, and on the label the group was titled Freddie Keppard's Jazz Cardinals. Dodds was with him again, but more importantly the trombonist was his old New Orleans band member Eddie Vincent, who had been with him in the Creole Band in Los Angeles and had appeared on the stage beside him for some of the years of the Creole Band's vaudeville success. Dodds was a brilliant sideman, but he was younger, and his style was so individual that in every group he recorded with his sound was always identifiable. With Vincent, whose playing had the same harmonic and rhythmic sense that Eddie Edwards and Emile Christian had demonstrated in their earlier recordings, Keppard was back in a familiar ensemble role. Also, for the session Keppard was working with material he knew, and it might have been that at this time he made the change from cornet to trumpet. For the instrumental "Stockyard Strut," Keppard's playing had an authority and a precision he never achieved again.

The session was in many ways an anomaly. It was 1926, not 1916, but Keppard and Vincent had stepped back into the raggy syncopations of their old band style. The rhythms in their playing were jagged, even stilted, while the rhythm sound was the same contemporary Chicago beat that was featured on dozens of South Side recordings. With majestic power, Keppard pulled the ensemble back with him into an almost forgotten era, but without apology or even a hint that this wasn't the sound of jazz at just this moment. For the other side of the single the band accompanied the vocalist Papa Charlie Jackson; the piece is an old New Orleans favorite, "Salty Dog," and in the lazy phrasing of the opening instrumental choruses by Keppard and Vincent there was a glimpse of what an Uptown band might have sounded like on a casual night at Johnny Lala's Big 25.

The first recordings that were made of the city's black orchestras are tantalizing in their incompleteness, but still they left an indelible record of tone and phrasing, rhythms and ensembles. The recordings had a fresh and expansive range that moved from the uninhibited bounce of the Piron orchestra to the stentorian drive of Keppard's Jazz Cardinals, and from the assertiveness of the sessions that mark the beginnings of the careers of Morton and Oliver. The Piron recordings, however, were the only ones made by a working orchestra that was still part of the New Orleans everyday scene of dances and small parties, restaurants and downtown theaters with their stage orchestras. In the next few years, though the record companies finally found their way to the city, and the sessions created a portrait of a flamboyant music that was still colorfully alive, none of the Creole orchestras recorded again. Piron, however, continued to play a leading role in the efforts of the sedate Downtown society to create its own world of dancing and entertainment.

For much of the early jazz period the only regular outlets for advertising and musical comments were the pages of the two white daily newspapers, the *Picayune* and the *Item*. The most important news source for the African American community was the national newspaper, the Chicago *Defender*, which began as a weekly but as its readership expanded became a daily. From the middle of the 1920s, however, New Orleans African American society had its own newspaper, the *Louisiana Weekly*. For many years its coverage of the Creole musical world enjoyed the enthusiastic services of the high school art teacher Edward Spriggins, who signed his articles with his middle name, as E. Belfield Spriggins. It was Spriggins who wrote in one of his columns about Buddy Bolden and his band. For Spriggins and the community he typified, there was still the interest in classical music and middle-class culture that had always been a major element in the new African American society.

Although local communities like New Orleans were far from the new black consciousness of the larger northern cities, there was an awareness that for the first time there were stirrings of a distinct African American culture, with its own aesthetic judgments and concerns, drawing on the uniqueness of the African American experience. The excitement centered on the movement in Harlem called the "Harlem Renaissance," heralding new work of writers like Langston Hughes, Claude McKay, Sterling Brown, and Countee Cullen. There was an interest in new black-inspired art, with exhibitions in New York galleries. There were major classical works: "Afro-American" symphonies by William Grant Still and Nathaniel Dent that used "Negro" melodies and harmonies as a distinctive dimension of their musical idiom. In New Orleans Camille Nickerson, the daughter of the well-known African American music teacher Professor William J. Nickerson, established the "B-Sharp Music Club in 1917 ". . . to help provide concert opportunities and college scholarships for aspiring classicists from the local African-American community."[3]

In New Orleans that community was as deeply split over the questions of racial identity as the rest of black America, and the situation was intensified by the struggle that had existed for decades between the Creoles of Color and the other black groups in the city. It was, at its most basic, a question of the most effective way to counter the virtually monolithic racism of white America. The issue of assimilation or separation was not effectively resolved until the 1960s, when young black radicals chose separation, and demanded the dismissal of distinguished African American writers, among them the poet Robert Hayden, from the faculties of major black universities because their work was not considered committed to the struggle for equality.

In Lynn Abbott's excellent analysis of Spriggins's writings in the newspaper,[4] it is clear that Spriggins often felt the awkwardness of his situation. On March 24, 1928, he wrote, "Just as 'jazz' is not solely for the musical rabble, so is the 'classic' not solely for the musical intelligentsia." On October 20, 1928, he complained about the record shops close to his school (McDonough 35 High School on South Rampart Street) and their habit of playing blues records on the sidewalk so loudly that his students could hear them. He clearly understood the element of exploitation that has always been an aspect of the white presentation of vernacular black culture. "Our group" is Spriggins's designation for African Americans.

> Through many of our group who are cashing in on "Blue" songs our group are getting more and more chances to have themselves heard on the phonograph records and over the radio.
>
> Now, it seems to the writer that those of us who are upon Rampart Street must surely be tired of listening to the "Race Artists" sing the blues. All day long we are forced to listen to this type of music. It just seems that we'll never outrun the blues. It's too bad, too, that our young people of high school age, just the time when they are highly impressionable, are greeted morning, noon, and night with these "haunting melodies."
>
> One solution to this problem is to urge our folks to keep moving when they hear these songs being rendered. The Rampart Street music stores play these songs just for us. Let them stay on their hands a while or let them wait until you come in and then play them.

The center for popular dancing and entertainment for Creole society was the Parisian Roof Garden on the roof of the Pythian Temple Building—home of a Masonic businessmen's organization on Gravier Street, described as "America's most beautiful pleasure palace, owned and operated by and for colored." Spriggins was a tireless promoter of its activities. On October 3, 1925 he wrote: "Two of the many reasons for the increasing popularity of the Roof Garden are the excellent music furnished by a ten piece orchestra under the able direction of Manuel Perez and the excellent order maintained at all times. These two items alone would make the place worth patronizing ... During the rest of this month and all of next month there will be several special dances given by the schools and high school clubs. These dances will be attended by many of the younger set. On one or two occasions the orchestra will be assisted by the Original Tuxedo Band."

The following week he mentioned three of the most popular numbers for the evening, two of them favorites recorded by the New Orleans Rhythm Kings. For their engagement, Perez's orchestra was now named the Parisian Serenaders. "The Parisian Serenaders seemed to have struck their stride and through their inspiring music worked the crowd up to a pitch where round after round of applause followed each selection played. The numbers to which they were virtually forced to respond several times were 'Moon of Waikiki,' waltz; 'She's Crying For Me' and 'Milneburg Joys.' There are few that will deny that at present the Parisian Serenaders are the exponents of some of the best music enjoyed by dance lovers of this city."

The Parisian Roof Garden, however, had already attracted competition; attendance at the dances slumped, and customers complained that the orchestra wasn't doing its best at all times. The competition was a second dance palace catering to Creole society, the Pelican, which opened a block away at the corner of Gravier and South Rampart. The orchestra playing for dancing on Saturday, Sunday, Monday, and Wednesday was Bebe Ridgely's Original Tuxedo Orchestra. On April 10, 1926, the Pelican advertised that the orchestra had added a "saxophone star," with a photo of David Jones, who had just returned from a successful southern tour with his Cotton States Orchestra, and who ". . . has planned a trip to Europe after his engagement at the Pelican. During his stay here he will conduct classes in jazz and harmony." Several years before, Davey Jones had played with Louis Armstrong in Fate Marable's orchestra, helping Armstrong with his reading. He was one of the most talented of the city's new jazz generation, an excellent arranger as well as brilliant soloist, and his presence alone would have been enough to give the Pelican an edge in their efforts to lure away Parisian Roof Gardens audiences.

Sometime early in 1927 the Garden was forced to close, and for a few months there was talk about what would happen to the location; but Armand J. Piron, still looking for larger opportunities for his music and his orchestra, reopened it on August 8, 1927, as "Piron's Garden of Joy." There was a large advertisement in the *Weekly* with the heading WHAT COLORED NEW ORLEANS HAS BEEN AWAITING. The ad featured the Victor publicity shot of the orchestra with the note that "Piron's Famous Victor Recording Orchestra, composed of eleven pieces, will furnish the latest dance hits at all dances." The new location offered entertainment as well as dancing to the orchestra. In Spriggins's column on October 11, he was enthusiastic over the success of the new dance hall—and inadvertently provided a glimpse of Piron speaking as a member of his social class.

Speaking of pep, poise, pleasing personalities, pretty faces, beautifully gowned ladies, we are reminded that the male of the species who attended the dance in the Garden of Joy on last Saturday evening . . . Got eyes full of visions of loveliness. . . . The consensus was that the Theophile Sisters are clever dancers and did their number quite pleasingly . . . Wasn't it nice to note that the affable Mr. Piron quietly asked that no money be thrown to the entertainers, as they were paid for their services. To throw money to our young women who are trying to show their art is indeed discourteous and out of place, as it tends to cheapen both the artist and her work. Let's put our women on a higher level by trying always to respect them, especially when they are trying to earn a livelihood by any legitimate means.

The basic personnel of Piron's orchestra hadn't changed since their recording sessions in New York, and he probably could have continued to present their familiar and still popular arrangements for as long as he chose, but in a burst of annoyance in 1928 he fired the entire orchestra, saying that their playing was "old-fashioned." The cornetist Peter Bocage's comment later, with a shake of his head, was that since they'd been together so long, Piron had to pay all of them reasonable salaries. When he brought younger musicians onto the bandstand at the Garden of Joy, he could get away with paying them considerably less. Bocage and others went on to form their own group that they named The Creole Serenaders. They were featured on a popular radio program in the 1930s—introducing their theme song "Purple Rose of Cairo"—and even without Piron they continued to be the city's most popular Creole dance ensemble.

By the next summer the Garden of Joy was so well established that Piron was able to turn over the music to Clarence Desdune, who led "Piron's Orchestra No. 2." The banjoist, playing one of his first jobs, was the eighteen-year-old Danny Barker. Piron was able to return to his profitable restaurant jobs and lead his new, younger "Cotton Pickers" orchestra on the SS *Capitol*. Although he was not to record again, Armand J. Piron left an indelible imprint on the cultural history of his own social group and on the story of New Orleans jazz.

The excitement, for the young crowds, however, followed the automobile, the new short dresses of "emancipated" women, and the slicked-down hair and surreptitious pocket flasks of their escorts to the city's newest dance emporiums. With the latest trends in New Orleans music, the new bands were leading the way.

14

Out to the Halfway House

New Orleans was what I like to call "The University of Jazz." Oh, lots of musicians and bands came from places like Kansas City and Chicago, but there was something—a certain combination of hot weather, dumps and dives and people that only New Orleans could provide.

There was one time I was driving out in the country and stopped at a place, a shed-like affair with a place to park your car, called the Half-way House. I dropped in for a cold drink or something to eat. The band that played there had five musicians, and I don't believe that any of them could read a note of music. Well, I sat there and listened and listened and listened. They didn't seem to know much of anything, but finally I asked them to play a favorite of mine, a waltz called Let Me Call You Sweetheart. *They knew that one all right. They knew it just well enough to tear it apart. A few weeks later I recorded that band playing* Let Me Call You Sweetheart, *and, believe me, it wasn't in three-quarter time either!*

FRANK WALKER, RECORDING DIRECTOR FOR COLUMBIA RECORDS,
RECALLING HIS VISIT TO HALFWAY HOUSE IN SEPTEMBER 1925[1]

The look of the places that New Orleanians went to dance changed in the 1920s. Instead of a saloon with dancing in a back room, or an amateurishly decorated one-story wooden hall in the middle of the next block that was hired for lodge meetings, political rallies, and neighborhood dances, some of the most popular jazz for dancing moved out of town. One of the busiest new dance places, the Halfway House Restaurant looked in photographs a lot like any other of the new wooden buildings that were edging out into what was then the outskirts of New Orleans, though its size would have loomed over an ordinary shotgun house, if there had been any close by. The building, at the corner of City

Park Avenue and Ponchartrain Boulevard, was about halfway between downtown Canal Street and the lake, so its name was a description of its familiar location. From the outside it was difficult to tell what it was. It was a square, sizeable one-story building with a wide pitched roof that sat on top of it like a squat lampshade. The edges of the roof were scalloped and projected out over the large windows to fend off the rain. The windows were the most distinctive part of the building. They were wide, double openings, extending from the floor almost to the edge of the eaves, and they were set only a few feet apart. If they were all opened to the air at once they would help keep the building pleasantly cool in the evenings.

One side of the restaurant was close to the New Basin Canal, a strip of water that drained south from Lake Ponchartrain. Next to the Halfway House was a small, steel frame bridge crossing the canal; on the other side it was only a short walk to the city cemetery. To the east and north of the cemetery the land was beginning to be cleared and drained, and the neighborhood of Lakeview was slowly expanding toward the lake over low-lying marshland.

On the western side of the canal, the road led out to the well tended grounds of the family resort of Spanish Fort at West End, and beside it on the lake was the noisier area of Bucktown, with the quieter resort of West End as a nearby neighbor. Bucktown still kept some of its character into the modern period, with its old-style wooden eating places built on pilings over the lake, but the New Orleans Yacht Club took over what was Spanish Fort in the modernization of the lakefront in the 1930s. When Katrina's winds struck, the rows of luxury boats were driven against each other, splintered against the piers, heaped against trees and walls, and for months afterwards the only sound was the gruff rumble of cranes as workers slowly picked through the wreckage.

A popular streetcar line ran north from downtown, along Canal Street and past Halfway House on the way to Spanish Fort. On pleasant afternoons the cars were loaded with families journeying out to the elegant gardens and the amusements at the lakeside. The younger crowd, who were free of the encumbrances of children and felt like making a day of it, could go out to the lake and enjoy the amusements at Spanish Fort, then take the streetcar back to the Halfway House for dinner and dancing. In the shadowy depths of the only known photograph of the Halfway House's interior, it is immediately apparent that the only thing for anyone to do there was dance. The entire room was a dance floor, with a fringe of tables backed up against the walls. The room had a quiet elegance: the tables had light colored, full tablecloths, there were neat bentwood backed chairs, tasteful, modest chandeliers, and a ceiling fan. The windows were tall and wide, and the walls had simple panels, but there was no elaborate décor. No paintings, no advertisements. At one end was a simple bandstand with a curtain behind it. The room may have seemed small, but the bandstand was wide enough for a grand piano, drums and bass, and a seven-piece orchestra.

What had changed in New Orleans that made the new dance places like the Halfway House so popular that they didn't even bother with much advertising was more than a nearby streetcar line. It was the automobile. The prosperity of the 1920s that was to bring profound changes to American social attitudes washed over New Orleans as well, and families who once couldn't think of owning a car before now were filling the streets with cars of their own. There were more miles of paved roads, and the cars themselves had improved—there weren't the uncertainties of breakdowns and unreliable tires that had plagued drivers before the war. The new models had self-starters, safer brakes, and they were much more comfortable. The doors and windows could be closed against the weather and against any interruption to whatever anyone might be doing in the front seat. For the flaming youth of the 1920s, the automobile became their way to get out of the house.

The favorite dance places that did occasionally advertise in the entertainment pages of the *Picayune* offered the same pleasures and accessibility as the Halfway House. They were restaurants with large dance floors scattered at the edges of the city. New Orleans jazz, in the 1920s, largely moved out of the downtown business district and the nearby neighborhoods to the suburbs, or to easily reached roadside destinations not far away. It was the newest trend, not only in New Orleans but in every large American city. The new bands were filling the tables and dance floors of large, sprawling, informal buildings that often were given the name "roadhouses." In New Orleans, although they weren't technically roadhouses, two of the best-known dance restaurants were at Spanish Fort, with a familiar suburban ambience. For older couples the most popular of the two locations was the sedate Tranchina's Restaurant, with its genteel atmosphere and the much-admired, infectiously swinging music by Armand J. Piron's Society Orchestra. The orchestra's series of successful dance singles on the Victor label had given their reputation a new polish, and they worked steadily for private parties as well as Sundays at the country club—at the same time playing nightly at the restaurant. The décor in Tranchina's included large potted plants in front of the elegantly raised bandstand, with a tasteful Japanese-style door brightened with paper lanterns in the wall behind them. Covering the wall and framing the doorway was a curtain, so the band could get on and off the bandstand without having to disturb the customers. In their posed photograph on the bandstand the orchestra was tastefully dressed in the customary tuxedos, with their black bow ties carefully aligned.

The other dance floor that advertised for customers at Spanish Fort was the Tokio [*sic*] Gardens, which didn't have a set orchestra policy. Some summers the music was provided by one of the many conventional dance orchestras who shared the bandstands with the New Orleans jazzmen. For the summer of 1924, however, the resort hired a jazz group, trumpeter Johnny Beyersdorffer and his Jazzola Novelty Orchestra. At twenty-five Beyersdorffer was one of the busiest of the new generation of white trumpeters, and the band had already built a steady following with young dancers. In their publicity photograph the atmosphere on stage was much looser than in the Piron orchestra photo, taken only a hundred yards away across the garden. The Jazzola Novelty Orchestra went for a youthful look: white trousers, dark, collegiate-style blazers, and straight neckties. From the photograph it looked as though the only ones in the band who played sitting down were the banjoist, the pianist, and the drummer.

Beyersdorffer's band was rougher and bluesier than Piron's Creole orchestra, but lacked their suave ensemble style. They made their only recording earlier in the spring, for OKeh Records, on the first trip any of the out-of-town record companies made to New Orleans to look for local groups. They did a dance single with two instrumentals, "I Wonder Where My Easy Rider's Riding Now?" and "The Waffle Man's Call." On both numbers Beyersdorffer played strong, driving solos using a mute, particularly on "The Waffle Man's Call," which stands out among the New Orleans recordings made during this same period. The band also included another of the Italian American instrumentalists, clarinetist Nunzio Scaglione, who was considered one of the best of the new musicians, and whose playing had a bright lift and spontaneity. The trombonist was Tom Brown, who had taken his band to Chicago nine years before, and his playing had rough echoes of the street-corner "ballyhoo" days, most reminiscent in a duet chorus with Scaglione in "The Waffle Man's Call."

The band's appearances were advertised in the *Picayune* in May and June as providing the music at the Dancing Pavilion, with dancing under the direction of Professor C. Eddie Morton. They were billed as simply a "Novelty" orchestra, and certainly that was how the management regarded them. The advertisement for June 3 depicted a rural farmer in straw hat, boots, and suspenders raising the dust with his stamping feet, and the next night at the Gardens was promised to be a BARN DANCE, with prizes for Rube Costume, Old Maid, and Best Barn Dancers, among other categories. Dancers who showed up wearing a costume were admitted free. A New Orleans band, whatever it called itself, was expected to play anything that the management requested.

During the spring Piron's orchestra was in New York playing at the Cotton Club, and for the time Tranchina's stayed open only as a restaurant, without a new orchestra. The other musical entertainment that was advertised at Spanish Fort was Tosso's Concert Band, which offered a free evening concert of Popular and Classic Airs. As a helpful hint to the resort's patrons who were looking for someplace to dance, the newspaper on June 6 noted that "Tranchina's is within a stone's throw of Tokio Gardens and many patrons of the popular dance pavilion visit the restaurant during the intermission."

In those first months of recording in New Orleans, beginning in the spring of 1924 and continuing through the winter of 1925, the two record companies, OKeh and Columbia, tried a number of local groups, returning over the next few years for additional sessions with the bands that had shown promise. Most of the new artists, like their music, were young, and for some of them this first notice by one of the record companies was all they would have for the rest of their careers. The recordings by Piron were the group's last, and the single recorded on March 16, 1924, by Fate Marable's disciplined orchestra from the SS *Capitol* is the only documentation we have of the celebrated Marable orchestras, as well as being the first session for drummer Zutty Singleton, a boyhood friend of Louis Armstrong who was to meet him again later when they both became stars in the swing era.

The dance rhythms and arrangements of both the Piron and Marable orchestras reflected their position as African American dance-band leaders whose own tastes and preferences mirrored their white audiences. Because Marable worked up and down the river, his dance beat utilized even more of the elements of white orchestras playing at the time. The most obvious difference was that although their white audiences danced with considerable enthusiasm and energy, because of society's restrictions they still moved more stiffly, which meant that the band emphasized the first and third beats of the measure, rather than sliding toward the second and fourth beats—the "backbeat"—that was more characteristic of the New Orleans jazz groups, both black and white.

Marable's arrangements were musically demanding, and if he had asked as much of his musicians a few years before, when the eighteen-year-old Louis Armstrong joined them, his orchestra would have been, as was often said, a "music conservatory." The two selections, "Frankie and Johnny" and "Pianoflage," also were the only recordings of the thirty-two-year-old trumpeter Sidney Desvigne, who took a flashing, authoritative solo on "Frankie and Johnny." He went on to lead his own riverboat orchestras, and in the 1930s directed a popular Uptown swing band. The orchestra Marable was leading in 1924, like most of his groups, included musicians from other stops on the river, but the rhythm section and the two trumpeters were New Orleanians. In his comments on the orchestra's recordings, Richard Sudhalter also singled out their high level of musicianship, quoting historian S. Frederick Starr:

> *It's their second title that attracts attention.* Pianoflage *was a 1922 piano ragtime novelty by Roy Bargy, best known as arranger and musical director of the Benson Orchestra of Chicago. It's a complex, rather formal piece, and Marable's men negotiate the turns and twists of this orchestration with considerable skill.*
>
> *The very fact that they would have chosen that piece for their recording debut speaks eloquently for the band's high musical standards—and for a certain lack of race consciousness. In Starr's words, membership in brass bands, particularly, "heightened respect for instrumental mastery, and led to the view that all should share it." It was a view shared by black and white.*[2]

The most prominent of the black orchestras who made their recording debut in these busy studio sessions was the Original Tuxedo Jazz Orchestra, still led by Oscar Celestin together with trombonist Bebe Ridgely; their recording career continued over the next four years. An interesting footnote to the band recordings was a blues novelty by veteran black vaudeville artists Billy and Mary Mack, which also made its way into the January 1925 sessions. The pianist for their stage band, Edgar Brown, played a standard accompaniment, with the addition of the local trumpeter Punch Miller. Miller was constantly on the road and it was only fortuitous that he made it into the studio. His playing had the acid tone characteristic of other local trumpeters like "Red" Allen and Lee Collins, and his solo chorus on "My Heartbreakin' Gal" displayed some of the busy virtuosity that was the trademark of his individual style.

Within this same stretch of the spring of 1924 to the winter of 1925, the companies captured the playing of a number of very young and very excited white cornetists with their dance bands. Among the musicians making their first recordings were trumpeters and cornetists Johnny DeDroit, Joseph "Skarkey" Bonano, Stirling Bose, and Joseph "Wingy" Manone, in addition to the session with Johnny Beyersdorffer. DeDroit was in his early thirties, but Manone and Bonano were just twenty, and Bose was eighteen. Although none of them displayed the ease and familiarity they demonstrated in their later recordings, they still brought a high level of skill and ambition into the studio. Bonano already showed his relaxed lyricism in his solo on "Dirty Rag" with pianist Norman Brownlee's orchestra, another group with Tom Brown on trombone and with the brother of Larry Shields, Harry, making his recording debut. Bose became a busy sideman with some of the major big bands of the 1930s, and his practiced playing on his sides with the Original Crescent City Jazzers hinted at his later ease in the swing era. Manone's first session also suggested that there was something to take note of, even if it was only his assertive attitude as he launched into his determined first solo. DeDroit was the most established of them, and his orchestra was recorded later in a last session in New York. Of all of the young lead players who were recorded, his playing sounds most centered in the mannerisms from the first New York "jazz" session of a few years before. Although his orchestras continued to be popular and to work steadily, he didn't record again.

For most of the years that the Halfway House was a popular stop on the West End streetcar line, the band was directed by the same leader, trumpeter Abbie Brunies. For most of their recordings the band took its name from the restaurant itself. The restaurant opened in 1914 and stayed open until the Depression forced it to close in 1930. It is Brunies's Halfway House Orchestra that gave the modest frame building its place in the story of New Orleans jazz.

Abbie was one of the innumerable Brunies brothers from Uptown. Albert, his full name, was born on January 19, 1900, two years before his younger brother George, the trombonist for the New Orleans Rhythm Kings. Like all of the Brunies Abbie was a solidly schooled musician, and by the time he was seventeen he was leading bands that Jack Laine sent out for jobs in Bucktown and Milneburg. He was said to be one of the first choices as cornet with the band that became the New Orleans Rhythm Kings in Chicago, but decided to stay with his local job driving a taxi, since he thought it would be more financially secure. He took over the job at the Halfway House, at least part-time, as early as 1919, leading a

THE HALFWAY HOUSE ORCHESTRA, 1923. FROM LEFT: CHARLIE CORDILLA, MICKEY
MARCOUR, LEON ROPPOLO, ABBIE BRUNIES, BILL EASTWOOD, JOE LOYACANO, LEO ADDE.

band called the Four New Orleans Jazz Babies. In a photograph the Jazz Babies
look very young and very excited with their job. Brunies was playing the trumpet,
Buck Rogers was the drummer, Mickey Marcour the pianist, and their banjo-
mandolin player was the blind musician who was said to have organized the first
white band to play jazz in New Orleans, "Stalebread" Lacoume. Brunies, like his
brothers, was as well-organized as he was talented as a trumpeter and continued to lead the band at the restaurant until almost the end of the decade. For
their final recording session in December 1928, the company decided to use his
name, and the single was released as by Albert Brunies and his Halfway House
Orchestra. Like Piron at Tranchina's, the Halfway House and its orchestra were
so popular that the restaurant didn't bother to do much advertising.

The band also played for excursions and afternoon jobs, and sometimes there
were both a white band and a black band. Pops Foster didn't know which of the
Brunies brothers was leading the orchestra, but he remembered jobs where they
worked together. Foster's reminiscence is particularly useful, because it is one of
the few times that any of the African American musicians recalled the white musicians, even though the bands and the musicians encountered each other often.

*Many times the Brunies band would have a job for another band and they
would call us. They'd also use Jack Carey's band, Amos Riley's band, or someone else. . . . Out at the Halfway House they had white bands. After a while the
Brunies Band got that job. They played for a lot of dances around New Orleans*

where I'd be on the same bill with them. The last time I played on a bill with them I was with Amos Riley's band and we were playing a country picnic out of Bay St. Louis, Mississippi. I missed the train with the other guys and had to get a later one. When I got to Bay St. Louis I hired a wagon for fifty cents to carry me out to the picnic. When I arrived they weren't there and I started eating sandwiches, having some drinks, and having a good time. When Amos's and Brunies' bands arrived they were sure surprised to see me. They'd gotten lost and couldn't find the place. The Brunies and their band played very good.[3]

Brunies himself showed considerable stability as a bandleader, keeping essentially the same band together for most of the years he worked at the restaurant. He was tall and lanky, standing in front of the group with a diffident slouch, but elegant in his band tuxedo and wavy dark hair that he kept trimmed short. As has always been the situation in New Orleans, the working musicians all knew each other and substituted freely in each other's bands. For some months in early 1925 he filled in with the orchestra led by a friend, clarinetist Tony Parenti, who was directing the band at the Lavida Ballroom in downtown New Orleans. Brunies was the cornetist with the group for their Victor Records sessions in March, which fell between his own sessions as leader of the Halfway House Orchestra in January and again in September. He also "loaned" most of the members of his orchestra to another friend, Paul Mares, who had returned to New Orleans after the breakup of the New Orleans Rhythm Kings in Chicago a year before. With the planned addition of the clarinetist Leon Roppolo, who also was with the Rhythm Kings and had just returned to the city, and trombonist Santo Pecora, the ensemble recorded five titles for Victor Records in March 1925 under the name The Original New Orleans Rhythm Kings, with five musicians from the Brunies band as part of the group.

As Brunies's recordings with his orchestra make very evident, the Halfway House thought of itself as a place to dance. The first time the band was recorded Brunies brought seven musicians into the temporary studio facilities that OKeh Records had set up on Canal Street. The idea, as far as OKeh was concerned, seems to have been to try to repeat the success of the New Orleans Rhythm Kings with another New Orleans band with a similar sound. This first session is still the best-known of the different early metamorphoses of the group, because the clarinetist on these first sides—and in the photo of the group posed on the bandstand—was Roppolo, already a jazz legend for his haunting solos with the Rhythm Kings. When he had left Chicago after the Rhythm Kings breakup, Roppolo played for a period in New York with a variety of groups, but he was already showing signs of increasing mental instability, and the two titles he recorded with the Halfway House Orchestra, "Pussy Cat Rag" and "Barataria," were his final recordings. There is a legend that in a fit of moody despondency he went out to the lake and threw his clarinet into the water. The story turned out not to be true, but can instead be thought of as a metaphor for the end of his short career.

The first session of the Halfway House Orchestra for OKeh Records had already been released a few months before, but when Frank Walker, the Columbia Records repertory director, stopped by the Halfway House for something to drink in the summer of 1925—at least to judge from what he later wrote about his first encounter with them—he didn't have any idea who the band was. It was the quintet that Brunies was leading that summer, when Walker asked them if they knew his favorite waltz, that Walker recorded late in September, including the fast foxtrot version of "Let Me Call Your Sweetheart" that had gotten them their Columbia contract. To be certain that the record buyers would know exactly what they were purchasing, the label read "The Halfway House Dance Orchestra (direction of Albert Brunies)." Dance enthusiasts who also enjoyed New Orleans jazz were getting something extra for their money. One of their most typical recordings opened their Columbia session, an assured, mature version of the new hit "Squeeze Me," with both Brunies and clarinetist Charlie Cordilla playing with easy confidence.

In the spring of 1926, when Frank Walker came on his second trip to New Orleans to continue working with local artists, Brunies had replaced most of the musicians he'd worked with for the "Let Me Call You Sweetheart" session the previous fall. The sound of the band he'd now assembled was to remain his basic stock in trade for the next three years. Essentially it was a classic dance jazz group. Of the six musicians, four of them played the rhythm—the tightest, most responsive rhythm section of any band to record in New Orleans in the 1920s. They had a sense of each other that shaped every accent, and they also all felt the beat at the same place. As all musicians know, everyone hears the basic pulse of the beat at a different time—even if the difference is only a fraction of a second. For the four in the rhythm section—pianist Red Long, banjoist Angelo Palmisano, brass and string bass player the experienced Chink Martin, and drummer Emmet Rogers—it must have felt that they even breathed at the same time. Against this beat there were only two horns, Brunies's cornet and the clarinet of Charlie Cordilla, who had played tenor saxophone on the first session with Leon Roppolo and stayed on as clarinetist for the new Columbia sessions. It was a pared-down, minimal sound without anything to distract the dancers from the beat and the melody. The dancers heard a strong, fleet, controlled rhythm with clear, sharply defined melodies played in arranged sections or as solos by the two horns. In the open space of the Halfway House dance floor their sound must have been irresistible.

In his discussion of the band's style, Richard Sudhalter also emphasized their strong rhythm section and ensemble clarity. "What strikes the ear is the clarity, each part defined, floating atop an unusually buoyant, unembellished 4/4 rhythm; Cordilla, an excellent journeyman musician, seems to improve as a soloist from date to date. On 'Won't You Be My Lovin' Baby' . . . Cordilla takes two solos; here and on the other side, the faster 'I Don't Want To Remember,' he's long-lined and fluent, with a rhythmic attack that has a certain parallel in the playing of Johnny Dodds."[4]

Across the canal to the west of the Halfway House and the new Lakeview suburb stretching out behind it to the lake was a different section of the city. The canal at that point was the dividing line between Orleans Parish, and Jefferson Parish. West of the canal was the Jefferson Parish suburb of Metairie, even newer than Lakeview. The new suburb sprawled over the flat bayou earth with even less plan or design than New Orleans itself, but with none of the consciousness of an old history that gave the river neighborhoods of New Orleans their distinctive character. Metairie is still as characterless today. If you get caught in one of its unending traffic slowdowns and glance glumly at the jangle of street signs for the nationally advertised business chains as you inch past them, you have the discouraged feeling that you could be anywhere in today's United States. When the rising water began its surge against the levee walls on August 29, 2005, it was soon evident that the earth berm bracing the Metairie side of the levee wall was two feet higher than the mounded earth on the New Orleans side, and Lakeview paid the price. For several months following the flood Metairie had the only functioning large shopping mall in the city, and one of the handful of functioning post offices, and its streets were more jammed than ever.

In the 1920s, however, Metairie was still new and exotic. The city's dog track, out on Metairie Road, attracted crowds almost as large as for the horse racing at the Fair Grounds. One reason for the popularity of the new roadhouses was that they generally were across county lines (or parish lines, as they're titled in Louisiana), so there was less harassment over the presence of liquor which, thanks to Prohibition, helped give a new and slightly risqué character to the "steamy" music most of the establishments featured.

One of the new dance restaurants, the Beverly Gardens, was close to the dog track and its advertisements assured their customers that the dancing wouldn't start until the last race was over. The house band in the early twenties was led by the trombonist Happy Schilling, who had exchanged band leadership with his friend clarinetist Johnny Fischer during the years that Jack Laine's bands were taking most of the jobs for the city's white musicians. Schilling's orchestra never settled into a steady lineup, but he had a pleasant personality and usually came up with jobs of some kind, so nearly every white musician in town played for him at least for an occasional date. Most of the bands working in the roadhouses eventually made recordings with the larger companies, so it's possible to sort out some of their personnel changes. Schilling, however, doesn't seem to have recorded at any point during his early career. In a photograph of his orchestra at about the time he was leading the house band at the Beverly Gardens, the musicians included drummer Monk Hazel and young cornetist Johnny Wiggs (then still using his own name, John Hyman). Guitarist/banjoist Freddie Loyocano, bassist Clay Pinner, and pianist Frank Pinero filled out the rhythm section; Schilling's son, George Schilling Jr., and Elery Maser were the reeds. For their formal publicity photographs they wore the obligatory tuxedos; in one of them the photographer posed them intently studying something in the center of

NEW ORLEANS ROADHOUSES ADVERTISE THEIR DANCE ENTERTAINMENT, LOUIS ARMSTRONG
PLAYS AT THE LINCOLN THEATRE, AND OKEH ANNOUNCES A NEW RECORDING BY A NEW
ORLEANS ORCHESTRA, 1925–1931. COLLAGE BY THE AUTHOR.

the photo—the shiny euphonium horn that Schilling was holding in his arms and
gazing at as tenderly as if it were a newborn baby.

Sometime early in the 1920s the Beverly Gardens became the Suburban
Gardens. In its new advertising it assured its customers that the road from downtown New Orleans was now paved all the way to Metairie, and it was a straight
drive out to their suburban location. Usually the band holding down the job was
Oscar Celestin's Original Tuxedo Orchestra, which was one of the most popular

bands in the new dance restaurants, and the Gardens advertised them almost weekly.

The A. J. Piron Orchestra returned to their old job at Tranchina's in the summer of 1924, after the band, much to Piron's disgust, voted to leave New York behind and return home. They weren't advertised as often as Celestin's Tuxedo Orchestra, though it could have been that Tranchina's and Piron were such an established part of the entertainment scene that advertising wasn't necessary. Some advertisements mentioned the band's talented pianist Steve Lewis, who had begun recording on his own as accompanist to the New Orleans entertainer Willie Jackson, and also cut an irrepressibly raggy piano roll of one of the songs that the band recorded, "Mama's Gone, Goodbye." The advertisements implied that he was so well known to the diners at Tranchina's that it wasn't necessary to write anything more than "Come Hear Steve Tickle the Ivories."

In 1926, two seasons after Beyersdorffer's summer at Tokio Gardens, another dance restaurant was busy at the lake, just west of Spanish Fort at the West End resort. It was opened by the downtown Roosevelt Hotel, and operated as the Roosevelt West End Roof. For two summers in the mid-1920s the house band was a new dance jazz group named The Owls, who memorialized their nights on the bandstand there with their composition "West End Romp."

The earliest photograph of the musicians who founded the band in 1922 is a backyard portrait of seven smiling white teenagers in schoolboy summer suits, white shirts, and informal neckties taken around the time of World War I. They are playing banjos, guitars, a mandolin, a ukulele, and a violin. The band's name was The Invincibles, and they were one of two ragtime string bands popular in the society world where their employers—usually their parents' friends—wanted music that was "hot but not too loud." The other band was the Six and 7/8s, some of whom ultimately joined with members of the Invincibles, continuing into the postwar years as a quartet.

The members of the Invincibles were middle class, most of them headed for college and careers or civil service. Their music was part of the comfortable social life in New Orleans before America's entry into World War I. Both of the youthful string bands had a precedent for the raggy elements of their music: string trios or small string ensembles were more popular in many Storyville cabarets than the noisier dance orchestras, and members of the Six and 7/8s used to sneak into Tom Anderson's saloon and buy beer for the musicians working there to learn some of their tricks.

Most of the musicians in both bands served in the military during the war; many returned to New Orleans after college to begin their professional careers. The members of the Invincibles decided to begin playing again, but it was now the beginning of the 1920s jazz craze, and they made a decision to learn other instruments and turn themselves into a dance jazz orchestra. Some were reluctant to make the change. Their brilliant jazz mandolin player Bill Kleppinger, who played the band's syncopated leads and breaks, made a halfhearted effort to learn the clarinet, then gave up and with his mandolin joined the members of the Six and 7/8s who still were playing. Edmond Souchon later described Kleppinger listening intently to the playing of Johnny Dodds, but Kleppinger insisted that he had never heard any of the black musicians Souchon often mentioned. The violinist Eblan Rau said that he'd stay with them as long as they didn't get "too serious," and when they began working as a regular orchestra he dropped out. The bass player, Red Mackie, was part of the orchestra for the first few months, but he was also starting up his own pine oil business, and there wasn't time to fit in a demanding schedule of rehearsals and performances.

In 1949 the musicians still active from the two string bands—Kleppinger, Souchon, Mackie, and Bernie Shields, who played the acoustic Hawaiian lap steel guitar—recorded two privately released singles on the New Orleans Originals label under the name the Six and 7/8s, and played with an ensemble flair and a rhythmic excitement that echoed the finest of the New Orleans classic bands. Kleppinger's mandolin version of the classic Picou solo on their rendition of "High Society" had the freshness of someone discovering the solo's intricacies for the first time. In the summer of 1954 I recorded a more extended session in Edmond Souchon's living room in Metairie, and an LP drawn from the materials was released on Folkways Records a few years later.

The noisy exuberance that was part of The Owls' approach to their music quickly won over their audiences. In a competition in 1926 sponsored by a downtown theater, The Owls were declared the most popular band in New Orleans, which trombonist Harrison Barnes, who had been part of the Chris Kelly orchestra and the Tuxedo Brass Band, confirmed in an interview in the 1950s. He often played on the excursion boat *Susquehanna*, which made day trips that featured music and dancing back and forth across Lake Ponchartrain to Mandeville. When the boat was docking at the end of the afternoon he could hear The Owls playing at Quirella's Restaurant, and as far as he was concerned they were the best band he knew of working in the city.

When Columbia Records began recording the band, they added "New Orleans" to their name, so the labels read The New Orleans Owls, but in the advertising that was done for the band in the city they were always The Owls. Their career was so short that they never lost their first sense of excitement over what they were doing, and they continually attempted new arrangements that demanded a high level of musicianship. They brought in a non-Invincible member: cornetist Bill Padrone, a thin, mustachioed, mousy-looking man who added a sharp, distinctive edge to their ensembles and was an exciting soloist. Columbia paid the band (along with their other dance group, the Halfway House Orchestra) the ultimate compliment by sponsoring a full-page advertisement in the *Picayune* on August 17, 1926. The four largest music retailers in the city—Grunewald's, Maison Blanche, the Dwyer Piano Company, and the D. H. Holmes Company—were gathered on the page with their own advertisements grouped around pictures of the two bands and Columbia's descriptions of the two new releases, The

THE NEW ORLEANS OWLS, PLAYING AT THE OLD SAZERAC BALLROOM SHORTLY AFTER
THEY ORGANIZED AS A DANCE BAND, 1924. FROM LEFT: DICK MACKIE, MONK SMITH, RED
MACKIE, BENJY WHITE, RENE GELPI, LEADER EARL CRUMB. STANDING BEHIND GELPI
IS VIOLINIST EBLEN RAU. THE MACKIE BROTHERS SOON LEFT, FOLLOWED BY RAU, WHO
DECIDED THEY WERE "GETTING TOO SERIOUS ABOUT THEIR MUSIC."

Owls' "West End Romp" and "Tampeekoe" and the Halfway House Orchestra's
"Since You're Gone" and "I'm in Love."

Latest Columbia Record Hits—Made by Local Bands!

*The New Orleans Owls, who play nightly at the West End Roof, need no
introduction to the dance lovers of New Orleans. The Columbia Phonograph
Company recently made several recordings by this talented group of local artists and have just released the first one of these recordings, which is on sale at
your favorite music store.*

---

*The Half-Way House Dance Orchestra have been famous for their hot
Charleston music ever since the Charleston rage hit New Orleans. This new
recording by them for Columbia is no exception and it is hot enough to bring
Charleston steps out of any lover of the dance. You will find this number on
sale at any of the stores advertising on this page but you'd better hurry as a
sell-out is expected on this record.*

The local piano distributor also wanted to be part of the excitement and the band's manager, drummer Earl Crumb, dutifully signed an endorsement of the piano.

What the Owls Say of the
Weber Grand

"We wish to say that the Weber Piano we used in these recordings proved valuable to us on account of its excellent tone quality."

Although there were some changes in personnel in their career, the principal members of the band were Padrone, cornet; Frank Netto, trombone; Pinky Vidacovich and Benji White, clarinet and saxophones; Lester "Monk" Smith, guitar and tenor saxophone; Rene Gelpi, banjo; Dan LeBlanc, tuba; and drummer Earl Crumb. Many of the arrangements they recorded, like the explosive "Picadilly" or the intricate "Goose Pimples," were complex and energetic, and they approached them all with the same bright enthusiasm. Perhaps because they never played as a dance orchestra before they picked up their instruments, their dance beat was edgy, without the smooth pulse of the Halfway House or the Piron Orchestra, but on the arrangements where they switched back to their original instruments the beat was calm and assured. One of the most unique moments, when they presented both sides of their musical temperament, came in their recording of the jazz standard "That's A Plenty." In the middle of the arrangement, during the short bridge that introduces the chorus, there was a sudden empty space when Monk Smith, who was playing tenor saxophone, dropped out to switch to the guitar, and for the next two repeats of the chorus, with the rest of the band silent, Smith and the banjoist Rene Gelpi, who also sounded as though he'd switched to guitar, played a finger-picked, lightly swinging string duet. In the repeat of the chorus one of the clarinetists, probably Pinky Vidacovich, added a gentle, low-register counterpoint. It is one of the loveliest moments of early New Orleans jazz.

The Owls still were playing in 1928, but most of the original Invincibles musicians had resumed their other careers, and among the new members were musicians like guitarist Nappy Lamare and saxophonist Eddie Miller, who would shortly leave for New York. After a few months the last lineup of the group disbanded. At the same time, with the opening of new, lavish theaters for motion pictures, a new musical area was opening up for New Orleans musicians, and for many of them it was no longer necessary to think only of dancers and roadhouse dance floors.

A musician's life is always a precarious balance between periods of more work than they can handle, and just as extended periods with no work at all, but for much of the 1920s it must have seemed to New Orleans jazz musicians that they'd come into a land of plenty. There were still dances and parties everywhere

COLUMBIA RECORDS ADVERTISES ITS "LOCAL HITS" BY THE HALFWAY HOUSE ORCHESTRA
AND THE NEW ORLEANS OWLS. THE OWLS PLAY AT THE LAKE, AND "ALBERT BRUNIES
ORCHESTRA" OPENS AT THE MIDWAY, AFTER THE FLOOD OF 1927 TEMPORARILY CLOSES
THE HALFWAY HOUSE RESTAURANT. COLLAGE BY THE AUTHOR.

in the city; there were jobs at the new suburban roadhouses, at the dance restaurants along the lake, or at the camps at Milneburg; and they soon began finding jobs created by the new novelties, radio and the movies. Downtown New Orleans was rapidly replacing its legitimate theaters and vaudeville houses with "Motion Picture Palaces," and the latest technical innovation, air conditioning, gave the new movie palaces an even further advantage. The new cooling systems and elaborate fans meant that the indoor spaces could be kept comfortable all year around, which solved the problem that had made indoor entertainment difficult everywhere in the South. For the summer months the advertisements for the theaters devoted as much space to praising their air conditioning systems as they did the films they were presenting.

In the first fever of enthusiasm over sound on films it was feared that background music and song and dance numbers in the films would force orchestras out of the theaters; but with larger crowds accustomed to live entertainment filling the seats, theater owners found that they could continue to use their orchestras, and even began bringing in vaudeville acts. The theater jazz that was presented in the stage shows between the film showings was as distinct a musical style as the jazz that was presented in the restaurants for dancing. The bands shaped their repertory to the different kind of presentation; in a theater, the audience wasn't dancing, they were waiting to be entertained. To satisfy them arrangers began creating busier music formats, with short solo sections chasing each other in and out of the choruses, and abrupt sections of harmony placed between instruments in different sections of the bands—the reeds and the brass—or the saxophones playing as a choir. The bands sometimes even added elaborate miming to the show. Whatever else it was, theater jazz was entertaining. Several of the downtown movie houses were large enough to feature orchestras—the orchestra at the Saenger Theater had thirty-five musicians—but none of them were billed as jazz bands. Only two of the New Orleans jazz groups that recorded in the 1920s had steady work in the movie houses: clarinetist Tony Parenti and his Liberty Syncopators, and trumpeter Johnny DeDroit and his Syncopators.

DeDroit's group had been the first of the local bands to be recorded by OKeh on the company's initial trip to the city in March 1924, doing six titles over two sessions in the studio—finishing the day before Beyersdorffer's band from the Tokio Gardens went into the studio for their only session. The band was then called Johnny DeDroit and his New Orleans Jazz Orchestra, and the arrangements were still in the mid-1920s dance jazz mode, with the emphasis on stiffly accented rhythms and busy solos. Two years later, now as the Syncopators, DeDroit and his band seemed to be everywhere. They opened theater shows, appeared as part of elaborate stage revues, and were the featured band in new restaurant openings. Unfortunately, the one place they didn't get to was a recording studio, so there is no way to know what their theater style sounded like. The musicians included in a band picture from about this time include clarinetist Henry Raymond, pianist Frank Froeba, trombonist Ellis Stratakos, banjoist George Potter, and Johnny's brother Paul as drummer, all of whom were very established and successful musicians.

At the Liberty Theater, which was another in the national Saenger chain, Tony Parenti exchanged the job for some time with leader Max Fink, but even if they weren't playing jazz, the band continued to be billed as the Liberty Syncopators. Parenti had been leading the band at the big La Vida Ballroom at the corner of Canal Street and St. Charles Avenue, which was as close to the center of New Orleans as anyone could come at that time. Another of the city's numerous

Italian-American jazz musicians, Parenti was born in New Orleans in 1900 and was already playing professionally when he was twelve. After the customary apprenticeship with Jack Laine's bands, he played in the orchestra on the excursion boat *Majestic* that cruised on Lake Ponchartrain. He worked for a period with DeDroit but was anxious to direct his own group, and he led a band he called Anthony Parenti and his Famous Melody Boys for two titles recorded by OKeh Records on their second trip to New Orleans in January 1925. A good-looking, dark-haired man with a stylish mustache, in all of the photographs taken of his bands Parenti looks entirely at ease in his role as orchestra leader.

Parenti's taste for theater jazz began early, when he organized his own Symphonic Dance Orchestra, an eight-piece ensemble that he took into the elaborately decorated supper club The Cave, downstairs in the Grunewald Hotel. Its décor was hung with stalactites, and stalagmites rose from the floor in front of the bandstand. Heaps of imitation boulders filled the ceiling and the walls, and in its dark gloominess the room did achieve some of the feeling of a dank cavern. His groups also worked in, among others, the Triangle Theater and the Alamo Theater. As leader of what he wanted to be a sophisticated orchestra with a new sound, Parenti's arrangements sound as though he spent considerable time listening to the new singles by bands working in cities like New York, with complicated shifts of melody between the instrumental sections and unexpected instrumental voicings.

His own playing also seemed to have taken on a coloration from the recordings he was listening to, and for his first session his playing had some of the mannerisms of New York's Ted Lewis, with its klezmer-style tonal extravagance. As the 1920s passed, however, Parenti's playing took on a more distinctive intonation, and on recordings like the early "Creole Blues" with his Famous Melody Boys, he had already developed a confident, stylish personality. After an experiment using the Bix-inspired cornetist Johnny Hyman, he began working with young trumpeter Leon Prima, who had an authority and a brash presence in his solos that was characteristic of some of the city's younger and more ambitious new musicians. The theater arrangements for the Liberty Syncopators were typical for their time, but in one of the suburban restaurants the dancers would probably have spent as much of their time sitting at the table listening to the music's intricacies as they would have out on the dance floor, which wasn't anyone's intention in those dancing years. When Parenti left New Orleans in the late 1920s, the theater work continued to attract him, and he finally settled into the pit orchestra of the Radio City Music Hall in New York to wait out the Depression.

The most important theater job for the city's African American musicians, the Lyric Theater, was held for years by John Robichaux's orchestra. But throughout his career Robichaux wouldn't consider recording, maintaining that music must be heard in person. The Lyric was generally open only for black audiences, but on a regular basis the theater would advertise a "Midnight Frolic," which began after the regular performances were finished for the night, and included the orchestra as part of the presentation. The advertisements in the *Picayune* always printed very clearly, "For White" or "Whites Only," so that there would be no suggestion of racial mixing in the audience. New Orleans musicians may have achieved a new synthesis in the music they were playing, but the mingling of the two races couldn't go beyond the notes of the arrangements and the flash of the solos.

Although the Midnight Frolics were a popular feature in many southern cities, they were little noted in early jazz writing. Lynn Abbott, a researcher who has made a comprehensive study of jazz-related materials in the contemporary press, documented the Frolics in New Orleans in a two-part article "'For Ofays Only': An Annotated Calendar of Midnight Frolics at the Lyric Theater."[5] In a 1926 article in the Chicago *Defender* the well-known vaudeville personality "Tutt" Whitney commented that "Midnight Frolics for whites, in Race theaters, are quite the vogue throughout the South." He described the Frolics as a regular feature in theaters in Houston, Memphis, New Orleans, Atlanta, Greenville, South Carolina, Winston-Salem, North Carolina, Pensacola, and Dallas. Abbott has documented "midnight shows," as they were first titled, at the Lyric as early as 1920. The performances were a way to circumvent the strict laws against race mixing that made it impossible for white audiences to enjoy the African American variety entertainment at their local black theaters. A letter to the *Defender's* entertainment editor Tony Langston on January 15, 1921, from a performer named Frank Montgomery, described his experience at the Lyric on New Year's night, two weeks previously. "Well, Tony, the house was packed from pit to dome, and they were standing all up in the aisles, and they were sitting in all the aisles, in the balcony and the gallery. We showed to 2,500 people and turned away over 800. The mayor of New Orleans, his staff and some of the biggest business men and millionaires in New Orleans were there to see the show. We had Esta Bijou [*sic*] & Wells and Wells on as extra acts, and they went over wonderful. Miss Esta Bijou is doing the best act now that she ever did in her career."[6]

The "Miss Esta Bijou" Montgomery named was Louisiana singer Esther Bigeou, a veteran figure on the black theater circuit. Among her many recordings was a joyous version of "West Indies Blues" that she recorded later with A. J. Piron's New Orleans Orchestra. The Piron Orchestra was also presented at the Frolic on March 27, 1924, shortly after they returned to the city after their recording sessions for Victor, Columbia, and OKeh Records, and their engagement at the Cotton Club in New York.

Abbott described the complicated system that was put in place in New Orleans to allow white audiences to attend the theater.

Jim Crow protocol required that admission to the Midnight Frolics be "by invitation only." Printed "invitations," which could be secured at the city's "leading hotels" and newspaper offices, entitled bearers to pay an admission fee at the door. Also related to Jim Crow protocol were repeated assurances that the Frolics did not begin until after the local white theaters were closed for the evening. Frolickers were regularly advised that the doors opened at 11:00 p.m., the curtain rose at 11:15 and the shows lasted until "well after midnight." . . .

Race contradictions and advertising hype notwithstanding, whites who ventured to a Midnight Frolic at the Lyric Theater got a full course of "authentic," up-to-date African American variety entertainers, from blues shouters and blackface comedians to opera singers, "banjo kings," "harmonica kings," vocal quartets, male and female impersonators, high-stepping "bronze beauty" choruses, jazz bands, yodelers, jugglers, wire walkers, hoop rollers, one-legged dancers and more.

As a local favorite, Esther Bigeou was featured at many of the Frolics. Another popular entertainer who returned often to the Lyric and the Frolics was Ethel Waters, who began her long and influential singing career with her first releases on New York's African American–owned Black Swan Records. White audiences who followed the Frolics through the 1920s would have had an opportunity to hear classic blues artists like Clara Smith and Bessie Smith, among many others, and would have been left with a consciousness of the vitality and the sophistication of the entertainment on the other side of the racial barrier.

The dance jazz and theater jazz from the 1920s survived on the exuberant recordings the bands left behind them, though the places where they worked gradually disappeared. With the economic struggles of the 1930s, and the expected changes in their audiences' tastes, most of the roadhouses were forced to close, and even the buildings themselves were lost to the suburban building boom. The Lyric shut its doors. Spanish Fort and its venerable gardens and dance restaurants were turned into the yacht basin. The Halfway House Restaurant closed in 1930. The location still was convenient, halfway to the lake on the streetcar line, and it opened again as an ice cream parlor that stayed in business until the after World War II. In 1952 the building was taken over by the Orkin Exterminating Company. The historic dance place caught fire in June 1995, and for many years it sat vacant, slowly giving way to the inevitable deterioration that marks the passing of time.

15

Kings of New Orleans

It was a great thing in New Orleans. Everybody was trying to be the best, to be the King. But to be the best you had to work hard and fight for it. And everybody would be after the top man. They would go where he was playing, and when he was through playing they would get their horns out. They didn't take their horns out just to come help him play; they would take their horns out to try to carve him. They wanted to see if they could beat him playing, and if they did, they took over and became the King. Many times when a player became the King, New Orleans lost him. When he stepped out and said, "Well, I'm King of the trumpet players," or "I'm King of the clarinet," or the drums, or the bass, he caught a train and he'd be gone.

LEE COLLINS[1]

The 1920s answered many of the lingering questions about the first emerging sounds of New Orleans jazz, because there were now recordings—some of them documents of what the first generation of musicians might have sounded like. But a handful of names, some celebrated musicians, remain elusive. If Buddy (or Buddie) Petit (pronounced New Orleans–style, Peh-TEET) hadn't liked his red beans so much that he and Frankie Duson cooked them on the bandstand when they were working with Jelly Roll Morton in California, they might have stayed in Los Angeles long enough to get into one of the local recording laboratories, and it might have given us an answer to one of the most tantalizing questions about New Orleans music at the beginning of the 1920s: What did Buddy Petit sound like? Of all the Uptown cornet players, he was the one everyone had something to say about, and for once all of them seemed to be describing the same musician. George "Pops" Foster was five years younger than Petit, but he was part of the same scrambling crowd of hard-drinking Uptown dance hall

BUDDY ("BUDDIE") PETIT'S JAZZ BAND IN MANDEVILLE, ACROSS LAKE PONCHARTRAIN FROM
NEW ORLEANS, 1920. FROM LEFT: VOCALIST, EDDIE WOODS, GEORGE WASHINGTON, BUDDY
PETIT, BUDDY MANADAY, EDMOND HALL, AND CHESTER ZARDIS.

musicians that moved in and out of each other's bands. His memories of Petit's
cornet style matched most of what the others said. "He didn't hit a lot of high
notes like Louis Armstrong did, he played down in his horn, in the low range.
Everything he played was low, nothing way up there and he wasn't any loud trumpet player. He was strictly a jazz player and was very pleasing to listen to."[2]

Foster worked with Petit's band before the unsuccessful trip to Los Angeles,
but already Petit was drinking uncontrollably. "We'd have to tie him down to
keep him from knockin' himself out. I don't remember him getting into any
trouble except for hurtin' himself. Buddy was drunk all the time ..." Louis
Armstrong, in a letter shortly before his death, still remembered Petit and the
street corner cutting contests. "Buddy Petit—Kid Rena—all of us youngsters
used to meet on the corners in the advertising wagons and do some carving. Of
course we all had our moments, because we were all good at blowing on our
cornets. So if Buddy carved me once it's OK by me. I liked the way he blew very
much indeed."[3]

One of the best-known photographs of Petit and his band satisfies all of the
expectations we have of how an Uptown dance hall band in the late 1910s would
have looked. They're standing outside on a country dirt road with a white fence
a little way behind them. They're in shirtsleeves, some wearing neckties, some
either forgot their ties or they're wearing light ties that blend with their shirts.
Some of them are in white trousers, the others in black. The majority are wearing cloth caps, but two of them have fedoras. Petit himself, in the center, is slight,
his legs spread comfortably apart, staring at the camera while he fingers the keys
on his cornet. His face is thin, with wide puffed lips and what in the fuzzy photograph looks like a callus on his lower lip from the cornet mouthpiece.

Lee Collins had already known Petit when he was just beginning to learn the cornet himself, and when he returned to New Orleans from Chicago in 1924, where he'd been with Joe Oliver's band, he often saw Petit in his final years, when alcohol had taken its toll.

> I remember one night when I was playing at the Entertainers and Buddy came in. He was a very sensitive guy, and he wasn't doing so good—almost burnt himself out on whiskey. He hadn't heard me since I got back from playing with Joe Oliver. I asked Buddy to sit in and play a bit, and he didn't play so well; he sounded like a different cornet player altogether. So, I hated to turn him down, but I had to tell him. "Buddy, I'll come back and play." Buddy just sat on the bandstand and looked at me, and he made me start drinking and I got drunk. Because he made me feel bad, he started crying. He said, "Lee, I'm so glad to see you playin' like that, you put me in mind of myself, like I used to play."[4]

Petit was the kind of rough figure who symbolized so much of the romance in the jazz of these years. His name was Joseph Crawford, but he adopted the family name of his stepfather Joseph Petit, a valve trombonist who played with many of the early orchestras. Buddy was born about 1887. His best playing years were probably when he was in his early thirties, about 1920—before the recording companies began sending their mobile studios to southern cities. So it was the moment in time, as well as the racial situation, and finally his alcoholism that left us without a document of his playing.

In any naming of "kings" among the black musicians, three names come up again and again: Petit, Chris Kelly, and Kid Rena. Collins also played beside Chris Kelly, the blues player, and Kid Rena, the high-note specialist, the other two cornetists whose sound is undocumented. (Rena's name is also pronounced in a particularly New Orleans manner, Reh-NAY.) What Collins remembered about Kelly was the piece that everyone else who talked him remembered, "Careless Love." "Chris Kelly was another fine New Orleans cornet player, but he wasn't as great as, say, Louis Armstrong. He had a different style from all the other cornetists; I have never heard any style anyplace just like his. Chris was a popular player for dances and had a big following. When he would play the tune "Careless Love" the people would stop dancing and just listen."[5]

At least it's possible to know how often men like Chris Kelly worked, and what kind of money his band earned, because his engagement books—small notebooks listing all the jobs and the salary for the musicians from the years 1921 and 1922—survived. One afternoon I was sitting on the porch of the trombonist Harrison Barnes, who had been in Kelly's band during this period. I'd brought a tape recorder over to his modest frame house in Algiers two or three times to ask him about the early days. He got up, went into the living room, and returned with two small memo books. They were worn, small enough to fit into a pocket, and the pages at the back had most of the band members' telephone numbers.

A granddaughter had used some pages for her lessons. Barnes turned over the pages, talking about the jobs and what it was like to work with someone as undependable as Kelly, then handed me the books and insisted that I take them to keep them safe.

For the last week of December 1922, Barnes had jotted down in quick penciled entries:

Sunday, 24th	Ad St. Charles	$3 $8 (advertising and dance)
Monday, 25th	Corporaters Hall	$6
Tuesday 26th	St. Joseph roman	$5
Saturday 30th	Midway	$8

It was a $30 week, which with some tips came out to a decent week's pay in 1922.[6]

When Collins first heard him play, Kid Rena was the other acknowledged "king,"; like Petit and Kelly, alcohol did the worst damage to his career. Collins remembered, "One of the kings of the New Orleans trumpet players was Kid Rena. He came in the days of the Waif's Home with Louis Armstrong, and he was another of my idols. It's too bad he drank so much and his lip gave out early. Rena had a most beautiful tone and a range which was more perfect that any cornet player's I ever heard. He could play the high register so clear and beautiful. In the early days he used to really cut me when we would meet on the corners advertising some club."[7]

Rena was three years older than Armstrong, and like him spent some time in the Waif's Home. He was another pupil of Armstrong's teacher, Peter Davis, and when the band was hired for parades, the two apprentice cornetists marched together in their short pants and long stockings. Unlike Petit and Kelly, Rena was recorded, but it was in 1940, as part of the historic first revival session. After years in taxi dance halls, and with his lip gone, there was only a nostalgic, labored reminder of what he might have been.

Other cornetists who came out of the Uptown musical scene—Mutt Carey, Freddie Keppard, and Joe Oliver—had recorded when they were working steadily, though all of them had to find studios outside of New Orleans because the city was then without recording facilities. Oscar Celestin, who was a year older than Oliver, never left the city but was to be one of the most durable artists of this early generation. When I would stop by the two clubs on Bourbon Street in 1950 that were presenting jazz, the Paddock Lounge and the Famous Door, Celestin was the nominal leader of the band at the Paddock Lounge, though he didn't appear often, and on a nightly basis the band was led by trombonist Bill Mathews. When Celestin did squeeze onto the cramped, oval shaped bandstand above the bar, it was difficult to imagine that when he'd begun playing, nearly fifty years before, his nickname was "Sonny." For the new audiences, he was always "Papa." I was also aware, from his flicking glances toward us and his immediate, ingratiating grin and serious, bowed head when we applauded, that

Celestin still had some of the cautious mannerisms he'd learned when he began playing for white society audiences before World War I. For him, his role as an African American entertainer in a white society was as clearly defined as the line of tracks of the St. Charles Avenue streetcar.

Celestin's orchestra was one of the most popular playing in the Metairie roadhouses when OKeh came to New Orleans with portable equipment in the 1920s. By the time his group recorded for the first time in January 1925 they had already been influenced by King Oliver's Chicago recordings of two years before. Conscious of his own technical limitations, Celestin often worked with a second cornet player. At no moment in his long career did any of the young horn players who were in and out of his bands, playing second to his lead, consider him to be a great trumpet player—but he gave them so much room in the arrangements that they seemed as easy with him as he was with them. Another obstacle in his career was the complicated racial sorting that separated the social groups in New Orleans. His two main rivals for the best-paying jobs, John Robichaux and Armand J. Piron, were both light-skinned Creoles. Robichaux was older, with an avuncular manner, Piron broodingly handsome. In contrast, Celestin was dark-skinned, his face broad and heavy with a strong jawline, and he often had a disconcertingly fixed expression. The geniality he projected from the bandstand, however, managed to make his society audiences feel as comfortable with him as he had learned to be with them.

Although Celestin was considered one of the most representative of the New Orleans musicians, he was born in southeast Louisiana, in Napoleonville, on January 1, 1884. He learned to play the cornet when he was a boy, and when he moved in New Orleans as an eighteen-year-old in 1904, he quickly picked up jobs with the Algiers Brass Band. His first job as leader was in the District sometime after 1910, when his orchestra appeared in the balcony bandstand at the Tuxedo Dance Hall on North Franklin Street. The differences between the Uptown and the Downtown musicians that were carefully observed in New Orleans went unnoticed by the white audiences they played for, and to keep up with requests for new numbers he hired some of the best-known Creole dance musicians. Peter Bocage was the violinist; George Filhe, the trombonist; Lorenzo Tio Jr., the clarinetist; and he had a rhythm section of drummer Louis Cottrell, pianist Manuel Manetta, and bassist T. Brouchard.

After a bloody gun battle in the bar in the front room of the Tuxedo on the night of March 25, 1913, the newspapers described the dance hall in some detail. The *Daily Picayune* made it clear that Celestin had already begun to pick up a following, comparing him to three of the best-known entertainers appearing in vaudeville or working in blackface on the minstrel stages. "The leader of the band at the Tuxedo was the pride of the house. Harry Lauder, Billy Van or George Evans never had anything on him in funny facial expressions or funny twists of his legs. When he led the band people stopped to watch his antics . . ."

THE TUXEDO BRASS BAND PLAYING FOR A MASONIC LODGE CORNERSTONE LAYING, ABOUT 1919. FIRST ROW, FROM LEFT: EDDIE JACKSON, TUBA; ALBERT JACKSON AND HARRISON BARNES, TROMBONES. SECOND ROW: GEORGE HOOKER, BARITONE HORN; ISADORE BARBARIN, MELLOPHONE. THIRD ROW: ABBIE FOSTER (IN DARK COAT), SNARE DRUM; CHARLIE LOVE, WILLIE PAJEAUD, AND OSCAR CELESTIN, TRUMPETS. AT REAR RIGHT IS BASS DRUMMER ERNEST TREPAGNIER. COURTESY OF HARRISON BARNES.

The shooting occurred on Easter morning at 1 a.m. There had been animosity between the owner of the Tuxedo, Harry Parker, and the owner of the 101 Ranch across the street, Billy Phillips. In the exchange of fire both Parker and Phillips were killed, and three of their men with them. The police were determined to keep tight control and immediately closed down the District. When it was reopened, the dance halls were no longer permitted to operate. After a few weeks Celestin opened at the Villa Café with a new orchestra, this time with more of the ragtime musicians, including clarinetist Louis Nelson DeLisle, and trombonist Eddie Atkins, who would leave for California with Freddie Keppard the next spring. Among the young drummers who worked with the band was Baby Dodds, who with his brother Johnny would go into the King Oliver orchestra several years later. Celestin also organized a Tuxedo Brass Band, which played in a looser style than the Creole organizations, the Onward and the Excelsior, and many of the younger musicians spent some time marching with him on the streets. When Clarence Williams and A. J. Piron began rehearsing their musical group for a projected vaudeville tour in 1915, Celestin was the cornetist.

RIDGELY ORIGINAL TUXEDO JAZZ BAND, ABOUT 1925. FROM LEFT: BILL MATHEWS, WILLIAM "BEBE" RIDGELY, SHOTS MADISON, WILLIE JOSEPH, EMMA BARRETT, ARTHUR DERBIGNY, UNKNOWN (SAX PLAYER FROM ST. LOUIS), "JESSIE" (TUBA), ROBERT HALL, WILLIE BONTIN. COURTESY OF WILLIAM RIDGELY.

One of the musicians Celestin worked with often was trombonist William "Bebe" Ridgely, a soft-spoken, pleasant man who worked steadily as much because of his dependability as for his skills as a trombonist. In 1916 or 1917 (when Ridgely thought back to the early years he was always careful to make it clear if he couldn't remember an exact date or the entire personnel of one of his bands) he decided to organize a "tuxedo" orchestra, and he brought Celestin in with him as a partner. Tuxedos were to become standard on the nation's bandstands a few years later, but in New Orleans at this time the orchestras still generally dressed in high-collar, military-style tunics with stiff parade band caps. With tuxedos, the two partners hoped to be able to attract the society jobs, as well as to demonstrate that they were up with the newest trends. To pay for their new outfits they arranged to play advertising jobs for several months for the tailor shop that made them. The tuxedos became their trademark, and they never played in less formal costumes. In the outdoor photo of Buddy Petit's band they were wearing shirtsleeves and caps; but in a photo that Ridgely lent me to copy, although they were also entertaining outdoors—at a company picnic—they posed behind the band's banner in their black tuxedos, despite the summer heat.

Since they worked steadily, the personnel of the group was much more stable than bands like Kelly's or Rena's. Two of the Marrero brothers—John on banjo and Simon on string bass—were generally with them, and Manuel Manetta continued as pianist. If they were using one saxophonist, it was usually William

Thoumy, who also doubled on clarinet. Their opportunity to record came on January 23, 1925, when OKeh Records returned to the city for their second series of sessions. In three hectic days the OKeh engineers and recording director succeeded in making successful masters with the Halfway House Orchestra, entertainers Billy and Mary Mack (accompanied by another young New Orleans cornetist, Punch Miller), Anthony Parenti's Famous Melody Boys, John Tobin's Midnight Serenaders, Russ Papalia's Orchestra, Norman Brownlee's Orchestra, the Original New Orleans Rhythm Kings, the Original Tuxedo Jazz Orchestra, the Scranton Sirens Orchestra, as well as two truncated sessions of Creole song material.[8] The recording sound was sometimes muffled, and the sessions were hurried, but from an historical perspective the early OKeh trips provide an invaluable glimpse into a New Orleans jazz scene that was undergoing steady changes.

The three singles by the Tuxedo Orchestra have an energetic bounce, with a full ensemble sound that adopted many familiar elements from the King Oliver recordings of the previous two years. To fill out the sound a second saxophone player, whose name has been forgotten, and a second cornetist, "Kid Shots" Madison, were added, presenting the engineers with the same acoustic problems they had already faced when they'd recorded the Oliver band itself. Although the balance once again emphasized the saxophones, the biting lead of the two cornetists could be heard cutting through the cluttered ensemble, harmonizing tightly in the style of Oliver and Armstrong. The arrangement for Celestin's "Original Tuxedo Rag," which included a carefully rehearsed two-cornet break, was even more reminiscent of the Oliver band's sound. The slide whistle (with Madison playing a harmony background) on "Careless Love," which imitated Armstrong's slide whistle melody with Oliver on "Sobbin' Blues" two years before, was the closest to a solo that the band came. New Orleans was once again showing its habit of nurturing its own styles.

Celestin's orchestra played with relentless power and exuberance that surged through the recordings, even with the bass almost inaudible and the drummer limited to the usual clatter of a woodblock. The choppy rhythm, however, was much closer to the relentless 4/4 of Chicago's South Side bands, and sounded so unlike the looser beat of the other New Orleans groups recorded at the same time that it's a possibility the band's sound was "adopted" for the sessions, to present them with a style that would be more familiar to record buyers.

When OKeh returned to the city only a few months later, in April 1926, the orchestra came into the studio again and this time the ensemble style was much closer to the current New Orleans mode. Celestin and Ridgely had quarreled over money, and Celestin left to form his band, taking John Marrero and drummer Abby Foster with him. Ridgely kept the old name, while Celestin used his own for his Celestin's Tuxedo Jazz Orchestra. His new musicians included a fine clarinet and alto saxophone soloist, Paul Barnes; a much more flexible trombonist, August Rousseau; a tenor saxophonist, Earl Pierson; and one of the handful of women jazz musicians in the city, pianist Jeanette Salvant, who continued to work with Celestin for the rest of his career. One of the more characteristic arrangements—on a two-strain pop dance melody recorded in the first session, "My Josephine"—makes it clear why Celestin was, for years, one of the best loved African American personalities playing jazz in New Orleans. Following a vocal by new singer Charles Gill, the rhythm section broke off into soft offbeat chords and Celestin "talked" through his muted cornet in a stately rephrasing of the melody that was theatrical, sentimental, and irresistible. Behind his solo the vocalist insisted admiringly, "Yes play it, Papa Celestin, play it. You know you can play it, boy, play it!" and was joined by another voice for a hummed moment of harmony. To a couple out on the dance floor on a summer night at the Suburban Gardens, the musical moment would have made an unforgettable interlude in an evening of dancing. For his growing audiences, "Sonny" Celestin had become the enduring "Papa" Celestin.

Celestin's Orchestra, like the Halfway Orchestra and The Owls, was recorded over a relatively extended period. In their succeeding sessions, especially by Celestin and the Halfway House band, changes in tastes of the dancing public were reflected in the arrangements and dance rhythms. The most free-spirited of the white orchestras, The Owls somehow resisted the policies of the companies of this period, which was to record black groups playing jazz arrangements, while white groups generally were restricted to dance music with vocals and a minimum of solos. By the later half of the 1920s, the record companies were making New Orleans part of their regular schedule, and the bands they had under contract were recorded once or twice a year. The white musicians were clearly affected by the new recording policies. Abbie Brunies's Halfway House Orchestra had always been presented as a dance band, and with their jazz style now in question, there was no way for them to get around Columbia Records' interest in danceable popular ballads.

There had been one change that opened the studios up to some of the musicians in new combinations. Just as in New York or Chicago, the companies were letting some of the local musicians organize their own studio sessions, giving some of the leaders the chance to call up friends who were working in other clubs or in dance orchestras for an afternoon jazz date. The two popular styles, dance music and jazz music, were drawing apart. The jazz artists began to see themselves as different from the dependable instrumentalists who filled out the orchestras and were satisfied to leave the jazz fast lane to others. Pianist Johnny Miller, drummer Monk Hazel, and the itinerant trumpeter Wingy Manone each put together sessions using musicians they had worked with often in a variety of groups.

Despite Manone's boisterous personality and uninhibited vocals, if the white musicians had thought in terms of "kings," the trumpet player they would have chosen would have been Sharkey Bonano. Bonano was in the same New Orleans tradition as cornetists like Buddy Petit. He didn't push for high notes, staying in the middle of the horn's range, and his tone was beautifully focused. His leads were strong and decisive, and he was continually probing for new ways of phrasing and for unexpected melodic changes. His solos were cleanly structured and in his recordings from this period the solos contribute much of the excitement to the arrangements. He was a band musician more than a showman, but each of the bands that brought in his distinctive lead responded with a new energy in their ensembles. For all his local reputation, however, Bonano was clearly uncomfortable on the first recordings he made with other groups outside of New Orleans. He was an early substitute for La Rocca in New York, when Eddie Edwards organized his version of the original band as he awaited the return of the others from London; Bonano also failed to keep the job when the Wolverines brought him to New York as a replacement for Bix Beiderbecke.

Even with the new policies of the record companies that had to be negotiated, it was a heady time to be playing jazz in New Orleans, and as the new sounds came down from New York, the local bands picked them up. The influence of the musicians playing with the Gene Goldkette Orchestra in Detroit—Bix Beiderbecke, Frankie Trumbauer, Bill Rank, Eddie Lang, Joe Venuti—as well as the harmonic and structural innovations of their arranger, Bill Challis, were a flood tide that abruptly swept up virtually every jazz musician in the United States, and for an extended period American jazz was carried along with it. The harmonies, the instrumental voices of the arrangements, the lyric solos, all became the new jazz sound, and the effect carried over to the new jazz performers working in Europe and South America. Beiderbecke imitators seemed to be performing in most of the European capitals as well as in dance bands everywhere in the U.S. Not even Armstrong, whose influence extended largely to his own solo style, had as clearly identifiable an effect on the next two or three years of jazz recording, for both black and white groups. Entire saxophone sections, in orchestras like Fletcher Henderson in New York and McKinney's Cotton Pickers in Detroit, played scored arrangements of Beiderbecke solos.

For the Crescent City's jazz community there was a proud sense of kinship, since Beiderbecke considered New Orleans, and La Rocca and Mares, as his musical roots. With the Goldkette band no longer together, Beiderbecke had joined the others in Paul Whiteman's thirty-seven-piece concert jazz orchestra, touring the country as a member of the brass section and appearing in occasional specialty numbers that featured him with a small group of the jazz instrumentalists. The inimitable bass player Steve Brown, who was Tom's brother and had been with the New Orleans Rhythm Kings for their first session, anchored the jazz choruses even when, as often happened, they were sandwiched into a larger, popular-styled orchestral arrangement.

For the white New Orleans jazz community, one of the climactic moments of the 1920s was certainly the night of October 28, 1928. Whiteman and his orchestra were playing at the St. Charles Theater, and Beiderbecke and Trumbauer were to be featured. It was almost as memorable a moment for Beiderbecke; backstage at intermission he met two of the earlier lead horn men whose playing had influenced his. Both Nick La Rocca and Paul Mares were there, leading the local group, which also included pianist Armand Hug, drummer Monk Hazel, and a young tenor saxophonist Eddie Miller. Beiderbecke was touched to see the two leaders, and one of his first questions was about Roppolo, who was unable to leave the institution where he'd been committed. The musicians were impatient during the first half of the concert, since there had been almost no opportunity for the orchestra's small jazz ensemble to perform, and when Monk Hazel saw Whiteman passing, he called loudly to him, "... if you don't let Bix play more this half we'll tear the place down." Whiteman laughed and agreed that Beiderbecke would have "plenty to do this time."[9]

Mares had been doing well in his family's muskrat pelt business and had bought a large house, where he and the others brought Beiderbecke, Trumbauer, and another man from the Whiteman reed section, Izzy Friedman, for a jam session that lasted most of the night. At one point Armand Hug asked Beiderbecke for some help with the chords of his solo composition "In A Mist" and Bix obliged, leaning over Hug's shoulders and showed him the part he was having difficulty with. Hug was only seventeen, and it was a moment he never forgot.

Even if the New Orleans dancers still talked about New Orleans as the home of the real jazz, the recordings that were popular everywhere in the country were steadily advertised in the New Orleans newspapers, and it was obvious to the local musicians that they'd lost the edge they had taken for granted for so many years. The bands recording in Kansas City, led by Benny Moten and Jesse Stone, had worked out the role of the saxophones in their arrangements and were already moving into the riff style that would take them into the 1930s. In New York the studio bands led by busy leaders like Red Nichols and Phil Napoleon, with an array of gifted sidemen who were working in the New York theaters—among them Benny Goodman, Jimmy and Tommy Dorsey, Miff Mole, and Jack Teagarden—were turning out dozens of skillful, if routine, singles in the New Orleans ensemble style. Two Philadelphia artists, Italian American guitarist Eddie Lang and violinist Joe Venuti, had pioneered a new jazz sound with their string instruments. Even in Chicago, where the New Orleanians had been such a strong influence, the young Chicagoans—some of them associated with the Austin High Gang that had hung around the New Orleans Rhythm Kings: Frank Teschmaker, Pee Wee Russell, Gene Krupa, Jimmy McPartland, Bud Freeman—were playing the old New Orleans repertoire with a raw new energy. The new styles that New Orleans jazzmen had helped to create ten years before had hurried past them, and they found themselves struggling to keep up.

If Abbie Brunies at the Halfway House tried to give his customers a sample of the Challis style, however, the orchestra's own playing was still rooted in the New Orleans idiom. The band's sessions of April 26 and 27, 1928, the spring before Whiteman came through town, were the most obviously influenced by Challis, and even with the impeccable and exciting new clarinetist Sidney Arodin joining them for the first time, the two days' work, as far as the Columbia recording director was concerned, was their least productive time in the studio. Only two of the six masters they recorded were released by the company at the time they were made. A third title—a composition that came closest to their old style, an instrumental piece with masterful bass playing by Martin titled "Wylie Avenue Blues"—turned up years later on a single released in Australia.

The first of the pieces the band recorded on April 27, "I'll Go Back To That Dear Old Pal Of Mine," mirrored the stylistic uncertainty. For this session Chink Martin had switched to string bass, but he bowed the opening verses with a sound that borrowed a little of the smooth rhythm of Wellman Braud's technique on several of Duke Ellington's recordings. The style of the arrangement, however, soon began to drift steadily back to New Orleans. The band had begun working with a singer, Joe Spano; after his particularly saccharine vocal, and a repeat of the melody played on alto saxophone by Joe Loyocano, for the last choruses Martin finally picked up the rhythm with a syncopated slap bass that made it clear that he and Steve Brown, who was generally considered the best bassist of that style in the 1920s, both came from New Orleans.

The same day that the Halfway House recorded their second session, Columbia also recorded two singles with Tony Parenti's current orchestra, now called Tony Parenti's New Orleanians, and for the session Parenti used cornetist Johnny Hyman. Of all the city's young musical hopefuls, Hyman was the most strongly influenced by the Beiderbecke recordings, and on the two singles he recorded with his own band, John Hyman's Bayou Stompers, for Victor Records in the spring of 1927, the others in the group also managed to imitate the sound of the different soloists with Beiderbecke, with a passable attempt at the on-edge New York rhythms. Like Hyman's Bix-styled lead a year later, both of the titles Parenti recorded with his New Orleanians in April 1928, "In The Dungeon" and "When You And I Were Pals," echo many of the mannerisms of the Goldkette musicians. Even The Owls, who continued on their own way through all of the distractions, recorded an arrangement of one of the pieces associated with Beiderbecke, "Goose Pimples," but their recording was made a month before his, in October 1927, and the similarities probably were built into the stock arrangement.

Of all the city's lead trumpeters, Sharkey Bonano was the least affected by the new wave. On his first recordings, with Norman Brownlee's orchestra in 1924, the cleanly focused tone and legato flow that marked his first recorded solo is centered in the New Orleans mainstream. Wingy Manone was as impervious to the Goldkette sound as Bonano, but he was only occasionally in the city. In the Depression years, with the popularity of vocal singles in a jazz setting, Manone was to have the most success of all the white New Orleans horn players, but he was mostly to be found in New York or Chicago, wherever he could find a job.

It was in these earlier months, when the record companies let the leaders put together their own sessions, that Bonano made most of his best-known recordings. The nominal title of the group for a April 1928 session for Brunswick Records was Johnny Miller's New Orleans Frolickers, but pianist Miller had borrowed clarinetist Sidney Arodin and bassist Chink Martin from the Halfway House Orchestra, and added a second reed, the fine Hal Jordy on alto saxophone. The first title, "Panama," opened with a Challis-style introduction, then quickly returned to the classic New Orleans ensemble idiom, and Bonano's solo was assured and beautifully phrased. The second title, the Creole Band's "Dippermouth Blues," was as strongly played but the arrangement less distinctive. It drew heavily on the King Oliver recordings, and Bonano's crackling solo was a preview of the many swing versions of Oliver's solo choruses that were to make their way into arrangements in the swing decade.

Bonano was already playing with the flow of melody that never left him, even in his later years as a Bourbon Street entertainer. His solo work also was the center of a second pick-up date, this time under the name Monk Hazel and his Bienville Roof Orchestra, when Brunswick returned to New Orleans eight months later. Hazel played both drums and mellophone—a brass instrument in about the same tonal range as the trombone, but with keys instead of a slide. He also played cornet but didn't feel he was enough of a cornetist to lead the band in the studio. On the label Bonano is named the musical director. The Bienville Hotel building, just off of Lee Circle in downtown New Orleans, has survived the modernization of the downtown area, as well as the clearing that was done for the approaches to the Mississippi River Bridge; if you look up from Lee Circle you can see where the roof garden was situated. Hazel was leading the dance orchestra there at the time, although the musicians he used in the studio probably were not all those who he used on the job. Hazel was the orchestra's cornetist.

Drawing on some of the same musicians who had recorded with Johnny Miller, Hazel used Arodin and Hal Jordy as the two reeds, and this time the guitarist Joe Capraro, one of the finest of the city's new string players, was featured in his own composition "Sizzling The Blues." It brought the guitar into the ensemble with breaks and a solo, in a clear acknowledgment of the influence of Eddie Lang's recordings. In his discussion of the recordings in his excellent study *Lost Chords*, Richard Sudhalter emphasized that the New Orleans musicians, consciously or unconsciously, now were being influenced by the New York studio groups, like Phil Napoleon's or Red Nichols's bands. In the local recordings, however, there was still is an overall rhythmic feel and a relaxation with their material that continued to give the music a New Orleans flavor. For the band's brightly energetic version of "High Society" Jordy switched to baritone sax for a solo chorus, then added a low-register countermelody to Arodin's interpretation of the classic solo. On all four of the band's singles Bonano's playing was fresh and compelling, with an optimistic attack that set the tone for the other soloists.

The musician who, with Bonano, gave the strongest stylistic coherence to these disparate groups was the clarinetist Sidney Arodin, who was also recording at the same time with Abbie Brunies's Halfway House Orchestra. Arodin's name is usually not included among the city's better-known clarinetists, but his playing on these sessions defined the clarinet style that continues to dominate small-band jazz performed in the New Orleans idiom today. The clarinet's obbligato role in the ensemble had been shaped into a coherent form by Larry Shields; Leon Roppolo remade it into a subtler, more personal melodic voice, but one ultimately too introspective for the band style as it changed over the decade. Arodin refined the style a step further, without losing the joyous strut that had always characterized the music of the best of the New Orleans white bands. Each of his solos was brilliantly shaped and emotionally assured, and he had the ability to fit whatever he was playing into the style of the arrangement.

Perhaps Arodin also is not better known because he was an elusive figure. He was born in 1901 in Westwego, just outside of New Orleans, and his family name was Arnondin. The name is unusual, and researcher Bruce Raeburn has suggested that it might be Belgian, rather than Cajun or Creole, the usual suppositions. There later were rumors that he was an African American who passed as white, but all of the New Orleans musicians, white and black, who played with him in the years he was in the city insist that as far as they knew he was white. His playing was so classic in its style that it would be meaningless to fix a racial tag to it. When he joined Abbie Brunies he was twenty-seven and had already had a more varied musical life than the others. He had begun his career in New York, and he had done his first sessions there as early as 1925. In New Orleans he not only recorded with the cream of the city's white musicians, but Lee Collins brought him in as a replacement for his regular clarinetist Louis Nelson DeLisle for the historic session with the Jones-Collins Astoria Hot Eight a year later. In one of the occasional steps across the racial line that gave New Orleans music so much of its richness, Collins and Arodin became friends. Collins's reminiscences are the clearest glimpse we have of Arodin when he was working in the city.

> After that [Collins had been working with Jack Carey's band] I went with Sidney Arodin, a fine clarinet player and a fine man in an all-white band. This was in a hole-in-the-wall place on Decatur Street run by a Spanish pimp who was a swell dresser. This guy had about seven women working in his place. One of them was known as Sis, but for various reasons I can't call her real name. In those days there was a tough New Orleans police captain named Smith. One night he came into this joint, so Sis warned me that if he asked any questions about me working in the white band I should tell him I was Spanish in order to avoid trouble.[10]

Arodin also composed a great deal of music, and he probably is best known as the composer of the melody for the song that with Hoagy Carmichael's lyrics became the jazz and popular standard "Up A Lazy River." Collins remembered that he played the melody before it turned into the song. "Sidney Arodin and I were crazy about stuffed peppers, so after we got off from work we would go to the French Market, buy them by the dozen, and walk along the street eating. Sidney loved to go down to the river and sit for hours, just watching the water.

I happened to have my cornet with me there the time he was making up 'Lazy River,' I know I was the first musician to ever play that tune."[11]

When he was first starting to play professionally, Arodin was part of the younger group of hopeful jazz artists, including Wingy Manone and Sharkey Bonano, but he dropped out of the crowd of local musicians, and most of his career was spent somewhere on the road. He married and moved to New York in the early 1920s, and his first recordings were made there in 1922. He went into the studio first with Phil Napoleon, and then for an extended period beginning in 1924 he recorded steadily with a New York group calling itself the New Orleans Jazz Band. For the first session they remade the New Orleans Rhythm Kings' "Tin Roof Blues," Arodin closely following Roppolo's original solo. In 1927 he played briefly with Wingy Manone in New York, then moved to New Orleans in time to do the recording sessions with the Halfway House Orchestra, Johnny Miller, Monk Hazel, and Lee Collins. He drank heavily, but it never affected his music—though, as Collins remembered, marijuana occasionally got in the way.

When work was slow in New Orleans Arodin moved on again. In 1928 he was in Memphis with Mart Britt and his Orchestra, returned for a few months, and left again in 1929 as local jobs began to dry up. This time he joined the popular San Antonio dance orchestra led by Sonny Clapp, and recorded for some months with them. Their last session was made in New York in 1931; the vocalist was Hoagy Carmichael, which means that by this time Arodin and Carmichael had met. As far as other musicians knew, Arodin usually lived in New York with his wife and their child. He seems to have stopped playing for the first years of the Depression, but the growing interest in the small New Orleans–style groups brought him back into the studio. In 1934 in New York he joined Manone again and went into the studio with Manone's New Orleans Rhythm Kings. One of the pieces they did was another version of "Tin Roof Blues." The same year he was also with New Orleans trumpeter Louis Prima's New Orleans Gang. Arodin was among most talented of his generation of New Orleans musicians, but his musical world was broader than the roadhouses and Ponchartrain resorts where many of the other musicians made their living.

For many of the city's white musicians there was enough work and camaraderie among themselves that they hesitated about leaving. It was not until the 1930s, when most of the New Orleans jazz scene collapsed, that they drifted away again. In March 1927 the pit orchestra in the largest theater downtown, the Saenger, employed thirty-five musicians, now earning union pay. Tony Parenti was leading his Liberty Syncopators at the Liberty Theater close by. Two months later the Metairie Inn announced "We Have a New Orchestra!" The new group was led by popular Jules Bauduc, and the advertisement described them as "The band with Personality, Rhythm & Pep." The music in New Orleans might have lost some of its lead over the jazz being played in other cities, but it was still a vital part of New Orleans life. It even managed to come through the unimaginable disaster that threatened the city later in the spring of that year.

16

The Tiger's Paw

*There below, in green of a beauty incredible, stretch the landscape gardens of
the Lord and the swollen river of gleaming tan. Its chopping waters, seen from
above at high speed, dissolving into streaming furrows, save where an angry
current boils.*

*A city's ordered precincts pass, strangely parklike from on high for all
their squat ugliness when seen as they really are. Now down in within spraying
range of the tawny flood, now up into the clouds serene where floods seem pal-
try things, on and on the seaplane drones. The sugar refinery buildings loom,
and other of the lower city's industries, below like an obsession in a madman's
brain, is the mighty Mississippi, Father of Waters. As a silver thread tortu-
ous, or as a broad lake from lesser ranges, his magnificent distances cut by the
earth's faults of vision; he is eminently there, at times like a great tiger sleeping
in twisted pose, twitching as he dreams of his awakening when he will scratch
and claw and blot out broad acres.*

ON THE FRONT PAGE OF THE *TIMES-PICAYUNE*, MAY 1, 1927

The pages of the city's daily newspaper, the *Times-Picayune*, were usually as
plainly and as dully written as a report of a meeting of the Sewerage and Water
Board, but the overblown prose of the piece on the front page of the paper on
May 1, 1927, as the writer struggled to find an adequate response to the vast floods
of that spring, gives, in its own way, a sense of the catastrophe. New Orleans, from
its first weeks in the swamps beside the Mississippi more than two hundred years
before, had always lived uncomfortably beside a sleeping tiger that someday might
reach out a paw and ". . . scratch and claw and blot out broad acres."

Unlike the catastrophe of Hurricane Katrina, which smashed the city in less
than a day, the Mississippi flood of 1927 was a growing menace that the readers

273

of the newspapers could follow day by day, with a playful slash of the tiger's paw to remind the city of the threat inexorably moving downstream toward them. The entire course of the Mississippi and its tributary rivers were a long, swollen tide, driven by the runoff of heavy winter snows and continuing torrential rains. On April 9 the *Picayune* included a small column on the front page with the disturbing news that there had already been deaths on the river's tributaries in Kansas and Oklahoma. There was a respite as the waters began subsiding in Oklahoma and Kansas, but a tornado wiped out the town of Rock Springs, Texas, on April 12, and by April 14 the waters were rising again in Oklahoma.

A foretaste of disaster struck New Orleans on Saturday, April 16, when an overnight storm drowned the city in 14.01 inches of rainfall, fives inches more than the previous record. Under the weight of water, the storm sewers failed, as they would in the levee breaks of Katrina nearly eighty years later. There were news stories that tragically would be repeated in the later catastrophe.

> *Piteous appeals for food for children were sent forth by mothers marooned on the second floors of houses in flooded sections of New Orleans more than fifteen hours after the record-breaking rainfall of 14.01 inches had ceased at 4 a. m. Saturday. Apparently no organized relief for the thousands of men, women and children held prisoners in their homes throughout Saturday by the water was effected by the city authorities, although informed by George Earl, general superintendent of the Sewerage and Water board, that the flood water would not be pumped off until Sunday morning. While Mayor Arthur J. O'Keefe announced Saturday that he had ordered policemen into the inundated sections to render what aid they could, this task was undertaken with the policemen doing regular patrol duty. These orders were issued after Mayor O'Keefe received constant telephone calls from the stricken sections, expressing protest and indignation.*[1]

When the city's fire fighters were asked why they hadn't responded to calls for aid, Fire Chief Evans replied,

> *"Mayor O'Keefe told me to instruct my men to do whatever they could in aiding distressed persons," said Chief Evans Monday. "However, we are equipped only for fire fighting. We have no equipment for flood relief. Our engines are too big to go through, and we have very few smaller cars. We were pretty busy the night of the big downpour, for there was one big fire and several smaller ones. Besides that practically all our trucks were busy pumping out flooded buildings in the business section."*
>
> *The Red Cross was ready to bring relief to the sufferers in flooded sections of the city, but Mayor O'Keefe said the situation was well in hand and its assistance was not needed.*[2]

For the first time the newly built area of Lakeview, behind the Halfway House and stretching out to Lake Ponchartrain, was flooded. On April 19 the local

Property Owners' Alliance blamed the disaster on ". . . inadequate levee protection from the waters of the Orleans Canal and of Lake Ponchartrain." In Lakeview in 2006, more than a year after the collapse of the 17th Street levee, which let water from the lake flood the area, most of the homes are still empty, many still filled with the rotting debris left by the floodwaters.

As the swelling waters from the new storm were added to the surge of water moving downstream, the engineers in charge of the state's levees assembled a workforce of ten thousand men to strengthen the earth walls against what they predicted would be a rise of three to four feet of the water level around the city. By April 19 the Mississippi had begun to wear at the line of levees protecting the lowlands of the Mississippi delta and the Arkansas riverbanks. On April 20 the Arkansas levees gave way, and the levees on the Mississippi banks followed within hours. The flood soon turned into the largest natural disaster in American history. The fast-rising water rushing through the levee breaks trapped hundreds of thousands of people, most of them impoverished black sharecroppers isolated in small shack communities strung along the levees. Many of the people who had time to flee crowded onto the only high ground that was left—the narrow strip of earth that had survived from the crumbling levee.

On April 22, under a headline that two thousand people were clinging to one of the levees screaming for help, the governor of Mississippi, Dennis Murphree pleaded, "For God's sake send us all the skiffs and the boats you can to Vicksburg." On April 25 the water was still rising and the Mississippi delta region had been drowned. Tent cities were hurriedly erected to house the refugees, and the towns that were still above water struggled to deal with the masses of people who were jammed into their houses and streets.

In New Orleans the water was still rising. If the levees hadn't given way upstream the wall of water probably would have already swept the city away, but the danger still was increasing daily. On April 24, in another preview of the 2005 tragedy, a tanker, driven by the winds, crashed into the earthen wall of the levee downstream and opened a sixty-foot "crevasse" as the paper termed it, in the levee wall. Two days later, as the water continued to rise, the decision was made to dynamite the levees twelve miles below New Orleans at Poydrous to save the city. The governor of the state immediately issued the necessary orders. In a less dangerous flood in 1921 a small crevasse had been opened near Orange Grove, a picnic spot where many of the bands performed, and the levee was considered to be vulnerable at that spot. The dynamite charges were to be set off at noon on Friday, April 29.

One of the persistent stories surrounding the Katrina disaster in 2005 is that at the height of the hurricane winds, some residents of the black Ninth Ward, the area that was devastated first by the wall of water driven by the winds, and then by the breaching of a levee behind it, claimed to have heard the sound of dynamite blasts over the winds. They accused "some white men" of setting off dynamite blasts to blow enough of a hole in the levee to drown their neighborhood and save white New Orleans. The efforts to breach the levee in 1927, however, make it clear that something as desperate as isolated dynamite charges against the reinforced walls of the Industrial Canal levee would have had no effect at all.

The charges used to open the low earth levee at Poydrous took a crew of sixty black laborers struggling from dawn to dusk with earth augers to set the charges, and even with the 1,500 pounds of dynamite they used, it was necessary to work in stages, blasting a layer of earth, then setting new charges to blast away the next layer. Even with this massive effort they only managed to open a gap of 150 feet, and the blasting continued for the next five days to open the gap sufficiently to lower the water levels threatening the city. Then upstream, a levee gave way at Tallulah, and with the land east and west of the city a swollen lake, the danger to the city was past.

The massive efforts that were made over the next decade to shore up the city's defenses against the "sleeping tiger" curled up beside it brought many changes to New Orleans, turning it into a city more like the rest of the United States, and also altering the dynamic that had helped sustain so much of the city's musical life. The Halfway House, home to Abbie Brunies and his dance orchestra for most of the 1920s, had to close briefly for repairs, but the band was only out of work for a few weeks. On May 14, advertised as Albert Brunies Orchestra, they opened at a lakeside restaurant in Seabrook called the Midway Bath House and Restaurant. It was an old-fashioned, rambling frame building on pilings, with old-style elongated wooden pillars on the porch and a wooden walkway out over the water to reach the entrance. It had some of the look of the old dance hall at Milneburg, Quirella's, which had been home to most of the younger musicians at one time or another. Quirella's itself, however, would soon be only a part of New Orleans history.

To deal with the threat of future flooding, the decision was made to build protective walls along the shore of Lake Ponchartrain, which meant that the loosely creative seedbed of musical activity at Milneburg would come to an end, and West End itself would be turned to other purposes. The renewal that affected the downtown areas razed streets around the Gravier and Liberty areas that had seen so many bands working their first jobs in the neighborhood saloons. The railroad station at Basin and Canal was moved, and the area that had been Storyville eventually was destroyed to make way for a modern housing project.

With the danger of the flood past, the record companies that had been traveling to the city to work with the New Orleans bands continued to show an interest in what was happening in the city's dance halls and restaurants. Ironically, the policies of the companies, who insisted on popular dance arrangements with vocal refrains from the white orchestras, for once worked to the advantage of the black orchestras, because they were expected to record their jazz specialties. At the end of the 1920s an unexpected burst of recording activity in the city by Columbia and Victor Records almost compensated for the years when they hadn't been willing to take chances on the bands led by musicians like Buddy Petit and Chris Kelly, artists with a reputation for undependability. In the spring

LEE COLLINS BAND, PLAYING IN TEXAS IN 1925. FROM LEFT; ARTHUR JOSEPH (?), MARY BROWN, FREDDIE MILLER, OCTAVE CROSBY, HENRY JULIEN, SHERMAN COOK, COLLINS, PERCY DARENSBURG.

and fall of 1927 Columbia recorded the band led by cornetist Sam Morgan. Victor Records, after 1927 sessions with Louis Dumaine, made its final 1920s recordings in New Orleans with the December 1929 session by the band led by Lee Collins and his close friend, Davey Jones.

Victor Records had begun recording in the South some time after the other companies had already established their session schedules. Victor's recording director was Ralph Peer, who had already had a substantial career in the "race" record industry, beginning with OKeh in its earliest days and continuing with Columbia Records. Despite his experience and his sound musical judgment, however, he had a problem signing important groups, since most of the artists with a loyal local following had already been signed to an exclusive contract with the labels that had gotten to them first. Peer, however, was also interested in acquiring publishing rights to song material for his own new publishing company, and he occasionally seems to have made recording decisions based more on the nature of the song material that was being auditioned than on the artist's sales potential.

Like the Melrose brothers in Chicago, Peer was conscious that the compositions he secured the rights to publish in those years could become the foundation for a successful publishing business. Although the recordings he supervised in New Orleans didn't create sales records, a series of sessions he produced at the same time (the summer of 1927) in the small town of Bristol, Tennessee, with white country artists were a different story. With artists like Jimmy Rogers and the Carter Family, the sessions became the foundation of the modern country music industry and secured the future of Southern Music, Peer's company.

Louis Dumaine, whom Peer recorded on March 5, 1927, only weeks before the flood, was an unlikely choice for a company of Victor's importance, since the city's black musicians never had considered Dumaine to be one of the indispensable artists. It took him some time to learn to play, and he was always associated with the Creole orchestras, though the eight sides the band recorded included musicians who were from both of the city's black communities. He was a tall, thin-faced, serious man, always formally dressed in coat and tie. He was also a well-trained musician, and when the emergency musical program, the Emergency Recovery Act, was set up to aid the city's musicians in the mid-1930s, Dumaine was appointed the director of both the large W.P.A. band and the equally large E.R.A. orchestra. Four of the band's singles were as accompaniment to blues singers: Genevieve Davis, whose voice was in the vaudeville mode, and a rougher, much more interesting singer, Ann Cook, who was also recorded later in the revival period.

Part of the interest in the Dumaine singles is that the band is one of the roughest to be recorded in the 1920s, anticipating the sound of some of the revival groups who recorded in boomy dance halls or musicians' living rooms fifteen years later. Their ensemble sound was particularly ragged, giving the impression that the band had been hastily assembled for the session. Dumaine's lead, though stiff, was pure and restrained, with a proud elegance, while the clarinetist Willie Joseph scurried noisily around Dumaine's melody, returning again and again to a handful of set phrases, while the saxophonist Louis James restricted himself to harmony tones. Considering that the group were playing dance music, their unsteady tempos and the clumsiness of the sousaphone player would have given the dancers considerable uneasiness. To add to the awkwardness, the young banjo player rushed the beat. With all the weaknesses, however, the recordings were a useful measure of how many of the city's less organized, casual bands sounded on ordinary jobs. On the first of their instrumentals, an uptempo piece titled "Pretty Audrey," Dumaine's lead had a kind of stiff-legged, syncopated feel that took it back to the beginning of the century. He was born about 1890, so he was from the same generation as Bunk Johnson, who was also born in that year, and the playing of the two cornetists was often described as very similar.

The best known of the pieces they recorded was a two-strain blues titled "Franklin Street Blues." The band's roughnesses took on a beguiling mood of nostalgia with a low-register clarinet solo and Dumaine's simple and eloquent solo chorus. The group also presented one of the few chances for the third of the Humphrey brothers, trombonist Earl, to record. His better-known brothers, trumpeter Percy and clarinetist Willie, were to become mainstays of the revival years. The uneasy blend of Dumaine's courtliness and the rough shout of Ann Cook's blues was probably like the sounds young Louis Armstrong heard up and down Gravier Street when he was growing up—with all the uncertainties, as the arrangements threaten to break down in the middle of the performance.

Only days after the floodwaters began to subside, Columbia Records had success with one of the Uptown bands with more of a reputation, Sam Morgan's Jazz Band. Once when we were talking, Danny Barker, one of town's sharp young banjo players at the time the band did their sessions, shook his head at their rhythm. "That was the old-time beat. They played for the old people, you know, like it was an old two-step." Most of the band's musicians weren't much older than Barker, but Sam, the oldest of the three Morgan brothers in the band, was born in 1895, and he set the tone for the ensemble. One of his brothers, Isaiah, who was born in 1897, played second cornet, and a second brother, saxophonist and clarinetist Andrew, born in 1903, was the youngest of the brothers. A fourth brother, Al, who played the bass, was not with the group for the recordings, though he might have lent his striding, four-beat acoustic bass style to bassist Sidney Brown, who at thirty-three was the oldest member of the band.

Sam Morgan was born in Bertrandville, Louisiana, and began playing the cornet when the family moved to New Orleans. He led one of the many small Uptown bands from 1916 to 1925. He was short, dark skinned, and a limited but strong cornetist who managed to work often enough to keep his band together. He was never considered one of the "kings" during this period. Sam's brother Andrew remembered the band rehearsing on Sam's steps in the evening, since most of them kept their day jobs. Sam worked as a track laborer for the Grand Island Railroad. He suffered a stroke in 1925 and for some time was forced to stop playing. The band continued for a few months under the leadership of trumpeter Willie Pajeaud, as the Magnolia Orchestra, but eventually disbanded. By now all three brothers were playing regularly. Al was usually on tour, but Andrew and Isaiah were working together in New Orleans in a band that Isaiah was leading. After a period of convalescence, Sam was able to join Isaiah's band, but within a few months he had assumed leadership. When they expanded the band to include an alto saxophone, Earl Fouche, who had been born in New Orleans but had grown up in New York, was added to the group.

In the 1950s many of the members of the band were still playing. Andrew was a large, generous, sincere dark-skinned man who marched on parades with his tenor sax and brought his clarinet to dance jobs in the backrooms of bars around the city. He was always willing to answer questions about the band, and let me copy the two old photographs of them I used in the book *Jazz: New Orleans*. He also cooked unforgettable red beans and rice, and the recipe I use today is the one he let me copy. His brother Isaiah was leading a band in Biloxi, Mississippi, and often came over to spend some time with his brother and to see old friends. I was able to record Isaiah's band playing for a private dance in Biloxi in May 1954, the only time he was recorded after the 1927 sessions with his brother. The Sam Morgan band's trombonist, "Jim Crow," became much better known as Jim Robinson, a mainstay of the George Lewis band through the revival years. The alto saxophonist, Earl Fouche, who was the same age as Andrew and as a boy lived in the same neighborhood, was also leading a small band, but following his discharge from the Navy in 1942 he had moved to Santa Barbara, California, and he ended his playing days there. When I located him, he hadn't heard the old records since he'd left New Orleans many years before, and hearing them again brought tears and pleased laughter.

The band was recorded twice, in April 1927 and then in October of the same year. There were four songs from each of the sessions, and they have had to do as an expression of all of the rougher New Orleans music that never made its way into a studio. What seems clear from the problems the Gennett engineers had with the King Oliver band in the studio, and the OKeh engineers had with the first Celestin recordings, was that the Uptown musicians played with unrestrained volume. The sessions were done in the Werlein Music Store's upstairs space on Canal Street, and the engineers seem to have had some of the same problems that were part of the acoustic recording era, though they were using new electrical microphones and turntables. The perpetual problems of recording a bass had been solved, but there was still concern about the volume jumping the cutting needle out of the groove, so the cornets were backed off into the distant spaces behind the others. On the first session, the cornets, piano, and drums were virtually inaudible, with the trombone only occasionally contributing a muted phrase. What was insistently audible, and made the recordings different from anything else done in New Orleans, was the bass—not only the emphasis in the balance, but in the instrument's surging rhythm. The engineer obviously was interested in Sidney Brown's loping, four-beat bass style, and the bass was given the most prominent role in the band.

The melody instrument that survived the sound tests was the lyric alto saxophone of Fouche, with occasional echoes of Andrew Morgan's clarinet or tenor saxophone behind him. Fouche's omnipresent saxophone throughout all of the eight singles could have been distracting, but he played with an unusually direct style, generally content with paraphrasing the lead, and his solo passages were thoughtful and melodic. There is some irony in the enthusiasm writers who were important figures in the later New Orleans revival had for the band's recordings, because they generally were dismayed by saxophones. For the first Columbia session, a saxophone, with a surging blend of horns behind it and accompanied by the bass, recorded at an exaggeratedly high level and placed in the center of the tonal balance, was largely what there was to hear. The band balance was so skewed that it is almost impossible to say what they sounded like on the bandstand, when the bass would have been either behind the horns or at the edge of the stage beside them, and the two cornets and the trombone could open up their horns, saving the mutes for occasional effects.

Despite the perplexities of the sound, the recordings have a loose, exhilarating power. Brown's brilliant bass playing presented a new rhythmic style on record, a style that was to become the basic 4/4 beat of the 1930s. One of the great bass players striding through the swing era with the New Orleans beat was the fourth of the brothers, Al, who anchored the rhythm section of the Cab Calloway

Orchestra from 1936 to 1939. With their crowded ensembles, the Morgan band probably sounded like the Celestin band might have sounded if they were jamming among themselves, but Morgan borrowed as freely from the Piron Orchestra's recordings. The chorus of a song from the second session, "Short Dress Gal," cheerfully reprised the chorus melody of Piron's "West Indies Blues."

For the second session the balance was corrected a little; the piano was occasionally audible and there was a trombone interlude on "Short Dress Gal"—details probably also borrowed from an impression of the Piron arrangement. Sam's exuberant vocal, however, came from a different part of town. The second number in the October session, "Bogalusa Strut," named for a small town northeast of New Orleans toward the Mississippi line, became the band's trademark. The ringing cornet duet led the ensemble and Sam's definitive muted tone could be heard throughout the arrangement. After a saxophone duet Fouche followed with a lyric solo of his own, then the horns came striding in, and on the final chorus for the first time it was possible to hear an exhilarating offbeat cymbal ride under Sam's riffed, insistent melody.

The band, however, might not have had the second opportunity to return to the studio if it hadn't been for the final piece they did in the studio in April. Almost as an afterthought, they finished with the traditional hymn "Sing On," the first time any New Orleans band had recorded a gospel song. The single was never a large-selling release—copies of the original release are rare collector's items—but among other musicians it was a musical breakthrough. When Columbia returned to New Orleans two of the four pieces they recorded with the band were hymns, "Down By The Riverside" and "Over in the Gloryland." For "Down By The Riverside" Sam was brought forward for a cornet statement of the melody, and to emphasize the ties to the gospel roots, the band sang a chorus of the traditional verses. The rhythm itself was subtly altered. For the opening verse statement Brown played the bass with a bow, then went back to pizzicato for the chorus. There had been so much antagonism toward jazz and the blues among southern religious people, that it was difficult to anticipate what the reaction would be when the first single was released, but these three jazz gospel performances were to open the gate for the glorification of the gospel sound that would become one of the most distinctive elements in contemporary New Orleans street jazz.

The records sold well locally. Sam would stand in front of the Morris Music Shop on South Rampart Street offering copies of "Everybody's Talkin' 'Bout Sammy," and the band carried singles with them to sell when they toured along the Gulf Coast. They played a excursion trip on the L&N Railroad, which took them to Chicago, where they played at the Warwick Hall on 47th Street. Andrew remembered that they played at a party for Kid Ory and were paid $150 for three hours playing for a dance sponsored by the "Two Black Dagos." The economic collapse of the Depression years, however, meant that the band never recorded again. Sam suffered a second stroke at a dance in Bay St. Louis in 1932, but he stayed with them for a few months, taking tickets at the door and trying to resume playing. The band finally gave up in 1933, and Andrew said that in February 1936 his brother contracted pneumonia watching the night Carnival parades pass by his house. Sam died on Mardi Gras Day, and Kid Howard's Brass Band, with clarinetist George Lewis, and the Tulane Brass Band played for his funeral.

In the summer of 1929 still another dance emporium with an enthusiastic following from Creole New Orleans opened, not far from The Garden of Joy venue that Piron had been operating on the roof of the downtown Pythian Temple. The new establishment was on the second floor of the Astoria Hotel on South Rampart Street. On August 3, E. Belfield Spriggins announced in the *Louisiana Weekly*,

> *Just had a chat with Messrs. H. E. Braden and Edwin Fauna [sic], the proprietors of the Astoria Hotel and they told me that have planned something new and entirely different to be opened on Friday, August 16. It will be known as the Astoria Gardens.*
>
> *Music for the place will the under the able directorship of Prof. David Jones, the man who made Ridgely's Tuxedo Orchestra famous, so you may rest assured that the music will be "all there."[3]*

In his column two weeks later, Spriggins described the opening as a "brilliant social success" and continued,

> *The frescoed walls, vari-colored soft lights shedding their dreamy influence, the hundred or more white-clothed tables and several hundred white-covered chairs, the floral decorations were really inviting . . .*
>
> *The big, happy crowd that attended showed their marked approval of things by their continued hilarity, which lasted until the final moment of the closing hour. The "whoopee makers" were there in big parties, and their spirit of enthusiasm was so infectious that at times the shouts of joy drowned everything, even the music, which the splendid orchestra rendered more loudly.*
>
> *Prof. Jones and his artistic musicians rendered a program that kept feet and shoulders moving even when the entertainers were showing their wares.[4]*

In the 1950s the Astoria still offered dancing (to a jukebox) and a dimly lit bar, but it was only open to black customers and was close enough to Canal Street and its occasional police officers that everyone was a little uncomfortable if an outsider crossed the color line. The "ballroom" itself, still called the Astoria Gardens, was upstairs above the seedy hotel and cocktail lounge. It was on South Rampart Street, not far from Canal Street on the lake side of Rampart. It was a dark, heavy, two-story stone building, with a narrow staircase up to the dance floor. It was still operated by Beansie Fauria (the spelling in Spriggins's column was either "Fauna" or "Fauvia"). Beansie was one of the laid-back New Orleanians still left from the old days, and he often took a break from the Astoria to walk over to the French Quarter and talk over business with gallery owner Larry Borenstein, who was running the Associated Artists' Studio on St. Peter Street, the roomy gallery space that he later turned into Preservation Hall. Since I was working for Larry, and Larry often had to meet customers—the gallery stayed open until midnight—I'd talk to Beansie while Larry was busy. He and Larry were involved in a number of things I never was told about. Beansie was a friendly, heavy, neatly dressed Creole, light-skinned enough to pass, and he once laughed that when he visited some of his relatives he could come up the front steps, but with others he had to go around to the kitchen door.

The first steady job that Lee Collins took when he came back to New Orleans after the Oliver band broke up was working for Johnny Lala at what had been the old 101 Ranch on Franklin Street. After several name changes it was now called the Entertainer's Club. Collins had matured into a sharp, lean, ambitious musician, and his reputation as Oliver's second lead made him a local celebrity. He was good looking, and continually managed to involve himself with women who burned with jealousy over all the other women who came to his jobs to smile at him. He met Fauria not long after he took the job with Lala. Collins recalled,

There was a guy named Beansie Fauria that ran a place called the Creole Fantasy. It was in a good location, right next to the Lyric Theater, but business was very bad at Beansie's place at this particular time. So Big John Evans—that was the bartender at the Creole Fantasy—told Beansie that the Entertainers was packed and jammed because of me playing there. All the show people from the Lyric Theater were going to the Entertainers, and with all those celebrities you could hardly get in the place.... One night while I was on my intermission, Beansie stopped by and asked me how I was doing. Then he offered me a big price to come and work for him. I told him, "Beansie, I never run out on a man or do him any harm unless he do me some." However, I did talk Beansie's proposition over with Udell [Udell Wilson, the band's pianist], and he said my musicians were with me; whatever I wanted to do was okay with them. My going to Chicago had changed everything—after I left Joe Oliver's band I didn't know my own power.[5]

Danny Barker, who was, like Collins, a, young, ambitious instrumentalist, joined the band later playing banjo and guitar, and one day when we were talking about Collins he laughed and told me about his audition with Collins band.

They were going to play a job over on the Mississippi coast, it might have been Biloxi, and I had never played with them, but Lee knew who I was. Now he was sharp. Very sharp. He had clothes and he had style, and I took my banjo

LEE COLLINS, 1925.

over to do the audition and he just looked me up and down. I was sharp too and I had put on my best outfit and he just studied me, then he looked down and studied my shoes, and I had on very sharp new leather shoes. So he looked at me and he said, "How' your mother?" And I looked back at him and I smiled and I said, "How's yours?"

Then he just shook his head and he told me where I was supposed to meet them for the job. You see, what he figured was that if I had sharp shoes like that and I knew the Dozens, I knew how to play the banjo.[6]

The "Dozens" was the old street-corner exchange of insults that was a widespread custom in African American urban life.

In 1926 Collins left the Entertainer and moved into the Club Lavida in the French Quarter, at the beginning of the music scene along Bourbon Street. Earlier in the 1920s it had been the La Vida Dance Hall, across Canal Street at the corner of St. Charles Avenue, and Tony Parenti's orchestra had recorded a "La Vida Medley" when they were working there the year before. Within a few months, however, Collins and the band moved to the Astoria to help out Davey Jones, who was a good friend. Jones had agreed to take the job but didn't have any musicians.

I was working at the Lavida, and Davey came to me and wanted me to take the job with my band, so I promised him I would. Then Beansie—he was the boss of the Astoria at this time—went ahead and had posters made, and we went out on the truck, advertising that my band would open at the Astoria. I went to my boss at the Lavida and told him that I was leaving, but somehow he talked me into staying. So I told Davey that I wouldn't take the Astoria job after all. The next night Beansie came to see me and said that if I didn't work for him I wouldn't work any other place in New Orleans, either. So that is how I took the job at the Astoria.[7]

After the crowded opening on August 16, the band's popularity steadily increased. On their next trip to New Orleans Victor Records brought them into the studio, even though it was late in 1929 and there were already ominous signs of the economic catastrophe that was waiting. The recordings done in the previous two or three years by the city's white bands had reflected the larger jazz world of the New York and Chicago recordings, and the band that Jones and Collins were leading together at the Astoria also reflected the new sounds from New York. The bite and the tension of their music sound as though they were responding to the brilliant singles that had been released only a few months before by one of the city's own musicians, trumpeter Red Allen, who was in New York with the Luis Russell Orchestra. He had released two singles in the spring with a small group drawn from the orchestra called Red Allen's New Yorkers. The Astoria orchestra's arrangements, with the structure and the complexity of Allen's studio group, had a sophistication that was worlds away from the exuberant jamming of Sam Morgan musicians. For the session that Collins and Jones recorded, the compositions by the members of the band, were new, and they were a showcase for the band's musicianship and exciting solo styles. Collins remembered, "Finding names for the numbers we recorded for Victor was easy. 'Astoria Strut,' of course, was named for the place we were playing at, and we called another tune 'Damp Weather' because it was raining that day. The way the saxophonists took the breaks together gave us the title for 'Duet Stomp.' And 'Tip Easy Blues' came about because Theodore Purnell would beat his feet when he was really tipping. 'Purnell's tippin' easy,' the guys in the band used to say."[8]

It was also the first racially mixed session in the city. Collins had decided to replace his regular clarinet player with his friend Sidney Arodin. When Arodin gave up his job on Decatur Street he would sometimes drop by wherever Collins was playing and sit in, and there were nights when he was too high to go back to his regular job. Collins liked his playing so well that he brought him into the studio for the session, which finally had to be done in the boomy Italian Hall on Esplanade, since they weren't offered any other facilities, probably because it was a black session. The engineers, despite the problems, succeeded in creating a tight, cleanly articulate recorded sound. The four singles had an explosive energy—the trumpet set against the section work of the reeds, the rhythm fueled by the 4/4 driving bass style—reminiscent of the stride of the Sam Morgan recordings. This time the bass player was the other Morgan brother, Al, and his bass again led the rhythm, as Sidney Brown's had done with his brother's band. Morgan was already a premier instrumentalist, and his playing was one of the strengths of the session.

In the slashing breaks of the first piece they recorded, "Astoria Strut," Collins playing had a power and assertiveness that suggested Red Allen's "It Should Be You," the signature piece of Allen's New York session, but what is startling in Collins' ensemble lead is how close his style was in phrasing and melodic structure to the clear, assertive leads of Sharkey Bonano, with an overlay in his tone from Armstrong and Red Allen. The New Orleans idiom continued to be a common asset shared by all of the local musicians. Each of the soloists in the Astoria orchestra was brilliant, and Arodin's lucid playing, in breaks and in his extended solos in "Damp Weather" and "Tip Easy Blues," was a continually exciting foil to the brashness of Collins' trumpet. In musical terms it was perhaps the most accomplished of the sessions made in the city, showing how deep the reservoir of musicians was in New Orleans, even though so many had decided to leave. Collins, as he'd said about the "kings" of the city, quickly followed the trail out of town, and in a few months was working in Chicago. He was lost to New Orleans. Of the important members of the band, only the pianist Joe Robichaux continued to be part of the city's musical scene, with his own swing group. None of the others, Collins, Arodin, Jones, or Morgan were to be part of the New Orleans world again.

17

The Prodigal

*Speaking of 1931—we did call ourselves Vipers, which could have been any-
body from all walks of life that smoked and respected gage. That was our cute
little name for marijuana, and it was a misdemeanor in those days. Much different from the pressure and the charges the law lays on a guy that smokes
pot—a later name for the same thing which is cute to hear nowadays. We
always looked at pot as a sort of medicine, a cheap drunk, and with much
better thoughts than one that's full of liquor.*

LOUIS ARMSTRONG DISCUSSING HIS MARIJUANA USE IN A
LETTER WRITTEN SHORTLY BEFORE HIS DEATH[1]

1931 wasn't much of a year for anyone in the United States, as the economy
crashed, banks closed, a third of the nation's workers were without jobs, and
the only encouragement from the government was the promise that prosperity was "just around the corner." For Louis Armstrong, New Orleans's most
famous jazz celebrity, it was an especially bad year. The difficulties began with his
arrest for possession of marijuana in Los Angeles. On the one hand, his career
was soaring. His nightly radio broadcasts from the Frank Sebastian's New Cotton
Club and his decision to use popular songs for recording material and to feature
his own vocals with a large band accompaniment was reaching beyond the small
audience for jazz that had already gotten the message of his revolutionary playing a few years earlier. On the other hand, the day-to-day business of managing
his career was continually threatening to careen off the rails, in part because of
his casual attention to his bookings, in part because of the ineptness of his management, but also in part because of the pressure on both Armstrong and John
Collins, a dapper, usually anxious-looking young white man who was his agent,
from the various criminal syndicates that controlled virtually all of the country's

major nightclubs, as an unintended result of the chaos caused by Prohibition. The bust in March, however, wasn't completely unexpected—he'd been arrested in Chicago the previous November on marijuana charges. In Los Angeles he and drummer Vic Berton had gone out into the parking lot of the Cotton Club during an intermission and were smoking a joint. As he wrote in the letter about the drug arrest, which Max Jones and John Chilton quoted in their biography *Louis*,[2] ". . . Vic and I were blasting this joint—having lots of laughs and feeling good enjoying each other's company. We were standing in this great big lot in front of some cars. Just then two big healthy Dicks (detectives) came from behind a car—nonchalantly—and said to us, we'll take the roach boys. (Hmm)"

One of the detectives led Armstrong back into the club and sat in the audience while he played the last set—which the detective assured him he enjoyed—and on the way to the station in the police wagon he confided to Armstrong that he was a fan.

> *First words he said to me were, Armstrong I am a big fan of yours and so is my family. We catch your program every night over the radio. In fact, nobody goes to bed in our family until your program's over. And they're all good—which I was glad to hear, especially coming from him. HaHa. Then I confidentially told him—Since you and your family are my fans they'd be awfully sad if anything drastic would happen to me, the same as the other thousands of my fans. So please don't hit me in my "chops", when he said to me, why, I wouldn't think of anything like that. That's all I wanted to hear. Immediately I said, OK let's ride I also told him—after all, I'm no criminal. . . . Hell, he said, you ain't doing any more 'n' anybody's doing. It's when they get caught is when they're found out.*

On the way downtown the detective told him that a bandleader playing in a club up the street had turned him in in a moment of jealousy because of the success of his appearances.

Marijuana surfaced as an exotic new arrival to the jazz scene during the 1920s, and at that time it wasn't generally illegal. Someone Armstrong's age had to deal with the anomaly that in the first half of their careers marijuana was legal and the use of alcohol was a criminal offense, and for the last half of their careers alcohol was legal and marijuana had become a crime. He dealt with the contradictory realities by using marijuana for most of his life. The "weed" turned up in many jazz song titles during the period, including the well-known "Chant of the Weed," "Reefer Man," "Weed Smoker's Dream," "The Viper's Drag," "If You're A Viper" (with its hyperbolic opening line, "Talk about a reefer five feet long"), Barney Bigard's "Sweet Marijuana Brown," and Ella Fitzgerald's "When I Get Low, I Get High." His own contribution to the genre was a 1928 instrumental titled "Muggles," which he slipped through presumably because none of the record company executives knew that muggles was one of the Chicago terms for a marijuana cigarette. Marijuana wasn't the only drug to be celebrated.

Cab Calloway had a 1931 hit with a song celebrating opium, "Kickin' the Gong Around."

Alcohol, the one drug the society had openly used until the experiment with Prohibition, has been the subject of songs and poetry, festivals and celebrations, for thousands of years. It was the scourge of the New Orleans jazz world; hundreds of local musicians had their careers sidetracked because of alcohol problems. Armstrong's enthusiasm for marijuana certainly had less effect on his music than the drugs that ravaged the bop scene a decade later, the heroin and cocaine that left their dark imprint on a generation of jazz artists, but at that moment in the parking lot behind the Cotton Club in Los Angeles it was a local criminal offense.

Once he was booked in the Los Angeles city jail, in a room filled with police who also were fans of the radio broadcasts, Armstrong spent nine days in a cell with two men who had been picked up for street crimes that he never got straight, but whom he'd known before, since they'd blown a lot of gage together. When he was brought out of the cell to stand trial, his suit was returned to him, and he found that all the seams and the lining had been torn out in a search for more drugs. The courtroom was jammed; a number of reporters had come from Chicago because of his popularity there, and the headlines had been threatening that he faced a six-month sentence. At the brief trial he was warned and given a suspended sentence, and to his relief and surprise he found himself back on the bandstand the same night. In his letter he insisted that the experience, like so many things that happened to him, did have a funny side. As he wrote, "What struck me funny though—I laughed real loud when several movie stars came up to the bandstand while we played a dance set, and told me, when they heard about me getting caught with marijuana they thought marijuana was a chick."[3]

Armstrong returned to Chicago in April to spend some time with his wife Lil and to play an engagement before ecstatic audiences at the Regal Theater. He then put together a ten-piece band to begin a tour that finally, and momentously, found its way to New Orleans. But the year's bad vibrations caught up with him again. The band was still working at the Showboat Club in Chicago, rehearsing on the bandstand for the southern tour, and one night late in April the door of his dressing room was pushed open and he was confronted by a man who took out a pistol. He was ordered to call a number in New York and confirm that he and the band were going to leave Chicago and take a job at a club called Connie's Inn there. Armstrong looked at the pistol and did as he was told, though he refused demands that he pay several thousand dollars for what the man claimed were damages resulting from a booking in New York that had been canceled the previous summer. When John Collins turned up a few days later, he warned Louis to stay out of New York for a while, and Armstrong with equal vehemence insisted that he wasn't going to stay in Chicago. Their final decision was to take a job for the summer at a Metairie roadhouse, the Suburban Gardens, where Celestin's Tuxedo Orchestra had been the house band for the last two or three seasons. Armstrong finished out the job at the Showboat Club with security guards to bring him back and forth from his apartment, and he could only be certain of protection inside the Showboat because another of the large Chicago clubs was owned by gangster Al Capone, who was a fan. Except for occasional periods of furious disagreement, the mobs that had divided up Chicago's nightlife respected each other's territories.

The unexpected decision to leave for New Orleans also caused problems with the city's musicians' union local, and there was still the unresolved issue of a cancelled booking the summer before, which had now been taken up by the New York musicians' union. Armstrong stayed in his apartment, letting Collins clear up the situation, and Collins booked the band for a grinding series of one-night appearances on the way down to New Orleans and again on the trip home at the end of the summer. They somehow squeezed in between fifty and sixty dance engagements in their travels. On the first leg of the tour, however, they left the one-nighters behind them in Louisville and took an L&N train south to New Orleans. It was the same railroad line that Armstrong had ridden nine years before when he had received the telegram from Joe Oliver, asking him to come north and join the Creole Jazz Band. He hadn't been back since that first trip, and there was some concern about what would meet them when the train got in. What they found waiting at the station was a procession of most of the city's black brass bands, led off by the marching band of the Zulu Club, a jubilant crowd of thousands of fans—white and black—a contingent of police to keep everything as calm as possible, and a motorcade for Armstrong and the members of the orchestra through the city, with stops along the way in his old Uptown neighborhood. The newspapers, the *Picayune* and the New Orleans *Item*, and the African American *Louisiana Weekly*, had been tipped about his arrival by his personal valet and secretary, who had also decided to take on the job of publicizing their stops.

For once, however, there was a justification for all the noise and flash. Armstrong was without question one of the most celebrated jazz artists performing anywhere in the world, and he was coming back home for a three-month engagement. The excitement at his homecoming was genuine. The Prodigal had returned!

In one of his autobiographies Armstrong wrote that he was told five thousand people filled the club for their first night at the Suburban Gardens, with thousands more sitting outside trying to hear the music. The band was opening in the old roadhouse—it originally had been the Beverly Gardens on Jefferson Highway at Labarre Road—and it's difficult to imagine a crowd of five thousand squeezing into one of the Metairie roadhouse restaurants. There were, however, crowds of people sitting outside along the levee close to the building. The Gardens, like every other club they would play in the South, was strictly segregated, and for the three months of his stay there Armstrong played for white audiences only. The crowd outside were the black fans who couldn't get into the club, so they sat in the darkness along the levee, coping with the mosquitoes, straining to hear his voice and his trumpet. In his description of the night he marveled that there could have been ten thousand of his fans gathered outside. "Well, they wasn't allowed in there, so quite naturally they gathered outside right along the levee, hoping to catch the music through the open windows. I'll never forget that sight." Inside, he saw many familiar faces scattered through the white audience. "Among them was people I'd grown up with, white boys you understand, I used to play games with on empty lots after school, and they were there calling me by name, you know, pleased to see me again."[4]

What the people sitting outside in the darkness wouldn't have heard was the terse reminder to Armstrong that, whatever success he was having as a performer, he was still back in the South, and he was still black. The Gardens had a nightly radio broadcast, with a white announcer who presented the bands. He opened with his usual introduction to the Suburban Gardens as Armstrong waited behind the stage curtain. Then he stopped, broke off, and said to the crowd in front of the stage, "I just haven't the heart to announce that nigger on the radio," then he walked off. To cover the confusion Armstrong came out through the curtain, and the ovation that greeted him continued until the storm over the announcement had been forgotten. He thanked the crowd and immediately went into a new song he'd recorded in April that was to be his theme song for the rest of his career, "When It's Sleepy Time Down South."

The rest of the summer passed quickly. The crowds held up at the Gardens, and Lil came down from Chicago to try to save what she could of their marriage. He and Lil had grown apart in the years he'd been on the road, and he had decided to marry one of his current girlfriends. It was the classic dilemma that so many musicians face at some point in their careers, spending so much of their time away from their homes and families. Just before the band closed at the gardens, Lil took the train alone back to Chicago.

Armstrong's return to the city was more triumphant than anything he could have anticipated. In the pictures that were taken of his meetings with friends he is smiling broadly, and he's certainly the most slickly dressed of the men in the crowd, with tailored suits and snappy hats. For a visit to the Waif's Home, where he'd had his first cornet lessons from its band director, Peter Davis, he brought along most of the band, and they posed for a photograph with Armstrong and his musicians sitting on wooden chairs lined up in a row, grinning into the camera, all of them elegantly dressed in the dark suits and ties they wore on the bandstand. Davis was standing modestly a few rows behind them, his face shining with a proud grin. Armstrong was holding his floppy brimmed white fedora on his lap, obviously as touched to be there as his old teacher. There were other New Orleans men from the band in the photo: bass player Johnny Lindsay, who'd worked around the District, then moved to Chicago and recorded with Jelly Roll Morton, and trombonist Preston Jackson and drummer Fred "Tubby" Hall, both of whom had left when they were too young to begin playing in the city. Behind them on the steps going into the home, was the current batch of young musicians, dressed in their white band uniforms and holding their instruments. Two or three of them managed to grin, the others looked solemn or nervous.

LOUIS ARMSTRONG VISITING THE WAIF'S HOME, WHERE HE FIRST LEARNED TO PLAY THE
CORNET, SUMMER 1931. HIS TEACHER, PETER DAVIS, IS STANDING TO THE RIGHT OF THE
BOYS' BAND. WITH ARMSTRONG ARE MEMBERS OF THE BAND HE WAS APPEARING WITH AT
THE SUBURBAN GARDENS, INCLUDING JOHNNY LINDSAY, FAR LEFT, DRUMMER TUBBY HALL
IN CENTER, TO THE RIGHT OF ARMSTRONG. TROMBONIST PRESTON JACKSON IS SECOND
FROM RIGHT.

The bass drum was lettered with their official title, MUNICIPAL BOYS HOME
Colored Boys Brass Band.

Armstrong spent time with his family, and even met his first wife again, who
was still living in the city. He bought uniforms for a black baseball team, with the
name Armstrong across the shirts, posing with them on the baseball field in a
sporting outfit of the band's dark jacket and white, striped trousers. This time he
was wearing his floppy brimmed hat again and leaning on a baseball bat beside
the team members, resplendent in their new uniforms, and his own grin has
even more of a gleam. They became known around town as Armstrong's Secret
Nine. He'd put on a lot of weight in Chicago, but even after some weeks of his
mother's old-style New Orleans cooking, he was looking trimmer.

The broadcasts from the Gardens continued to spread his name nationally, and
he had already settled into the entertainment format that would have as much
of an effect on the style of jazz performances as his brilliant playing. Between
1928 and 1930 he had recorded a string of successful singles using popular song
material as a vehicle for his voice and trumpet. Some of the songs are still identified with him, among the best known, "Ain't Misbehavin'," "Black And Blue,"
"Shine," "When You're Smiling," "Rockin' Chair," "I Can't Give You Anything

But Love Baby," "Confessin'," "Some Of These Days," "After You've Gone," "If I Could Be With You," and "St. James Infirmary." The treatment was simple; a short introduction, a melody chorus led by the trumpet, usually muted, a vocal chorus, a half chorus with one of the other soloists to give him time to pick up the trumpet and get back a little from the microphone, then a trumpet solo, inevitably ending in a slow, spiraling, breathtaking display of high notes. On stage he added a repertoire of flourishes with a pile of handkerchiefs, a stream of verbal asides, laughter, and mugging to keep the show alive. What had been evident in his brilliant series of instrumental recordings in the late 1920s with artists like pianist Earl Hines was that instrumental jazz had no market outside the jazz community. With popular songs, and late-night radio programs and the new jukeboxes to sell them, Armstrong had found his way out of the constricted jazz market.

The formula was so successful that for the next ten years virtually every new trumpet player, white or black, who was offered a recording contract found himself singing more than he was playing. Their voices didn't have to be good; the idea was to sound as engaging and as upbeat as Armstrong was. The bands that didn't have a singer were told that they had to hire one, since it was songs that were selling the instrumental sound and not the other way around. Once he'd found his formula, Armstrong essentially never varied it, though the size of his backing group changed with the newest trends, and from time to time he added a new pop favorite to the basic repertoire. He performed essentially the same show for forty years, spending his life on tour in an unending series of concert appearances. He evolved into one of a handful of universally known entertainers who could appear anywhere in the world and find a tumultuous audience waiting to welcome him.

The summer engagement ended with a final flush of down-home racism to remind him of where he was. They had played one day's shows at the Lafayette Theatre shortly after they arrived in June, but otherwise they had played for white only audiences the entire summer. As a gesture for the African American community that hadn't been able to hear him in the Metairie roadhouse, the band offered to present a free dance at an army installation outside of New Orleans the day after they'd closed at the Gardens. Thousands of people showed up, some of them coming by wagon from local small towns. When the band arrived they found that the gates had been locked and the crowd was drifting angrily away. It had been announced that the dance was cancelled. The reason given was that dancing wasn't permitted on military property.

Their troubles, however, were not over. They traveled by bus to Texas for a job in Houston, then when their tour bus arrived in Memphis on their way to Little Rock, they were arrested. The wife of the manager, Mary Collins, was traveling with the musicians, a lone young white woman sitting in the front seat with the band's guitarist, Mike McKendrick, a black man, beside her. The official reason the police gave for arresting them was that they refused to change from the bus they were traveling in to a different bus that had been hastily arranged as a substitute for them. They had arrived in a large, comfortable Greyhound bus, and were being told they had to change to one that was smaller and in poor repair. Mrs. Collins protested that she had paid $50 extra for the better bus, and the band was jailed at that point. The trombonist Preston Jackson said that they were directed to the bus terminal, and when they got there, ". . . it looked like half the Memphis police force met us around there. 'All right, you niggers,' they said, 'You're in Memphis now, and we need some cotton pickers, too. . . .' They put us all in one big cell. A guy came through: 'Louis, I heard you fellers in Houston last week, you know.' Well, we didn't care where he heard us, we wanted to get out of jail and make Little Rock."[5]

Armstrong and his musicians might have gotten away with traveling on a decent bus, but the South wasn't ready for the sight of a white woman sitting in the front seat of the bus with a black man.

If New Orleans in that summer of 1931 had still been having the street-corner battles of music that Armstrong had grown up with, the incandescence and the power of his playing would have closed out every new trumpet player who tried to blow against him. The sobering reality, however, was that there wasn't anyone there to challenge him. The economic disaster of the early 1930s had devastated the New Orleans economy, but the swift shift in tastes to larger swing groups also meant that even though there were jobs, most of them were in other places.

When Armstrong was still a teenager and just beginning to work in the brass bands and on the riverboats, Chris Kelly was leading his band for steady dance engagements and street advertising, and Armstrong certainly heard him play his famous "Careless Love" solo. Kelly continued his raw, alcoholic lifestyle, however, and died in 1927, only thirty-six years old. The cornetist Louis had admired for his swing and his tone, Buddy Petit, was still playing when Armstrong opened at the Suburban Gardens, but alcohol had also taken its toll, and his playing was often confused and erratic. He died a few weeks after Armstrong's opening, supposedly from overeating at a Fourth of July picnic where his band was performing. He was forty-four. Armstrong was one of the pallbearers at the funeral. Older musicians he'd known, or musicians with families, stayed behind and took whatever work they could find, but New Orleans continued its role as an exporter of jazz artists.

One of the most successful of the exports was Henry "Red" Allen, son of the brass band leader Henry Allen Sr., who had hired Armstrong as a very raw beginning cornetist. Allen was one of the most promising of the younger musicians, and in 1927, when he was only nineteen, he was hired by King Oliver to join his band in New York. Oliver's career was running down, and Allen joined pianist Luis Russell from New Orleans, who had also been working with Oliver and was organizing his own group. Allen became part of the brilliant Russell band that was soon working and recording in the New York area. It was perhaps the finest of the New Orleans bands to emerge in the late 1920s, even though they never played in New Orleans, and there were musicians in the band who hadn't made the train trip North, especially the fluid, imaginative alto saxophone soloist Charlie Holmes. Holmes was born in Boston, and first studied the oboe, for a period playing in one of Boston's symphony orchestras. He was a close friend of Johnny Hodges, of Duke Ellington's band, and when he moved to New York as a seventeen-year-old in 1927, he worked first with drummer Chick Webb before moving to the Russell Orchestra.

The band's rhythm section, built around its light, agile, pressing beat, anchored the band solidly in the New Orleans idiom. Luis Russell, the pianist and leader, was from Panama, and he'd made his way to New Orleans in 1919, after his mother won a lottery. A modest, hard-working musician, he had served his apprenticeship in the clubs along the "tango belt," at the edge of the old Storyville district. When he left New Orleans it was to join King Oliver's new band, the Dixie Syncopators, in Chicago. The drummer Paul Barbarin, with his understated, press roll technique, like trumpeter Allen also came from a venerable New Orleans musical family. His father Isadore Barbarin played alto horn or baritone horn in the city's elite brass bands, including the Onward and the Excelsior, and Paul began playing professionally while he still was a teenager. He and Russell worked together in Tom Anderson's Annex in 1919, after Storyville closed, and he was photographed on the bandstand with the group, a diffident looking nineteen-year-old behind a large bass drum. The trumpet player with the group was the legitimate Creole musician Arnold Metoyer, and the clarinetist was Albert Nicholas, who later made the same trip north, first to King Oliver's orchestra, then to Russell's new orchestra.

George "Pops" Foster had been one of the best of the early generation of New Orleans bassists, and he had been working steadily since he left New Orleans. His insistent bass was the final ingredient that sparked the band's unquenchable rhythmic drive. With Allen's soaring solos buoyed by the rhythm section's swagger, and Holmes, Nicholas, tenor saxophonist Teddy Hill, and trombonist J. C. Higginbotham trading solos that seemed almost to come out of the sky, the band created some of the most exciting jazz of the late 1920s. They were fulfilling the promise of the New Orleans sound more than leaving it behind them, even though their book of arrangements was one of the most advanced in New York.

In his autobiography Foster emphasized the band's New Orleans style and New Orleans beat when they opened at the Savoy Ballroom in February, 1929.

We were really romping then, really bouncing. The rhythm was playing great together and the trumpet players were screaming soft so you could hear the people's feet scraping on the floor. You could stand right in front of the band and they weren't blasting you out. We had Red Allen, J. C. Higginbotham, Paul Barbarin, Albert Nicholas, Charlie Holmes, Teddy Hill, and a whole bunch of great guys. We worked seven days a week and we loved it. We'd rather be working than be at home. It was like it was back in New Orleans. Back then

GEORGE "POPS" FOSTER, ABOUT 1928.

I used to sit around wishing I could go to work. It was a pleasure to work in those days. Russell's band was romping so good we had everything sewed up around New York. We were playing the same style we played back in early New Orleans.[6]

In 1929 the orchestra's trumpet soloist Red Allen had an opportunity to make a solo recording, and he used a small group from the Russell orchestra. The bite and fire of the first single, "It Should Be You" and "Biffly Blues," influenced many new groups, including Lee Collins with his group at the Astoria Ballroom. Some writers have dismissed Allen as another of the many imitators of Louis Armstrong, but there were essential differences in their solo styles. On Allen's early recordings his tone was without the swelling vibrato that Armstrong began to use to end virtually every held note, and Allen's style of improvisation was based on crisply articulated arpeggios to a much greater extent than Armstrong's, who generally developed his solos as a variant of the vocal melody. The rhythmic emphasis characteristic of Allen's uptempo solos on these recordings was also more tightly phrased. The entire generation of New Orleans trumpeters who matured in the 1920s, including Lee Collins, Armstrong, Allen, Guy Kelly, Punch Miller, and Herb Morand, as well as Sharkey Bonano, Wingy Manone, and Louis Prima shared many of the same stylistic influences, and the similarities in their playing were probably products of their New Orleans background as much as a response to the popularity of Armstrong's recordings.

The success of Allen's first single led to other single sessions, and as the 1930s wore on he was in and out of recording studios. The companies, however, were conscious that it was almost impossible for them to sell instrumental jazz, even in times not as desperate at the early 1930s. As the producers had learned with Armstrong, it was much less of a problem to sell a cover version of a popular song as a "novelty jazz" release. The same predictable style of arrangement became the pattern for virtually all of Allen's releases. With only occasional exceptions his warm, persuasive voice was featured singing every number. The material he was given was often lackluster, and there were only glimpses of the power of his trumpet, but he made it through the lean years still with a career.

Although as he began touring after the war and he had a steadily growing international audience, Allen always thought of himself as a "home boy," and he returned home often on visits. His father was still leading his brass band, and in 1950, on one of his visits to the city, Allen found that his father had a Sunday parade. He impulsively returned to the house for his trumpet, and joined his father's band in his New York clothes as the band swung down the street. For Henry Allen Sr., it was one of his life's proudest moments.

Others of the promising young generation of trumpeters, like Allen and Lee Collins, also found work outside of New Orleans, and spent the next decades on the road or working small club jobs. Punch Miller had an early opportunity to record in New Orleans in 1925 with the popular vaudeville team of Mack and Mack, adding his trumpet to the duet's vocals. His playing on these recordings already had the slightly acid tone and edgy rhythmic style that was his trademark when he returned to New Orleans in the 1950s. Much of his career was spent on the road. For a period in 1927 he was in Chicago with a colorfully costumed group called Francois' Louisianians. Herb Morand had moved to Chicago at the beginning of the Depression and was having a successful run with a fine small Chicago jazz/blues group, the Harlem Hamfats, who made a series of popular records through the 1930s. Guy Kelly, the exciting young soloist who had recorded with Celestin in 1928, left a few months later to join Dave Peyton's band in Chicago.

Many of the city's most promising younger musicians, like Allen and Collins, and virtually all the best of the new generation of white jazz artists were forced out of New Orleans in the economic collapse of the thirties—which was exacerbated by the city's long slide into poverty—but they never stopped thinking of themselves as New Orleanians. When trumpeter Wingy Manone found himself with a band in California that was led by a black bass player from back home, the other man looked at him, smiled, and said, "Hi, Home." New Orleans was home. New Orleans and its jazz artists had left an indelible mark on the sound of jazz in the 1920s, and although their influence now was more subtle and blended more successfully into the new jazz mainstream, the New Orleans sound was to leave almost as distinctive a mark on the next decade. With the playing of the city's prodigal Louis Armstrong, however, when he left his summer at a Metairie roadhouse and went on to bring his music to Europe two years later, the New Orleans style was to leave its broad, swaggering imprint on the jazz that was flourishing everywhere in the world.

Armstrong never strayed far from his New Orleans roots, and when he returned from Europe he soon began touring with his old friends in the Luis Russell Orchestra. Russell had never been able to find a musical formula that would bring his band closer to the kind of vocal/ballad material that was becoming more and more popular through recordings and the radio networks, and their instrumental brilliance wasn't enough to draw the dancing public. By the early 1930s they were finding it difficult to keep working as a band. Even Foster became discouraged. "We started fooling around with big band arrangements and quit romping or playing what you call Dixieland. While we were playing Dixieland we were great. When we started playing like all the other bands, finding work got rough. Why should they hire you when they've already got the same thing?"[7]

With Armstrong fronting the orchestra, everything changed. Their stage show opened with a feature spot for Allen, who played, sang, and introduced one of his new singles, then the stage was turned over to Armstrong, who had matured into a consummate entertainer. They had already recorded with him in 1929, and the rhythm of the orchestra and their featured soloist fit together seamlessly. In a mid-1930s photograph the new stage presentation was lined up in front of a shimmering curtain, Barbarin's elaborate drum kit behind them as a stylistic prop for the pose. The original group had expanded to a seventeen-piece stage troupe, with Armstrong and the band's two vocalists in the center. Armstrong and vocalist Sonny Woods, in the center, were in dark suits, the others in gleaming white, with matching shoes, dark shirts, and contrasting ties. They stood with their hands clasped behind their backs, with grins that would light a theater without any additional help. For Armstrong and Foster, those years on the dirt streets in New Orleans when Foster would sleep on the wagon he was driving to a delivery, letting his mule pick its way through the ruts, and when Armstrong was hauling his coal wagon from Storyville cribs to Uptown corner cabarets, must have seemed like memories of life from some other planet. The comfortable partnership between Armstrong and his New Orleans friends continued until the war finally closed down the big band industry.

18

Jazz Nights

One time I blew into New Orleans with nine hundred simpletons in my pocket and nobody would speak to me. They didn't like my clothes. I came in town wearing a sweat shirt, slacks, and sandals, and driving a V-8, but when I went in the saloons I was ignored.

As soon as I caught on I drove fifty miles out of town, bought me a sharp new suit and came back in style.

"Now you're talkin'," they said, and Cousin, what a welcome I got then.

WINGY MANONE[1]

As the thirties and the bitter years of the Depression ground on across the United States, the reckless optimism of the jazz of the previous decade seemed more and more like someone's misplaced memories. Many of New Orleans's younger musicians, however, had already been through their own slump at the end of the twenties, and they had sweated through a new direction in their music. With an emphasis on vocals and popular song themes, and on the colorful individuality of the soloists, the music made an attractive entertainment package. Louis Armstrong had found a style of jazz that could smile its way through the hard realities, and for the small clubs and theaters that came through the dark years the musical mood was an upbeat grin—like Armstrong's.

In the first months following the crash no one could have foreseen the troubled decade that was to follow, and for the first years of the Depression New Orleans limped along trying to be as much like the old Big Easy as it knew how. If you had a little money the neighborhood restaurants still offered music and a night out to dance for a decent price. The movie palaces still offered the same shows with their theater orchestras, a taste of vaudeville, and on some nights free dishes for the ladies. The Suburban Gardens hung on in Metairie and had a successful summer in 1931 with the steady crowds that came to hear Armstrong with his big band. Halfway House, however, continued its old formula of unlimited dance music, and with audiences looking for entertainment and some kind of a floor show it suddenly had fallen a step behind the more sophisticated dance restaurants downtown. It closed the summer before Armstrong's return.

In the early Depression years many younger African American musicians for once had an advantage in the struggle for jobs. The excursion steamers had never openly announced a policy of not hiring white bands, but the bands working on the boats still operating were generally black, and they continued to provide the kind of solid musical training in reading big band arrangements that Fate Marable's bands had presented to musicians like Armstrong and "Pops" Foster a decade before. The jobs weren't well paid, but the excursion steamers still offered work, and the other jobs that were to be found didn't pay much better. Through much of the thirties the most talented of the young black instrumentalists all did some time on the boats operating on the Mississippi or across Lake Ponchartrain.

Sidney Desvigne, who was light-skinned and slight, thin-faced with a small mustache and usually with a serious expression, led the band on the SS *Capitol* for several years, occasionally bringing his swing groups into town to one of the larger restaurants whenever a job turned up. He served his apprenticeship as a trumpet player with Marable in the early 1920s and had played the jazz solos on the single that Marable's orchestra recorded in 1924. When Marable began working on another riverboat further north on the river, Desvigne took over the band; in his first group he kept on banjoist Johnny St. Cyr, another riverboat veteran, who would soon leave for Chicago and the New Orleans scene there. Another Marable veteran, bassist Foster, also stayed on before he headed east to New York.

In 1929 Desvigne was leading the orchestra on the SS *Island Queen*, and the band included a very young, skinny, and uncomfortable-looking trombonist named Louis Nelson, who in the 1950s was to become one of the mainstays of the city's revival bands. The pianist, a cheerful entertainer and vocalist named Walter "Fats" Pichon, became a local institution as a cocktail pianist in the hotels serving the trickle of tourists who still came to the city. The trumpet player was an equally young Gene Ware, and Ransom Knowling was the bassist. In the one battered photo of the band that has survived, six of them are standing in the typical band lineup, half turned away from the camera, hands in pockets, in broad striped jackets with white shirts and bow ties. When Desvigne and his band posed again two years later, they were back on the SS *Capitol*, and had expanded to an eleven-piece group. Another familiar figure of the 1950s revival, guitarist Emanuel Sayles, was part of the rhythm section. Louis Nelson was still with the orchestra, looking as wary but with a better-fitting suit. The band had left their striped coats behind and were now in sober, dark business suits, white handkerchiefs folded neatly into their breast pockets. Both Ware and Knowling were to go on to other bands where they did considerable recording, Knowling, in one

THE SIDNEY DESVIGNE ORCHESTRA ON THE SS *CAPITOL*, 1931. FROM LEFT: LOUIS NELSON, UNIDENTIFIED, GENE WARE, EMANUEL SAYLES, ADOLPH DUCONGE, SIDNEY DESVIGNE, "WILSON," RANSOM KNOWLING, TATS ALEXANDER JR., TED PURNELL, WALT COSBY.

of those unexpected sideways moves often characteristic of a musician's working life, became a busy accompanist for many of Chicago's popular blues singers later in the 1930s.

For some of the white musicians there were still jobs in restaurants, although they had to dress to blend in with the new sophisticated décor. In some band pictures from this era the musicians seem to be sitting uneasily in the middle of a set for a Hollywood musical. In 1930 the most talented of the white trumpeters still in town, Sharkey Bonano, joined another trumpeter, Leon Prima, as co-leaders of the Prima-Sharkey Orchestra at the Little Club on Rampart Street, near Common. Like Desvigne's riverboat orchestra, the band had moved on from the typical instrumentation of the 1920s New Orleans jazz ensemble—it had grown to a ten-piece group, playing swing arrangements along with the repertoire of old New Orleans standards their audiences still expected. The band adopted the instrumentation of the popular recording orchestras—three reeds, two trumpets, trombone, and four rhythm—which gave them a more forceful ensemble sound but bound them into increasingly elaborate arrangements. With trombonist Charlie Hartman, clarinetist Irving Fazola, and pianist Frank Pinero, the band included some of the best young white musicians still in town. In their smiling publicity photograph they are seated on a broad, comfortable bandstand with a bright, patterned curtain drawn across the wall behind them. The sparsely decorated dance halls and dimly lit cabarets where jazz had first emerged only twenty years before were already now a part of New Orleans's colorful past.

THE PRIMA-SHARKEY ORCHESTRA, PLAYING AT THE LITTLE CLUB, 1930. FROM LEFT: SEATED, CHARLIE HARTMAN, SHARKEY BONANO, LOUIS PRIMA, IRVING FAZOLA, DAVE WEINSTEIN, NINO PICONE; STANDING, AUGIE SCHELLANG, LOUIS MASINTREE, FREDDIE LOYACANO, FRANK PINERO.

The months that the bands could count on steady work were numbered, however, and groups like Desvigne's and Sharkey's faced an increasingly difficult future. The economic situation in New Orleans was as discouraging for musicians as it was for everyone else, and many of the younger instrumentalists made strenuous efforts to find work outside of the city. In poignant snapshots taken in 1930, one of the bands leaving town, the "New Orleans Rhythm Masters," photographed themselves as they set out for New York. The members of the seven-piece band were crammed into a canvas-topped touring car, with a large wooden crate strapped on behind to hold the drums, some of the instruments, and their suitcases, and a folding gate rigged along the running board to hold the rest of the instruments. They had painted "Danger T.N.T., New Orleans to !N.Y.!" on the crate. When they posed in a cluster around the car before it was packed for the road, most of them tried to smile. Guitarist Joe Capraro was the driver, and the band included some of the best of the white veterans, with bassist Chink Martin, drummer Leo Adde, clarinetist Sidney Arodin, and trumpeter Bill Gillen. Charlie Cordilla, from the Halfway House, was dressed in sporty checked plus-fours, argyle knee socks, and a white band shirt with flowing sleeves, but his expression reflected a more realistic understanding of their situation. He looked as if he were on his way to a funeral.

For the next decade the most common place to find musicians still playing New Orleans–style jazz was in a hotel room in New York or Chicago. There weren't many more jobs in the northern cities than there were in New Orleans, but at least there was a music scene, and the musicians who were flexible in what they were willing to play could find places to work, if they had to scuffle along on miserable salaries. Guitarist Danny Barker, who had been working with

Lee Collins band, tried New York in 1930, when Collins left for Chicago after his breakthrough recordings with the Jones-Collins Astoria Eight. Barker's experiences would have sounded familiar to most musicians of the time.

For the most part it was the Depression and the Depression for musicians in New York—man, it was a bitch! I was working, I remember, in the Lenox Club, and there was a ten-piece band, eight chorus girls, four waiters, two bartenders, two managers, a doorman, a porter, and a "whiskey man." The whiskey man was the cat who used to hide the whiskey downstairs so when somebody wanted to drink he'd go down and come up with it mysteriously.

On weekdays they had but one or two parties a night. On weekends it was a little better. The hours were like from ten in the evening to five in the morning. Well, whatever they picked up in the register in the course of the night, at the end of the night they would pull a table into the middle of the floor and spill out the receipts of the night on the table and give everybody an equal share. Some mornings we'd make seventy-five cents, other mornings we'd get twenty-five. Everybody cooperated because there was nowhere else to go and, in fact, nobody had nothing . . .[2]

Everybody moved in with somebody else to keep expenses down. Paul Barbarin, who was playing with Luis Russell's orchestra, was Danny's cousin, so Danny at least had someone from down home to turn to for a little help and for some New Orleans food—which the wandering musicians often seemed to miss even more than they missed the struggling city itself. All of them did some time in the taxi dance halls that were part of the scene in every city. Barker turned to the taxi dances and their grueling working conditions when even the clubs, with their policies of dividing up whatever money they took in, couldn't keep going.

Also during the depression there were a few jobs for musicians in dance schools. We'd go to work at eight P.M. and play until three A. M.—without stopping. These were taxi dance halls. There were thirty to forty dime-a-dance girls. We played on a commercial kick—all the current pop tunes. We only played a chorus or a chorus and a half to make the dances shorter. You'd keep your bottle, if you could afford one, on the stand with you and you'd bring your lunch and each of us would take turns taking a break while still on the stand to eat or drink while the drums kept playing. The only time they had a real full band were on the introductions and the ending of the tunes.[3]

With the election of President Roosevelt in 1932, and his determination to use the resources of the government to bring some kind of stability to the desperate economic situation, ambitious programs of public works were instituted everywhere in the country to give jobs of some kind to the army of unemployed.

Much of the environment that had seen the birth of the New Orleans jazz style disappeared during the decade. Storyville was demolished to make way for an elaborate public housing project, which at the time was regarded by many leading architects and city planners as the model of what should be done to create a more healthful and safe environment for the urban poor. The buildings, abandoned and in poor repair, are still standing across Basin Street from the French Quarter, while there is continuous debate over their eventual fate. Louis Armstrong's old Uptown neighborhood was demolished to make way for the Union Railroad Station and the broad, divided street that led to Canal Street.

The Army engineers and the new construction along the lake took away the florid jazz scene at the Milneburg camps, and a new lakeside summer resort took its place, this time with a beach and an amusement park. In the summer of 1935, the new "Playground" of New Orleans, Ponchartrain Beach, was advertising "Safe Swimming, Thrilling Rides, Amusing Games" and a new Casino for dining and dancing. It was at the end of Elysian Fields Avenue, where Milneburg had been, and now there was frequent city bus service instead of the railroad line and its doughty engine Smoky Mary. In the newly developing Gentilly area along Elysian Fields, construction had begun on the drained marsh land, though the economic situation insured that there wasn't much new building. Like Lakeview just to the west, close to Spanish Fort and West End, Gentilly was developed on reclaimed bayou land, and when the Katrina catastrophe struck in 2005 it was obvious that development in both areas had been ill considered.

The new, and more sophisticated entertainment that New Orleanians were enjoying—at least the people who had some money to go out—had little to do with the kind of swinging dance music that the bands had presented a few years before. The music had steadily grown in harmonic sophistication and rhythmic subtlety. The Blue Parody Orchestra at Ponchartrain Beach presented three shows a day, and there was a continually changing offering of acrobatic stunts and animal acts—the usual summer fairground entertainment for cities like New Orleans everywhere. The publicity release for the opening of the season for the new Casino on June 2, 1935, makes it clear that the old days of the free and easy Milneburg camps and their jazz bands making the trip with the instruments loaded on to Smoky Mary was already a dim memory, even though it had been one of New Orleans's most popular summer places only a few seasons before.

The Blue Parody Orchestra, under the direction of Angelo Quaglino, which has been popular among the sororities of New Orleans, will be a nightly feature of the Casino at Ponchartrain Beach starting today.

The Blue Parody Orchestra has made frequent broadcasts over radio station WDSU. These broadcasts will be a regular feature brought to radio listeners by remote control from the Casino at Ponchartrain Beach. The Casino has been completely modernized, with new lighting effects, gay and colorful decorations, and a new dance floor.

> *As Ponchartrain Beach is a state park, no admission fee is charged to those desiring to spend an evening on the boardwalk, and the Casino makes no charge for dancing privileges other than that incurred in drinks or food obtained at the tables.*
>
> *The melodies of the Blue Parody will be broadcast over the entire beach by means of magnifying units and a series of speakers placed along the boardwalk and the beach. Bathers as well as strollers can enjoy the melodies from any point within the confines of the park.[4]*

For most New Orleanians, at least there was the familiar reassurance of an orchestra leader with an Italian name.

Other locations where there had been steady work for the bands moved to a non-jazz policy. In the summer of 1935 the Blue Room at the Roosevelt Hotel was presenting Bernie Cummins and his orchestra, with a floor show that offered a duo of "Superb Dancers." The Hotel Jung, which for years had used Ellis Stratakos and his Orchestra, now featured Ray Teal on the Jung Roof, "Under the Stars," with his Orchestra and Entertainers. Stratakos began his recording career as trombonist with Johnny DeDroit and The New Orleans Jazz Orchestra in 1925, and he continued to be an important local jazz artist, with a group that included several important younger musicians, among them cornetist Johnny Wiggs, trumpeter Louis Prima, clarinetist Irving Fazola, saxophonist Joe Loyocano, pianist Freddie Neuman, and drummer Augie Schellang; but the trend had moved on to less demanding—and more brightly optimistic—musical performances.

Black dance orchestras faced the same problems, and also were forced to adapt their orchestra styles to the new trends. John Robichaux was in his sixties when the Depression closed in on the city. The fire that destroyed the Lyric Theater in 1927 had already ended one of the longest steady engagements of any New Orleans orchestra, but he continued playing with most of his orchestra at the La Louisiane Restaurant on Iberville Street into the late 1930s. Celestin continued to lead his orchestras, but he was also older, and less active than he had been for many years. Kid Rena, the only one of the classic black 1920s jazz trumpeters still playing in the city, led the band at the Gypsy Tea Room, a large new club that opened in the mid-1930s, with Harold Dejan playing saxophone and bassist Burke Stevenson. In a club photograph the band members, in informal uniforms of light suit jackets and darker trousers, sit in a smiling group with the show's entertainers and well-dressed customers.

Another Robichaux (though they were not related), Joe Robichaux, organized the most successful large swing group in New Orleans in the 1930s. It was the same Robichaux who had played the piano with the Jones-Collins Astoria band for their Victor recording session. He was born in New Orleans in 1900. For a period around 1917 he played in Chicago with the Tig Chambers Orchestra. When he returned to Louisiana he worked the circuit of small towns around New Orleans in the early 1920s with the Black Eagles Orchestra led by trumpeter

Evan Thomas, his piano style absorbing some of the distinctive phrasing and rhythm of the Piron Orchestra's Steve Lewis. Robichaux assembled his swing group for The Entertainers, a club on Franklin Street, close to the corner of Custom House. It had a long history as one of the busiest dance locations within the Restricted District, known earlier as the 101 Ranch, the 102 Ranch, and Billy Phillip's Café. Robichaux's band included most of the newest generation of jazz instrumentalists. They played with an easy brilliance that caught the essence of the New Orleans style, at the same time moving it into the contemporary dance mode. Gene Ware, the fine trumpeter player from Sidney Desvigne's SS *Capitol* orchestra, anchored the brass section, and with Robichaux's supple piano setting the rhythms the band had an easy, infectious swing. Fortunately, Robichaux managed to interest Vocalion Records in a contract, and the earliest version of his group, still with only seven pieces, took the train to New York in the summer of 1933. Between August 22 and August 26 they recorded twenty-two singles, most of them instrumentals. The band's vocalists, guitarist Walter Williams or clarinetist Alfred Guishard, sang on five of the arrangements, and busy New York studio vocalist Chick Bullock was added for the final two sides, but otherwise the band brought the New Orleans rhythmic lift into the studio with a series of exciting instrumentals. Many of the pieces they recorded were their versions of new swing successes, but their sound was their own. By some clerical error Robichaux's name was misspelled as Robechaux, but what was most important was that all of the sides were issued and had enough sales for the band to hold on to its job in New Orleans.

As the new swing style grew in popularity, Robichaux expanded the band to fourteen pieces; the brass section included trumpeters Gene Ware, Kildee Holloway, and John Girard, and trombonists Frog Joseph and Clement Tervalon. In March 1936 Decca Records had a recording unit in New Orleans, and four numbers were recorded by some of the members of the new orchestra. For some reason the masters were never released, but one track has recently been located, and the small ensemble plays with a classic New Orleans feel. Joe Robichaux played an important role in opening up the local musicians to new melodies and new ensemble styles.

By the mid-1930s, as the Depression showed no signs of lightening, there was even less work in the small neighborhood clubs, and the jobs often offered salaries of a dollar a man for the night, with tips expected to bring in something on top of that. When the recovery programs set in motion by the government began registering musicians for publicly funded performances, most of the musicians still in the city signed up for the Emergency Relief Administration Orchestra. The two photos of the African American program include hundreds of musicians, carefully posed with their instruments in crowded rows, with the leader, trumpeter Louis Dumaine (who had recorded with his band in the 1920s), either standing to one side or sitting in the center of the ensemble. The photograph taken on January 15, 1935, in Jackson Square was included in *New Orleans*

Jazz: A Family Album.[5] A second assembled group portrait taken on February 2, 1935, at the Fifth Ward Boxing Club was included in *Jazz: New Orleans.*[6]

In the hurried struggle to get some kind of aid program started, the orchestra was open for anyone who showed enough interest in music to sign up, whether or not they were working musicians, so many faces in the photographs have never been identified. There was still a scattering of performers who went back to the ragtime days; Albert Glenny, Frankie Duson, Ernest Trepangier, Sam Morgan, Shots Madison, and Harrison Barnes. But also bundled into their jackets against the winter chill were many of the young performers who would become better known in the 1950s, including Cie Frazier, Israel Gorman, Willie Humphrey, Andrew Morgan, Manuel Paul, Sonny Henry, John Casimir, George Cola, Jimmy Clayton, Kid Howard, and Oscar Henry. Mingled on the tiers of steps were musicians who had played with Buddy Bolden and younger instrumentalists who were experimenting with the new swing idiom. This jazz panorama could only have been found in New Orleans.

At the same time, outside the city there were the stirrings of what would become a new interest in the small ensemble New Orleans style that had its roots in the ragtime of Jack Laine and his Reliance Orchestra. The first impetus that had come with the Original Dixieland Jazz Band still had reverberations among many musicians, and the next of the Crescent City bands to achieve a wide success, the New Orleans Rhythm Kings, further refined the white small band sound. Their effect on the young Chicagoans who heard them—the musicians of the Austin High Gang, and out-of-town visitors like Bix Beiderbecke—was decisive. Jazz was to lose whatever stylistic cohesion it had as the 1930s passed, but one of the diverse streams that became permanently established was the essence of the New Orleans style. It finally became known generically as "Dixieland," a tacit acknowledgment of the influence of the ODJB. With the end of Prohibition in 1934, small clubs could openly serve liquor again, the mobs that had controlled the music scene through their ownership of the cabarets and restaurants moved on to other activities, and there was work, more or less steady, for small bands everywhere. The classic New Orleans style became the style of choice. By the end of the decade, for New Orleans musicians the years turned into a hectic jazz band ball.

One of the New Orleans jazz vagabonds was trumpeter Wingy Manone. He had recorded with his New Orleans Boys in 1927 and was restlessly moving back and forth from Chicago to New York, wherever he could find a club that would hire him, sometimes spending days on the street and riding a freight to get from one town to the next. For Manone, the jazz band ball never stopped. His autobiography *Trumpet on the Wing*, written with Paul Vandervoort II and published in 1948, captured some of the feeling of these heady years. He had found a place to stay at 912 Wilson Avenue in Chicago, close to the lake, when he ran into pianist Art Hodes in the musicians' union. Hodes began hanging around Manone's place so much he was finally invited to move in.

Guys would come in town who played our kind of music, and look us up because we had the town wrapped up. They'd move right in and sleep on the floor because there were so many kicks goin' on. They had money to check into a hotel but they'd rather come up there where we were.

They spent all their money for records, gin, food, and stuff, and stayed right there.

Mrs. Broknick, the landlady, liked all the friends that I had who came there from out of town. She saw that they would never leave, and that they were gonna sleep on the floors, so she brought in extra blankets and pillows.

The boys would offer her money for the courtesy, but she wouldn't take it. She was a fine lady.

The victrola was going all day and all night long. When one batch of guys left another bunch would come in to say hello and never leave. If any of the big-time leaders wanted to find out where they could get a musician they called up Wingy's place, and there was always somebody there to answer the phone.[7]

Manone's autobiography is as colorful and as uniquely individual as Louis Armstong's, though it can be a little confusing to try to put together precise itineraries out of what were written as loose personal memoirs. One of his memories was of a Chicago recording session that he put together with the crowd hanging out in his apartment on Wilson Avenue. The group that made it to the studio included clarinetist Frank Teschemaker; George Snurpus, who played tenor sax; Art Hodes, piano; Ray Biondi, guitar; and drummer Augie Schellang, who had been with the Prima-Sharkey Orchestra at the Little Club. Manone remembered that they had rehearsal at Schellang's apartment, going through the two tunes over and over until the head arrangements got the sound he wanted, then the band broke off and "beat it" to the studio.

Some of the Chicago musicians were beginning to cross the racial lines that were still firmly in place everywhere. When the brilliant new pianist Earl Hines began working and recording with Jimmy Noone's Apex Orchestra in the spring of 1928, then a few weeks later with Armstrong's recording group, the Savoy Ballroom Five, he effectively changed the whole melodic style and rhythmic techniques of jazz piano. He and Manone enjoyed each other's company, and they sometimes managed to do what Manone called "guest shots." Each of them was a strong, extroverted personality; both sometimes showed up for their jobs wearing black raccoon-skin coats. Manone found that Hines's style was so advanced that sometimes when Hines had finished his piano introduction, Manone was so struck by what the pianist had just invented that he stood there holding his trumpet, silent with admiration, and Hines had to begin the introduction again.

The New Orleans instrumentalists who would become the nucleus of the Bob Crosby Orchestra in 1935 had also found that they could do better if they got out of town and went north. Drummer Ray Bauduc, the precocious son of band

WINGY MANONE, 1938.

leader Jules Bauduc, left in 1927 to join Joe Venuti's group in New York. Eddie Miller, who had for a brief time played tenor saxophone in the final incarnation of The Owls, left at the beginning of the Depression to join Ben Pollack's orchestra in New York. Guitarist Nappy Lamare, who had also spent some months with The Owls, and done his first recording with Johnny Hyman's Bayou Stompers, was also working in New York, and would join Bauduc and Miller with the Crosby orchestra.

The Bob Crosby Orchestra was to become for the late 1930s what the Luis Russell was for the early 1930s: a refuge for New Orleans musicians and their unabashed enthusiasm for their hometown's musical flair. It began as a cooperative band led by instrumentalists who had been part of Ben Pollack's orchestra but were now freelancing with other groups in New York. In an atypical, businesslike move they brought in vocalist Bob Crosby, the younger brother of the extremely popular singer, film star, and radio personality Bing Crosby, as the band's nominal "leader." With a series of successful recordings—including their rousing tribute to their New Orleans roots, "South Rampart Street Parade"—they held their position as one of the most successful of the large swing orchestras until the coming of World War II effectively ended the swing band era. Their recordings in the late 1930s often caught some of the New Orleans strut, particular the sessions by the small group drawn from the orchestra that was known as the Bobcats. For the Bobcats recording date in October 1938, five of the musicians in the studio were New Orleanians—Fazola, Miller, Lamare, and Bauduc along with trumpeter Sterling Bose, who had been part of the New Orleans jazz scene as the cornetist with the Original Crescent City Jazzers in 1924.

The small clubs taking over the role of the old 1920s dance palaces were suited to the new small jazz groups who brought their musicality into the American entertainment mix. It was the New Orleans style that worked best; the rhythmic excitement, the flow of solos and the relaxed humor of the vocals. For several years the New Orleans style, as refocused by the Chicagoans, became a kind of musical *lingua franca* for a generation of musicians. With all of the new attention to the music in New York, even Sharkey Bonano was drawn away from New Orleans. With his Sharks of Rhythm, a small band that included his friend from the 1920s, trombonist Santo Pecora, he finished the 1930s working in a series of New York clubs. Louis Prima, the younger brother of Leon Prima, who had been Bonano's partner in the Prima-Sharkey Orchestra at the Little Club, was also having considerable success with the combination of New Orleans trumpet and unabashed vocals. With his wife Keely Smith he would become an entertainment fixture in Las Vegas until his death.

Wingy Manone continued to shift back and forth from New York to Chicago, settling as long as there was work, but he was becoming more and more a fixture in the New York club scene. He managed to keep recording steadily, slowly building the personal commercial niche that would last him through the rest of his career. No one was making much money from their recordings—the dance singles they were turning out sold for thirty-five cents—but the emphasis on popular songs meant that sometimes one of the bands might have a jukebox hit that could help them find club work. For his session in August 1934 Manone put together an eclectic group that included veteran musicians working beside younger performers. The clarinetist was a young Artie Shaw, and the pianist for two numbers was Jelly Roll Morton, one of the handful of occasions when the idiosyncratic Morton was hired by another leader. Morton's playing was skilled and professional, but Manone didn't use him again.

Manone seemed to be sailing through the 1930s with at least a degree of success when, to everyone's surprise including his own, he had a hit record. "I got a chance to make the record that really made a big man out of me, 'Isle of Capri.' I have to admit, now, however, that when I waxed 'Ol' Capra' I had no idea it would be so popular. When I loused up the lyrics I was just doing it for laughs. But, man, that record sold over a drillion copies."[8]

For the session in March 1935 Manone used three New Orleans friends, Ray Bauduc, Eddie Miller, and Nappy Lamare, along with bassist Harry Goodman, clarinetist Matty Matlock, and pianist Gil Bowers.

Ray Bauduc was the boy who gave me my beat. He gave me that New Orleans drop, that I had to have, to get gone, When I wanted to get feelin' just right, I'd tell him, "Man play those rims for me like you do for Eddie Miller."

Bauduc always wore his hat when working on a record date, and on the last master, when we were going for a good one, I'd tell him to put his hat on sideways, New Orleans style, and that would do it.[9]

With "Capri" a solid hit, Manone went home, and the reception, as he saw it, was something like what the town had given Louis Armstrong that summer of 1931.

> *A thousand pounds of people had come down to the station to meet me, and when I got off the Pullman they all started singing "Ol' Capra." Man, the tears came to my eyes to think that so many fine people liked me.*
>
> *As soon as the welcoming festivities were over they rushed me into a big Cadillac convertible with the top down. With a parade and a band behind, they buzzed me down Canal Street, with a police escort, to the Roosevelt Hotel, the best in town.*
>
> *The trip was about ten blocks, and as the train pulled in about noon a lot of people were on the streets. As we went down Canal, Rampart, Common, and Baronne they waved at me, sitting up there like a king on his throne. I had my horn in my hand and waved back.*

For Manone, the high point of the parade came when the procession drove past his uncle's pawn shop on Rampart Street. His uncle called out that if he got stranded in town, he'd be glad to lend him a little money on his trumpet.

The moments of easy joyousness, however, were few and far between for most of New Orleans as the Depression held its grip on the country. Through the hot summers most of the picnic grounds were empty, more of the clubs had closed, and even the brass bands swung out on the streets on fewer Sundays. The excitement over the New Orleans style of small-band jazz that was drawing customers into clubs in New York and Chicago was having little effect on New Orleans and its casual neighborhood dancing audiences. In the spring of 1939, the jazz writer Charles Edward Smith spent several weeks in New Orleans, as part of the research he and other writers were doing for the book *Jazzmen*. He found the inspiration for his writing not only by talking with the veteran musicians who could take him back to the old days, but also by hanging out in the clubs that still were open. He stayed through the Mardi Gras, and found that it was the only time he had an opportunity to hear much music, since so much of the city was silent. Some of the older names still were playing. He found trumpeter Abbie Brunies, many years after his success at the Halfway House, leading a band at a Bourbon Street club where they first played for a floor show, and then had time for a few numbers of their own. "Abbie . . . had a spot in the French Quarter, playing cabaret shows for the tourist trade. Between shows they tried to play standards, but the spirit was missing. The band just couldn't pull together. You could say it was because Ray Bauduc was in Chicago with Crosby or because Fano Roppolo was with Primo, but that would be unfair to Abbie's drummer and clarinet player. Actually, you couldn't expect much inspiration from a band whose members felt dangerously close to economic insecurity."[10]

Smith found the situation for the city's black musicians was equally bleak. "Except during Mardi Gras, most of the better Negro musicians will be working intermittently, if at all. They will tell you that Big Eye Louis Nelson is down to the Gypsy Tea Room two nights a week. Maybe you'll find him there and maybe not."[11]

Smith also spent some time with pianist Fats Pichon, who had worked on and off with Sidney Desvigne on the excursion boats, and had taken his own groups on the boats for several seasons. When Smith met him, Pichon was mostly arranging for bands who were on tour from out of town and needed a score for a new song that was being requested, but Pichon still played for dancers leading his own hot group.

> Walter Pichon . . . has a little band of his own at the Crescent Billiard Hall, a white place frequented by the best shaggers in town. Occasionally in the South you see a shag that's right on the floor, not the bouncing kind that makes a Manhattan dance hall a major hazard. And you can, in places like the Crescent, see dancing that is free from exhibitionism. Sometimes when the trumpet player, John Brunious, plays Dippermouth in a clean style, a jitterbug climbs the chandelier but aside from such lapses, the dancing is equal to the music. Usually when Brunious reaches the third chorus of Dippermouth the kids have stopped shagging and formed a semi-circle around the band platform.[12]

One of Smith's most illuminating encounters was with Steve Lewis, the pianist with the Piron orchestra who had been popular enough for Tranchina's Restaurant to advertise his appearances with the orchestra just by announcing that "Steve" would be there. Pichon had told Smith to look for him. Since it was the Mardi Gras season, nearly every musician in the city was working somewhere, and Smith found Lewis in a modest saloon in the French Quarter, close to Canal Street. Smith had already gotten to know Jelly Roll Morton in Washington, D.C., and it was the similarities of Lewis's playing to Morton's that first caught Smith's attention.

> . . . on a little red piano with the inevitable sugar can to catch tips he played sometimes for himself, sometimes according to the whims of the patrons. He was something like Jelly Roll Morton and it was hard to figure out at first. Then one realized it was the way he used chords. Watch a man's left hand and you see if he is a musician,. Jelly Roll said then, and watching Steve brought it back. How he got that half-pint piano to respond to his fingers was a constant puzzle to the customers, who would group about, drinks in hand, asking him to do that last chorus of St. Louis Blues over again, so they could see how it was done. Steve looked up with a leonine and very Latin grin, spoke with a slightly Creole intonation, putting his fingers on the keyboard. "They played this a long time ago," Steve said softly, without looking up again.[13]

In that spring of 1939, it still was possible to drift back into the first decades of New Orleans jazz. Smith finally was able to catch up with Big Eye Louis Nelson DeLisle at the Gypsy Tea Room, where for most of the night he and the band accompanied a floor show. When the band had a few numbers of their own, DeLisle agreed to try the old Picou chorus on "High Society," even though it wasn't a piece he played a lot and he was having trouble with his clarinet. DeLisle was only in his mid-fifties, but to Smith he was one of the links he hoped would lead him back to that first generation of ragtime musicians. "They went through the piece twice. Girls pushed back the portieres that separated the cabaret from the bar, stood in the doorway and listened. The dark-complexioned bartender (all the bartenders and managers seemed to be either Sicilians or Creoles) poked his head through the little service window, looking over at one of the girls. Suddenly on the last chorus, Louis was playing the *real* one, the one he had learned from Picou. When he asked afterward if that was all right, there was a gleam of self-satisfaction in his eye. He knew it was all right. He was just making conversation."[14]

In one of his most emotional encounters Smith found trumpeter Kid Rena playing in a taxi dance hall. Like taxi dance halls everywhere, the band at the place where Rena was working played from ten at night until almost dawn, without intermission, seven nights a week. The fiery high-note performer, who had challenged everyone in the city only a decade before, lost his lip in the long hours of the dance hall.

About eleven o'clock one of the boys left the platform to get a big container of black coffee. The band went right on. When the coffee came, each had a few sips while the others played. Kid Rena said that his lips began to feel the mouthpiece after that first drink of coffee. Around one o'clock he'd have another, and by then he'd have an embrouchure. The whole band felt it. Instead of changing the tune they'd stop, begin, stop, begin,—three or four choruses of the same number with pauses between! For the last chorus of Royal Garden Blues, *Kid Rena stood up and took it, a clean curving tone held taut, building up the chorus, the band coming up hard with the rhythm. In the semi-darkness you could see the gleam of someone in the band smiling at him.*[15]

As New Orleans came to the end of the Depression years, the excitement and creativity of the music had become as frayed and as worn as the city itself, waiting for some change in its fortunes.

19

Glories, Remembered

I haven't touched the trombone for a little more than a year, except last New Year's Eve, when I had an engagement at a country club. I tried to get into shape in seven days, but after the second I gave that up, knowing what a New Year's Eve society engagement was for work. I therefore picked up the fiddle, directed and looked wise and made three hours overtime which I could not have done on my horn, as my lips would have been swollen ten times their size after one hour's work.

EDDIE EDWARDS, TROMBONIST FOR THE ORIGINAL DIXIELAND
JAZZ BAND, WRITING TO NICK LA ROCCA ON JUNE 8, 1936[1]

New Orleans, with its complicated past and its ambivalent attitudes toward the present, had always seemed to stand outside the American mainstream, but by the 1930s the flow of ideas and fads and musical trends between New Orleans and the rest of the country had become less of a viable exchange. The dominance of nationally syndicated radio and the steadily widening influence of the movies, produced in Hollywood, were turning the city, along with the rest of the nation, into a passive audience for a popular culture that was almost exclusively created somewhere else. The city's unique jazz traditions continued to be part of its self-definition, but the consciousness of its role in the development of new jazz styles was also changing. The old dance halls had largely fallen silent, and more and more of the corner clubs were depending on the ubiquitous jukeboxes, with live music only one or two nights a week. There was a new dance craze, the fast "lindy" step called "jitterbugging," but it was an athletic step that needed a great deal of room, and most of the small New Orleans clubs posed signs saying "No Jitterbugging!" on the walls. For years New Orleans had gotten by with a complicated, flailing dance step for fast tempos with the couple hugging close as they stayed out of the way of each other's flying feet on the cramped dance floors. Exhibition-style jitterbug competitions were restricted to occasional dances at one of the larger auditoriums.

With the stream of recordings and late-night broadcasts by orchestras playing in all of the new swing idioms, it was impossible for local musicians to shut out the sounds of the music crowding around them. Writer Tom Bethel noted that in 1936 alone the city's black audiences had an opportunity to hear the Duke Ellington and Jimmy Lunceford Orchestras in April, Cab Calloway in June, Don Redman's Orchestra and Louis Armstrong fronting the Luis Russell Orchestra (which included several New Orleanians) in August, and Lunceford again at the Pelican Roof Garden for Christmas Eve.[2] For the white musicians there was this same procession of artists who had national audiences for their recordings and personal appearances.

At the same time, however, the first generation of musicians who had shaped the city's first syncopated styles, and then developed them a step further into jazz, were in their forties and fifties now, and like musicians everywhere, they were beginning to look back on what they had done, even if the bands they had created no longer were together and many of them had almost stopped playing. The New Orleans musicians realized that their jazz style was still a personal expression for them.

There are many reasons why bands break up—irritations, jealousies, disappointments—but there seem to be just as many reasons why musicians who have put away their instruments often decide at some point that they left some things still unfinished, that they still have things they want to prove, at least to themselves—things they want to bring back to life. There always seem to be reasons for bringing old groups together again, even if there are feelings just as strong suggesting that they just forget the whole thing. But it isn't only the bands and their members who have this feeling of something left unfinished. As they slip into middle age, the same mood that affects the musicians also affects the people who hung on every note when everyone was considerably younger. Fans of the bands also shared this sense of the music as a source of their own identity— and the music they remembered so passionately was also something they had enjoyed. Why couldn't they experience the excitement one more time?

In the dead months of the mid-1930s, the impulse for several of the older generation of the early New Orleans artists to try to turn back the clock—to find some of the remembered glories—was also driven by some promise that going back to playing could help them economically. Nobody was making much money doing anything, and picking up their horns and playing again wouldn't leave them in worse shape than they were already. For most of them there was also an even more personal reason. They had loved playing, they had loved the sense of being part of a group, they had felt they were creating notes and harmonies that hadn't been there when they started—so why not give their music another try before the instrument went back into the closet and nobody could remember the arrangements anymore? With different degrees of success, and with as much diffidence as confidence, four of the important New Orleans artists and groups from the 1920s emerged again briefly in the midst of the Depression. The economic situation was as despairing as it had been for most of the decade, but perhaps they felt that it was already so bad it couldn't get any worse, and they had reached the age where they didn't have so many years when they could wait for some signs of prosperity.

It was one of the old fans of the Original Dixieland Jazz Band who stirred the fires in Nick La Rocca. With the collapse of his band and his own breakdown in the mid-1920s, La Rocca had left behind him the music that he and his band had created. He gave up music after his return from New York and went back to his old profession as a contractor and builder, offering his services for electrical rewiring. He managed to keep his business going despite the economic crash, and of the five members of the band who'd left New Orleans in 1916, he was the only one with a measure of financial security. Edwards and Sbarbaro were still trying to keep their musical careers going in New York, but for a period in the early thirties Edwards had been forced to operate a newsstand in Times Square, and though he found some musical work—mostly as an orchestra violinist—in the mid-thirties, he was working as a baseball coach a few hours a day for a YMCA boys' team. La Rocca had lost contact with Shields.

As H. O. Brunn wrote in his story of the band, the person who contacted La Rocca was not quite the usual fan, though he'd spent hours at Reisenweber's and he loved their music. During the months that they'd played there a salesman named Lew Gensler from the Packard automobile showroom across the street had been a regular listener. He was a competent pianist and songwriter, and had once tried to teach the band one of his songs. In the mid-1930s, working as New York agent for a Hollywood studio, Gensler was putting together a cast of performers for a major musical film, *The Big Broadcast of 1937.* He got in touch with his old musical favorites through their pianist, J. Russell Robinson, who was working in New York as a staff musician for N.B.C. A call to the major booking agency for jazz artists, the William Morris Agency, put him in touch with Robinson, who was excited at the prospect of appearing in a Hollywood musical and passed Gensler on to La Rocca in New Orleans.[3]

La Rocca, however, was in the middle of building two houses, working as his own carpenter, and there was no way he could consider Gensler's offer. In his correspondence with other members of the band after the breakup he had still been interested in what they all were doing, but he had been upset enough at leaving music himself that he hadn't paid attention to what was happening in the emerging swing craze. Like any popular music style that begins to reach a broad audience, the new sound had absorbed as many of the old sounds as it had reworked them. When La Rocca began listening to radio broadcasts, in many of the arrangements the swing bands were performing—bands often led by instrumentalists who had been playing the Original Dixieland Jazz Band's compositions a decade before—he heard much more of himself and Shields and the old band's strutting ensemble style than he had expected.

Record companies also had found that there was still interest from record buyers in the band's old material. George Brunies, the original trombone player for the New Orleans Rhythm Kings, led a session in New York using the Rhythm Kings name and including two other New Orleans musicians, trumpeter Wingy Manone and clarinetist Sidney Arodin. The four titles they recorded in September 1934 were all ODJB compositions, "Bluin' The Blues," "Ostrich Walk," "Original Dixieland One-Step," and "Sensation." La Rocca found himself agreeing with their old friend Gensler: perhaps they should try it again.

Most of La Rocca's recent correspondence with Edwards and Sbarbaro—who was now performing under the name of Tony Spargo—had dealt with disputes over the use of the band's name, and disagreements that still hung in the air about the copyrights of the compositions. Spargo, in fact, had done a recording session in New York in October 1935, using the band's name, of four pop tunes featuring the vocals of pianist Terry Shand. Edwards complained in a letter that Spargo had recently taken a band to a job in Princeton using their old name, and he'd even told the band's trombone player to sign autographs as "Eddie Edwards." Edwards seemed particularly upset because the trombone player didn't play very well.

Even with so many indications pointing to a new audience for their old music, La Rocca still hesitated. Without Shields he didn't feel it was worth making the try, because Shields's clarinet had been the featured instrument on most of the arrangements. He'd lost track of him when Shields had moved to Los Angeles, but his brothers and other members of Shields's family were still in New Orleans, and La Rocca went looking for them. Larry, he learned, had come back to town, but he hadn't played the clarinet for several years and he was working in a religious book store. La Rocca claimed later that when he saw his old band member again, Shields had his arms full of bibles. La Rocca also saw that, although he was in his early forties, Shields's hair had turned white.

Shields was hesitant about picking up the clarinet again, not sure that he could recover his old skills, and La Rocca also hadn't been playing, but he and Shields eventually began practicing together. They were first noticed playing again in public on May 19, 1936, at the Old Absinthe House on Bourbon Street in the French Quarter. There was a startled response from a journalist for the New Orleans *Item*, Mel Washburn, in his column four days later.

Tuesday night I was sitting in the Absinthe House watching the floor show . . . "And now," said Eddie Barber, the master of ceremonies, "we've got a treat for you . . . two boys from the most famous band in the world, Larry Shields and Nick La Rocca of the old Dixieland Jazz Band." What's this, I says to myself . . . what kind of sandy are they putting over . . . and then onto the floor comes Nick and Larry . . . in the flesh . . . and they swung into one of their old favorites. Boys and girls THAT was swing music . . . just a trumpet and clarinet . . .

*but how those boys went to town. Maybe they have had a twelve-year layoff
. . . but you'd never believe it listening to 'em . . . and you should have heard
the storm of applause they provoked from the pop-eyed audience . . . pop-eyed
because they couldn't believe that a white-haired grandpop like Larry could
make that clarinet screech, wail and sob as it was doing . . . or how that left-
handed trumpeter could get such a seductive swing into the rhythm as Nick
was doing; Later I asked 'em how come . . .*

*"We're not working here," explained Nick, "but we come down here two
or three times a week and go into the show, just to get in tune again . . . get our
lip up and wear off the rough edges that the last 12 years have given us."*[4]

When everyone from the old band was assembled again, the first rehearsals
were clumsy and discouraging. It was difficult for them to find their way back
to their old feel for each other's playing style. Lips and fingers had lost some
of their flexibility. But by the second day, they were picking up some of the old
feel for their ensemble. There were new publicity photos, with them posed in a
new swing-style pyramid, grouped with the other members of the touring band.
Shields was at the peak of the pyramid, clarinet pointed upward, his white hair
shining in the camera lights.

The band went out on tour again with an attractive entertainment package
that featured the original small ensemble performing in a show that opened and
closed with a large swing group, which also included all of the members of the
band. The recording sessions actually began early in September 1936 with the
thirteen-piece swing group, which performed as "Nick La Rocca and his Original
Dixieland Band." Shields was still the featured soloist, and his style, for these
arrangements, was more conspicuously modern, with a freedom and musicality
that would have blended comfortably into the arrangements of most of the new
swing bands.

As musical documents, the reunion and 1936 recordings of the five members
of the Original Dixieland Jazz Band are particularly significant for the light they
throw on the early period of the New Orleans jazz style. There was a dispute in
the studio: the recording engineers assumed that the group would use the bass
player who was appearing with them on the stage. The bass had been set up in
the studio and was already being checked for sound balance when La Rocca
objected. He insisted that the band's original sound should be documented on
record, performing the same arrangements they'd featured when they achieved
their first success nearly twenty years before. It is a revelation to hear essentially
what the first dancers heard in Reisenweber's Restaurant in 1917, now with modern studio techniques that made it possible to hear the band's complex ensemble.
The old recordings, though often exciting, never managed to get all of the band
into the record grooves at the same time.

What is immediately clear in the 1936 sessions, released under the name The
Original Dixieland Five, is what a good band they were. Jazz writers like Rudi

THE ORIGINAL DIXIELAND JAZZ
BAND, 1937. TOP PHOTO, FROM
LEFT: ORIGINAL FOUR MEMBERS:
EDWARDS, SBARBARO (SPARGO), LA
ROCCA, SHIELDS. BOTTOM PHOTO:
THE ADDED BASSIST IN THE BACK IS
HARRY BARTH; PIANIST J. RUSSEL
ROBINSON, WHO JOINED THE BAND IN
1919, IS TO THE RIGHT.

Blesh, who had heard them during that first 1917 engagement, always insisted that the effect of their new style when audiences heard it in person was overwhelming, that all of the vitality and brash strut the first critics described was still present on the modern recordings. With the 1936 studio techniques and microphones, however, it was also possible to follow the tight, responsive interweave between the three horns. Edwards's trombone part gave the ensemble much of its unity—his anticipation of the melody and the subtle reinforcement of the harmonic changes. He generally used higher voicing of the chords than many trombonists who followed him, and he also emphasized La Rocca's lead in his staccato phrasing, continually shifting the listener back to the trumpet for the beginning of the melodic shifts. Shields's playing still had its muscular flow, and his tone was as warm and supple. The most obvious changes in the new versions of their old repertoire, though they were subtle and varied from piece to piece, occurred in the rhythm. Because both Sbarbaro and Robinson had been playing regularly, they sometimes had a newer feel in their beat. Perhaps unconsciously, they now phrased some tempos with a suggestion of an emphasis on the afterbeat. As one of the band's strongest defenders, discographer Brian Rust, wrote in his notes to an extensive reissue of their music,

> *To be sure, there are adjustments and a few alterations between the 1918 versions and these of 18 years later, but there can be no doubting that the original concept and the spirit that breathed life into it, are still there. In some ways, these 1936 performances are even more zestful than their 1918 predecessors; the tempo is somewhat slower, but La Rocca's gleeful whoops in the last chorus of* Tiger Rag *are not heard on the Aeolian, Victor, Columbia or OKeh versions, and the rhythm section of Robinson and Sbarbaro is fully audible throughout. Shields gets a long solo passage on* Original Dixieland One Step, *but it is interesting to note that Joe Jordan's* That Teasin' Rag *is still used as the trio strain, with no label credit—and no lawsuit.*[5]

Their advertising featured the name they'd adopted for the tour, "Nick La Rocca and his Original Dixieland Band," and the prominence of La Rocca's name was a forewarning of the tensions that soon arose in the group, despite a very enthusiastic response to their music. To bring that band back and support the first months of the tour it had been necessary to find financial backing, and La Rocca had invested some of his own money in the venture. The original members of the band had agreed that the money they earned would be divided into equal shares, but as an investor La Rocca insisted on having two shares. Despite the tensions, they stayed on the road for a year, and filmed an historic segment for a *March of Time* presentation that recreated their first studio recording. It is surprising that they managed to hold out for a year, but they were so successful and the salaries so substantial that they hesitated for months before there was a final quarrel. When they broke up for the last time, La Rocca, Shields, and Robinson went separate ways, and never appeared together again.

Edwards and Sbarbaro still worked together in New York into the 1950s, keeping some of the spirit alive in their uninhibited playing. Sometimes I'd encounter Sbarbaro riding the subway, standing beside the door of the subway car with his large bass drum in its canvas case beside him. If Edwards was with the band at one of the downtown barn-like places that featured Dixieland, I'd hear the boisterous tone of his trombone before I went inside the door. Robinson resumed his career as a radio staff musician. Shields finally returned to California, where he continued to play occasionally with pick-up groups despite a serious heart condition. La Rocca went back to New Orleans to his construction business, still defending the band against the critical attacks on what they had created so many years before. As he stubbornly insisted in a letter to Rust, "I think the world of Louis Armstrong and all those great men who took jazz and carried it far, but I still say we were the first."[6]

All of the members of the old bands, when they began playing again, found that their role in the emerging small jazz ensembles had changed. They were no longer America's dance bands. Instead of the dance tempos and the emphasis on familiar melodies that had shaped their music a decade before, they now found themselves playing in "jazz clubs" with miniscule dance floors beside the bandstand, if they had any space for dancing at all. The New Orleans restaurants that had presented their dance music, like the Halfway House, with their fringe of tables at the edges of the large spaces for the dancers, were only a memory. The musicians found themselves on cramped bandstands, where they were expected to feature a jazz repertoire instead of the standard popular melodies they had been used to performing. Also, what they were presenting was in essence a jazz exhibition, and the emphasis was now on solos and on individual musicianship. The audience that had once danced to their rhythms was now crowding into large ballrooms to dance to the slow rhythms of the large swing orchestras, with their near-symphonic instrumental textures, or for the specialty numbers that accompanied the new "jitterbug" craze. The acrobatics of jitterbug style needed more space than the small clubs could provide.

The familiar name of the New Orleans Rhythm Kings, the younger band that had shaped the Original Dixieland Band's sound for a new audience in a Chicago cellar in the early 1920s, had, like the ODJB itself, never quite gone away. George Brunies used the name for the September 1934 sessions in New York, and revived the old New Orleans standard "Panama," along with the band's old hit "Tin Roof Blues." For a subsequent session in February 1935, Brunies borrowed the old name again, coming into the studio with a group which was closer to the Chicago style, with cornetist Muggy Spanier and drummer Gene Krupa, but kept some of the New Orleans flavor with tenor player Eddie Miller.

The original trumpet player with the New Orleans Rhythm Kings, Paul Mares, had stopped playing for some time after the band broke up in 1925, when he returned home to go into the family's hides and fur business. He and his wife opened a restaurant in New Orleans; as the Depression tightened its hold, they moved back to Chicago and opened the popular Bar-B-Cue Restaurant near the Loop. He began playing again, though on a casual basis. Mares had always been affable and self-effacing, an easy friend to many of the Chicago musicians. He also seemed to get along with most other Chicagoans. Lee Collins was busy in the new Chicago jazz clubs in the mid-1930s, and he was leading a quartet at the Casa Blanca Club on Clark Street on the North Side, when one night he had a surprising glimpse of just how many people knew Mares.

I remember one night a squad car rolled up in front of the Casa Blanca and a couple of cops came in and asked if I was Lee Collins. When I said, yes, I was, they told me to get my horn and come with them outside to their car. As we were getting in the policeman asked me if I knew Paul Mares—he was the famous white cornet player that led the New Orleans Rhythm Kings back in the 1920s. I did know him, of course, and it turned out that Paul was opening a place of his own and wanted me there. When I got there I found Baby Dodds,

George Brunis, Muggsy Spanier, and some of the guys out of Bob Crosby's band all sitting on the bandstand. Paul was acting as bartender and blowing horn at the same time. From ten o'clock that night until eight the next morning we played all the great New Orleans standards. But my boss was some angry with me when I went to work the next night.[7]

Mares had an opportunity to record again in January 1935; Brunies was now using the old name of the band, so Mares instead chose their original name, the Friar's Society Orchestra. There were only four titles, and more of the session musicians were from Chicago than New Orleans, but Mares's playing had a fierce, insistent return to the fire of the best of the Rhythm Kings recordings. The essential quality of his playing hadn't changed, but from the first dominating phrases it was clear that at thirty-five Mares was a much better musician than he'd been at twenty-three, when he'd made his first recordings.

There were two New Orleanians in the group with him, and each of them added a distinct New Orleans tonality to the ensemble's overall sound. The trombonist was Santo Pecora, who had been with Mares for the first revival of the band in New Orleans in 1925, a year and a half after their breakup. The clarinetist for the new session was Omer Simeon, who had studied with Lorenzo Tio Jr. but had left New Orleans with his family and moved to Chicago before he was experienced enough to play with groups at home. His first recording sessions were with Jelly Roll Morton's Red Hot Peppers. Simeon played in a fluid New Orleans style, though he had absorbed many of his New Orleans mannerisms from Barney Bigard, who was featured with Duke Ellington's Orchestra. At the time of the session, Simeon was working with Earl Hines's Orchestra at the Park Terrace Hotel. The rest of the band were Chicagoans, among the best known and most exciting of the jazz-oriented younger musicians. The rhythm section included the brilliant pianist Jess Stacy, a few months before he joined Benny Goodman's Orchestra, and drummer George Wettling, whose playing combined an insistent push and an impeccable sense of timing.

The band recorded one of the old hits of the Rhythm Kings, "Maple Leaf Rag," and it is illuminating to listen to the two versions. Each of them was taken at a very fast tempo, and Mares's trumpet led the ensemble. The 1923 version, however, had only piano and drums in the rhythm section and their sound, acoustically recorded, couldn't equal the headlong drive of Stacy's piano, Marvin Saxbe's guitar, Pat Pattison's bass, and Wettling's drums. In 1923 the tempo was just a little beyond Roppolo and he was often enough off in his ensemble passages to be noticeably falling behind the beat in three or four sections. It was also not one of Brunies's most coherent performances. The tempo may also have made him a little uncomfortable, and for long stretches he fell back on basic chording, only occasionally suggesting one of his usually unified trombone counters to the lead.

In the 1935 recordings Santo Pecora's trombone was as coherent and as intrusive as Mares's trumpet. For the session they played two uptempo numbers,

"Maple Leaf Rag" and "Nagasaki": both moved with the relentless energy they'd borrowed from the Chicagoans. Pecora prowled the arrangements, shifting from broad legato passages to the kind of biting staccato, off rhythm figures that were characteristic of Eddie Edwards's playing. There was also an alto saxophone, the little-known but exciting Boyce Brown, and the arrangements involved the entire band, backing the solo passages with another horn or Pecora's trombone. In the center of the storm, Mares's role was to insist on the melody—and insinuate the rhythmic potential of the melody. He shifted accents, changed tone and vibrato, and drove the rhythm with a headlong energy. Like Shields's playing with the augmented swing group that was part of the revival of the Original Dixieland Band, Mares's new recordings sustained everything that had made his playing distinctive a decade before, but effortlessly brought it into the modern epoch.

The Dodds brothers, Johnny and his younger brother Warren "Baby," had never entirely stopped playing, even in the most chaotic years of the Depression. They had stayed in Chicago—after spending the 1920s there, it was Chicago that was home, and no longer New Orleans. In the 1930s they were part of the same shuffle of musicians drifting in and out of the small jazz clubs. There was also a small but determined crowd of friends who had never gotten over the effect that Johnny's old recordings had on them, and they followed him in his shifts from job to job, a kind of impromptu jazz circuit that was giving work to a number of displaced Crescent City musicians.

In the wave of interest in the old New Orleans jazz roots that helped return the Original Dixieland Band to the scene, Dodds also had an opportunity to record again. For the first session in January 1938 he was in New York, and the band with him were the members of John Kirby's very popular sextet, with one substitution. Pianist Lil Armstrong, who had been with Dodds in the old King Oliver band and worked with him many times over the years, took over the piano bench from Mary Lou Williams, the group's usual pianist and arranger. The band was called Johnny Dodds and his Chicago Boys. Two years later, however, probably through the continued interest in the people who were his steadfast fans (among them William Russell and two friends, Barbara Reid and John Steiner), Dodds had an opportunity to record again, this time with a band full of New Orleanians. The trumpeter who had worked with him on many of his 1920s recordings, Natty Dominique, was back; Preston Jackson played trombone, Richard M. Jones was the pianist, Lonnie Johnson, guitarist, Johnny Lindsay, bassist, and his brother Baby was the drummer. Under the name Johnny Dodds and his Orchestra, there were two titles, both of them characteristic blues, taking their names from their New Orleans past. "Red Onion Blues" memorialized the old club at the corner of Julia and South Rampart, and "Gravier Street Blues" used the name of one of the streets in the neighborhood where Louis Armstrong had grown up. Dodds's playing on the two blues was in his classic blues mode, the same throbbing, intense, decisive blues playing that had dominated his numerous small band recordings. A decade later, his tone and the mood of his playing had darkened. Unlike Shields with the large touring group, Dodds made no effort to adapt his playing to the lighter, more agile clarinet sound of the swing bands. With only a few notes of the new recordings it was immediately, insistently obvious that this was Johnny Dodds and that his feet were planted on the same ground where they'd been for most of his career. The recordings were to be his last. He died less than two months later.

If the 1936 recordings by the ODJB were, from the point of view of musical history, the most important of these later documents of the New Orleans style, perhaps the most sensitively musical of all the attempts to go back to the old glories was the group of ten piano solos Jelly Roll Morton recorded in New York in 1939 that were issued as a set under the title *New Orleans Memories*. Like so much of Jelly Roll's career, the way back to the recording studio had taken many twisting bypaths. His last session for Victor Records had been in the fall of 1930, and it had been obvious for some years that he hadn't succeeded in making the stylistic transition from his small group singles to a large band arranging style. He was still relatively young—he was only in his late thirties when he recorded his last commercial singles—but he was already becoming identified with a New Orleans that was bathed in nostalgia and had taken on the aura of myth, rather than commercial reality. Through the early 1930s he stayed in his Harlem apartment, hustling in the pool rooms when he could find someone he could take for a little money, trying to find jobs for orchestras he intended to put together, standing on Harlem street corners talking to any musicians who happened to come past, and covering sheets of music paper with sketches for arrangements. Moses Asch, who owned the small Asch label at that time, remembered seeing him often in the lobby of the Brill Building near Times Square where most of the music publishers had their offices,. He was always well dressed and kept to himself. He was waiting for any royalties that might arrive for his compositions that were being recorded again.

For Nick La Rocca the problem with the new histories of jazz that had forgotten him, along with his band and their accomplishments, was the effect of the interviews given to the young writers by older New Orleans musicians like Bunk Johnson and Clarence Williams. In the angry notes La Rocca added to the margins of the articles he encountered he railed at "lying Negroes." Morton's problems were more pervasive and troubling. He wrote in a letter in June 1940 to a friend and business associate, Roy Carew: "There is a new system being used to put every one out of the music business but Jews. Since the Jews are in a dominating position at this time, they are in control of the Union, radio stations, publishers, booking agents & etc. either Jews & Communists. The Union officials now in office was considered Communist before they entered office & believe me they have put most everyone out of business but the Jews or Communists."[8]

Morton had also caused some of his problems himself. For a period late in the 1920s he had been associated in a publishing venture with an agent and music publisher named Harrison Smith. Smith claimed that Morton sold twenty-eight of their company's songs, many of them by a composer named Ben Garrison, to Victor Records for enough money to get his car back from the finance company. As Smith recalled his difficulties with Morton, "He rode all around New York for about a year with Ohio plates on his car, so the finance company couldn't get him. The finance company was looking for him because he borrowed $1000 on a Lincoln car. They finally found him. He sold a lot of my tunes to Victor Records. Victor told me to give them to Jelly Roll to look them over to see if he wanted to record them. So he sold twenty-eight tunes to Victor for $700—my tunes. That was to get his car back. So I told the Victor manager, 'You bought stolen property.' Oh, it didn't mean anything in the old days, you know."[9]

Among the disputed titles were several that Morton did record, including "Fickle Fay Creep," "My Little Dixie Home," and "Smiling The Blues Away." Smith later brought suit against the Radio Corporation of America, the parent company of Victor Records, demanding restitution and the rights to issue the material himself as the original publisher. His suit was upheld and he released several of the Morton recordings that had used Garrison's material on his own small label. Smith also maintained that an Italian-American musician named Hector Marchese gave Morton a number of his compositions to arrange, mistakenly assuming that if he sent registered copies to himself that this would constitute a copyright. Among the material Smith claimed Marchese had given to Morton, one was a song that became one of Morton's most enduring later recordings, "Sweet Substitute."

By the mid-1930s Morton had established himself in Washington, managing a deteriorating upstairs night club on U Street that went through a number of names, among them The Jungle Inn or The Music Box. It had a piano and a small dance floor, and the clientele was mostly neighborhood drinkers. By this time he was also being discovered by some of the enthusiastic fans who were to collaborate on the book *Jazzmen*, including Charles Edward Smith, who was working in Washington at the time, and William Russell. The very young Ertegun brothers, Nesuhi and Ahmet, who would go on to found the legendary Atlantic Records label, often climbed the stairs to listen to Morton perform. In a letter to Russell in 1967 Smith commented, "Some people got the idea that only whites visited Jelly's club, but of course that was untrue. I remember many a night of mixed audiences, one when some Howard University people, including Sterling Brown, were there and he and Jelly exchanged blues verses."[10] Brown was one of the most accomplished of the writers associated with the Harlem Renaissance, and his abiding interest in black vernacular culture included the folk blues.

As word spread, other people with some interest in jazz history began dropping by, and Morton greeted them with unfailing courtesy. He was already suffering from asthma and a heart condition, but he attempted to function as the entertainment, the host, and the manager of the depressed establishment at the same time. Occasionally a small swing group played at the club, and on those nights Morton worked the room as a host. He still could be moody and temper-amental, and one evening he was stabbed by an angry customer. Although the wound wasn't serious, it contributed to his mounting worries. In his perpetual hope of making some kind of comeback, he also rehearsed with a semiprofes-sional band in nearby Baltimore; their home recordings, with Morton playing a small electric organ, were released many years later.

The first step toward what would be an important reevaluation of his old career and at the same time the beginning of his new role as an unforgettable raconteur of the New Orleans past came in May of 1938, when Alan Lomax, the young director of the recently established Folklore Division of the Library of Congress, asked Morton to play some of his compositions and tell a little about his life for the Folklore Division. The circumstances that brought him to the small auditorium in the Library of Congress were among the few good things that happened to Morton during this period. Morton's paranoia about what he considered to be the theft of his compositions and performance styles had grown as he watched other artists whose careers he had followed from their rough beginnings achieve the kind of success he dreamed of for himself. He decided that he might get some help from the Library of Congress, since it was there that copyrights were registered, and somehow he was given an opportunity to talk with Alan Lomax. Alan and his father, John Lomax, had been collecting folk songs for years, publishing them in popular song collections in versions that they sometimes copyrighted in their own names, which meant that Lomax had con-siderable experience with questions about copyrights of traditional material.

Lomax at this point actively disliked both jazz and the blues, which he felt were destroying the country's heritage of Anglo-American folk song. As he wrote later, ". . . jazz was my worst enemy. Through the forces of radio, it was wiping out the music that I cared about—American traditional folk music."[11] Morton had dressed in his best suit and tie for his foray into the official realm of music copyrights, which made Lomax even more uncomfortable. "I looked at him with considerable suspicion. But I thought I'd take this cat on." What interested Lomax was the opportunity to find out ". . . how much folk music a jazz musician knows. The first recording began by [my] asking if he knew 'Alabama Bound.' He played me the most beautiful 'Alabama Bound' that I had ever heard."

In his extensive notes to the award-winning CD boxed set of the complete Library of Congress recordings, John Szwed quoted Lomax's excited decision to follow up his hunch about Morton's musical memories.

> I said, "Just a minute." We were on the stage at the Coolidge Auditorium. [Busts] of Beethoven and Brahms were there. We were where the chamber music of the United States was being played. Jelly Roll felt that was just the proper setting for him . . . He wasn't the least bit awed by that. I ran all the way upstairs into the office of my chief—Chief of the Music Division—and said, "Harold, we have absolutely a great jam here. I want to get permission to use

fifty blank aluminum discs. I think he'll have something to say." I think they probably cost about $100, maybe $200 to record this man. On the way back down I decided to do a full-scale interview. I was at top-speed. . . . I had a bottle of whisky in my office. I put it on the piano. . . . I sat down on the floor, looked up, and said, "Jelly Roll, where did you come from and where did it all begin?" He then began to play the piano and talk. It came out of nowhere, the fact that he decided to do that. We hadn't agreed on it at all. Sort of half closing his eyes, he gave that immortal definition of his family, and New Orleans.[12]

In their first sessions together it was clear that Lomax hadn't any idea of what he'd gotten himself into, and his questions and his approach to jazz as a musical genre got in the way more than they opened out the subject. Morton, however, seized the opportunity, and the sessions went on until July, whenever his health made it possible for him to get to the Library.

The result of his hours in the Library auditorium is one of the vital documents of American cultural history. The complete sessions, lasting more than twelve hours in total, grew into a rich saga of a part of the American past that seemed to have already become lost to the relentless passage of time. Morton related stories he'd heard as a boy, described the musical life of New Orleans when he was a teenager, and played songs he said he'd heard from the musicians who were part of wandering underworld of ragtime entertainment when he began his own travels. He also performed his own personal cache of compositions in extended, freely inventive solo improvisations. The material, in the beginning, was simply there in the archive, on the original 12-inch acetate discs, and anyone with a serious interest in Morton who visited the archive could listen to the original aluminum discs that Lomax had recorded.

The war years interrupted the revival of interest in New Orleans music, but there was immediate pressure on the archive to allow the material to be commercially released when the war ended in 1945. Finally a small, independent company named Circle Records, owned by jazz critic and art historian Rudi Blesh, managed to clear the necessary releases with the Morton estate and find a way through the regulations that controlled the use of what was in essence material owned by all of the people of the United States. Blesh was then living, for part of the year, with a woman named Harriet Janis, who with her husband Sidney Janis owned and directed the Janis Gallery, a prestigious New York gallery that consistently presented new and challenging art. Blesh lived in a cluttered basement apartment on New York's Lower East Side, where my wife and I often visited them. He asked Harriet—who was called Hansi—to edit the material on the discs into albums that could be presented as musical "chapters" of Morton's story.

The twelve albums that Hansi compiled from the original sessions were released in a series on 12-inch Circle 78 r.p.m. singles, in a limited edition that quickly became coveted collector's items. She made it clear that she left some of the material off the releases, and she didn't hesitate to put together albums that she felt had a theme, emphasizing different aspects of what Morton had created, giving the albums imaginative titles like *Bad Man Ballads* or *The Spanish Tinge*. The first album was titled *Jazz Started in New Orleans . . .* The blend of music and story as she presented it, however, lost none of Morton's complex personality, his unique memories of what he had heard in his youth, or his pianistic abilities. When the complete original recordings were made available in 2005 on CD in a beautifully presented, Grammy Award–winning package by Revenant Records, it was clear to all of us who had grown up with the Circle albums—later issued on LP—that Hansi had done us an important service. Her sensitive sorting and assembling had given the long sessions a coherence that was almost lost when the old discs simply rolled by.

The interest that had grown up around jazz, now that for the moment it was commercially the most successful new musical style in the world, turned its attention to the past, and the success of the new recordings by the Original Dixieland Jazz Band became an economic incentive for other companies. Many of the visitors who climbed the stairs to Morton's club in Washington were trying to interest one of the major companies in new recordings, and Morton himself had been actively proselytizing his own cause with indignant letters to the press claiming that he had been the inventor of "jazz and stomps," and suggesting in interviews that he was the "only living fountainhead."

The efforts finally succeeded in September 1939, when Bluebird Records, a Victor subsidiary, brought him back into the studio with a pick-up group of "Dixieland" instrumentalists that included four New Orleanians: soprano saxophonist Sidney Bechet, clarinetist Albert Nicholas, bassist Wellman Braud, and drummer Zutty Singleton. The other musicians were trumpeter Sidney DeParis, trombonist Claude Jones, tenor saxophonist Happy Caldwell, and guitarist Lawrence Lucie. The group was titled Jelly Roll Morton's New Orleans Jazzmen. Morton sang on three of the arrangements, played the piano, and sketched the arrangements. The records had an enthusiastic reception even though musically they didn't have the distinction of the singles he'd recorded in the mid-1920s. The three reeds made it difficult to balance the ensemble, and there was already a hint of the musical mannerisms that were to overtake the Dixieland style as the years passed.

Lomax was acquainted with producer Gordon Mercer at a small company called Musicraft Records that was bringing out folk song material, and he suggested to Mercer that Morton might do something for the company in the same style as the sessions he'd recorded with him. Mercer was enthusiastic about the concept, but about the same time he moved to a new and even smaller company, General Records. Morton had returned to New York, where he was living with his wife Mabel in Harlem, and Mercer asked Charles Edward Smith to work with him to select a the group of solo recordings to create a *New Orleans Memories*

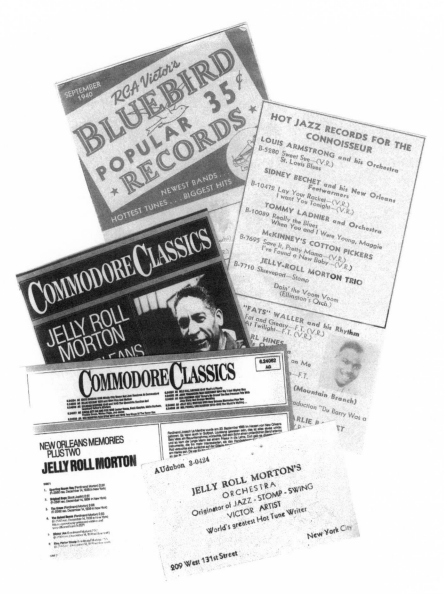

JELLY ROLL MORTON MAKES A COMEBACK. BUSINESS CARDS, A BLUEBIRD CATALOG ANNOUNCEMENT, AND AN LP OF A NEW RELEASE OF THE NEW ORLEANS MEMORIES SINGLES. COLLAGE BY THE AUTHOR.

album. Smith was also asked to write an essay that would be included with the package. The album's concept grew out of the long documentation Morton had already created in his Library of Congress recordings. Smith began visiting Morton regularly in his Harlem apartment, working with him in the choice of material to record, talking about the concept behind the album, and listening to

Morton talk. There was a grand piano in the apartment of a downstairs neighbor, and sometimes Morton would play through songs for him there.

The recordings were done in mid-December 1939, a little more than two months after the Bluebird band sessions; Mercer was the producer. The records were originally issued in a 78 r.p.m. album with Smith's notes. In almost a reprise of what he had done for the Library of Congress, Morton sang, played, and reminisced on one of the songs. Part of the effect was the intuitive pairing of the singles as they were originally released, and it is almost impossible to recreate their effect today, since the series of recordings is now presented in different formats. On the original five releases vocal selections were pressed on one side of the single and instrumental solos on the reverse, each chosen to complement some element of the vocal number. In their original order the singles were programmed:

Mamie's Blues/Original Rags	General 4001
Michigan Water Blues/The Naked Dance	General 4002
Buddy Bolden's Blues/The Crave	General 4003
Winin' Boy Blues/Mister Joe	General 4004
Don't You Leave Me Here/King Porter Stomp	General 4005

As the listener played through the singles, one at a time, turning each of them over to follow Morton's voice and then his solo piano, it was as though a personal history of those early years of New Orleans jazz were unfolding. The first of the songs, "Mamie's Blues"—with its spoken introduction, "This is the first blues I no doubt heard in my life. . ."—was nominated for many of the year's Best Recordings lists, and even today is often performed just as Morton created it so many years ago.

Smith had been asked to contribute to the album notes for Morton's new recordings for Bluebird, but he couldn't get to New York, so he asked Fred Ramsey to go to the studio and take notes for him. Ramsey's account was detailed and extensive, and he added a deeply personal reminiscence of his own about Morton. He had met Morton only two or three times, but he, Smith, and Gordon Mercer met with Morton on December 31, 1939, at the office of General Records on 7th Avenue to go over details about the *New Orleans Memories* album.

*Charlie had asked me to come up with him to talk about technical points and which records were to be included in Jelly's New Orleans Memories album, whether they should put in two more titles—*Sporting House Rag *and* Animule Ball. *Jelly sat and listened. He was completely his normal self, not his blustery self that a lot of people were accustomed to think of him being. And he had a sort of sad wistful quality about him, and I shan't forget that. When he was ready to leave, a warm smile lit up his face, driving out the coldness of the New York office building. Saying, "I wish you the happiest of New Years and may you all prosper," he picked up his briefcase and left.*[13]

In the notes he kept for Smith for the first Victor/Bluebird session, Ramsey commented that Morton never stopped playing, even when the rest of the band was taking a break. At first Ramsey thought it was a kind of entertainment on Morton's part; then he realized that Morton was playing all his compositions in the hope that the record executives in the control room would decide to include them in the session. When Ramsey thought back to that moment, he recognized the deep sense of sadness in Morton, beneath the bravado. "There was almost an acceptance of defeat about Jelly, although he never lost his punch, you know. You never really had the feeling that he was giving up. And I felt this in his playing that day at the Victor session. He started playing those long solos, and knowing they were never going to be recorded, and, well, it was sad, sad and tragic, and I had the feeling that this guy was going to be gone soon and all that stuff we're going to lose."[14]

The next month, January 1940, General recorded a series of band pieces with Morton leading a more flexible New Orleans ensemble, this time with trumpeter Red Allen playing a strong New Orleans lead. The singles were released under the general heading "General Tavern Tunes," designed for jukeboxes in places that featured jazz, which meant that the band could be more flexible than the all-star session for Bluebird the previous September. Another of Morton's enduring classics, his vocal on the Hector Marchese composition "Sweet Substitute," from the first of their three sessions, was the first release. The final session, on January 30, opened with a medium-tempo instrumental, "Dirty Dirty Dirty," which also took its place in the Morton canon. In the arrangement he took his final band solo, and played with a soft, understated tenderness, as though he knew himself that there wouldn't be an opportunity again.

In the summer Morton finally had a chance to present his own story of his role in the creation of jazz on the nationally broadcast program, "The NBC Chamber Music Society of Lower Basin Street." (N.B.C. are the initials of the National Broadcasting Corporation.) In the winter he made a long and arduous trip to Los Angeles, driving his two old-fashioned touring cars coupled together, in an attempt to sort out his personal affairs, and to be with Anita Gonzalez once again. His health never recovered, and after signing over to Anita his entire estate he died in her arms the next summer. Morton continues to be a controversial figure, but in his *New Orleans Memories* he achieved what all art attempts to do, to shape and to create its own reality. In many ways we will always experience New Orleans as Morton recreated it in his memories and his imagination.

20

Revival Days

. . . Louis's band was playing a Catholic dance in New Iberia, Louisiana, and I saw Louis talking with this old guy. After we started playing, I said to Louis, "Who's the old guy?"

Louis said, "That's Bunk Johnson."

I said, "I didn't even recognize him."

Louis said, "I didn't either."

GEORGE "POPS" FOSTER, REMEMBERING HIS 1937 MEETING WITH
VETERAN NEW ORLEANS TRUMPETER BUNK JOHNSON[1]

Two casual conversations that occurred about the same time, but in different places, were to change the perceptions of New Orleans and its music for all time, in ways that even now are difficult to sort out. By the late 1930s the fresh, uncomplicated spirit and communal store of musical ideas that had made the classic New Orleans ensemble style so distinctive had spread to a large audience that knew only the name, but responded with endless enthusiasm. This uncomplicated popular response, however, was abruptly to be confronted with a new perception of New Orleans jazz and its history. Nothing in reality is ever quite this uncomplicated, but in this moment it was possible for a number of things to coalesce; and, in a metaphoric sense, what was born in these two conversations was the New Orleans Jazz Revival.

The first conversation was the unexpected meeting beside the bandstand when Louis Armstrong and his touring band were making a series of one-night appearances in Louisiana. At this point he was fronting Luis Russell's orchestra, still with its core of New Orleanians. They were playing at a Catholic dance in New Iberia, a small, poor town in the sugar growing area about ninety miles west of New Orleans, on wet bayou country close to the Gulf. While they were playing, an old-seeming man came close to the bandstand to listen. He was poorly dressed, thin and rundown, without any teeth. In the intermission he called out to Armstrong and they talked for a few moments. When the band's bass player, George "Pops" Foster, asked Armstrong who it was, he replied that it was Bunk Johnson, the cornet player who had been with the Superior Orchestra when Louis was still a boy. Foster, who was nine years older than Armstrong and had often encountered Bunk when he was working in his first bands, also hadn't seen him since Johnson had left, probably sometime around 1910, to go on the road with a minstrel show band. Neither of them recognized him. He was only forty-seven, but looked years older. Foster also talked to him when the band got off the stand. "The next intermission I went over and talked to Bunk for awhile. He said he'd been driving sugarcane wagons. He sure had changed in those twenty-seven years. He didn't have no teeth at all. He said he'd been with the minstrel show a long time."[2]

The second conversation was between a twenty-two-year-old named Fred Ramsey, who in 1937 had just found a job with a New York book publishing house after successfully completing his Princeton University thesis on the writings of James Joyce (whom he'd interviewed in Paris as part of his thesis), and the senior editor that he was working for at Harcourt Brace & Company. Out of the conversation came the book *Jazzmen*, which was published in 1939. In the summer of 1954 Ramsey came to New Orleans to spend a few weeks as part of his travels for a Guggenheim Fellowship he'd been awarded to document African American musical roots in the South. It was the first Guggenheim awarded in the field of African American musical studies. *Jazzmen* had had a decisive effect on my life, and one afternoon after I'd gotten to know him, I asked him how he and his friends had come to write it. Fred was a large, friendly, slow-moving man with bristling black hair cut short. He wore glasses and his expression was usually serious. After recording music in rural Alabama and Mississippi he arrived in New Orleans with his wife and their one-year-old son, and the only place he could find to rent was a stuffy apartment without air conditioning near Coliseum Square. The sweltering summer heat and the cramped space were too much for his family, and they returned to New Jersey. Fred dealt with the suffocating air by spending most of his time in tee shirts and rumpled shorts.

Fred shook his head at the series of coincidences that had led to the book. He said that the editor he was working for knew about his interest in jazz, and when a jazz manuscript came into the office he asked Fred to read it and give him his opinion. It was written by the New York klezmer-style clarinetist and entertainer Ted Lewis, whose squalling clarinet had been a conspicuous element in the sound of Earl Fuller's Famous Jazz Band, one of the early bands that attempted to exploit the success of the Original Dixieland Jazz Band. Lewis had gone on to lead a successful band, and in his manuscript claimed that he was the inventor of this new jazz music that was sweeping the country. Ramsey shook his head and told me that he'd begun buying King Oliver records when they were new and he was still in school, and had shelves filled with records by the Original

JAZZMEN, THE 1939 BOOK THAT BROUGHT NEW ORLEANS INTO THE CENTER OF THE JAZZ STORY. (THE COVER IS A LATER EDITION.) COLLAGE BY THE AUTHOR.

Dixieland Jazz Band, the New Orleans Rhythm Kings, Oliver, Jelly Roll Morton, Bix Beiderbecke, and the Chicagoans. He managed to read all the way through the manuscript, but when he came back to the office with it, he banged it down on the editor's desk and said a little testily that he could write a better history of jazz himself. The editor looked up at him, and after a moment said, "Then do it."

With the offer of a contract, Fred called several friends who were as obsessed with jazz as he was. One of the recruits was a knowledgeable record collector

334

named William Russell. Russell spent some time talking to veteran musicians in Chicago, and he said later that they kept telling him about someone named "Bunk" who had played the trumpet and could tell them anything they wanted to know. The problem was that none of them could remember his last name. In an effort to sort out the situation Russell talked to Louis Armstrong backstage at the Strand Theater in New York in January 1939. He told Armstrong that he'd heard the name Bunk, but nobody could tell him the last name. As writer Tom Bethel described their conversation, Armstrong replied, "What do they say it is?"

"Either Campbell, Robinson, or Johnson," Russell said.

"Well, it's Johnson."[3]

Armstrong went on to say that he'd seen Johnson only a few months before in New Iberia, but he didn't have an address for him. A letter sent to Johnson the next month in care of the New Iberia postmaster reached him, and the correspondence that followed became the basis for the early chapters in the book. Russell had never heard Johnson play, but pieced together a lyrical description of his playing from accounts he got from other musicians.

The seeds that would take root as the New Orleans Jazz Revival had been planted.

Just as there are musicians and arrangers who through their performances change the direction and the content of the music they play, the editors and writers of *Jazzmen* were to have a decisive effect on jazz as it meant to them. When the book was published in 1939, the radical Bop revolution that would decisively change the perception of jazz and the role of its musicians was still several years in the future. The outbreak of the war in 1941 also postponed the inevitable confrontation between the historical emphasis in the book and the innovative directions younger musicians in New York were taking. What the book and the jazz upheaval a few years later had in common was that the two groups—the jazz fans like Ramsey and Charles Edward Smith, who identified with the older jazz styles, and rebellious young musicians like Dizzy Gillespie and Charlie Parker—were each sourly disappointed by the commercial edifice that jazz had become by the end of the Depression years.

Each of the groups was concerned that jazz musicians, always a restless minority in the cramped dimensions of the popular music industry, were increasingly confined within the context of the large bands, in which their success—even their economic survival—depended increasingly on the distinctive backgrounds they were expected to contribute to the vocal arrangements featuring the bands' singers. The freedom that jazz represented had been reduced to one of the elements of a multitiered entertainment package, and for most of the soloists the freedom lasted eight (or occasionally sixteen) measures in the arrangements. It was a richly creative period for many of the more adventurous swing groups, but maintaining the kind of cash flow that could keep a fifteen-piece orchestra on the road meant more and more an omnipresent commercialization of their music.

The career of a group like the Bob Crosby Orchestra, with its New Orleanians, often resembled a kind of complicated economic bargaining: in return for their arrangements of popular ballads and the emphasis on sweet dance music, they were also given the opportunity to record music with a much looser jazz flavor, though almost always in the context of the small "Dixieland" unit, the Bobcats. In essence, the large orchestras needed their distinctive soloists, but they didn't need them to do very much. The soloists added a distinct melodic excitement for the few measures they were asked to play, but in a night on the bandstand the orchestras presented more ballads and popular dance pieces than they did the occasional uptempo speciality for the jitterbuggers. For most of the jazz soloists, what they were doing was an uncomfortable artistic compromise, but for the record companies and the theaters and ballrooms where they were appearing, it was only an acceptance of the realities of the popular music industry.

This same conviction that jazz was losing some of its distinctive character was behind the emotional response of the two loose camps, the swing musicians and the jazz writers whose interest was in the historic New Orleans ensemble style. The difference between them lay in the fact that the musicians—who were searching in after-hours jam sessions for a new jazz idiom—felt that the way out of their dilemma was to break free of the rules and go forward, while for the group of enthusiastic fans and writers who created *Jazzmen*, the way out of the dilemma was to go back to jazz's earlier roots. What was unexpected about the division that opened between the two sides in the debate was that enough people identified with one or the other of the two ideas for the jazz world in the late 1940s and early 1950s to become an emotional battle ground between the modernists and the traditionalists. It was the period of the rancorous "mouldy fig wars," named for the dismissive term the progressive jazz musicians used to describe the traditionalists. At one point the bandleader Stan Kenton, whose orchestra was one of the most discussed and admired of the adventurous new ensembles, said with some acerbity, "I'm open minded about Dixieland music. I don't care who kills it."

Jazz historian Bruce Raeburn has suggested that when the young Nesuhi Ertegun—who would join his brother Ahmet at Atlantic Records during this period—became editor of the influential magazine *The Record Changer* in 1946 and backed away from the magazine's negative response to the new jazz trends, the emotions had cooled. The antagonisms, however, still soured the jazz scene. When one of the contributors to *Jazzmen*, William Russell, was asked to serve as one of the judges of the *Esquire* magazine annual jazz poll, he refused to nominate anyone who played a saxophone because, as he explained, the saxophone wasn't a jazz instrument. Magazines and newsletters devoted to the traditional jazz revival have remained insistently uninterested in current jazz trends, with only an occasional, and often grudging, inclusion of names like Charlie Parker in their columns. When the Eureka Brass Band was assembling for a parade in the 1950s, someone often would call out to trumpeter Willie Pajeaud, "Willie, play

THE EUREKA BRASS BAND PLAYING A FUNERAL, DECEMBER 1950. MUSICIANS IDENTIFIED
ARE ALBERT WARNER, TROMBONE (BACK TO CAMERA), EDDIE RICHARDSON (BACK
TO CAMERA), WILLIE PAJEAUD, ERNEST ROGERS, ROBERT LEWIS, RUEBEN RODDY.
PHOTOGRAPHS BY SAMUEL CHARTERS. COLLAGE BY THE AUTHOR.

us some bebop." He would respond with a flurry of out-of-tune, rushed notes and then join in the laughter.

The controversy was only resolved by the unexpected appearance on the scene of rock and roll in the mid-1950s, which overnight swept the field as the popular music culture of the United States and made the jazz predicament largely irrelevant. In New Orleans, however, the traditionalists dominated the music scene, and much of the underpinning of what they were attempting to achieve with their "revival" had been articulated a generation before in *Jazzmen*.

It isn't possible to understand what lay behind the creation of the complex of ideas that went into *Jazzmen* without knowing something about its editors and writers, since the jazz world they envisioned was one in which they projected their own personalities. At this point I must make the obligatory acknowledgment that I knew three of them, and for many years one of them, Frederic Ramsey Jr., was one of my closest friends. Charles Edward Smith, co-editor of the book with Ramsey, was associated with Folkways Records in the late 1950s and early 1960s, as I was, so we met often in the office, and once or twice Fred and Charlie and I went out drinking together. Smith is generally considered to be the first serious jazz writer; he began publishing informed articles on jazz artists in the early 1930s. His writings appeared in journals as disparate as the literary magazine *Symposium* and *The Daily Worker*, the newspaper sponsored by the American Communist Party in the early Depression years. His perceptive response to jazz artists and their milieu, as well his richly nostalgic writing style were an important influence on both Ramsey and Russell, and I was one of the neophyte writers for whom his prose became a stylistic model. When we met, however, Smith by that time was a self-destructive alcoholic, so any kind of friendship was impossible.

The third of the three key figures behind the book was the complex composer, musician, record label owner, and ideologue William Russell. He was older than the other two, born in 1905 in the town of Canton, in rural Missouri. His family was German, and he began studying the violin when he was still a boy. He was already composing music by the time he was in his teens, and also played the violin in the local movie theater. He entered a music conservatory at the age of thirteen and graduated when he was eighteen. He began his career as a music teacher, but when he was twenty-two he moved to New York City to continue his violin studies with a noted violinist from the New York Philharmonic. At the same time he was pursuing his classical studies he became excited by the new jazz music, and his compositions straddled the two musical idioms. In 1931 his pioneering fugue for percussion instruments was given its world premiere in New York. In 1932 he had an opportunity to spend six weeks in Haiti, and the percussion ensembles he heard there focused his interests on African-derived instruments and their rhythmic possibilities.

Russell spent much of the 1930s touring the United States with a theater group that presented Chinese shadow plays, accompanying the performances on a Chinese dulcimer, a two-string violin, and a moon guitar. He briefly visited New Orleans in 1937, and contributed short pieces about boogie woogie piano style to jazz publications in the United States and Europe. During this period he also studied composition with Arnold Schoenberg in Los Angeles, although his hesitations about the compositional path he was taking prevented him from completing more than a handful of his revolutionary works for percussion ensemble. At the time he joined Ramsey and Smith to create *Jazzmen* he had recently completed a Bachelor of Science degree and was working as a chemist in a factory in Pittsburgh that produced electrical transformers.

Russell often visited New Orleans when I was first there; then while I was living with my first wife on Royal Street in the mid-1950s, Bill opened a small shop on a Chartres Street corner a few blocks away. A loosely organized group of us who had the same enthusiasm for traditional New Orleans jazz, along with veteran clarinetist Raymond Burke, managed to drop by most evenings. Although I knew Bill for more than thirty years, our differences of opinion were too decided for us to be friends. He also felt that, as someone who had come late to the scene, I was an interloper and was appropriating ideas and concepts that had been initiated by other people. For long periods I was conscious that he disliked me as much as he allowed himself to dislike anybody. Our most comfortable working relationship was during the period twenty years later when I was the record producer for the New Orleans Ragtime Orchestra, which included Bill as their violinist, and there was no need for either of us to question whatever the other one suggested about anything.

Nine writers contributed chapters to the book—Charles Edward Smith, Frederic Ramsey Jr., William Russell, Stephen W. Smith, E. Sims Campbell, Edward J. Nichols, Wilder Hobson, Otis Ferguson, and Roger Pryor Dodge— though the three main editors contributed the largest share of the writing. Russell wrote two chapters and collaborated on a third, Ramsey wrote two chapters, and Charles Edward Smith wrote two chapters and the highly charged romantic evocations of the scene for each of the four settings of the book: New Orleans, Chicago, New York, and the jazz environment everywhere in the United States. The editors and contributors worked with intense concentration and the manuscript was completed within a year. The book was intended to be a history of jazz, which at that point ended in 1939, and reading it again, it's clear that they did the job with considerable skill and tireless enthusiasm.

Each of the book's writers was passionate about his area of jazz, and despite its truncated story—ending with jazz only thirty years old—it is still, as a literary and stylistic achievement, one of the most satisfactory of all the jazz histories. Modern readers will find that its presentation is remarkably balanced. There were detailed chapters on the white Chicago jazz school, an intelligent appraisal of Bix Beiderbecke's career, and although the blues material was sketchy, Russell contributed a groundbreaking introduction to boogie woogie. There was even an evocative chapter about the white musicians in New Orleans. It was, however,

the first section about New Orleans, subtitled "Callin' Our Chillun' Home"—
with its opening interlude by Charles Edward Smith, the opening chapter "New
Orleans Music," written by Russell and Stephen W. Smith, and Ramsey's chapter
"King Oliver and his Creole Jazz Band"—that created what has become the legendary account of the development of early jazz.

Before *Jazzmen*, the only published appearances of Buddy Bolden's name
had been E. Belfield Spriggins's brief paragraphs in the pages of the *Louisiana
Weekly* in 1933 and the mention of Bolden in Louis Armstrong's *Swing That
Music* in 1936. Until American readers opened the pages of the book there had
been nothing in jazz history describing moments like a blues cornet contest
between Freddie Keppard and Joe Oliver. Storyville was only a red-light district,
and jazz hadn't made its way up the river after the Storyville brothels closed.

The story that emerged in the book's pages would not have achieved such
immediate acceptance if it didn't fill a need for a myth. For its editors and writers
it was an act of faith to create a story that would lend the beginnings of jazz in
New Orleans a closer indebtedness to black musical sources. With the shadowy
figure of Bolden, the *Jazzmen* writers created a figure who had an even more
decisive mythic value. Without any consciousness of what they were doing—or
even, I think, any intention—they shaped their story around a musician who left
no recordings of his playing. Bolden's music could be imagined as whatever anybody wanted it to be, and the idea of a romanticized figure like him who could
have "invented jazz" could be used to satisfy anyone's fantasy of what early New
Orleans music might have sounded like.

Jazzmen would not have had such a decisive influence on the music of New
Orleans had there been only the book, with its emotional evocations of the city's
past. But what followed over the next half century was a flood of recordings of what
came to be known as the music of the New Orleans Revival. Within a few months
of its publication there was interest in finding and perhaps recording some of the
musicians Charlie Smith described in his final chapters about what he'd heard in
the Mardi Gras bars and dance halls. In the summer of 1940 a friend of Smith and
Ramsey, Heywood Hale "Woody" Broun, was the first to journey to New Orleans
with the aim of recording some of the men in Smith's pages. Broun was the son
of the sportswriter, journalist, war correspondent, and founder of the American
Newspaper Guild Heywood Campbell Broun, who had died the year before.

Charlie Smith, in his account of nights in the music bars and dance halls where
he found the older musicians still playing, had devoted several paragraphs to Kid
Rena, and wrote tantalizingly about Rena drinking hot coffee late at night, then
playing with some of his old vigor. Broun had no difficulty locating him, and he also
found several of the others Smith had heard, including the two Creole clarinetists
Alphonse Picou and Louis Nelson DeLisle. In the early years of the revival recording sessions, the first few days were always spent finding anybody who was in town
and felt like playing. It was to be some time before the visitors began circulating
addresses and telephone numbers of the musicians who might be interested.

For some years the sessions were done entirely with nonunion musicians, which meant staying away from the working professionals, who were invariably union members. If the producers of the recordings *had* been interested in working with union musicians, they also would have had to pay union recording scale, which was out of reach of their miniscule budgets. This meant that many of the best-known of the New Orleans instrumentalists couldn't be considered—musicians like Paul Barbarin, pianist Fats Pichon, or Johnny St. Cyr. It also meant that, of the musicians working on Bourbon Street with the Papa Celestin band or the Bill Mathews band at the Paddock Lounge, only the older Alphonse Picou was regularly involved. There was also, throughout the beginnings of the revival, a clearly demarcated color line. The young enthusiasts who journeyed to New Orleans to record veteran musicians were emotionally committed to recording African American musicians. The policies of the record companies in the 1920s, which had led to the refusal of the recording directors to consider black musicians who were not in the commercial mainstream, like Buddy Petit or Chris Kelly, were now turned on their heads. Among the revivalists it was almost exclusively older black musicians who were considered worth recording. The city's adventurous young black instrumentalists who were experimenting with new progressive styles found themselves ignored by everybody.

The trombonist Broun found for the sessions he envisioned was Jim Robinson, who had been with Sam Morgan's band. Albert Glenny, the seventy-year-old bassist, had played with Bolden's band. The drummer was Kid Rena's brother Joe. There was no piano available, so the rhythm section was filled out by guitarist Willie Santiago, who had played with Louis Armstrong at Tom Anderson's saloon in 1920. Broun had difficulty finding some kind of rehearsal space—or a recording studio that would allow him to record a nonunion African American band. Finally a local radio station, WWL, in the Roosevelt Hotel close to Canal Street, made its facilities available. The rehearsal session that Broun recorded on August 14, 1940, was the first New Orleans revival session. A week later, on August 21 the band returned to WWL and recorded nine masters that were released on what was virtually a private, nonprofit label, Delta Records.

Although the companies involved in the first years of the revival were all like Delta, small and with virtually no distribution, the records were made by people closely associated with the growing numbers of record collectors as well as the specialty jazz record stores that had emerged around the country. The singles that were released immediately became the subject of intent listening and heated discussions by the new generation of jazz writers and musicians. One of the pieces Broun recorded, a nostalgic nineteenth-century march tune in 6/8 rhythm titled "Gettysburg March," became a new addition to the traditional jazz repertoire within a few months of its release.

The sound of the group that Broun assembled was not to become the characteristic revivalist style, but of all the bands that were recorded, it perhaps came closest to the sound of the dance music that the small orchestras were playing before World War I. The rhythm was gently lilting, with an understated swing, and the melodies in the horns were played in a bare style that was as carefully unadorned. Rena's playing had none of the fire that was supposed to have been his signature in the 1920; the fire had been extinguished in the taxi dance halls. The melodic flow of his leads, however, echoed the playing of Peter Bocage and Louis Dumaine on their recordings nearly twenty years before. Each of the clarinetists played with a pattering, articulated style, a near-staccato sound as they tongued each note. The legato flow that became the standard sound of the New Orleans clarinetists by the 1920s was clearly a later development. One of the most charming moments on the recordings was the duet chorus by the two clarinetists on Picou's classic chorus in "High Society."

With the Delta recordings it was clear that there still was music in New Orleans to be recorded. They also held out the possibility that the secrets of the first moments of jazz in the city could perhaps be unraveled through more sessions with the surviving veterans. The most colorful figure of *Jazzmen* was Bunk Johnson, and in the photographs of him with the trumpet that the group who had found him had purchased, he looked serious and prepared for whatever challenges that might appear. Broun had intended to use him for his session, but it was too difficult for him to consider the problems of finding Johnson in New Iberia and bringing him to New Orleans. As time passed there was growing impatience to bring Johnson into a studio, which was complicated by the December 7, 1941, attack on Pearl Harbor and the first months of World War II. The situation was also complicated because Johnson hadn't played in New Orleans for decades, his home was on the other side of the state, and except for a short example of his playing by himself that he'd made on a home recording machine for the group of people associated with *Jazzmen* who'd helped him with the horn and new dentures, no one had heard him play.

Bill Russell and a friend, Gene Williams (who published the traditionalist magazine *Jazz Information*, and produced recordings with a strong commitment to the concept of the revival), decided they would travel to New Orleans to record Johnson in the spring of 1942, when Russell could take a vacation from his Pittsburgh job. As they were preparing to leave, they learned that another group from Los Angeles who shared their enthusiasm were also on the way. The Los Angeles group included Dave Stuart, who owned the Jazz Man record shop and label, along with two others with the same interests, Hal McIntyre and Bill Coburn. The two groups decided to pool their resources, and when Russell arrived from Pittsburgh on Saturday, June 6, they began trying to put a band together. Russell had traveled south by way of Chicago to ask his friend clarinetist Jimmy Noone if he could recommend a clarinet player for the sessions, but after listening to the Delta recordings Russell had already decided that the playing of the musician Noone suggested, Big Eye Louis Nelson DeLisle, who had recorded on that first session, wasn't "hot" enough.

The question of a clarinet player hung over their efforts to put a band together. Virtually every reed player in the city had switched to the saxophone. The group were also just getting to know Johnson, who arrived in New Orleans on Monday, June 8, two days after Russell. They weren't aware of that a clarinetist Bunk had worked with in the early 1930s had returned to New Orleans from a job out of town the day before Bunk came to the city. For two days no one could quite work out who the musician was. Bunk told them a name that they thought sounded like "George Strode" or "George Stewart." Jim Robinson, however, who had played for the Delta sessions, was their choice as trombonist, and when they found him the next day he told them that the man's name was George Lewis and that he lived on St. Philip Street. They quickly found Lewis and after a pleasant time talking with him and meeting his family they decided he would be their clarinetist, though no one thought of asking him to play for them.

When Charles Edward Smith stayed in New Orleans at the end of the 1930s trying to trace the roots of New Orleans music, he missed another musical world that was home to musicians like George Lewis. If Smith had stumbled across the clubs where these bands were still playing for dancing, he would have written a different ending to his New Orleans chapters. Despite all the difficulties of the Depression years, musicians like Lewis, pianist Billie Pierce and her husband Dee Dee Pierce, clarinetist Albert Burbank, trumpeter Kid Howard, and trombonist Jim Robinson, worked steadily, even if it was at hole-in-the-wall clubs or restaurants and their guaranteed pay was often as little as a dollar or a dollar and a half. Their style of New Orleans ensemble playing grew out of the style of the 1920s, but was shaped now over the steady 4/4 pulse of the swing bands. No one played the banjo anymore, and the electric guitar was standard everywhere. Several of the clubs where the nonunion musicians worked were along Decatur Street, which in the 1930s was one of the city's rough areas, and they played for crowds of seamen and workers on the river. At clubs like the Popeye or Luthjen's there was music at least two or three nights a week. There were still a handful of more solid jobs at the Gypsy Tea Room, but they were held down by the union musicians in bands led by Sidney Desvigne or Joe Robichaux. The musicians from this other New Orleans musical world were out of the commercial spotlight, but they were creating the music that was to be at the heart of the revival.

That evening Russell finally got to hear Johnson. As he wrote in the diary he kept during the sessions, he followed Bunk up to his room in the house where he was staying. "I went up with him and carried his horn. I asked Bunk to play a few notes on his horn, 'to show me how *it* sounded' if he wasn't too tired. He sat down, put in a mute, and *tried* to play a scale and a few other sputtery notes, terrible tone, no volume, no force, and half of notes missed; he talked about his mouthpiece, and said it wasn't just right. He likes a wider rim . . ."4

Despite any misgivings Russell might have felt, there was nothing to do but continue with their plans, and the band met the next afternoon at the home of the pianist Walter Decou for a rehearsal. The only musicians who were there

LUTHJEN'S BAR AND DANCE
HALL, 1954. PHOTOGRAPH BY
SAMUEL CHARTERS.

were the three horns; Johnson, Lewis, and Robinson, with Decou playing simple, chorded rhythm. Russell's notes continued: "The band got together, tuned up briefly, and Bunk had to play *Oh Lord I'm Crippled, I Can Not Walk* to show them the tune. Spit around, not very impressive, soft tone (as always when playing alone). Then Bunk stomped off. Bang! What tone and drive and go the band had. No rhythm instruments needed. Bunk a real teacher and leader, in absolute command, the real boss, yet ready to give everyone a chance to be featured. After another try Bill Coburn and I went round the corner to get some drinks, no soft drinks, but we got a big bottle of ginger ale, ice, and three or four beers."

At that afternoon rehearsal the outlines of what would become the revival's approach to New Orleans traditions was already clear, with two of the key figures, Johnson and Lewis, giving a personal character to the forms that the music would take. They found someone still playing banjo, and there would be a strong, chugging rhythm section, with both the bass and banjo playing an unaccented 4/4 beat in the style of the old Sam Morgan Band recordings. The melodic instruments would be the trumpet, trombone, clarinet ensemble that Russell and the others had seen in the old jazz photos, and the musical material would be a mix of pieces from the city's old shared repertoire, with occasional popular songs that someone remembered and felt like playing. There would be as much of an emphasis on the ensemble as possible, with solos generally limited to one-chorus reprises of the melody. Saxophones—except for a few later exceptions—and arranged instrumental passages—except for anything that might be used from the old ragtime, "Red Backed Book" orchestrations—were not considered. This was the formula that established the pattern for the large majority of the revival recordings that followed.

The session was to be held at a small third-floor studio of the Grunewald Music Store on June 11, five days after Russell's arrival. Jim Robinson finally arranged for a banjo player, Lawrence Marrero, and a drummer, Ernest Rogers on the morning of the recording. The out of town group had heard a bass player Bunk liked, Austin Young, who agreed to play, although he was a union member. Of all the revival recordings, these first discs had probably the poorest sound quality, despite a number of trial discs to solve some of the problems of balance and sound quality. As Russell wrote in his diary, "First playback sounded terrible. I was afraid Dave would try to make settlement with musicians and call the date off. Trombone was too loud, moved to side; piano, bass and banjo moved closer, but still no bass could be heard. Bunk told to face mike more. Tried one of my 10" blanks, but wouldn't cut. Using aluminum base, the first side was cut."[5]

When Stuart sent the masters to the cutting laboratory he used for his Jazz Man singles, he later learned that the engineers were about to throw them away, since they felt the sound was so poor there was no reason to release them. However, eight titles were released on four singles, beginning with "Panama" and "Down by the Riverside" as Bunk Johnson's Original Superior Band on JM 8. As a final comment at the end of the long day, Russell added in his diary, "We took Bunk home in a car. As we turned onto Rampart Street I saw the Eagle Saloon and I said, 'Tell me, Bunk, did the Eagle Band ever play any better than that?' He didn't hesitate at all—'no,' and he implied that they never swung out like that."

The collectors' world was divided over the singles, in part because of the disappointing sound quality. At the same time, for many listeners Johnson's playing was a revelation, and the sound of the entire band, as they "swung out," had a gutsy, raw energy and spontaneity that had not been suggested by the Delta recordings. For Russell, Johnson, and Lewis, the first singles were to change their lives. Russell was so disappointed with the sound quality of the recordings that he decided he could do just as well himself; he acquired a disc cutting machine of his own and began returning to New Orleans as often as he could scrape together the resources, visiting the city to record new sessions on his vacations from his job. Ultimately he founded his historic small label American Music to free himself from any dependence on recording technicians or record companies.

Other enthusiasts immediately became interested in documenting more of Johnson's playing. There was a second session four months later, in October 1942, for Gene Williams, with Lewis and Decou again in the band, but with brass band musician Albert Warner playing trombone, Chester Zardis playing the bass, and Edgar Mosley, drums. This recording was done at the more professional setting of the WSMB radio studio. In April 1943, just as Russell was planning to return to New Orleans with better recording equipment, Bunk was suddenly invited to San Francisco by jazz writer Rudi Blesh, to participate in a series of lectures on jazz history. Johnson spoke to the audience and joined the band for the final concert. He remained in San Francisco for more than a year, playing weekly concerts at the Maritime Union Workers' Hall, and recording with the musicians of the San Francisco revival, Lu Watters and his Yerba Buena Jazz Band.

George Lewis remained in New Orleans, taking work on the docks as a stevedore, and initially there was some question about his role in the unfolding scenario of the revival, since it was assumed that he was essentially on the sessions as Johnson's sideman. In May 1943, however, Russell returned to New Orleans with his new disc cutter, and with Johnson in San Francisco, Russell made the decision to record a band led by Lewis, using a musician he'd played with often, Avery "Kid" Howard as the trumpet lead. The recordings were made at the popular black club the Gypsy Tea Room, a shambling wooden building at the corner of Villere and St. Ann Streets that was larger than the previous locations that had been used, and Russell's new recording equipment was considerably better than what had been available before. Howard had been performing for some time as a Louis Armstrong soundalike, and there was some concern about the mix of his "modern" sound and the revival style band Lewis assembled, but Howard brought to the band a bristling energy and a soaring musical range. On some of the numbers, like the piece that opened the sessions, "Climax Rag," his brash tone exploded into the ensemble. Since Russell didn't have his own company at this time he sold the masters for $300 to a new company called Blue Note Records, which had slightly more distribution than the other companies involved in the revival. The royalties were to go to Lewis. Because the owners of Blue Note, two recent German immigrants, Alfred Lyon and Francis Wolfe, were worried about potential problems with the musician's union, the records were released in October 1943 on a lookalike label titled Climax Records as George Lewis and His Ragtime Stompers. For the first time the revival had a hit. As Bethel chronicled the excitement, "A jubilant Francis Wolfe wrote to Russell: 'Climax Rag came out today and was an immediate hit at the shop. The record sounds fine and could not be better in any respect. . . . It was an exciting day for us, when we opened the first box containing 'the very incarnation of the spirit of New Orleans jazz,' and put the first record on the machine. The Stompers are the best, no doubt about it in our mind.' "[6]

For many writers, Bethel among them, the sessions were Russell's most successful achievement as a producer, and the recordings made it clear that Lewis could successfully lead a group of his own. Two of George Lewis's solo performances that Russell recorded later, with Lewis playing in his living room accompanied only by Marrero's banjo and Alcide "Slow Drag" Pavageau's bass, were to become even more closely identified with the revival epoch: a lyric blues improvisation given the title "Burgundy Street Blues," recorded on St. Philips Street in July 1944, and the nostalgic, reminiscent "Over The Waves," recorded in May 1945. Both performances were to become emblematic of the revival, and have been performed and recorded in Lewis's style by generations of clarinetists over the last half century.

Over the next few years there were a number of new revival recordings featuring Johnson and Lewis, often including drummer Baby Dodds, who was brought down from Chicago to join them. The interest in the new releases was

GEORGE LEWIS, 1960S. PHOTOGRAPH COURTESY OF BILL COLYER.

still largely limited to collectors and to people who had read *Jazzmen*, but Bill Russell and Gene Williams, who had traveled together to New Orleans hoping to produce the first Bunk Johnson session in 1942, were convinced that there was a large audience waiting to dance to the band's music in New York. After futilely attempting to interest local promoters in the idea, they decided to go ahead themselves, and with Williams's financial backing they rented a vast, run-down hall named the Stuyvesant Casino on the lower East Side of Manhattan, on 2nd Avenue near 9th Street, for $300 a month and arranged to bring the band north. Williams had a large apartment in Greenwich Village, and the band would live in the four empty bedrooms. By this time the band members were in constant friction with Johnson, who had reverted to the heavy drinking that Pops Foster remembered from the early days. Johnson would miss rehearsals, and a search of the streets would find him in a drunken stupor, without his horn or his dentures. He began the New York adventure on a sour note by missing the train, and turning up a day later alone. By the time they had their first rehearsal in the hall the mood had grown so rancorous that Russell searched for Lewis later, and found him in tears on a bench in Union Square Park, so upset at the insults Johnson had

347

BUNK JOHNSON

AND HIS NEW ORLEANS BAND

FEATURING

GEORGE LEWIS	BABY DODDS
JIM ROBINSON	SLOW DRAG
LAWRENCE MARRERO	ALTON PURNELL

DANCING

TUESDAY, WEDNESDAY, THURSDAY and FRIDAY NIGHTS
From 8:30 P. M. to 12:30 A. M.

and SUNDAY AFTERNOONS from 2:00 to 5:00 P. M.

STUYVESANT CASINO

140 SECOND AVENUE   Near 9th Street   NEW YORK CITY

Two Blocks East of Wanamaker's

Easily reached by all main subway, "L" and bus lines. From West Side Lines, take 8th Street crosstown bus to Second Avenue.

ADMISSION: $1.00. Incl. Tax   Sundays, 80c. Incl. Tax

BUNK JOHNSON'S BAND, WITH GEORGE LEWIS, OPENS AT THE STUYVESANT CASINO, NEW YORK CITY, 1944.

directed at him that he was determined to go back home. It was only after long, emotional pleading that Russell convinced him to stay. The band opened for what they hoped would be a dancing crowd on Friday night, September 28, 1945.

Not many dancers turned up to try their rhythms, but in the first audiences were other writers from *Jazzmen*, including Fred Ramsey and Charlie Smith. For the people who understood what the band represented, it was a powerful emotional experience. A young pianist, Bob Green, described the effect of the music on him when he heard the band for the first time.

It was a startling experience, walking in and suddenly hearing this sound . . . It was overwhelming. The band played in this huge ballroom with the walls a sort of cream color, tables all around, a dance floor cleared in the middle with a great crystal chandelier hanging down that had these little surfaces on it, and as it revolved lights played off it and reflected rainbow colors off the walls. And over in the far end, this great band with Bunk and George, Baby Dodds and Jim Robinson. It was incredible . . . suddenly walking into this room and hearing this power coming off the bandstand, with Bunk really going and George cutting through and filling in, and Jim bringing up the bottom, was something I had never experienced. . .

With this band you felt you were on a locomotive and just holding on for all you were worth and it was just chugging, and the wind was blowing back. Instead of just one ensemble and then everyone taking solos and taking turns, there was this whole band, this great machine that worked and seemed to envelop everyone, the hundreds of people that were in the Casino.[7]

Many of the artists, writers, and intellectuals who became part of the steady audiences were even more rhapsodic in their response to the music. The same impulse that had led to their feeling of disappointment over the commercial highroad that jazz seemed to be taking drew them to the band's unstudied excitement. The poet William Carlos Williams, who had always sought out what he felt was the original impulse, the deeply rooted force within the natural world as well as the society around him, was moved to write one of his most emotional poems after sitting in front of the bandstand for an evening. His exultant conclusion, echoing one of the most popular judgments of the day, was that the members of the band were "men!"

There was national press coverage of the band's appearances, and although the crowds were smaller than Russell and Gene Williams had anticipated, within a few weeks the venture was beginning to be economically viable—though for Williams, who had a family income, this wasn't a concern. For the growing audience just discovering New Orleans music, what was more important for anyone who couldn't get to New York were two major recording sessions with the band, both by major companies with extensive national distribution. The first was an album for Decca Records titled *New Orleans Revival* by Bunk Johnson and His New Orleans Band, recorded on November 21. The second album, recorded by Victor Records two weeks later on December 6, with a follow-up session on December 19, was titled *New Orleans Jazz—Bunk Johnson*. Both albums, especially the Victor release, reached an audience largely unaware of what had been occurring in the New Orleans dance hall sessions. For some listeners who had been excited by the rough spontaneity and the hand-hewn quality of the first recordings, the professional recording sound and the commercial album presentation were a disappointment, but for nearly everyone else they were an abrupt discovery. The band played with the same headlong rush of the rhythm and there was the same emphasis on the complex ensemble sound of all the instruments that had characterized the first sessions, but for years there were complaints in traditionalist publications that the band sounded better on almost any of their previous recordings than they did for the New York commercial labels.

The New York recordings had a profound effect on the contemporary jazz scene, reaching a new nationwide audience. There had already been stirrings of interest in the older styles. In California Kid Ory was already performing with members of his old Sunshine Orchestra and Louis Armstrong would soon return to the small-band New Orleans format with his All-Stars. The recordings by Bunk Johnson made it clear, however, that there was still a deep well of music in New Orleans, and within a few years the French Quarter had become the gathering place for enthusiasts of the revival musicians, as well as a popular stopover for a stream of photographers, writers, and musicians interested in absorbing and documenting the revival style. After my first visit to take clarinet lessons from George Lewis in 1950, a series of apartments in the French Quarter were to be my home for most of the 1950s while I interviewed jazz veterans, followed the brass bands, spent at least one night every weekend listening to Billie and Dee Dee Pierce at Luthjen's, and went through newspaper files for the book *Jazz: New Orleans, 1885 – 1957*.

The number of recordings that were done as the revival became more and more popular with collectors and aficionados is almost incalculable. Since the impetus behind the sessions was to preserve and document a musical style, rather than achieve any kind of economic success, the only limit to the amount of recording was the interest of the people involved. The discography that Tom Bethel included in his biography of George Lewis is seventy tightly spaced pages long, listing releases on thirty-seven labels. At a rough count there were 145 sessions, but Bethel adds that there are many private recordings that probably will be released sometime in the future. If sessions by other leaders and bands are added to the total—sessions led by musicians like Punch Miller, Billie and Dee Dee Pierce, Emile Barnes, Percy Humphrey or Kid Thomas, as well as innumerable releases by various groups presented by the revival halls that opened later—it is obvious that the New Orleans revival was one of the most exhaustively documented musical genres in the recorded era. Like nearly everyone else I knew in New Orleans I also contributed to the total. I did sessions in the 1950s by Billie and Dee Dee Pierce, the Eureka Brass Band, Israel Gorman's Band, Isaiah Morgan's band in Biloxi, street cries and Mardi Gras musicians, the first recordings with a group of Mardi Gras Indians, and the historical white string jazz group, the 6 & 7/8s String Band. Today new sessions are continually added to the mountain of material that has already been preserved, even after the disaster of Katrina and its devastating effect on the city's jazz community.

In the New Orleans African American community the feelings about the revival were often ambiguous. To an extent it was a question of age: older musicians were generally pleased to be earning a little money and getting some recognition, while younger musicians were often upset with the choice of being offered work if they played in the revival style, or being left to jam in neighborhood bars if they didn't. In their book *Bourbon Street Black* Jack V. Buerkle, a sociologist and a former musician himself, and New Orleans guitarist Danny Barker, who had spent most of his very successful career in New York, interviewed a number of musicians and included their responses to the question of the revival style. The answers were often undecided, but there was always a consciousness of the dilemma. In a summary consideration of the revival phenomenon, Buerkle and Barker were much more critical of the scenario as it had evolved.

All over the United States, musicians began forming groups based on the New Orleans motif so they might possibly supply part of the demand for the old music. Whenever possible, instrumentation was exactly like the Crescent City groups. Bunk and a few of the other old-time New Orleans Negroes did tour, and for a time they caused considerable stir among the relatively "pure" jazz buffs and their friends. But there were not really that many jazz buffs who followed the New Orleans style; certainly not enough to financially sustain the movement by themselves on any extensive scale. Within a few months, though, numerous white groups copied the New Orleans Style as best as they could. . . . An important characteristic of these groups was that they were all white. What had begun as a revival of an essentially black art form ended up being a financial windfall for some white groups.[9]

The two writers became increasingly strident concerning white musicians playing what they considered to be a uniquely black music, though I think I recognize Barker's voice more prominently in this passage, since it echoed things he said to me many times in the French Quarter. "It becomes even more remarkable when we realize that the complete revival and its ultimate waning occurred with the belief (at least by those who thought about it) by most Americans that a group of white musicians had revived 'their' music. We are able to understand this when we recall that most people had given credit for the creation of jazz some years back to either the Original Dixieland Jazz Band or Paul Whiteman. As one would expect there was a great deal of bitterness in the veteran black jazzmen as they began to notice this new chapter of their 'invisibility' unfolding before them."

For whoever wrote the passage, it was only a short step to extending the argument by drawing in the thesis of Ralph Ellison's epochal novel *The Invisible Man*, and including any white musicians playing in a New Orleans style in their attack on the white racism that they felt was endemic in the jazz world. "While we recognize that the motives of the white musicians on the surface, at least, were just to get more and better gigs, a somewhat more exact explanation is that this has happened in a national culture that at least overtly professes the black man to be incapable of innovation or creation of any substance. The cultural milieu that has permitted this reaction by the white man is one that stereotypes all Negroes, making no allowances for differences of personality, creativity, motivation, intelligence or social class."[10]

Although both Buerkle and Barker might have found enough in the New Orleans scene to feel some justification for their interpretation of the revival years, they might also have been reacting to isolated events like the success of English clarinetist Acker Bilk, who had a worldwide hit single with a performance of "Over the Waves" that was an uncomfortably direct copy of the solo version George Lewis had recorded in his New Orleans living room in 1945. With the exception of a handful of musicians in the United States and England who had a sure commercial sense of their audience's tastes, however, the musicians playing in the hundreds of revival bands that sprang up everywhere in the world were recreating the recordings they loved as a gesture of faith in New Orleans and the music it had created.

I played in revival bands for many years, and for us even the dizzying heights of ordinary union scale were beyond our ambitions. We would have welcomed any African American musicians who chose to join us, but it was not until the 1990s that I met any young black musicians who felt easy enough with the New Orleans past to join the bands. If the groups were generally composed entirely of white musicians, it was because during these years there were no young African American musicians that any of us knew who elected to play New Orleans—style jazz. In addition to whatever misgivings they might had had about the compli- cated racial dynamic of the revival, they realized, quite sensibly, that there was no way to make a living being part of it. In their enthusiasm, the white bands made every effort to hire veteran black New Orleans musicians whenever they had some economic support, and for many of the New Orleans veterans there were years of extensive tours appearing as the featured soloist with a young revival band. The young black musicians I encountered had a visceral response to the new sounds and challenges of bop, to Miles Davis and John Coltrane. The New Orleans idiom was something they left to us.

Interest in the older jazz styles, certainly in part as a reaction to the discomfort many of the older listeners felt with the progressive jazz styles, also had its paral- lel universe in the Bourbon Street world of white New Orleans musicians. It was not only the established names like Sharkey Bonano and Santo Pecora who were able to ask for more money from the tightfisted club owners; there were new young artists like trumpeter George Girard and the commercial Dixieland music of the Assuntos, Frank and his brother Freddie, who emphasized the visual and showy aspects of the music. Jac Assunto, a trombonist who was the father of the two brothers, had been part of the white jazz scene of the 1920s; he'd recorded a novelty muted solo with John Tobin and his Midnight Serenaders in 1925. The Assunto Brothers turned the Bourbon Street Dixieland style into a slickly pre- sented package that they eventually took to Las Vegas for years of success in the casinos.

The white musicians also had a record company, Southland Records, which endeavored to preserve as much of their music as possible. It was owned by Joe Mares, the younger brother of New Orleans Rhythm Kings trumpeter Paul Mares. Joe Mares idolized his older brother, and at the very beginning of the band's career he had loaned George Brunies an overcoat so he could travel to Chicago to join the new group. Much of the Southland output was commercial Dixieland music, as strictly defined in its instrumentation and its repertoire as the recordings of the black revival bands, though stylistically it was sometimes difficult to find some common dimensions to their music, even though both groups of instrumentalists had their roots in New Orleans. Mares also recorded historical sessions, bringing older musicians back into the studio again, includ- ing veterans like Tom Brown and Chink Martin, who was playing with Bonano's

GEORGE LEWIS PLAYING WITH
KEN COLYER'S BAND, LONDON,
1960S. PHOTOGRAPH COURTESY
OF BILL COLYER.

band. It was one of the unreleased Southland tapes that producer Barry Martyn
and I found on the shelves following Katrina that included Jack Laine playing his
bass drum with a pick-up band. Southland didn't draw the kind of color line that
was more characteristic of the many revival labels, and often the finest sessions
were bands that included musicians from the entire rainbow of the city's artists,
including Raymond Burke, the fine clarinetist who had been part of the crowd
often dropping by Bill Russell's shop on Chartres Street.

One of the New Orleans Dixieland–style trumpeters, Al Hirt, had a national
hit with a recorded novelty instrumental titled "Java," and he returned to
Bourbon Street and opened his own club for the steadily increasing crowds of
tourists. A few years later he was joined by another well-known New Orleans
figure. A popular national television program had featured a local clarinetist,
Pete Fountain, who returned to his hometown and opened another successful
Bourbon Street club a few blocks from Al Hirt's. The two clubs anchored a new
business in conventions and tours that were increasingly including New Orleans
jazz in their offerings. Fountain's home and his collection of instruments and
mementos was destroyed in the Katrina disaster, but as he concluded wryly, "I
have two of my best clarinets. I can still toot."

Beginning in 1961, audiences who were fans of the revival sound were drawn
to Preservation Hall on St. Peter Street, which presented veteran black musicians in an atmosphere that was close to the old dance halls where their music
had grown up. George Lewis and his musicians were often included in the band
whenever they were in town between their perpetual tours. The mists that had
obscured so much of the early New Orleans jazz story finally were dispersed for
the generation of artists who had somehow survived the years of silence.

21

Struttin'

Musically, what's going to happen around here—it's about maintaining the past. But that isn't a good word, because if I say maintain the "past," what I really think about is that it's something that's growing. It's a kind of machine. That's the way music was around here, constantly growing, and it has the past in it. So if we can maintain that, then we'll do what we've always been doing— maintaining a music that has a past that's very much alive today. That's what we have to work for.

To me, that's the way I see the living body of music in New Orleans. It's something that's very old, but it's still growing. It's like a tree that has a big, big trunk and old roots, but if you look up at the top, you can see it's still sprouting little leaves. It's still coming out, waving in the breeze.

That's what we have to do, make sure the tree don't get sick.

NEW ORLEANS DRUMMER JOHNNY VIDACOVICH, AFTER
THE HURRICANE AND FLOOD OF 2005[1]

The flood that drowned New Orleans in the wake of Hurricane Katrina on August 29, 2005, left more then 80 percent of the city an empty wasteland of abandoned houses and waterlogged debris, strewn with the shapes of 250, 000 automobiles covered in a dried gray layer of silt that left them the lifeless color of dust. It seemed, three months later, that the city's music would have drowned with its neighborhoods and its economy. But crowded onto the stage of the Café Brasil on Frenchmen Street, the Hot 8 Brass Band blasted out an uptempo melody that was part street music, part old brass band style, part new club rhythm, and all New Orleans. The members of the band, from the city's African American neighborhoods, were in their twenties and thirties, in sweatshirts and jeans, baseball caps sideways, the trumpet players a little overweight, but all of the band giving themselves totally to the music, sweat already running down their faces. It was as if they'd just flung open a door and there was a loud street parade outside. Like the rest of the city, the members of the band had been driven out by the flood, but even with the city still only a numb shell of itself, they'd come back. One of the trumpet players and a saxophone player beside him seized the microphone at the front of the stage and shouted,

We're back y'all!

People will tell you that when we get up here to play we give you that spirit of New Orleans. You know what I'm saying. But what's the TRUTH is that we get it from you. It's you that's giving us the spirit that's in our music! Without the spirit of the people of New Orleans, there couldn't be no New Orleans music, and that's the truth!

And y'all KNOW IT!

The blast of sound leaked through the painted windows to the winter darkness outside. The casual crowds that had come to look into the music clubs that lined the two blocks of Frenchmen Street, where it joins Decatur Street close to the French Quarter, drifted from one club to another. In all of the small establishments there was some kind of music: string band jazz with a clarinetist, new jazz with a New Orleans beat, washboard blues, Cajun songs accompanied by an ancient pedal steel guitar, or one of the New Orleans jazz elders—pianist Ellis Marsalis, father of the Marsalis brothers—entertaining in the neighborhood's one upscale lounge bar. The clubs were small, so small they always had the feel of a crowd, even though in some of them there was still room at the back for more customers. From the street it was like a musical jambalaya—a little bit of everything, with the overlay of sound from the Hot 8 Brass Band like a pungent spice lending it all a distinctive flavor. But across the street a military patrol moved slowly along the sidewalk, talking to each other as they glanced into the open doors at the crowds. Later, driving along the lifeless blocks that were all that was left of the city's center, the low silhouette of the military vehicles, the Humvees, silently passed me on the empty curve of South Claiborne Avenue, still cruising before they would begin to enforce the night curfew and close down the streets.

It seemed often in those weeks after the flood that the only thing coming to life again in the city was its music, even though during the uncertain journey that New Orleans music had undertaken over the previous decades it had seemed sometimes that the music itself would be one of the things that was most threatened. In the 1970s and the 1980s the jazz revival still had its enthusiasts, Bourbon Street still had its bands, but only a few of the veteran musicians were left to take their places on the bandstands. Usually the places like Preservation Hall or The Palm Court Jazz Restaurant that tried to keep the old traditions alive, could still find enough musicians to present a band that had the expected

PRESERVATION HALL, 1983, THE
ENTRANCE ON ST. PETER STREET.
PHOTOGRAPH BY SAMUEL CHARTERS.

look and the expected feel, but in other places around the city the traditional bands usually were made up of a blend of older New Orleans veterans and enthusiastic young newcomers, white and black, combining race and age, sometimes even two or three nationalities.

In the 1950s and 1960s, to those of us who were involved with traditional sounds, it seemed like we were continually saying to each other that we'd just heard the last of something, or we'd just experienced the end of something. The older music we had come to the city to find was losing its vitality at the same time that a new New Orleans style that had never been part of our obsessive agenda had become vibrantly alive, even if it didn't have a familiar sound. For the first time since the 1920s New Orleans was once again providing a pulse and a direction to American popular music. The two-way musical exchange that had ceased to work between New Orleans and the rest of the country in the Depression years had been patched up and was functioning again. The city was no longer simply the passive audience for things being created somewhere else.

By the mid-1950s, when I turned on the AM radio in the picture frame shop where I was working on Royal Street, what filled the room was the rocking beat of New Orleans rhythm and blues. It was a different kind of beat; it didn't represent the revolutionary musical changes that jazz had introduced thirty years before, but it had a loose, casual, swaggering sound that captured the other side of New Orleans life—the shadows of the evening trees along the streets of the Treme neighborhood, or the morning sun on the rows of "shotguns" along First Street. For the next few years, whenever I was in the city, I turned on the radio to the songs of Fats Domino, Ernie K. Doe, Professor Longhair, Irma Thomas, Earl King, Huey Smith, Allen Toussaint, and Lee Dorsey. In the kind of cultural continuity that gives New Orleans so much of its uniqueness, when I was working as a producer with the traditional group the New Orleans Ragtime Orchestra, I learned that the band's bass player, Walter Payton Jr., was not only the father of the modern-style trumpeter Nicholas Payton, Walter had also played electric bass on Lee Dorsey's classic R&B hit "Working In A Coal Mine."

The new excitement over New Orleans R&B, however, didn't give much work to its jazz musicians, except for occasional recording sessions backing up local recording artists. The only steady work was in the tourist bars, with their insistence on the old New Orleans jazz sound. Young musicians who were exploring the new jazz sounds continued to leave, just as they had in the 1920s. A generation of ambitious instrumentalists took their skills to other cities that offered more possibilities for their careers to develop. The talented sons of pianist Ellis Marsalis—Branford, Wynton, Delfeayo, and Jason—all left to pursue their careers elsewhere. Young trumpeters like Terence Blanchard, Nicholas Payton, or Leroy Jones followed the same trail that had taken Lee Collins out of New Orleans in the 1920s. As Collins had summed it up, ". . . when a player became the King, New Orleans lost him." One of the most talented of the young pianists and singers, Harry Connick Jr., the son of the city's District Attorney, spent more time in Las Vegas and Hollywood than he did in any of the modest clubs along Magazine Street or in the lounges of the new tourist hotels at the foot of Canal Street.

When I returned to the city after Katrina I found the devastation I had anticipated, but I couldn't have expected that there would be a musical scene that still was exploring new sounds and directions—and at the same time bringing along a sense of the styles and musical discoveries that New Orleans had already given us. One night as I was driving in the muffled darkness along Carrollton Avenue, its streets still without illumination, I saw a light a few blocks away on a building on Oak Street. I turned toward it and found that the Maple Leaf Bar, one of the run-down small clubs that had helped keep the city's musical traditions alive, had managed to open again. Inside, on a much scuffed, low bandstand in the grimy dance hall next to the bar, a jazz trio was playing with a new-sounding hard swing. It was jazz of the new era and they played with a taut energy—but it had a beat I'd heard before, and the piece they were playing was an old New Orleans standard, "L' il Liza Jane."

I didn't find out the names of the musicians until I was leaving two hours later. The bass player was James Singleton, who occasionally plays with the traditional bands at the Palm Court Jazz Restaurant. The tenor saxophone player,

Tim Green, was obviously as much at ease with New Orleans roots as he was with his intense personal explorations. The leader of the group, the most exciting drummer I'd ever listened to in New Orleans, was Johnny Vidacovich, whose uncle Pinky Vidacovich had played the clarinet with the New Orleans Owls. Holding a bottle of beer, I danced along with the trio in the shabby room for two sets, surrounded by perspiring college students who found the beat as irresistible as I did. After the first set, as Johnny Vidacovich was leaving the bandstand, I called out to him that this was the first modern jazz I'd ever heard that I could boogie to. He gave me a quick, knowing smile, and held up two thumbs.

Of all the slowly fading elements of the city's musical heritage that we mourned in the 1950s, it was the brass bands whose last years we felt the most intensely. The brass bands—for us it was mostly the Eureka Brass Band or the Young Tuxedo Brass Band—still took anyone interested in the old styles back to the beginnings of jazz, when bands like them had marched down the streets and emptied school classrooms of kids who rushed outdoors to run alongside. In the brass bands, with their familiar repertoire of dirges, marches, and spirituals, we still could hear what jazz had been like in the years that were lost in the past. On many afternoons I found myself walking along a quiet street in one of the old neighborhoods, listening for the sound of the Eureka and the soaring trumpet of its leader, Percy Humphrey. If I didn't hear him down the block, I knew that eventually I'd hear his trumpet somewhere around the corner.

What we didn't see when we followed the brass bands—not only with the older veteran bands like the Eureka and the Young Tuxedo but also with the casual pick-up bands that hit the streets on Mardi Gras—were young musicians ready to take over the music. Perhaps it was this, as much as anything else, that discouraged us. How could this music go on if no young musicians stepped forward to join the bands? It was during the period when many young African Americans were impatient to leave the past behind them, and the sight of the cluster of white faces around the brass bands and the few still performing dance hall bands set a discordant stamp on the musical traditions the performers represented.

But New Orleans wasn't ready to let the brass bands go. One night in the 1980s a friend, pianist Lars Edegran, told me he was taking me to a club called The Glass House, and for the first time I heard the Dirty Dozen Brass Band. It used a smaller version of the familiar brass band instrumentation, but their repertoire had expanded to modern jazz, modal experimentation, and new jazz compositions played with a stunning virtuosity and assurance. It was too soon to tell if the appearance of the band meant that there would be a brass band renaissance or if they would continue to be an intriguing concert group, like the orchestras assembled by avant garde jazz artists like Anthony Threadgill or Oliver Lake.

At about the same time, a new street musician began playing for tourists in Jackson Square, the center of the French Quarter and the most visited of all the French Quarter's tourist destinations. He was a large, heavy man, usually in a white shirt and dark trousers, who smiled broadly, played the tuba, and led a brass band that was even smaller than the Dirty Dozen. His band, to go with its size, was called the Chosen Few, and though his name was Anthony Lacen, he was always known as "Tuba Fats." Perhaps to make up for his band's size, or perhaps simply to make his presence known, Tuba Fats turned his instrument into a noisy, breathy, unmistakable interruption in the French Quarter's streets. With Fats, the tuba didn't play an accompaniment, it blasted out long, barreling introductions and wayward melodies, and at the end of the performance, there was Tuba Fats smiling broadly and looking around with satisfaction at the rest of his mini-band.

New Orleans has turned to its own people time and time again in the long story of its music, and it was one of New Orleans's own who finally lit the fuse for what has become an explosion of brass bands and their new jazz style that has taken over the city's streets. The young brass bands are what the ballyhoo bands were a century ago. They are the "now" of New Orleans jazz. It was Danny Barker, who had begun playing with Lee Collins in the 1920s, who combined his sense of New Orleans jazz history with his years of experience as a working musician to throw wide the doors that the Dirty Dozen Brass Band and Tuba Fats had pushed open a crack. Barker's role began as a social project. Reverend Andrew Darby, the pastor of his suburban church, the Fairview Baptist Church,

THE HOT 8 BRASS BAND PLAYING AT
CAFE BRASIL, 2005. PHOTOGRAPH BY
SAMUEL CHARTERS.

asked him if he might consider starting a boy's brass band to help keep some of his young parishioners out of trouble. Barker agreed to try, and he brought his own jazz background, as well as his knowledge of the brass bands traditions, to the project. His Fairview Brass Band, with Barker incongruously marching along in the group with his banjo on a cord around his neck, soon was a regular part of the street scene. His youthful musicians could strut for their friends in their own neighborhoods, just as the band men had done decades before.

The black public high schools in New Orleans also had brass bands, though the style was a faster, riff-dominated ensemble roar that made up in raw energy what it lacked in subtlety. The crowds of young musicians helped add their own excitement to the new movement and the brass bands brought back the sense of in-your-face challenge and laughing risk that had been missing in New Orleans music for too many years. Bands like the Rebirth Brass Band, the Soul Rebels, the Hot 8, the New Birth Brass Band, Coolbone, the Stooges, and their white counterparts Bonerama, with its front line of four trombones, have brought new life to the New Orleans music scene. Already younger instrumentalists, like trumpeter Kermit Ruffins, who was a teenage member of the Rebirth Band, and Leroy Jones, another trumpeter who first marched with the Fairview Band at the age of thirteen, have gone on to distinctive careers as solo artists.

Perhaps what makes the rebirth of the brass bands so expressive of the city and its history is that once again it's the dance beat that they've brought back to New Orleans jazz. In New Orleans in the months following Katrina's destruction I heard the brass bands playing indoors in the clubs for dancing more often than I heard them on the street for parades. The Dirty Dozen have gone on to become part of the international touring circuit, playing every major festival and adding to their already lengthy list of albums. In a return to their roots in 2004, for the funeral of their friend Tuba Fats, who died in January, they recorded a classic New Orleans funeral album, with the dirgelike opening of a hymn, then quickening to the familiar street marches. The album, *Funeral for a Friend*, was one of the most exciting returns to the old traditions that any band has achieved in many years.

One afternoon I was talking with drummer Johnny Vidacovich and asked him how he felt about the new brass bands, since he'd grown up marching in his junior high and high school bands on those same streets. He laughed and threw up his hands.

I feel great about them. Because they're young guys who have put a spin on all of it. They're using the character of traditional marching music, but what they do isn't exactly like it, so now a lot of old guys don't get with it and there's where you have a problem . . .

Now it's true the young guys are just using brass band instrumentation and a few ideas and they play very fast, on top of the beat, you know, where the older, traditional brass bands didn't play fast that way. Their beat was more lazy, a strolling kind of laziness, and they played songs and their style was not so loud and fast and edgy and straight.

But hey now! Some of these guys grew up in the projects. They saw people using crack. They saw people using heroin, but this music isn't heroin or anything like that. . . . It's a social problem. It's nothing to do with what belongs to the tradition. So I mean, hey, it's like all other kinds of music, it's only just on the outside like a disguise. What's important to me is the nature of the music and what's important to me is the fact the tradition is going on.

These young cats have picked up sousaphones and snare drums and bass drums and saxophones and trombones. And that's not cool? Let's think about it and get a little positive here. . . . Now they don't know how to play "Way Down Yonder in New Orleans" or maybe they don't know how to play "Bogalusa Strut"—some complicated tunes like that. They're ghetto kids, they're project babies, some of them. For a cat dealing with that, who knows where their mommies and daddies are, much less getting a music lesson. Gimme a break! We're lucky some of the cats are picking up a trumpet and not a gun.

You know what I think about the brass bands today?

I say, "Thank you, God! Thank you, God!"[2]

THE REBIRTH BRASS BAND PLAYING
AT THE ROCK 'N' BOWL, 2005.
PHOTOGRAPH BY SAMUEL CHARTERS.

Those of us close to New Orleans and its music have always felt that there was a world of notes and sounds we could have heard if we'd just come a few years before, but we always had the certainty that if we stayed long enough, we'd hear at least some echoes of what we were seeking. It has always been a city that saves as well as it renews. It doesn't discard its past. What is difficult to accept at this moment in the city's long and rich history is that New Orleans itself seems threatened. How can the city come back if the people still scattered in other cities don't feel they can come back? How can the owners of the thousands of wooden houses that sat with polluted water up to their roofs for weeks find the resources to repair electrical wiring and toilets and kitchens? How can neighborhoods that survived so many disasters and difficulties face the uncertainty of more storms and more inadequate protection from the water that lies all around it? As you fly into the city after the flood, the sheen of the lakes and the spiraling crescent of the Mississippi River no longer seem passive. They seem only to be waiting for the next stirring of the winds in the Gulf. But from the beginning, it wasn't a good idea to put the city where it was, and three hundred years later it continues to be a city like no other. If the music of New Orleans and its irreplaceable jazz traditions can be continually renewed and replenished by memories of the past, then perhaps for the city itself there is this same hope for the future.

Notes

INTRODUCTION

1. Charters 2006, 168.
2. Rose and Souchon, vi.
3. Beurkle and Barker, 119.
4. Beurkle and Barker, 11.
5. Ibid.
6. Charters 1963.

1. A CITY LIKE NO OTHER

1. Latrobe, J. C., 239.
2. Hayward, 479.
3. Latrobe, J. C., 238.
4. Kmen, 4.
5. Kmen, 49.
6. Kmen, 38.
7. Kmen, 56.
8. Bremer, vol. 2, 211.
9. New Orleans *Daily Picayune*, 16 Feb. 1842, 4.
10. Latrobe, vol. 2, 241.

2. PEOPLE, FACES

1. Saxon, 219.
2. Whitman, 1199.
3. Saxon, 220.
4. Saxon, 229.
5. Twain, 473.
6. Twain, 475.
7. Twain, 473.
8. Hearn, 1.
9. Hearn, 79.
10. Hearn, 70.

11. Ferrier.
12. Latrobe, B. H., 179.
13. Laine.
14. Roberts.
15. Roberts.
16. Charters 1963, 4.

3. A SOCIETY TO ITSELF

1. Shapiro and Hentoff, 30.
2. Abbott and Stewart.
3. *Daily Picayune*, 30 June 1910, 6.
4. Bethel.
5. Bethel, 25.
6. Bethel, 80–81.
7. Collins, 33.
8. Abbott, 2003/2004.
9. Shapiro and Hentoff, 30.
10. Shapiro and Hentoff, 63.

4. PAPA JACK'S BOYS

1. Shapiro and Hentoff, 58.
2. Ramsey and Smith, 42.
3. Laine.
4. Laine.
5. Laine.
6. Laine.
7. Christian.
8. Ramsey and Smith, 41.
9. Rose and Souchon, 179.
10. Rose and Souchon, 188.
11. Ramsey and Smith, 44.
12. Ibid.

5. THE OTHER SIDE OF TOWN

1. Charters 1963, 57.
2. Foster, 12.
3. Armstrong, 7.
4. Ramsey and Smith, epigraph, n.p.
5. Marquis.
6. Shapiro and Hentoff, 38.
7. Foster, 16.
8. Armstrong, 21.
9. Spriggins 1933.
10. Spriggins 1933.
11. Foster, 9.
12. Foster, 26.
13. Foster, 41.

14. Foster, 47.
15. Foster, 87.

6. ON THE CIRCUIT

1. Charters 1963, 56a.
2. Ramsey and Smith, 21.
3. Shapiro and Hentoff, 45.
4. Foster, 52.
5. Charters 1963, 36.
6. Gushee.
7. Gushee, 71.
8. Gushee, 76.
9. Rose and Souchon, 147, 162, 164.
10. Gushee, 35.
11. Shipton, 108.
12. Gushee, 99.
13. Gushee, 106.
14. Ibid.
15. Gushee, 162.
16. Charters 1963, 42.
17. Gushee, 206.

7. "JASS"

1. Shapiro and Hentoff, 81.
2. Lowry.
3. Holbrook.
4. Shapiro and Hentoff, 81.
5. Shapiro and Hentoff, 82.
6. Sudhalter 1999, 7.
7. Gushee, 138.
8. Gushee, 299.
9. Holbrook, 138.
10. Holbrook, 139.
11. Brooks, 83.
12. Rose and Souchon, 254.
13. Sudhalter 1999, 25.
14. Brunn, 187.

8. THE FIRST SENSATIONAL MUSICAL NOVELTY OF 1917!

1. Nunez material in Internet entry.
2. *The Encyclopedia of Jazz*, New Edition, 1960, 307.
3. Shipton, 102.
4. Ibid.
5. Brunn, 21.
6. Kenney, 11.
7. Letter in *Esquire Magazine*, January 17, 1946.
8. Brunn, 43–44.

9. Gracyk, 3.
10. Brunn, 52.

9. SOME RECORD!

1. Graycyk, 5.
2. Brunn, 67.
3. Beurkle and Barker, 118.
4. Brunn, 84.
5. Gracyk, 5.

10. SOUTHERN STOMPS

1. Armstrong, 180.
2. Longstreet, 257.
3. Longstreet, 251.
4. Ibid.
5. Souchon, 341.
6. Kenney, 41.
7. Berrett, 32.
8. Kenney, 20.
9. Kenney, 70.
10. Kenney, 71.
11. Bergreen, 73.
12. Bergreen, 168.
13. Kenney, 46,
14. Bergreen, 178.
15. Carmichael, 203.
16. Souchon, 343.

11. RHYTHM KINGS

1. Sudhalter 1999, 84.
2. Brunn, 127.
3. Brunn, 138.
4. Sudhalter, 1999, 29.
5. Shapiro and Hentoff, 122.
6. Havens and Gilmore.
7. Sudhalter 1999, 29.

12. MISTER JELLY

1. Lomax, 160.
2. Russell, 87.
3. Russell.
4. Russell, 40.
5. Russell, 88.
6. Russell, 487.

7. Russell, 491.
8. Lomax, 160.
9. Lomax, 161.
10. Lomax, 162.
11. Russell, 145.
12. Stoddard, 49.
13. Russell, 550.
14. Russell, 564.
15. Ibid.
16. Lomax, 176.
17. Russell, 386.
18. Russell, 125.
19. Russell, 360.
20. Russell, 364.

13. BOUNCING AROUND

1. Spriggins 1927.
2. Russell, 564.
3. Abbott 1999, 13.
4. Ibid.

14. OUT TO THE HALFWAY HOUSE

1. Shapiro and Hentoff, 163.
2. Sudhalter, *New Orleans in the '20s*.
3. Foster, 62.
4. Sudhalter 1999, 73.
5. Abbott, 2003/2004.
6. Abbott, 2003/2004, 4.

15. KINGS OF NEW ORLEANS

1. Collins, 50.
2. Foster, 81.
3. Jones and Chilton, 53.
4. Collins, 53.
5. Ibid.
6. Charters Archive.
7. Collins, 54.
8. Sweetman.
9. Sudhalter 1999, 258.
10. Collins, 32.
11. Collins, 32.

16. THE TIGER'S PAW

1. *Times-Picayune*, 17 Apr. 1927, 1.
2. *Times-Picayune*, 19 Apr. 1927, 2.

3. Abbott 1999, 34.
4. Ibid.
5. Collins, 43.
6. Barker.
7. Collins, 47.
8. Collins, 48.

17. THE PRODIGAL

1. Jones and Chilton, 133.
2. Ibid.
3. Ibid.
4. Armstrong, 148.
5. Jones and Chilton, 152.
6. Foster, 139.
7. Foster, 141.

18. JAZZ NIGHTS

1. Manone and Vandervoort, 98.
2. Shapiro and Hentoff, 196.
3. Ibid.
4. *Times-Picayune*, June 2, 1935, 6.
5. Rose and Souchon, 275.
6. Charters 1963, unnumbered page.
7. Manone and Vandervoort, 83.
8. Manone and Vandervoort, 115.
9. Manone and Vandervoort, 119.
10. Ramsey and Smith, 269.
11. Ibid.
12. Ramsey and Smith, 271.
13. Ibid.
14. Ramsey and Smith, 270.
15. Ramsey and Smith, 276.

19. GLORIES, REMEMBERED

1. Brunn, 208.
2. Bethel, 112.
3. Brunn, 205.
4. Brunn, 207.
5. Rust, 16.
6. Ibid.
7. Collins, 82.
8. Russell, 248.
9. Russell, 507.
10. Russell, 474.
11. Szwed, 9.
12. Ibid.

13. Russell, 505.
14. Ibid.

20. REVIVAL DAYS

1. Foster, 164.
2. Ibid.
3. Bethel, 125.
4. Bethel, 133.
5. Bethel, 137.
6. Bethel, 155.
7. Bethel, 194.
8. MacGowen, 149.
9. Beurkle and Barker, 107.
10. Beurkle and Barker, 168.

21. STRUTTIN'

1. Charters 2006, 9.
2. Charters 2006, 164.

Bibliography

Abbott, Lynn. "Mr. E. Belfield Spriggins, First Man of Jazzology." 78 *Quarterly* 10 (Nov. 1999).
———. "'For Ofays Only': An Annotated Calendar of Midnight Frolics at the Lyric Theater." *The Jazz Archivist* XVII (2003/2004).
Abbott, Lynn, and Doug Seroff. *Out of Sight.* Jackson: University Press of Mississippi, 2002.
Abbott, Lynn and Jack Stewart. "The Iroquois Theater." *The Jazz Archivist* (Dec. 1994).
Armstrong, Louis. *Satchmo: My Life in New Orleans.* New York: Signet Books, 1955.
Barker, Danny. Conversation with the author. 1956.
Bergreen, Laurence. *Louis Armstrong: An Extravagant Life.* New York: Broadway Books, 1997.
Berrett, Joshua. *Louis Armstrong and Paul Whiteman.* New Haven: Yale University Press, 2004.
Bethel, Tom. *George Lewis: A Jazzman from New Orleans.* Berkeley: University of California Press, 1977.
Beurkle, Jack V., and Danny Barker. *Bourbon Street Black.* New York: Oxford University Press, 1973.
Bremer, Fredrika. *The Homes of the New World: Impressions of America.* 2 vols. 1853; rpt. New York: Negro University Press, 1968.
Brooks, Tim. *Lost Sounds.* Urbana: University of Illinois Press, 2005.
Brunn, H. O. *The Story of the Original Dixieland Jazz Band.* Baton Rouge: University of Louisiana Press, 1960.
Carmichael, Hoagy, with Stephen Longstreet. *The Story of Hoagy Carmichael.* New York: Farrar, Strauss & Giroux, 1965.
Charters, Samuel. *Jazz: New Orleans, 1885–1963.* 2nd ed. New York: Oak Books, 1963.
———. *New Orleans: Playing a Jazz Chorus.* London: Marion Boyars, 2006.
Charters Archive. Dodd Research Center, University of Connecticut.
Christian, Frank. Interview with Dick Allen, with William Russell and Al Rose. 6 Sep. 1965. William Hogan Jazz Archive.
Collins, Lee, edited by Frank J. Gillis and John W. Miner. *Oh, Didn't He Ramble: The Life Story of Lee Collins as Told to Mary Collins.* Urbana: University of Illinois Press, 1974.
Cott, Jonathan. *Wandering Ghost: The Odyssey of Lafcadio Hearn.* New York: Alfred A. Knopf, 1991.
Ferrier, Maude K. Interview with the author. Berkeley, California. 1954.
Foster, George, as told to Tom Stoddard. *The Autobiography of Pops Foster, New Orleans Jazzman.* Berkeley: University of California Press, 1971.
Gehman, Mary. *The Free People of Color in New Orleans: An Introduction.* New Orleans: Margaret Media, 1994.
Gracyk, Tim. "The Original Dixieland Jazz Band" in *Popular American Recording Pioneers.* Online entry. http://www.gracyk.com/odjb.shtml/.
Gushee, Lawrence. *Pioneers of Jazz: The Story of the Creole Band.* New York: Oxford University Press, 2005.
Havens, Dan, and Richard Gilmore. "Conversations with George Brunis." *Mississippi Rag* 25 (Sept. 1998): 1–10.
Hayward, John. *A Gazetteer of the United States of America.* Hartford: Case, Tiffany, 1853.

Hearn, Lafcadio. *Creole Sketches*. Boston: Houghton Mifflin, 1924.

Holbrook, Richard. "Mister Jazz Himself—The Story of Ray Lopez." *Storyville* 64 (Apr.–May 1976).

Jones, Max, and John Chilton. *Louis: The Louis Armstrong Story, 1900–1971*. London: Mayflower Books, 1975.

Kenney, William Howland. *Chicago Jazz: A Cultural History, 1904–1930*. New York: Oxford University Press, 1993.

Kmen, Henry A. *Music in New Orleans*. Baton Rouge: Louisiana State University Press, 1966.

Laine, Jack. Interview by William Russell. March 26, 1957. William Hogan Jazz Archive, Tulane University.

Latrobe, Benjamin Henry. *The Journal of Latrobe*. New York: D. Appleton, 1905.

Latrobe, Joseph Charles. *The Rambler in North America*. Vol. 2. New York: Harper & Brothers, 1835.

Lomax, Alan. *Mister Jelly Roll*. New York: Pantheon Books, 1993.

Longstreet, Stephen. *Sportin' House*. Los Angeles: Sherbourne Press, 1965.

Lowry, Ed, with Charlie Foy. Paul M. Levitt, ed. *Joe Frisco: Comic, Jazz Dancer, and Railbird*. Carbondale: Southern Illinois University Press, 1999.

MacGowen, Christopher, ed. *The Collected Poems of William Carlos Williams*. Vol. 2. New York: New Directions, 1988.

Manone, Joe "Wingy," and Paul Vandervoort II. *Trumpet on the Wing*. London: The Jazz Book Club, 1964.

Marquis, Donald M. *In Search of Buddy Bolden: First Man of Jazz*. Rev. ed. Baton Rouge: Louisiana State University Press, 2005.

Pastras, Phil. *Dead Man Blues: Jelly Roll Morton Way Out West*. Berkeley: University of California Press, 2001.

Ramsey, Frederic, Jr., and Charles Edward Smith, eds. *Jazzmen*. New York: Harcourt Brace, 1939.

Roberts, John Storm. *The Latin Tinge*. New York: Oxford University Press, 1979.

Rose, Al, and Edmond Souchon, M.D. *New Orleans Jazz: A Family Album*. Baton Rouge: Louisiana State University Press, 1967.

Russell, William, ed. *"Oh, Mister Jelly!"* Copenhagen: JazzMedia Aps, 1999.

Rust, Brian. Notes for *Original Dixieland Jazz Band: The Creators of Jazz*. Watford, England: Ovid Records, 2000, 16.

Saxon, Lyle. *Fabulous New Orleans*. New Orleans: Robert L. Crager, 1950.

Shapiro, Nat, and Nat Hentoff. *Hear Me Talkin' To Ya*. New York: Dover Publications, 1966.

Shipton, Alyn. *A New History of Jazz*. London: Continuum, 2001.

Souchon, Edmond, M.D. "King Oliver: A Very Personal Memoir." In *Reading Jazz: A Gathering of Autobiography, Reportage, and Criticism from 1919 to Now*, ed. Robert Gottlieb. New York: Random House, 1999.

Spriggins, E. Belfield. *Louisiana Weekly*, 11 Oct. 1927.

———. "Excavating Local Jazz." *The Louisiana Weekly*, 22 April 1933.

Stoddard, Tom. *Jazz on the Barbary Coast*. Berkeley: Heyday Books, 1998.

Stuart, Jay Allison. *Call Him George*. London: Peter Davies, 1961.

Sudhalter, Richard M. *Lost Chords: White Musicians and Their Contribution to Jazz, 1915–1945*. New York: Oxford University Press, 1999.

———. Notes for *New Orleans in the '20s*. Timeless Historical Records, CBC 1-014 Jazz.

Sudhalter, Richard M., and Philip R. Evans, with William Dean-Myatt. *Bix: Man and Legend*. London: Quartet Books, 1974.

Sutton, Allan, ed. *Cakewalks, Rags and Novelties*. Denver: Mainspring Press, 2003.

Sweetman, Ron. *Recording Activity in New Orleans in the Twenties*. 2005-03-21, http://www.bluesworld.com/NODiscog.html/.

Szwed, John. "Doctor Jazz." Notes to *Jelly Roll Morton: The Complete Library of Congress Recordings*. Cambridge: Rounder Records, 2005.

Twain, Mark. *Mississippi Writings* (including *Life on the Mississippi*). New York: Library of America, 1982.

Whitman, Walt. *Whitman, Poetry and Prose*. New York: Library of America, 1982.

Index

Page numbers in *italics* indicate illustrations.